Made in NuYoRico

MADE IN NuYoRico

**Refiguring American Music**
A series edited by Ronald Radano, Josh Kun, and Nina Sun Eidsheim

MARISOL NEGRÓN

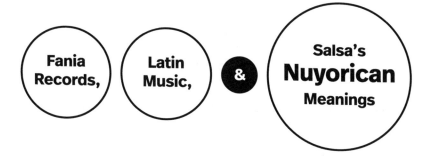

Fania Records, Latin Music, & Salsa's Nuyorican Meanings

DUKE UNIVERSITY PRESS
*Durham and London*
2024

Printed in the United States of America on acid-free paper ∞
Project Editor: Lisa Lawley
Designed by A. Mattson Gallagher
Typeset in Minion Pro and Real Head Pro
by Westchester Publishing Services

Library of Congress Cataloging-in-Publication Data
Names: Negrón, Marisol, [date] author.
Title: Made in NuYoRico : Fania Records, Latin music, and salsa's Nuyorican meanings / Marisol Negrón.
Other titles: Refiguring American music.
Description: Durham : Duke University Press, 2024. | Series: Refiguring American music | Includes bibliographical references and index.
Identifiers: LCCN 2023057416 (print)
LCCN 2023057417 (ebook)
ISBN 9781478030898 (paperback)
ISBN 9781478026662 (hardcover)
ISBN 9781478059875 (ebook)
Subjects: LCSH: Salsa (Music)—New York (State)—New York—History and criticism. | Salsa (Music)—Puerto Rico—History and criticism. | Salsa (Music)—Social aspects—New York (State)—New York. | Salsa (Music)—Social aspects—Puerto Rico. | Puerto Ricans—New York (State)—New York—Music—History and criticism. | Puerto Ricans—New York (State)—New York—Ethnic identity. | Fania (Sound recording label)
Classification: LCC ML3535.5 .N44 2024 (print) | LCC ML3535.5 (ebook) | DDC 781.64—dc23/eng/20240430
LC record available at https://lccn.loc.gov/2023057416
LC ebook record available at https://lccn.loc.gov/2023057417

Cover art: *Salsa band, Lower East Side, NYC, 1976.* © 2024 Hazel Hankin.

*Le dedico este libro a mami y papi, a Elías, and all the salseros and salseras who danced, sang, and played their way through salsa's everynight life.*

# Contents

# Illustrations

## Acknowledgments

Ultimately, this research was possible because of the generosity of salsa fans, artists, music industry executives, and promoters who shared their time, experiences, memories, and resources. Just about everyone I met extended themselves in ways too numerous to detail fully, including Berto Álvarez, Evelyn Calderón, Henry Calderón, Elizabeth Colón, Iván Colón, Mildred Cortez, Jimmy Delgado, DJ Berto, María Dominguez, José Encarnación, Lillian Jiménez, Felipe Luciano, Orlando Marín, Eddie Montalvo, Frankie Morales, Lisa Morazzani, John Navearez, Nydia Ocasio, "Cookie" Pacheco, Johnny Pacheco, Dylcia Pagán, Angel René, Antonio Rivera, Melba Sánchez, Migdalia Suárez, Ralfi, and Wanda. Special thanks are due to the many people who provided guidance during my trips to New York, particularly those who opened their Rolodexes (yes, Rolodexes). Charlie Candelario, then president of the Old Timer's Festival, and promoter Richie Blondet introduced me to friends and colleagues. Luis "Máquina" Flores, a dance legend since the days of the Palladium, drove me around New York to show me the locations of nightclubs and afterhours. His descriptions of New York's Latin music scene not only provided insight into salsa's ways and everynight life but provided an alternative history of the Palladium days that included the spaces and clubs frequented by patrons who did not meet the famous nightclub's standards of respectability. Musician, journalist, and Latin music historian Aurora Flores and musician Angel René both invited me into their homes and welcomed me to Julia's Jam at the Julia de Burgos Cultural Center in East Harlem. Yeyito Flores took me to spots in Central Park where *rumberos* met regularly to play music. I joined *salsera* Paula Connil at La Maganette, where she introduced me to fans who had been dancing salsa since the 1960s and 1970s. Sadly, La Maganette ended a thirty-year run in 2005. Izzy Sanabria, graphic artist, editor of *Latin N.Y.*, and emcee for the Fania All-Stars, showed me original artwork for the many album covers he designed.

One of the highlights of my research was the opportunity to watch Típica 73 rehearse for their thirtieth-anniversary concert, and Son Boricua prepare for a gig at Orchard Beach, thanks to *timbalero* Nicky Marrero and percussionist José Mangual Jr., respectively. Mangual and timbalero Jimmy Delgado talked with me for *hours*, painting an evocative and emotive picture of the salsa boom and their professional and personal trajectories in Latin music. Both Ralph Mercado and Larry Harlow provided unvarnished histories and detailed accounts of the concert at the Cheetah and how it came to be filmed. Bassist and composer Gui Duvignau spent many hours talking with me about Colón and LaVoe's music and breaking down arrangements.

I benefited immeasurably from the opportunity to hang out and talk to fans and musicians at various places in New York thanks to Vicente Barreiro, owner of Casa Latina Records in East Harlem (since closed); Mike Amadeo, renowned songwriter and owner of Casa Amadeo (La antigua Casa Hernández), a New York historical landmark included in the National Register of Historic Places; Kenneth Giordano, who owned Willie's Steak House in the Bronx and hosted live music—and where I saw Dave Valentín play for the first time; and Efraín Suárez, owner of Made in Puerto Rico in East Harlem, which housed the International Salsa Museum in its back room, and who encouraged me to hang out at the store so I could meet folks to interview. It was there that I talked at length with Willie Medina, coproducer of the radio show *Rincón Caliente*, who invited me to join him at the Old Timer's Festival. He introduced me to promoters, fans, and musicians, many of whom I interviewed there and on future occasions. Angel Rodríguez gave me a tour of the Point Community Development Corporation in the Hunts Point section of the Bronx and invited me on a "Mambo to Hip Hop Tour" of Latin music clubs in the neighborhood. I joined Andrew Padilla on his "El Barrio Tours: Gentrification in El Barrio."

While information about the Fania catalog is now widely available on the internet, that was not the case when I began my research. Victor Gallo provided a list of the Fania catalog that included SLP numbers and release dates. He also connected me to Ernesto Aue at Palacio de la Música, S.A., a Venezuelan record label that released international titles for Fania Records and the various related labels. Mr. Aue provided a color copy of the cover art for the Fania albums released by Palacio de la Música. Juan Otero Garabís surprised me with a copy of *Our Latin Thing* when the only copies available were bootlegged.

This book has benefited incredibly from the support, generosity, and guidance of my extraordinary colleagues. At the University of Massachusetts, Boston, my American studies colleagues shared their time, leveraged their experience, and provided feedback on the manuscript. Rachel Rubin reviewed the entire manuscript, Aaron Lecklider read almost every conference paper related to the book, and Lynnell L. Thomas continues to be a dedicated mentor whose support throughout the writing process is immeasurable. My colleagues in Latino studies have demonstrated immense enthusiasm for my work and professional trajectory at UMass Boston and stepped up to share the administrative leadership of the program so I could finish the manuscript. I am especially grateful to Luis Aponte-Parés, Devin Atallah, Chris Barcelos, María Carvajal Regidor, Daniel Gascón, Albis Mejía, Rosalyn Negrón, Lorna Rivera, Ester Shapiro, Tim Sieber, Mirén Uriarte, Raúl Ybarra, and the late Glenn Jacobs, who generously gifted me his personal collection of *Latin N.Y.* issues dating from 1973 to 1976. It is a privilege to be at an institution with a critical mass of scholars whose scholarship, student outreach, and community-based projects center the histories, knowledges, and everyday lives of racialized minoritarian communities. Colleagues from across the university attended my talks, provided feedback on my work, and generally supported me in this process, including Ping-Ann Addo, Nada Ali, Elora Chowdhury, Chris Fung, Holly Jackson, Peter Kiang, Patricia Krueger-Henney, Denise Patemon, Aminah Pilgrim, Rajini Srikanth, Karen Suyemoto, Shirley Tang, and Cedric Woods. The institutional support I received from the College of Liberal Arts, particularly from Tyson King-Meadows and Pratima Prasad, helped me finish the book. The Brandeis University Women's Research Center provided space and administrative support as I prepared the manuscript for publication. The warm greeting I received from Harleen Singh, Kristen Mullin, Stephanie Lawrence, Abby Rosenberg, and the various scholars who welcomed me to Brandeis set the tone for a marvelous year.

My research benefited tremendously from the early guidance I received from Richard Rosa, who nurtured my interest in tracing salsa's social life;

Yvonne Yarbro-Bejarano's insights when I began outlining the project; and Renato Rosaldo's mentorship as I embarked on my first research trip to New York. Juan Flores read an early version of the manuscript and suggested avenues to explore. He and Miriam Jiménez Román, mentors to so many of us and steadfast champions of diasporic Puerto Rican scholarship, encouraged the work and followed my progress. The encouragement I received from José Esteban Muñoz when I presented at a Mellon Mays University Fellows summer conference encouraged me to think about salsa's potentiality in new ways and buoyed me more than he could have ever known. Alberto Sandoval Sánchez has supported my growth as a scholar for too many years to count. He gave his advice freely on the direction of the manuscript when I most needed it and introduced me to Marc Anthony's "Vivir mi vida," with which I open the book. Deb Vargas was a generous mentor during my tenure as a Woodrow Wilson/Andrew W. Mellon Junior Faculty Career Enhancement fellow. She, Arlene Dávila, and Sharon Holland passed on their experience, knowledge, and advice as I prepared to submit my manuscript to various university presses. Deborah Pacini Hernández gifted me published and unpublished materials from her personal library. Nicole Fleetwood, Zaire Dinzey-Flores, and Khari opened their homes to me while I conducted research in New York.

The two chapters I workshopped at the New England Consortium of Latina/o Studies benefited from the detailed feedback provided by respondents and other scholars who participated in the discussion that followed each of my presentations. I am particularly grateful for the collegiality of Ginetta Candelario, Mari Castañeda, Kaysha Corinealdi, Israel Reyes Crespo, David Hernández, Irene Mata, Petra Rivera-Rideau, Vanessa Rosa, Silvia Spitta, Wilson Valentín-Escobar, and Carmen Whalen. I am fortunate to have an extended network of colleagues who supported me throughout the various states of my research and through the publication of the book: Frances Aparicio, Michelle Boyd, Claudia Castañeda, Dolores Ines Casillas, Roxanne Donovan, Loan Dao, Kate Epstein, Reebee Garofalo, Patricia Herrera, Denise Khor, Lawrence La Fountain-Stokes, Sonja Lanehart, April Langley, Marisol LeBrón, Marcia Ochoa, Jessica Pabón, Melanie Pérez Ortiz, Marjorie Salvodon, Ramón Rivera Servera, Liana M. Silva, Faith Smith, Jenny Stoever, Kyla Wazana Tompkins, and Lourdes Torres.

Archivists and research librarians are superheroes. The UMass Boston Healey Library team provided access to *Claridad* and *El Nuevo Día*, including the digital archive for the latter. The staff at the US District Court for the District of Puerto Rico provided space for me to scan legal documents and, once I left, made copies of any additional materials I needed and mailed them to me in Boston. The US District Court for the Southern District of New York and the National Archives and Records Administration (NARA) helped me search for a wayward case file. I received additional research support from librarians at Harvard University, especially Peter Laurence at the Archive of World Music and Deanna Barmakian at the Law School. Ramón Rodríguez at Boys Harbor (now Harbor Conservatory for the Performing Arts) in East Harlem provided access to issues of *Latin N.Y.* that were part of Colección Raíces. Victor Otoño Nieves and Reinaldo González Blanco at the Fundación Rafael Hernández Colón provided materials not available through the digital archive. And the research staff at the Amherst College Archives and Special Collections guided me to the Marshall Bloom Papers.

I also worked with various digital archives available free of charge to the public: Archivo Histórico *Claridad*; Discogs Music Database and Marketplace, which hosts an extensive collection of images from LPs, album covers, and the liner notes for Fania's original releases; the now-defunct Descarga.com, a marketplace for tropical Latin music that published the *Descarga Journal*; Salserísimo Perú, which produces interviews, profiles, and investigative reports related to salsa; and World Radio History (WRH), a digital archive created by radio broadcaster and consultant David Gleason, who received the inaugural Library of American Broadcasting Foundation award for Excellence in Broadcast Preservation in 2023. The archive contains more than nine million pages of magazines and other publications, Federal Communications Commission documents, technical manuals, and more.

Thanks are also due to the phenomenal research assistants who worked on the project. Elix Colón conducted research at the Supreme Court of the State of New York, the US District Court for Southern New York, and the New York Public Library for the Performing Arts. Katsyris Rivera Kientz collected, reviewed, and organized primary sources. Monique Pabón provided administrative support as the files for the project grew, and Danielle Slaughter helped prepare the manuscript for production. I also want to thank Ken Wissoker at Duke University Press for his long-term support of this project; series editors Ronald Radano, Josh Kun, Nina Sun Eidsheim, and Charles McGovern; the production team that shepherded the book to publication, including Lisa Lawley, Kate Mullen, and Chard Royal; and the copyeditors who helped me clean up the manuscript, Sheila and Kim.

Sadly, many of the persons whose art I write about, who formed a core part of Fania or the salsa boom, whom I interviewed, or who contributed to this project in other ways have passed away. Vicente Barreiro, Ray Barretto,

Willie Bobo, Charlie Candelario, Milton Cardona, Joe Cuba, Manu Dibango, Cheo Feliciano, Juan Flores, Luis "Máquina" Flores, Gertrude Fredd, Joe Gaines, Leon Gast, Kenneth Giordano, Andy González, Irving Greenbaum, Agustín Gurza, Larry Harlow, Miriam Jiménez Román, Tato Laviera, Willie Medina, Ralph Mercado, José Esteban Muñoz, Johnny Pacheco, Frances Rodríguez, Roberto Roena, "Little" Ray Romero, Professor Joe Torres, Willie Torres, and Yomo Toro left us a remarkable legacy of music, poetry, journalism, and the cultural history of Black, Latinx, and queer communities.

I am eternally grateful to my parents, Digna and Primitivo, whose hard work, hopes, and dreams for my brother and me propelled us forward; my brother, Héctor, for his love, support, and sacrifices; mis primas hermanas Martiza y Socorrito for their unwavering love, dinners, and nights out; and my dear friend Charlene for her steadfast encouragement and inspiration. My in-laws in Virginia cheered me on through every stage of the book, and my mother-in-law, Judith, traveled to Boston to help with childcare while I conducted archival research in New York. Liora helped me find my way time and again. I am beholden to the women whose labor contributed to the completion of this book, especially my comadre Verónica, Doña Elvira, and Doña Aparecida.

I am blessed by the love and support of my partner, who has been on this ride with me since I began working on the project. He is my confidante, sounding board, occasional copyeditor, champion, and dearest friend. He has celebrated the highs, boosted my spirits when necessary, and took the lion's share of responsibilities in our household when I needed to conduct research, travel, or meet deadlines. My son, whose hugs give me life and whose encouragement fills my heart, es la luz de mis ojos.

# Introduction. Rican/Struction

## THE SOCIAL LIFE OF SALSA

NuYoRico: n. that space between the Empire State and El Morro

**La Bruja,** "Nuyorico Interlude" (2006)

In April 2013, singer-actor Marc Anthony released the single "Vivir mi vida" (Live my life), a Spanish-language salsa cover of the song "C'est la vie" released by Algerian *raï* singer Khaled a year earlier.[1] The music video accompanying "Vivir mi vida" was filmed on location in New York's East Harlem, or El Barrio, the symbolic home of the Puerto Rican diaspora in the United States. The video follows Anthony from the Fifth Avenue offices of Marc Anthony Productions in Midtown Manhattan, where he ruminates on his legacy as a father-son-brother-friend-and-musician, to East Harlem, where Anthony grew up. A police escort leads Anthony's entourage through the streets of New York to East Harlem, where fans greet him with cheers and requests for autographs as he makes his way to a temporary stage in the middle of the street. The camera shots inserted throughout the video provide a panorama of life in East Harlem. A close-up of the bodega on the corner shows its name to be La Marketa. The name calls to mind the historical East Harlem public marketplace created in 1936 to regulate pushcart vendors.[2] La Marqueta, as it came to be known, became a cultural and economic hub for the growing community of Puerto Ricans and other

Latina/o American and Caribbean peoples in New York. A shot of young men playing stickball in the street and another of one wearing a "Thunder Stickball" jersey invokes modern stickball's quintessentially New York character and its popularity among Puerto Ricans since the 1950s. A banner of La Virgen de Guadalupe, the Catholic patron saint of Mexico and Latin America, signals the growing Mexican presence and "Latinization" of the neighborhood since the late 1980s and 1990s, as do the various flags from Latin America and the Caribbean waved by fans who surround the stage on three sides. The Puerto Rican flag, however, is exceptional. It is the first to appear on-screen and the only one shown by itself. While New York stands in for a cosmopolitan Latinidad, the video links salsa's meanings to a New York Puerto Rican history.

Anthony's rendering of "Vivir mi vida" departs from Khaled's original dance-driven recording, which emphasized heteronormative romantic love and the pleasure of collective dance that transcends the legacies of colonialism and racial hierarchies. Composed by writer-producer Julio Reyes Copello, the cover riffs on the title and chorus of the original while the verses emphasize individual desire.[3] Anthony's rumination in the song's prologue about his legacy precedes verses that center instantaneous and continuous pleasure. Preferring to "vivir en el momento" (live in the moment) rather than dwell on a painful present, the singing subject declares his intention to "live his life." "Vivir mi vida" moves beyond this seemingly self-reflexive referential system by underscoring the potential of salsa's performative excess for envisioning a future beyond the challenges of the here and now. The song turns toward laughter, dance, dreams, and pleasure to "entender el destino" (understand fate) and "encontrar el camino" (find the way). The synthesis of salsa, R&B, and soul in the song's arrangements brings in Anthony's musical influences and early career in freestyle—a genre with formative cues derived from Latin soul, doo-wop, salsa, house, and Hip Hop—as well as those of Anthony's longtime collaborator Sergio George, who produced the song and, like the vocalist, came of age in East Harlem.[4] The song's fast tempo and prominent bass line, a departure from many of Anthony's earlier salsa recordings, invoke the instrumentation and arrangements by salsa pioneers such as bandleader-trombonist-producer Willie Colón, whose explosive trombone line characterized the music's foundational period during the mid to late 1960s and 1970s.[5] Anthony's swagger, in turn, recalls the image of Colón and vocalist Héctor LaVoe, two of salsa's most beloved figures, as salsa's "bad boys."[6]

Anthony's improvisational utterances, timbre, and articulation encourage parallels with LaVoe's performative practices. When Anthony, who played LaVoe in the 2006 biopic *El Cantante* (The Singer), calls out to the audience as *mi gente* (my people), he draws on the meanings of LaVoe's signature song by that name. "Mi gente," as Wilson Valentín-Escobar asserts, "addresses the listeners as belonging to Hector Lavoe, and him to them. Lavoe is positioned as the spokesperson and signifier" of Puerto Ricans.[7] By placing himself into that relationship, Anthony constructs himself as heir to LaVoe's performative legacy and affective relationship with diasporic Puerto Rican communities, who considered the late vocalist one of their own. Anthony's physical frame, long and lanky like LaVoe's, accentuates the role of the body in memorializing the vocalist endowed with the title of "El Cantante de los Cantantes" (The Singer's Singer).[8] The affective economy of pleasure in "Vivir mi vida," both the song and the accompanying music video, insists on the liberatory potential of laughter, dance, and pleasure in the face of suffering, a theme familiar to LaVoe's fans:

¿Pa' qué llorar?
¿Pa' que sufrir?
Empieza a soñar, a reír . . .
Siente y baila y goza
que la vida es una sola

[Why cry?
Why suffer?
Start to dream, to laugh
Feel and dance and celebrate
Because there's only one life]

The persistence of desire in the cultural politics of pleasure is particularly salient for poor and working-class diasporic Puerto Rican communities, whose relationship to salsa is foregrounded in the music video. The migration of almost half a million largely rural and working-class Puerto Ricans to the United States during the 1950s made possible the success of what *Time* magazine heralded as "Democracy's Laboratory in Latin America" on its June 1958 cover, featuring Puerto Rico's first elected governor, Luis Muñoz Marín. Puerto Rico's entrance into modernity as a "showcase" of US Cold War economic development policies depended, however, on massive migration to the United States when the shift toward an urban-centered manufacturing economy, however labor intensive, remained unable to fully absorb displaced agricultural workers.[9] Puerto Rico's colonial status facilitated the migration and provided US employers with a source of cheap labor. In both the United States and Puerto Rico, diasporic Puerto Ricans were situated structurally, historically, and symbolically through "differential inclusion," defined by Yen Le Espiritu as one "whereby a group of people is deemed integral to the nation's economy, culture, identity, and power—but integral only or precisely because of their designated subordinated standing." Constituted as integral to the performance of modernity and reviled as its impediment, diasporic Puerto Rican communities were imagined as failed and expendable subjects.[10]

Together, the song and music video draw on not only salsa's Nuyorican histories but the liberatory potential of salsa's foundational moment to imagine Latina/o and Nuyorican futurities.[11] The music video reclaims the streets of New York, and East Harlem in particular, for Puerto Ricans. Policies like "stop and frisk" targeting Black men and Latinos always already interpellate residents as a waste population that threatens public safety. On the day of the video shoot, however, the sirens that accompany Anthony's police escort signify his status as a world-renowned artist. The sirens, the cheering fans, the pulsing rhythms of the band, the female background vocalists, and the singer's own emotive performance combine to produce a moment of *gozo*, of pleasure, a moment in which to transcend tears, sorrows, and the suffering of the here and now vis-à-vis salsa. Anthony's memorialization of salsa's foundational period and East Harlem's Puerto Rican histories reanimates the music's Nuyorican epistemologies even as it recognizes the neighborhood's pan-Latina/o demographics and symbolic status as a transnational space of Latinidad.

## Made in NuYoRico

*Made in NuYoRico* offers a cultural history of salsa that traces the music's Nuyorican meanings across a fifty-year period, beginning in 1964 with the creation of Fania Records, the "Latin Motown" of salsa. The book traces how a Nuyorican imaginary became embedded within salsa as it flourished across New York's streets, parks, rooftops, afterhours, living rooms, stages, dance floors, and recording studios during the mid to late 1960s and 1970s. I center the music's Nuyorican aesthetics together with the imbrication of social, cultural, political, and economic relations. Mapping salsa's meanings beyond New York and this initial moment, the book examines how salsa's Nuyorican imaginary was mobilized across various musical, social, legal, and geopolitical contexts in the United States and Puerto Rico over the next four decades. The history of Fania Records and its associated labels and publishing companies forms a core part of this cultural history. *Made in NuYoRico* recuperates the foundational role of New York's Puerto Rican communities in salsa's development. In so doing, I explore how salsa's Nuyorican imaginary remained embedded within the music long after the legendary label closed its doors.

I draw on a diverse and broad archive that illuminates salsa's Nuyorican imaginary, the performative excess of racialized masculinity, and the music's complex, sometimes conflicting, and always danceable meanings. Interviews I conducted with fans, artists, and music industry personnel contribute to the creation of a living archive that not only reveals alternative genealogies of Latin New York and salsa previously rendered invisible, but transforms our understandings of how New York Puerto Ricans impacted salsa's emergence and development over time. Interviews and profiles published in a variety of mediums, including online repositories like *Descarga Journal* (now defunct), digital programs such as SDRB (*El show de Rubén Blades*), and the videos produced by *Salserísimo Perú* expand access to previously undocumented or inaccessible histories. Close readings of songs triangulate lyrics, musical arrangements, and performance. I also work with liner notes and album covers, magazines and newspapers, press releases, and legal documents to examine salsa's significance across a variety of musical and nonmusical contexts. This wide array of primary sources underscores how salsa's Nuyorican meanings shaped the music's formation, aesthetics, and transformation into a global commodity.

*Made in NuYoRico* does not provide a history of salsa. Nor am I interested in proposing an origins narrative or making claims of Puerto Rican ownership, or authority over the music and its meanings. The book emphasizes the contributions and importance of salsa's multiethnic and racially diverse foundational figures and musical influences. I foreground this issue because the cultural hierarchies embedded within debates about salsa's origins reanimate the coloniality of power. In her groundbreaking work on Puerto Rican music in New York during the interwar period, Ruth Glasser explains how ethnomusicologists and music critics make "Puerto Rican music the loser in an ahistorical Darwinian scheme that closely parallels social science condemnations of Puerto Ricans as a failed ethnic group" whose musicians "have left their own ostensibly meager musical resources behind and 'merely' adapted Cuban sounds." These assessments leave Puerto Rican music as "more or less a footnote to the history of the rumba and to subsequently popular Cuban genres."[12] This truism, reflected in Hollywood films like *Dance with Me* (1998) and *Dirty Dancing: Havana Nights* (2004), reifies an understanding of salsa as Cuban music.

The imposition of modernist frameworks on salsa's musical development minimizes not only the ways Puerto Rican musicians and fans in New York informed the music's emergence but also the transnational flows of Black diasporic expressive culture within the US-Caribbean world over a century.[13] As Lise Waxer notes in the introduction to her anthology *Situating Salsa* (and cultural critics such as Frances Aparicio, Marisol Berríos-Miranda, Wilson Valentín-Escobar, and César Rondón have likewise shown), "Even a casual listening to salsa from the 1960s and '70s (e.g., Eddie Palmieri) and its Cuban antecedents from the 1940s and '50s (e.g., Arsenio Rodríguez) provides empirical grounds for distinguishing between the two."[14] These statements echo those of Eddie Palmieri, who cites Afro-*Caribbean* rhythms as the heart and soul of the music, thereby refusing a nationalist framework and placing salsa within a Caribbean and Black diasporic context. Attempts to fix salsa's origins within a particular national musical tradition privilege the nation-state, recur to a rubric overdetermined by US colonialism, and ignore the multidirectional flows of culture among Latin America, the Caribbean, the United States, and other sites of Black diasporic expressive culture.

The Rican/Struction in *Made in NuYoRico* recuperates salsa's social and relational contours, illuminating the music's Nuyorican imaginary and its multivalent meanings in New York and Puerto Rico over half a century. My use of "Rican/Struction" as an analytic finds its inspiration in the eponymous album by the Bronx-born and East Harlem–raised Nuyorican percussionist and bandleader Ray Barretto, whose musical chops and innovation extended across salsa, charanga, boogaloo and Latin soul, R&B, and jazz. Born in 1929, Barretto came of age listening to the Puerto Rican music of his parents as well as the swing and jazz bands of the era. Barretto has widely credited Dizzy Gillespie's foundational Latin jazz–bebop recording of "Manteca" (1947), composed with Afro-Cuban percussionist Chano Pozo and arranged by Gil Fuller, for propelling his desire to play professionally. Barretto began his professional career in the 1950s with jazz and bebop greats like Charlie Parker and Max Roach. His debut in 1961 with *Barretto para bailar* (Barretto to dance to) marked the beginning of a long and illustrious career. He released more than forty albums and collaborated on dozens more with artists like Herbie Mann, Cal Tjader, and even the Bee Gees. Barretto released his first album with Fania Records in 1968. *Rican/Struction* (1979) was his thirtieth album and marked a return to Fania after recording with Atlantic Records. The album cover was conceptualized by Izzy Sanabria, the editor of the magazine *Latin N.Y.* and a graphic designer who often emceed concerts for Fania. The cover finds its inspiration in *Gulliver's Travels*.[15] Painted by Jorge Vargas, it features Barretto's disembodied head emerging from a mountain while his disembodied hand stands poised over a drumskin. Small figures work atop the hand while scaffolding keeps the head upright. According to Sanabria, the small figures on the *Rican/Struction* cover represent band members working on the album, signaling their role in Barretto's creative and professional Rican/Struction. This collaboration is also marked by Barretto's reunion with former lead vocalist Adalberto Santiago, who had previously left the band with several other musicians to form Típica 73. *Rican/Struction* brought together Afro-Caribbean and other Black diasporic forms of musical expression, including jazz and funk, underscoring the continued possibilities for experimentation and musical fusion after the decline of the 1970s salsa boom. *Rican/Struction* celebrated Barretto's vision of both his and Latin music's past, present, and future. Rican/Struction, as an analytic, signals a recuperation of New York Puerto Rican histories that highlights the experimentation and creativity of Nuyorican social and artistic movements.

My use of "Nuyorican" returns to its earliest uses by diasporic Puerto Rican poets, playwrights, and other artists, for whom it signified a racialized colonial subject position intertwined with counterhegemonic aesthetic practices. For the late Miguel Algarín, cofounder of the Nuyorican Poets Café on the Lower East Side, Nuyorican referred to much more than "a Puerto Rican born and/or living in New York," instead indicating "a 'way of being' through which 'individuals practice and embody Nuyoricanness through culture, language, and the spaces they inhabit.'"[16] This Nuyoricanness, similar to the "Neo-Rican" elaborated by poet Jaime Carrero, signifies a counterhegemonic position grounded in the status of diasporic Puerto Ricans as racialized and colonial subjects in the United States as well as cultural agents who draw on Black diasporic, Puerto Rican, and US social and cultural practices in the performance of liberation.[17] Nuyorican was initially a pejorative term used in Puerto Rico to refer to diasporic Puerto Ricans, and its resignification by Algarín and Nuyorican Poets Café cofounder Miguel Piñero highlights the racialized and colonial landscape navigated by Puerto Ricans in New York and Puerto Rico. They claimed the term at a time when the physical and audible presence of Puerto Ricans in public spaces was perceived as a threat to Americanness.

I.1    Album cover for Ray Barretto's *Rican/Struction* (1979)

Part of the Nuyorican Arts Movement, salsa transformed the stages and streets of New York into a space of Puerto Rican collectivity, performance, and colonial resistance. Nuyorican aesthetics, which *Made in NuYoRico* traces within salsa, repudiate normative mobilizations of Americanness *and* Puerto Ricanness.[18] Rather than attempt to constitute a diasporic Puerto Ricanness within narratives of whiteness and respectability, Nuyorican aesthetics celebrate the status of diasporic Puerto Ricans as "revolting subjects," impediments to modernity in both the United States and Puerto Rico whose presence pollutes the racial, linguistic, and moral fabric of the national symbolic.[19] Patricia Herrera and Karen Jaime similarly emphasize the celebration of the abject in Nuyorican aesthetics and cultural politics since the 1960s. Piñero's creative work, Jaime explains, centered "a vibrant neighborhood full of poor and working ethnic people, illicit economies and activities, and local and international liberatory politics."[20] As Herrera stresses, Piñero's emotive performances, improvisational practices, and vocal aesthetics drew from the soundscape of everyday life, "transform[ing] social realities into artistic and political possibilities."[21] While print and visual culture "centered the male body literally, figuratively, and performatively," scholar-performers Herrera and Jaime demonstrate that feminist interventions and queer art-making and sex practices at the Nuyorican Poets Café were integral to the cultural politics of a Nuyorican aesthetic rooted in the everyday lives, historical experiences, and cultural imaginary of Nuyoricans.[22] These cultural politics connected diasporic Puerto Ricans to other racialized groups engaged in liberatory praxis and global anti-colonial struggles.

Salsa's Nuyorican aesthetics overlap with the conceptualization by Jaime and Herrera, including its "masculinist-centric ethos" that necessitates attention to the roles and agency of women in Latin New York and salsa.[23] Salsa's aesthetic contours include the "oral expression of the self; the negotiation between New York/American culture and Puerto Rican/Caribbean culture through music and language; and the transformation of the performer into a conscious cultural worker before the public" that Algarín considered fundamental to a Nuyorican aesthetic.[24] The development of salsa's Nuyorican aesthetic must also be understood, as Herrera outlines, in relation to both Puerto Rican and Black diasporic traditions, including Afro-Caribbean musical expression and African American vernacular traditions.[25] I capitalize Nuyorican to designate its signification in *Made in NuYoRico* with diasporic Puerto Ricanness, Puerto Rican abjection, and the historical moment in which salsa's foundational narratives developed.

My use of "NuYoRico" draws on what Nuyorican feminist Hip Hop artist, poet, and playwright Caridad de la Luz, aka La Bruja, describes as "that place somewhere between the Empire State and El Morro," a military fort from the Spanish colonial area located at the edge of Viejo San Juan in Puerto Rico.[26] In this book, NuYoRico is a symbolic site where cultural expression, racial and colonial subjectivity, rootedness in physical location, and a recuperation of public space—both the stage and urban streets—are constitutive of diasporic Puerto Rican subjectivity. It signals the continuum of meanings within Nuyorican, with all its possibilities and contradictions.

## Music Making and Puerto Rican New York

As Ruth Glasser documents, the history of music making in New York's Puerto Rican communities extends back to the 1920s and 1930s, when recent arrivals established *colonias* (neighborhoods) in which residents formed part of informal networks that supported the professional development of musicians. As Glasser explains, a small cadre of Afro–Puerto Rican musicians that included Rafael Hernández, his brother Jesús Hernández, and Rafael Duchesne were recruited directly from Puerto Rico to play in the African American military regiment led by Captain John Reese during World War I and settled in New York after the war. Other musicians, many of whom also worked in sectors of the economy unrelated to music, formed part of the migration to the United States propelled by structural shifts in Puerto Rico's economy in the late 1920s that produced a surplus labor force. New York's position at the center of the entertainment industry and recording opportunities played a key role in their decision to settle in New York, where Puerto Ricans played an integral role in the city's musical landscape.[27] Compositions by Rafael Hernández and the *plenas* of Manuel Jiménez (El Canario), who moved to New York in 1925 and remained there for more than twenty years before returning to Puerto Rico, were among the first contributions by diasporic Puerto Rican composers and songwriters to Puerto Rico's musical canon.[28] Puerto Rican musicians had to be versatile to make a living, and thus they were often broadly familiar with US popular music, including African American musical traditions, as well as Latin American and Caribbean repertoires. Yet, as Glasser chronicles, racist practices among nightclub owners and promoters bifurcated the careers of Puerto Ricans musicians. Those that audiences might read as "white" benefited from a broader array of opportunities to play in uptown (e.g., Harlem) as well as the downtown clubs denied to Black Puerto Rican musicians.[29] The birth of Cubop, or Latin jazz, in the 1940s, forged through the collaboration of Afro-Cuban musicians Machito (Frank Grillo) and Maurio Bauzá with Gillespie, brought together Black diasporic musical traditions in new and innovative ways. By the late 1940s and 1950s, the mambo craze spilled beyond the largely Puerto Rican and Cuban neighborhoods in New York and created additional opportunities to play throughout the city to racially and ethnically diverse audiences.[30]

The careers of Puerto Rican musicians during the interwar period foreshadowed a generation of artists born or raised in New York after World War II who were, as Latin soul artist Johnny Colón (no relation to Willie Colón) described himself, Puerto Rican "all the way" down to their bones but were "born with the American Hit Parade."[31] The demographic changes propelled by the migration of African Americans and Puerto Ricans to New York after World War II accelerated social, cultural, and musical reciprocity. During the 1950s and 1960s, Puerto Rican musicians continued to engage with Caribbean, Latin American, and US popular music, particularly rock 'n' roll's continuum of African American musical styles.[32] The US blockade of Cuba, however, suspended access to a vibrant source of musical innovation. According to musician Elliot "Yeyito" Flores, it also created an opening for Puerto Rican musicians to challenge cultural hierarchies that privileged Cuban music and Cuban musicians in the *rumbas* that took place regularly in Central Park.[33] While mambo, *cha cha chá*, and *charangas* remained largely unchanged during this period, Puerto Rican engagement with African American musical styles like doo-wop flourished.[34]

Living and working alongside each other, African Americans and Puerto Ricans also went to the same nightclubs, which often featured Black and Latin bands on the same billing. The burgeoning boogaloo music scene, with its celebration of Black and Latin American musical traditions, layered a deceptively simple musicality with what Juan Flores describes as an "emotional depth and homespun creativity" that epitomized the synthesis of Black and Latin rhythms. The departure from established musical practices within Latin music is most clearly seen, Flores notes, in the intertwined funk, soul, and Afro-Caribbean rhythms of boogaloo. The boogaloo compositions of artists like Willie Bobo (William Correa) sounded the cultural and musical reciprocity between Puerto Ricans and African Americans that had existed since World War I. Boogaloo emphasized the musical and social reciprocity between African Americans and Puerto Ricans in multiple ways. Juan Flores highlights the synthesis of musical styles, outbursts that invoked a raucous crowd at a party, and the counterpoint between the "crowd" (that is, the chorus) and the piano. The racialized excess of songs like "Bang! Bang!" by Joe Cuba and "I Like It Like That" by Pete Rodríguez influenced the development of salsa, although the latter largely turned away from foregrounding African American rhythms in favor of Afro-Caribbean musical styles.[35]

## Puerto Ricans in the City

Even as Latin music sounded the spatial and social relations on the streets of Latin New York, the presence of Puerto Ricans raised concerns for politicians and public officials at the local and federal levels. As the political and economic control of the United States increasingly created conditions catalyzing migration from Puerto Rico in the 1930s, the number of people arriving to New York raised the specter of future congressional representation for a population deemed racially inferior. Puerto Rican participation in the 1935 uprisings in Harlem became fodder for these anxieties locally, raising concerns about the criminality of a population that could not be deported.[36] Lorrin Thomas has shown how the "flood" of Puerto Ricans arriving to Harlem in the 1940s likewise raised fears about their exemption from the "rigorous physical, political and economic examinations applied to all other immigrants" just as concerns of a fifth column increasingly circulated in the United States during World War II.[37] Puerto Ricans also posed a threat to the nation's borders. "We were reliably informed," stated Representative Ed Gossett, a Democrat from Texas, "that one can purchase in New York itself a Puerto Rican birth certificate," thereby making New York "a haven" for illegal entry into the United States.[38]

The *New York Times* characterized the "infiltration" of the Lower East Side by Puerto Ricans as a contributing factor to the spread of "disease, dirt and crime" in the city. The same reporter contrasted the "tidiness of Puerto Rican housewives" in Spanish Harlem with the practice of "tenants who throw garbage from windows in paper bags." The writer, who identified "traditional" practices in the Puerto Rican countryside as a cause of the unseemly behavior, emphasized that East Harlem remains "dirtier than just about any other place in the city despite daily pickups by the Department of Sanitation." The representation of Puerto Rican women as "tidy" thus appeared as an individual anomaly amid unseemly cultural proclivities that polluted the city. Accordingly, the 1949 profile of East Harlem and its residents included commentary on the high rates of tuberculosis in the neighborhood and the violent clashes with Italian residents who "resent[ed] the *invasion* of East Harlem by Puerto Ricans."[39]

The 1950s brought mixed attitudes toward recent Puerto Rican arrivals. As Thomas outlines, social service agencies emphasized the need for understanding between New Yorkers and recently arrived Puerto Ricans. Likewise, the skill, reliability, and work ethic of Puerto Rican workers were praised by employers who, encouraged by Cold War patriotic fervor, gave "a patriotic tone to the hiring of citizens, including Puerto Ricans."[40] Newspaper articles in the *New York Post* and the Spanish-language *Diario de Nueva York* highlighted the increasing importance of Puerto Ricans to the city as a voting bloc and consumer group, respectively.[41] These changes notwithstanding, the 1950s also saw increasing xenophobia around the growth of Puerto Rican communities in New York, and the media and public officials circulated narratives of them as an economic, structural, and public health threat to the city.[42] Public discourse constructed the large migration of Puerto Ricans to New York as the cause of political instability and declining resources in the city. Rather than looking at the "excesses of private low-income housing and labor market instability," city officials blamed Puerto Ricans for the spread of slums. The Mayor's Advisory Committee on Puerto Rican Affairs, previously named the Advisory Committee on the Puerto Rican Problem, stressed the economic burden placed on New York's resources.[43]

The racialization of Puerto Ricans in New York became entangled with colonial, anti-Black, and anti-immigrant ideologies. Puerto Rican migrants were not African American, but they were Black. And those who were not Black were not racialized as white. That the mass migration of Puerto Ricans at midcentury coincided with that of African Americans further linked Puerto Rican racialization with that of African Americans.[44] By the late 1950s, mainstream media began publishing stories that pointed to the post–World War II migration of African Americans and Puerto Ricans to New York as a contributing factor in exploding public school enrollments in New York City. A 1958 *New York Times* article implied that abnormal reproductive practices among African Americans and Puerto Ricans resulted in a surge of school-age children that "more than offset the loss caused by the migration of many families to the suburbs."[45] Insofar as the *Times* had already framed white flight from the city in terms of African American and Puerto Rican migration to New York, it reinforced attitudes that the $100 million the city spent on facilities and teacher hires was a drain on the city's resources by the very residents who had replaced white children as the majority in Manhattan and the Bronx. A 1966 front-page *New York Times* article that reported the exodus of twenty-five thousand "non-Negro" and "non-Puerto Rican" children from the city's public schools over the course of a single year reproduced the distinction between "New Yorkers," on one hand, and African Americans and Puerto Ricans, on the other.[46]

In the 1960s, the structural problems encountered by both groups would be described in terms of cultural deficiency by Nathan Glazer and Daniel Moynihan in *Beyond the Melting Pot: The Negroes, Puerto Ricans, Jews, Italians, and Irish of New York City* (1963). Historical and social science research also contributed to the pathologization of poverty among Puerto Ricans. Oscar Lewis won a National Book Award for his ethnography *La Vida: A Puerto Rican Family in the Culture of Poverty* (1966), which centered Puerto Rican communities in New York and La Perla in San Juan. The "culture of poverty" elaborated by Lewis blamed systemic and persistent intergenerational barriers on "absent fathers, matriarchal families, women having children while still very young themselves, poor work habits, violence and obsession with sex."[47] Puerto Ricans and African Americans would be singled out within social and economic policies as the primary causes of New York's fiscal crisis of the early 1970s.[48] The public policy of benign neglect enforced drastic austerity measures and provided the template for neoliberal initiatives that developed more fully in the 1980s.

The pathologization of Puerto Ricans brought together representations of economic dependence and racialized inferiority with concerns about local and national security. Anti-imperialist critiques from the Puerto Rican community that framed migration and settlement within the context of broader economic and political forces faced anti-Communist rhetoric that questioned Puerto Ricans' loyalty to the US government. In 1944, the Federal Bureau of Investigation (FBI) interrogated political activist and journalist Jesús Colón, who would also be subpoenaed by the House Committee on Un-American Activities (HUAC), about his ties to the Communist Party. Locally, Democrats questioned Antonia Denis, the only Puerto Rican woman who formed part of the Democratic political machine in Brooklyn during the early 1950s, about her presumed Communist sympathies. As Thomas explains, the Democrats based their assumptions about Denis not on her actual participation in the Communist Party but rather on their beliefs about the propensity of poor, racially mixed, morally degenerate Puerto Ricans to be targeted by the Communist Party.[49] Red-baiting persisted as HUAC scheduled a series of hearings to investigate reports of a "Communist conspiracy . . . attempting to penetrate Puerto Rican nationality groups in New York City and to establish conduits between these groups in the United States and Communist conspiratorial operations in Puerto Rico" in 1959. The committee insisted that Puerto Ricans remained susceptible to Communists, who wanted only to further the Soviet agenda and thus had no actual commitment to Puerto Rico.[50]

Even when local politicians, social services, and mainstream media painted more sympathetic portraits of and emphasized the structural challenges faced by Puerto Ricans, they reproduced hegemonic narratives of racialized cultural inferiority. In New York's cultural imaginary, Puerto Ricans and African Americans presented an obstacle to the geopolitical priorities of urban renewal projects and the performance of "national cultural maturity and urban resurgence that could be brandished in the Cold War with the Soviet Union."[51] Concerns over juvenile delinquency were high among politicians and moneyed interests. New York's newspapers, for their part, overrepresented violence between Puerto Ricans and African Americans, downplayed the role of whites, and underreported interethnic tensions among white ethnics, a practice that supported the city's logic for managing space.[52]

Even the Spanish-language newspaper *La Prensa* contributed to the image of Puerto Ricans as "hoodlums" or gang members that threatened the city.[53]

By the early 1960s, the development of public housing for middle-class residents exacerbated tensions over real estate by "balkanizing" neighborhoods like the Lower East Side. Urban renewal projects left middle-class white ethnics in new housing living alongside the old and dilapidated buildings where Puerto Ricans, who remained a "problem" in need of "management and regulation" by the New York City Housing Authority despite being "excellent" tenants, continued to live.[54] Efforts directed at stopping the spread of "unsalvageable slums" disproportionately focused on Black and Puerto Rican residents.[55] Throughout the city, one group displaced another as local government agencies moved them around. In parts of East Harlem, for instance, African Americans replaced Puerto Ricans, who in turn had already displaced Italians.[56] Often dubbed "Puerto Rican removal programs," urban renewal frequently resulted in Puerto Ricans finding themselves shuffled from one apartment to the next.[57] The San Juan Hill/Lincoln Square neighborhood, where *West Side Story* was filmed, was a thriving eighteen-block multiracial neighborhood composed of working-class and lower-middle-class residents and their businesses. It was razed by the time the film premiered in 1961 as part of city planning efforts. As Samuel Zipp explains, "The force of culture and the arts, newly rescued from feminized inertia and recruited for manly duty in the Cold War, would also be deployed to offset the threat to racial purity and stable cultural lineage looming in an era of urban transformation." Spurred by urban renewal and Cold War ideology that promoted the fine arts as the apogee of democracy, the neighborhood would be replaced by twenty-eight luxury apartment buildings and the Lincoln Center for the Performing Arts.[58]

The abjection of Puerto Ricans as colonial-racial others informs how whiteness *among* Puerto Ricans became unmarked, and racism within Puerto Rican communities in the United States considered "inconceivable." This refusal to mark whiteness reifies persistent racial hierarchies within Puerto Rican diasporic communities—at times even while acknowledging and condemning racism in Puerto Rico.[59] The failure to contend with racialized privilege risks attributing the structural challenges faced by Black Puerto Ricans to individual choices or a "culture of poverty." Moreover, as the Know Collective reminds us in their founding statement, dominant attitudes dismiss private and public charges of racism by Black Puerto Ricans, whose own lives inform their "thought, knowledges, and epistemologies."[60] Racist narratives and practices reproduce discourses that pathologize Black

Puerto Ricans while ignoring the persistence of racial hierarchies informed by histories of enslavement, classism, patriarchy, and anti-Black racism.[61]

Just as Black Puerto Rican bodies marked the "changing complexion" of New York, the sounds of noisy Puerto Ricans speaking in Spanish and Spanish-inflected English racialized Puerto Ricans as linguistically, culturally, and intellectually inferior. Jennifer Stoever's analyses of the reciprocal relationship among sound, listening, and race in the racialization of Puerto Ricans in New York during the 1950s and 1960s reveals a "sonic color-line" wherein "racial difference [was] coded, produced, and policed." Puerto Ricans' aural presence was racially coded as "rough, rowdy, loud, and hilarious, terms that evoke the antithetical image of the disciplined decorum of body and voice demanded by (white) American cold-war norms and listening practices." Equating the city's Puerto Rican presence with noise, the *New York Times* used language similar to that of articles on white flight to describe the invasive and "unseemly" soundscape of Puerto Rican New York.[62]

Racialized anxieties about the presence of Puerto Ricans in the public sphere reveal how both sound and space emerged as loci for the construction of difference in the formation of Nuyorican identity in the geocultural space of New York. The film *Blackboard Jungle* (1955) echoed racialized anxieties about the learning (dis)abilities of Puerto Rican children. As Stoever argues, the Hispanicized English of Puerto Ricans marked their racialized aural dissonance as aberrant noise unassimilable with the reproduction of American national identity.[63] The depiction of Puerto Ricans as racialized others reached its fullest elaboration in the theatrical and film productions of *West Side Story* (1957 and 1961, respectively). The film became the a priori reference for Puerto Ricans in the national imaginary. The sound of drums that opened *West Side Story* reflected how aural markers worked in conjunction with visual and discursive representations such as images of cannibalism, delinquency, and poverty to cement, as Alberto Sandoval Sánchez has argued, the image of Puerto Ricans as "Latina/o domestic ethnic and racial other" that posed a violent threat to the city's social order.[64]

The interlocking discourses elaborated in the media, the political arena, academia, and popular culture produced a "disgust consensus" that shaped dominant perceptions of diasporic Puerto Ricans, in both the United States and Puerto Rico, as disposable populations responsible for the city's deteriorating social conditions.[65] Insofar as "debt represents an economic relationship inseparable from the production of the debtor subject and his 'morality,'" as Maurizio Lazzarato argues, the lack of racial capital and unequal integration into the US economy, as well as Puerto Rico's colonial relationship to the United States, produced a public identity through which diasporic Puerto Ricans were interpellated as failed citizen subjects indebted to the state.[66] Drawing on the work of Imogen Tyler, I propose that salsa's Nuyorican aesthetics cannot be separated from the social abjection of Puerto Ricans and "what it means to be (made) abject, to be one who repeatedly finds herself the object of the other's violent objectifying disgust." I propose that salsa became a site through which Nuyoricans, and here I turn once again to Tyler, "reconfigure[d] and revolt[ed] against their abject subjectification."[67]

Puerto Rican participation in grassroots social movements proliferated alongside the music that emanated from New York's streets. Like salsa, political activism redefined the meaning of public spaces by transgressing the roles that mainstream media assigned Puerto Ricans. The New York chapter of the Young Lords Organization, which formed in response to the growing needs of Puerto Rican communities, was labeled by critics as "the fifth column in the service of Castro and Moscow."[68] The clandestine Fuerzas Armadas de Liberación Nacional (FALN, Armed Forces for National Liberation) took up arms in the fight for Puerto Rican independence from within the United States. Other microlocal efforts focused on both citywide efforts and the needs of specific neighborhoods. The agenda for Lower East Side resident associations such as CHARAS Inc. included economic empowerment while the Lower East Side Puerto Rican Action Committee advocated "rapid and often radical social change."[69] In 1969, the cultural institutions El Museo del Barrio and Taller Boricua became part of social struggles that emphasized shifting away from the middle-class and Hispanophile desires of earlier organizations that endeavored to integrate Puerto Ricans and other Hispanics into the mainstream.[70]

The artivists of the New Rican Village Cultural Arts Center, founded in 1976 on the Lower East Side, combined creative expression, activism, and shared a commitment to "using art as a means to revitalize various dilapidated New York City neighborhoods, and to foster a cultural renaissance modeled around new diasporic Latina/o identities." Poets, dancers, visual artists, and musicians alike participated in an environment that fostered experimentation and creativity. Musicians like Jerry González, Andy González, Milton Cardona, Steve Turre, and Papo Vázquez purposefully departed from commercial limitations placed by Fania Records.[71] In the photographic essay by Marcos Echeverría Ortiz, the New Rican Village is described as follows by photographer Máximo Colón: "The New Rican Village was a place for 'Students, militants, and intellectuals—a place for people from our community involved in cultural and political stuff.'" In the same essay, Young Lord Miguel "Mickey" Meléndez notes that the New Rican village was "unlike any other traditional salsa club, 'this was a place for left Latin cultural development. It really took the Nuyorican cultural experience to a place where you can experience different things [poetry, theater, and music] under one roof.'"[72] Nuyorican poets like the late Tato Laviera and Sandra María Esteves, who was part of the New Rican Village collective and a founding member of the Nuyorican Poets Café, incorporated the music's rhythms and meanings into their poetry as the sounds of salsa filled their own lives in the streets of Latin New York and the nightclubs across the city.

### ¡Qué le pongan salsa!

Emerging in the mid to late 1960s in neighborhoods where Puerto Rican and other Latin American and Caribbean immigrants had settled in New York since the beginning of the twentieth century, salsa quickly became a cultural marker for the city's urban, poor, and working-class Puerto Ricans. The experimentation with instrumentation and incorporation of diverse stylistic elements characterized salsa but, unlike boogaloo and Latin soul, foregrounded Afro-Caribbean musical genres. The shift away from African American musical styles and toward Afro-Caribbean musical practices considered more conventional within Latin music did not, however, preclude stylistic developments that distinguished salsa from its predecessors in New York. Nor did it entail a complete departure from African American musical styles. The instrumentation, musical arrangements, and other stylistic elements cultivated an alternative musical soundscape grounded in a brash, urban musicality that sounded the cultural and spatial geography of the city.[73] Like the broader Nuyorican Arts Movement of which it formed a part, salsa both reflected and informed an emerging Nuyorican imaginary.

Often referred to as the Latin Motown, Fania Records developed an infrastructure for the creation, circulation, and consumption of salsa that far exceeded the capabilities of existing Latin music labels established after World War II. The label was cofounded by Dominican flutist, composer, and bandleader Johnny Pacheco and Gerald "Jerry" Masucci, an Italian American lawyer and former police officer. The label struggled financially during its early years, but by the early 1970s it emerged as the dominant force in the New York Latin music industry. Formerly signed to Alegre Records, which had gone bankrupt, Pacheco sought to create a label that, unlike his previous one, prioritized musicians and treated them as family rather than exploitable commodities.[74] Pacheco brought his experience as a musician and bandleader, his relationship with local performers, and his familiarity with the Latin music scene to the partnership. Most of Alegre's artists followed Pacheco to Fania, and his talent for identifying up-and-coming talent, like bassist Bobby Valentín, proved indispensable as Fania Records grew its stable of artists.[75] Masucci may have first been introduced to Afro-Caribbean rhythms while stationed at the US naval base in Guantánamo as a Marine, but he famously claimed to never have listened to Latin music prior to this venture. Like other labels of the 1960s and 1970s that saw themselves as fostering "innovative and creative oases for new or unconventional musicians in the midst of a capital-driven and profit-oriented record business," Fania Records emphasized its commitment to creative musical practices by signing both established musicians and emerging artists.[76] This corporate strategy allowed Fania to sign emerging musicians with little business acumen and few alternatives for relatively little.

Between 1971 and 1977, Fania expanded its stable of artists and its music catalog by acquiring several of its competitors, including Alegre, Cotique, Tico, Mardi Gras, and Inca Records. Masucci, who eventually became sole owner of Fania Records, also established Fania International; Vaya Records, which recruited talent in Puerto Rico; and Musica Latina International.[77] Fania International and Musica Latina expanded Fania's reach into Puerto Rico and other parts of Latin America, releasing albums by Argentine balladeer Sabu (Héctor Jorge Ruiz) and the Chilean Grupo Ángeles.[78] In 1968 Masucci created Uptite Records, a short-lived label that specialized in soul and R&B, and which has been ignored in histories of Fania's growth. Masucci also created the eponymous label Jerry Masucci Music (JMM and JM), which began releasing albums in 1976. In a 1997 filing with the Securities and Exchange Commission, the company then doing business as Fania (Fania Entertainment Group) reported a catalog of approximately 1,300 master recordings, 10,000 individual songs, more than 650 albums, and all the recording contracts and songwriter agreements signed with Fania's publishing companies. In 2005, the company that bought the catalog from Masucci's estate discovered a storage unit with a treasure trove of masters, including previously unreleased material. In 2018, Concord, the company currently doing business as Fania, reported that the catalog consisted of 19,000 audio masters and 8,000 compositions.[79]

By the mid-1970s, Fania Records succeeded in extending salsa's distribution networks well beyond the United States, where salsa has remained at the core of developments in the "tropical" Latin music market and played an integral role in the evolution of ballroom dancing. Fania established a distribution center in Panama in 1974 and, just two years later, became the first Latin music label in the United States to own its own recording studio. A year later, it procured a manufacturing plant in Puerto Rico.[80] This eliminated a principal challenge that independent labels faced at the time in predicting sales: Fania could keep production of a particular album modest to avoid overstock while responding to demand quickly.[81] But by 1978, the label was in decline. Masucci sold the catalog in 1979 to the Uruguayan company Valsyn, popularly believed to have been a shell company owned by him. He closed Fania Records and most of the network of additional record labels sometime in the early 1980s. Masucci went on to create and administer various labels that continued doing business as Fania. Each became the legal successor to the original Fania Records and the network of labels and publishing companies owned by Masucci, responsible for the massive catalog of music and publishing rights. Following Masucci's death, the catalog became one of the most coveted in the music industry and has since been acquired by successive entities.

Masucci's stewardship of this empire has led to the generalization of the names Fania and Fania Records to refer to the original label, the network of recording companies and publishing houses he owned, and the various successors who have controlled the Fania catalog. I use "Fania Records" to refer to the original label. I use "Fania" to refer to the original label *as well as* additional labels created or acquired by Masucci in the 1970s, the publishing companies he created, and, when appropriate, the labels' successors. I use "Fania successors" to refer to the series of companies since 1979 that have continued to do business as Fania by acquiring the rights to use the trademarked name, including Musica Latina, Sonido, Emusica, Codigo, and Concord. In some cases, such as that of Musica Latina and Sonido, they also assumed legal liability for unpaid royalties or breaches of contract involving artists signed to the original Fania companies. The "Fania catalog" refers to the music catalog for Fania Records, its network of labels, and successors Musica Latina and Sonido; all available master recordings for each of the labels; and the publishing rights owned by FAF Publishing, Vaya Publishing, and Vev Publishing, the companies to which most of the artists signed to Fania signed over their publishing rights. When appropriate, I use the name of an individual label for specificity.

My use of "Latin music" refers to the US music industry's production of "Spanish-language music of Latin American origins."[82] Deborah Pacini Hernández provides a useful definition of the Latin music industry, which historically has included recordings from Latin American countries, including the Spanish-speaking Caribbean, and "ethnic" recordings made in the United States, and clarifies my own use of the phrase:

> Although the commonly used term "Latin music industry" suggests a monolithic entity, this industry has always included multiple layers and players—some with strong connections to Latin America, some without—whose domains of activity have often overlapped and intersected with each other as well as with the mainstream music industry. Moreover, many of the most influential players in the Latin music industry—even in the case of small domestic independent labels—have *not* themselves been Latino. Some of these non-Latinos whose professional lives revolved around Latin music have been personally engaged with Latino communities, although for others, Latin music has simply been another product that could turn a profit if marketed effectively. All Latin music industry personnel, however, regardless of their own ethnic and racial backgrounds, have had to ply their trade with a complicated network of multiple ethnically, racially, and culturally defined communities and markets whose boundaries have always been porous and unstable.[83]

This quotation serves to highlight the complexity of the Latin music industry and the use of "Latin" as a referent for both a field of broad musical traditions and a sector of the music industry that, while distinct, remains embedded within larger musical and corporate structures. To this end, when I speak of "Latin" musicians, this refers to the music rather than serving as a marker of artists' racial, ethnic, and cultural backgrounds. In fact, as Pacini Hernández reminds us, during the first half the twentieth century, Latin music was often performed by artists who were neither Latina/o nor Latin American. Nor did it entail, as demonstrated by the mainstream circulation of Mexican music during this period while music performed by Mexican Americans remained primarily within these communities, interest in music performed by Latina/o musicians or music publishers.[84]

With each Latin boom since the 1970s, salsa's social imaginary has been increasingly separated from the communities, musical practices, and cultural matrix from which the music initially drew: largely Black, urban, poor, and working-class Puerto Rican communities. The Rican/Struction in *Made in NuYoRico* resides in foregrounding the entanglement of aesthetics, cultural politics, and economic and social relations with salsa. This understanding resists the ongoing tendency to describe culture as an opposition between commodified and authentic aesthetic culture. Accordingly, *Made in NuYoRico* considers the imbrication of "work, pleasure, consumption, spirituality, 'aesthetic' production, and reproduction" in salsa from the perspective of diasporic Puerto Rican artists and audiences.[85] Just as salsa did not emerge outside the market, commodification and commercialization cannot be reduced to the logics of the market, and of global media in particular. Such claims presume a monolithic market and passive consumer without considering the specificity of cultural products informed by the everyday lives and cultural practices of racialized and, as in the case of Puerto Ricans, colonial subjects.

Rican/Struction operates as both a methodology and an analytic for exploring the reiterative power of a Nuyorican aesthetic that transmitted ways of knowing and being in the world that drew on the past, present, and future amid the abjection of diasporic Puerto Ricans in both the United States and Puerto Rico. Rican/Struction illuminates the entanglement of pleasure's enduring possibilities with salsa's aesthetics and cultural politics. Salsa became a vehicle for diasporic Puerto Ricans not only to repudiate their structural coming into presence in New York but also to "speak"—by singing, playing, dancing, improvising, listening, arranging, composing—in ways that exceeded normative renderings of productive citizenship.

**Laying It Out**

*Made in NuYoRico* restages various moments between 1964 and 2014 during which, should we "listen in detail," as Alexandra Vázquez urges us, we may hear the possibilities and contradictions of salsa as a site for the expression of Nuyorican futurity.[86] Each chapter of the book centers on a particular moment that calls attention to how salsa's aesthetic contours, affective economy of pleasure, and Nuyorican imaginary coalesce in the public, cultural, economic, and/or legal fields. In each case, I tease out not what salsa is but what salsa *does* at a particular moment. That is, I attend to salsa's signifying practices and how its dissonant sonorities sound to particular publics, in particular places, at particular times. I explore salsa's meanings in each instance by bringing together Nuyorican histories with stylistic elements, affect, and market logics. Doing so requires "listening in detail" to music and the *people* who "came to be a part of [the music], what they contributed to, how they made it sound, and what directions" they took salsa.[87] It requires listening closely, carefully, and repeatedly to those people, periods, songs, and details that have been deemed insignificant. The goal is not to merely add to salsa's histories, fix the music's meanings, or ascribe new meanings to it but to be flexible, open to possibilities, to listen again and again to the music and the people who played it, listened to it, danced it.

I focus primarily on the musical collaborations of Colón and LaVoe from 1966 to 1978, a period during which they helped launch and consolidate Fania's position as New York's preeminent Latin music conglomerate. As two of salsa's foundational figures, they became a synecdoche for salsa's rebelliousness. I situate Colón and LaVoe within broader Nuyorican artistic, political, economic, and social expression, rather than as exceptional figures. The collaboration of salsa's so-called bad boys during this period consists of two phases. The first lasts from 1966 to 1975, during which LaVoe provided lead vocals for Colón's band. Colón's departure from his own band and LaVoe's solo recordings initiate the second phase in their collaboration.[88] LaVoe continued with the band and released *La Voz* (The Voice), his first solo album, in 1975. Colón, who produced *La Voz*, would go on to produce LaVoe's next albums, *De ti depende* (It depends on you, 1976) and *Comedia* (Comedy, 1978). Colón and LaVoe would reunite in 1983 on *Vigilante*, the score to the film by the same name.

*Made in NuYoRico* is made up of two sections wherein I trace salsa's social life, first through the streets of New York during the 1960s and 1970s as musicians, fans, and Fania reveled in the music's effervescence. The second part of the book traces the afterlife of the salsa boom. It highlights how the music's Nuyorican meanings informed salsa's aesthetic, commercial, legal, and social meanings in Puerto Rico and the United States. This latter section focuses primarily on salsa's meanings within the legal sphere, as part of public policy, and in relation to economic development. Each of the two parts highlights how salsa's imbrication with a Nuyorican imaginary impacted the music's trajectory, producing a plurality of meanings.[89] Similarly to Ana Ochoa Gautier, whose work examines sound and listening practices in Latin America, I endeavor to show how salsa's musical and nonmusical practices "invoke, provoke, and incarnate for different peoples."[90]

Three chapters compose Part I, which maps salsa's cultural history through the streets of "Latin" New York from 1964 through the end of the following decade. This period is demarcated by the creation of Fania Records, its increasing domination of Latin music in New York over the next fifteen years, and the precipitous decline that led to its closure. The first chapter takes as its point of departure the film *Our Latin Thing*, a musical documentary of the legendary 1971 Fania All-Stars concert at New York's Cheetah Lounge.

With a vision that extended beyond salsa to the communities in which the music emerged, first-time director Leon Gast intermingled scenes filmed primarily on New York's Lower East Side with the performance at the Cheetah. Linking salsa's aesthetic contours to the city's poor and working-class Puerto Rican communities, the film illuminates an ambivalent relationship between Fania Records and Latin New York: New York Puerto Ricans participated in the commodification of salsa while resisting their reduction to objects of consumption.

The inspiration for beginning *Made in NuYoRico* with the reciprocity and tensions between culture and the market, broadly conceived, came from both artists and fans I interviewed for this project. I was particularly moved by recollections of salsa's everynight life at nightclubs and afterhours across the city. These interviews, informal conversations, and opportunities to attend community events drew me to explore the salsa circuit of nightclubs, afterhours, hotels, and resorts. During salsa's foundational period, salsa's dance floors were not yet a site for the transformation of whiteness in the context of an exotic other but rather a space wherein the performative excess of Puerto Rican bodies across the city's landscape shaped salsa's cultural and commercial meanings.[91] Highlighting the proximity of dance and political life, salsa's everynight life illustrates, as Celeste Fraser Delgado and José Esteban Muñoz propose, how, "magnificent against the monotonous repetition of everyday oppression, dance incites rebellions of everynight life."[92] This first chapter foregrounds a performative excess that exceeded Fania Records' ability to fully control or appropriate salsa's meanings.

Chapter 2 examines how Colón and LaVoe cultivated an image of themselves as "los malotes de la salsa" (salsa's bad boys) who exulted in excessive behaviors of aesthetic and social incivility that defied established musical practices and social norms. The musicality and defiance form part of a Nuyorican aesthetic that "reclaims peoples, artistic practices, and subjectivities deemed abject and reconfigures them" in ways that resemanticize the streets of Latin New York and repudiate the status of Puerto Ricans as "revolting subjects."[93] Their *chusmería*, an often racially veiled term used to describe excessive "behavior that refuses standards of bourgeois comportment . . . and to a large degree, [is] linked to stigmatized class identity," embraced Puerto Rican abjection.[94] Their use of *relajo*, what Diana Taylor might describe as their "joyous rebellious solidarity" with poor and working-class Puerto Ricans, included those whom *salsero* Luis "Máquina" Flores described as the "pimps" and "whores" at the social fringes of Latin New York.[95] Colón and LaVoe embraced liminality and made visible their rejection of the respectability central to hegemonic narratives of Puerto Rican and American national identities.[96]

In chapter 3, I explore how Colón and LaVoe's performance of subjecthood regarded the feminine as both necessary and threatening to the performance of subjecthood. These gendered underpinnings necessitate, as Hazel Carby indicates, an interrogation of the ideological and political impact of how their music constructed the sonic, visual, and discursive field of representation.[97] I propose that the performance of subjecthood by salsa's bad boys depends as much on the performance of virile masculinity as the repudiation of *lo sucio*, what Deborah Vargas theorizes as the "surplus subjectivities who perform disobediently within hetero- and homonormative racial projects of citizenship formations."[98] I demonstrate that the racialized masculinity of salsa's ideal subject is predicated on the representation and expulsion of undisciplined desires and disobedient women and queer subjects.[99]

The second part of the book begins with an exploration of salsa's flows to and within Puerto Rico. Chapter 4 analyzes the attempt of then governor Rafael Hernández Colón to mobilize salsa's Nuyorican meanings and global popularity as part of a branding campaign curated for the Puerto Rico exhibit at the 1992 Universal Expo in Seville. Working with government press releases, speeches, newspaper reports, and documents related to the development of the Puerto Rico pavilion, I map how salsa's Nuyorican imaginary was mobilized as a repository of the nation's presumed cultural exceptionalism, cosmopolitan character, and economic aspirations.[100] I demonstrate that the nation branding campaign that culminated with the "Puerto Rico es salsa" (Puerto Rico is salsa) concert at the Expo reified a transatlantic world economy wherein the Caribbean serves to reinforce hegemonic cultural and economic practices invested in white supremacy and the structural inequalities that uphold it.[101]

The final two chapters of the book return to the music itself, following the trajectory of the song "El Cantante" (The Singer) from its initial recording in 1978 by LaVoe to its recording and performances by Rubén Blades, who wrote the song's initial verses. If LaVoe's early work and the public character of his tumultuous personal life endeared him to diasporic Puerto Rican fans, who considered LaVoe one of their own, then his performative persona coalesced around the image of the tragic clown like never before when he recorded "El Cantante." The song narrates the private trials and tribulations of a singer beloved by his fans. In the first of these two chapters, I trace the ways that, over the next fifteen years, "El Cantante"—both the song and its musical persona—became the lens through which a public narrative formed around LaVoe. By examining lawsuits wherein various parties claimed the rights to LaVoe's royalties, I show that his depiction within the legal system relied on representations of racialized excess and abjection. Chapter 6 turns to the tensions between LaVoe's performance of "El Cantante" and Blades's legal status as the song's sole author. Drawing on the work of legal scholar Rosemary Coombe, I propose that legal claims to "El Cantante" must be approached through an analysis of the constellation of images, narratives, and legal conventions that form part of hegemonic power within the courtroom.[102] To that end, my approach to the question of whether "El Cantante" should be considered a joint work under copyright law, or, at minimum, require a collaborative agreement between Blades and LaVoe's estate, is based on an understanding of law "not as rules and policies but as stories, explanations, performances and linguistic exchanges" through which social constructions of power are negotiated.[103] Rather than attempting to establish the truth of claims to LaVoe's royalties and the song's authorship, this final chapter examines how legal doctrines are established and protected over time and the ways they reify the coloniality of power through which LaVoe's status in the courtroom was (re)presented.

Salsa's social life across half a century reveals a complicated process whereby multiple concurrent claims circulate simultaneously in the artistic, social, economic, and legal spheres. *Made in NuYoRico* shows not only how salsa reclaimed the public sphere in New York from which Puerto Ricans were repeatedly expelled literally (through urban renewal) and symbolically but how the music's Nuyorican imaginary became the site for the performance of musical, cultural, political, legal, and economic authority. *Made in NuYoRico* illuminates how Nuyorican subjectivities embedded within salsa impacted the music's trajectory in both New York and Puerto Rico, sounding a colonial contestation that produced alternative meanings of Puerto Ricanness in each space. Salsa's ability to convey an "authentic" Puerto Rican subject in both New York and Puerto Rico hinged not only on the music itself but also on the ways the performers negotiated the terrain as they claimed the authority to represent Puerto Rico and Puerto Ricanness. This authority extended from the stages of the cuchifrito circuit to Puerto Rico and Spain, and from the streets of Latin New York to its courtrooms, where questions of cultural authority and representation become entangled with modern copyright law. Ultimately, I illustrate how artists, fans, music industry personnel, and even government institutions have produced competing and overlapping claims to salsa's Nuyorican imaginary for over half a century.

# Anatomy of a Salsa Boom, 1964–1979

PART I

# Our Latin Thing    **1**
## SALSA'S NUYORICAN HISTORIES

The musical documentary and cult classic *Our Latin Thing* (*Nuestra cosa*), released in 1972 by Fania Records, is generally considered the debut of the Fania All-Stars.[1] The film features concert footage from an August 26, 1971, performance by the All-Stars at the Cheetah Lounge, one of New York's most well-known clubs of the time, located at Fifty-Third Street and Broadway. The ensemble band included many of the most well-known musicians and vocalists signed to Fania, including bandleaders Ray Barretto, Roberto Roena, Willie Colón, and Larry Harlow alongside lead vocalists such as Héctor LaVoe, Ismael Miranda, José "Cheo" Feliciano, and Pete "El Conde" Rodríguez. In addition to the concert, *Our Latin Thing* incorporates a series of scenes filmed on New York's Lower East Side and in its primarily Puerto Rican and more broadly Latina/o community. *Record World* praised the film for its "spectacular" camerawork and montages that would contribute to the box office success of the "historic" film.[2] Salsa historian César Rondón appreciated seeing "where the musicians came from, what world they represented, and to what social and cultural circumstances the music played."[3] The film captures a rawness, creativity, and sense of possibility that drew precisely on a Nuyorican performative excess across the stages, nightclubs, and streets of Latin New York that could not be anticipated or fully appropriated by Fania Records.

The film begins with a shot of children playing on a rooftop and an aerial view of New York's streets below. The camera cuts to the roof where one boy appears to fly a kite while others watch, and the sounds of congas and bongos fill the air. The camera then follows a prepubescent boy across the roof, and the viewer gets another bird's-eye view of the neighborhood as he looks over the edge at buildings, children playing in the street, and trash strewn on the street and sidewalks below. The boy turns and runs to the roof door, and the scene changes to the street itself, where children pour out of one building as the percussion continues offscreen alongside Spanish-speaking voices that become increasingly distinct. The boy from the rooftop, smiling and seemingly carefree, emerges from the building where we last saw him and skips across the street, returning to view at the entrance of an alley. The clanging of the metal can he kicks reverberates across the concrete as the sounds of the city fall away and the film's theme song, Barretto's "Cocinando" (Cooking), begins to play.[4] The smooth groove of the largely instrumental Latin jazz track marks a transition from the streets and sounds of Latin New York to the music itself. The repetition of "Cocinando suave" (Cooking smoothly) suggests that the film is cooking up something for the viewer.

In the alley, the boy lingers to read the film credits on the concrete wall. Designed and hung on the wall to look like graffiti, the credits read like a greatest hits collection of Latin musicians in New York. Once the boy reaches the end of the wall and the credits, he disappears momentarily from the screen. In the next shot, he appears running across a small lot before darting through an opening in the chain-link fence that leads to a street lined with garbage piled in heaps and buildings obviously in severe need of repair. The *New York Times* review described them as "blocks where the city sanitation sweepers seem never to have visited."[5] Indeed, the mise-en-scène underscores the deteriorating economic conditions at the end of the 1960s and in the early 1970s, a period marked by the serial displacement of Puerto Rican residents, increasing unemployment, and disinvestment in Black and Puerto Rican neighborhoods throughout the city. The opening scene also summons memories of the Young Lords garbage offensive in 1969 in East Harlem. In response to the residents' concern about mounting garbage, the Young Lords moved the trash from the neighborhood sidewalks to the middle of the street. They lit the pile on fire because the Department of Sanitation refused to collect the trash or give them supplies to do it themselves.

With an ease that suggests familiarity with the neighborhood, the boy sprints through passages that appear innocuous from the sidewalk but provide shortcuts between buildings. A temporalization effect occurs as

**1.1** Still from Fania All-Stars' *Our Latin Thing* (1972)

Barretto's solo begins in "Cocinando." The boy, like the music, appears to pick up speed. "Cocinando" ends abruptly, what's cooking is ready, and the dissonant sounds of a *descarga* (jam session) taking place offscreen begin. The boy's smile conveys his excitement and anticipation as the camera follows him in and through buildings and alleys. He finally arrives at the descarga taking place on scaffolding erected in front of a building with a sky-blue, red, and white mural. He quickly picks up a bottle and stick and attempts to accompany the musicians on clave. The camera, which privileges the line of sight of children on the ground next to the scaffolding, moves along a horizontal axis to reveal various prepubescent and adolescent young people on each level. The oldest and most experienced musicians are perched on the top two levels, where several young men and a young woman play the congas and a younger boy accompanies them on bongo. Prepubescent boys sitting on the scaffolding alongside the musicians participate in the music making by tapping on their own bodies and found objects like boxes, cans, and bottles. The combination of actual instruments and found objects creates a discordant and raw musicality. While the dissonant sounds of the descarga contrast sharply with the melodious rhythms of "Cocinando," the aspiring musicians on the scaffolding follow a well-defined rhythmic pattern locked in by the percussionists.

The camera pans the children playing, watching, and dancing before lingering on one of the adolescent *congueros* on the top platform of the scaffolding. As he increases the tempo, the shot tightens around his hands until they occupy the entire screen and begin to blur. The swish pan effect continues as a different rhythmic pattern overlaps and eventually overtakes the first. Another object then begins to take form on-screen. A pair of hands, one the viewer has not seen before, comes into focus. The conga, like the rhythmic pattern being played on it, has also changed. As the camera pulls away, the shot reveals the transformation of the young conguero on the scaffolding into an adult man wearing thick, black, horn-rimmed glasses. Viewers familiar with the Latin music scene will recognize him as none other than renowned Nuyorican percussionist, arranger, and bandleader Barretto on *tumbadora*, rehearsing for the Cheetah concert with the other Fania All-Stars. His presence on-screen brings together Latin music's past, present, and future at the culmination of the film's opening scene.

A break in the rehearsal creates an opening for Sid Torin, a jazz disc jockey (DJ) known as Symphony Sid Torin who was among the first to play Spanish-language music on an all-English radio station in New York, to interview Barretto. Barretto sits on a chair with his tumbadora positioned between his legs as Symphony Sid asks about the percussionist's aspirations for Latin music. Barretto responds, "The thing that eventually I really hope happens is that [*strikes the tumbadora*] message and the feeling of unity we have here . . . and our Latin music and culture goes out all over the world." Positioning himself as an ambassador of both music and culture, Barretto highlights the intersection of salsa's aesthetic and affective contours with his hopes for the music's commercial success. Barretto, the only musician interviewed in the film, is known to have exerted creative control in the recording studio. His slap on the instrument draws attention to Latin music's sonic imaginary, the circulation of expressive culture, and the transmission of cultural knowledge. It expresses the music's development at the intersection of culture and market priorities. For Barretto, salsa's commercialization was not at odds with musical innovation or cultural authenticity. Instead, salsa's commercialization and potential crossover offered the opportunity for musical collaborations, creative innovation, and economic opportunities.[6] The desire for salsa's commercialization originates, within *Our Latin Thing*, from the musicians themselves rather than Fania Records. The transition from the streets of Latin New York to the stage at the Cheetah positions

Fania Records as the vehicle for Latin music to reach the potential referred to by Barretto.

As a marketing tool, *Our Latin Thing* proposes salsa's commercialization as part of an organic process, one embedded in the dense community networks in New York's Puerto Rican communities.[7] Scenes filmed outside the Cheetah with the various musicians reinforce this possibility while symbolically linking the All-Stars to Latin New York. In one scene, Johnny Pacheco, accompanied by a group of children who follow him, plays the flute.[8] In another, Barretto takes on the role of *piragüero*, handing out shaved ice to children at a music festival sponsored by Fania Records. During the same festival, LaVoe and pianist Mark "Markolino" Diamond form part of the crowd watching a performance by Orchestra Harlow. By linking the streets of the Lower East Side to the Cheetah, Fania Records presents salsa's commercialization as a natural progression of the music's emergence on the streets of Latin New York. Yet the film also suggests that Fania emerged in a vacuum. *Our Latin Thing* does not explore the history of music-making within Latin New York from which Fania benefited. Historian Ruth Glasser has shown that friends, family, colleagues, and small businesses provided an informal network that helped sustain Puerto Rican musicians after World War I. *Tríos* (trios) and *cuartetos* (quartets) looked after musicians arriving in New York, social clubs hosted dances with live music, civic organizations sponsored musical entertainment, and individuals hired bands to play at weddings and other private functions. Small business owners, particularly (but not exclusively) those who owned record stores, became intermediaries between artists and record companies when labels like Victor began to focus on the US market for Spanish-language music.

Victoria Hernández, who opened what is believed to be the first Puerto Rican–owned record store in New York in 1927, became an important patron of local musicians. She acted as booking agent, advanced recording fees to musicians, and likely collected a fee from record labels for identifying commercially viable artists. Glasser notes that Hernández, a professionally trained pianist in her own right, "never became a popular musician, [but] she was involved with popular music in every way short of playing it herself." Her success supported the musical career of her brother, renowned Puerto Rican composer, multi-instrumentalist, and bandleader Rafael Hernández. Glasser underlines how

> Victoria Hernández's business acumen not only gave her brother the time he needed to concentrate on his musical groups and com-

positions and the wherewithal to avoid more gruesome industrial experiences, but she was also indispensable as an organizer of his musical projects and became official manager for his cuarteto, which was named Victoria in her honor. Victoria organized tours and record dates and made sure that her brother and the other bohemios [bohemians] in his group fulfilled their contracts. In fact, she did everything possible to combat the image of the musician as bohemia [bohemian], down to making sure its members wore suits and ties rather than the stereotypical ruffle-sleeved rumba shirts.[9]

Victoria's business acumen, patronage, and involvement with her brother's musical career are indicative not only of the important role played by merchants in supporting local artists but of the ways women in Puerto Rican communities helped sustain musicians.[10] Casa Hernández in the Longwood section of the Bronx is now named Casa Amadeo after its current owner, Mike Amadeo. During the salsa boom, Casa Amadeo continued Victoria's legacy and "provided a safe space while the neighborhood was burning" in the 1970s and a place for young people to reconnect with Latin music.[11]

**From Car Trunks to the Cheetah**

Fania Records' early financial challenges form part of an origins narrative of an independent label committed, unlike major labels, to aesthetic sensibilities rather than market priorities. Pacheco and Jerry Masucci cofounded Fania Records in 1964 with $2,500 that Masucci reportedly borrowed from his mother, as well as what Pacheco told me was "fifty percent talent and fifty percent luck."[12] They famously delivered records out of the trunk of a car to stores in New York, including Casa Amadeo, Record Mart on Forty-Second Street, and Casa Latina on 116th Street. Pacheco and Masucci extended their marketing reach by relying on mom-and-pop record stores in cities like Miami and Chicago. These initial investments often failed to produce revenue. Some store owners claimed to have lost the product, which Pacheco suspected was generally untrue.[13] In Puerto Rico, the local distributor reportedly returned the label's first shipment there in its entirety.[14] Yet Fania Records endured despite these challenges. Pacheco advertised new releases during his own gigs. He would ask audiences if they had the record, and if they said no, he would ask where they lived so he could tell them the location of the nearest store that carried the album. With its tiny budget, the label also bought airtime on New York radio stations like WBMX

La Mega and WADO.[15] Lackluster record sales for even one album could put an independent label like Fania Records out of business due to limited capital resources.[16] Neither Pacheco nor Masucci took a salary from Fania Records for the first few years so that all revenue could go back into the business. During my interviews with Pacheco and Fania executive Victor Gallo, both emphasized tax strategies the label used to maximize the possibility of success.[17]

Masucci's gambit on *Our Latin Thing* turned the All-Stars into rock stars. A year after the film's release, they performed again, this time at Yankee Stadium, astonishing the music industry when the event drew somewhere between thirty thousand and forty-five thousand spectators.[18] Their first concert at Madison Square Garden in 1974 sold out, and the following year the All-Stars returned to Yankee Stadium. This salsa "boom," however, remained in its nascent stages in August 1971. When the idea to host the 1971 Fania All-Stars concert first arose, it was suggested that the performance take place in Central Park and that admission be free. Masucci reportedly balked at the suggestion. Unable to find a promoter to host the concert in venues like the Fillmore and the Manhattan Center, he chose the Cheetah, apparently at the urging of R&B and Latin music promoter Ralph Mercado.[19] A cavernous New York nightclub with a large dance floor and a two-thousand-person capacity, it provided an ideal space for the concert. The club's multilevel setup allowed director Leon Gast to position cameras so as not to interfere with the concert and the audience. The club's lighting only had to be supplemented, rather than completely replaced, to allow filming.[20] Mercado, the promoter for the Fania All-Stars show that had taken place at the Red Garter, takes credit along with Masucci for the decision to hold this second concert. Mercado booked events at the Cheetah on Thursday nights. He reportedly agreed to schedule the concert on one condition: Fania was to pay all expenses and let Mercado take all the money at the door from admission.[21] Masucci begrudgingly accepted the offer. Several days before the concert, Pacheco expressed concern about the state of the music for the show. According to Harlow, Pacheco asked Masucci to postpone the performance, but a film crew had already been contracted.[22] So Pacheco "holed up" in a hotel with bass player and arranger Bobby Valentín for two days to write the music. The night before the performance, he and Valentín were still working on it.[23]

Mercado, who would become one of the foremost Latin music producers in the United States by the early 1980s, usually began advertising a week before an event. For this concert, though, with the funds Masucci provided, he undertook an extensive publicity campaign to promote the concert a month in advance. As Mercado put it when we met in his Manhattan offices, he "advertised the hell out of" the Cheetah concert within New York's Puerto Rican and broader Latina/o communities.[24] The publicity campaign added posters to the usual circulation of flyers as well as radio spots on Latin music shows like those hosted by local DJs Symphony Sid and Dick "Ricardo" Sugar.[25] On the night of the concert, the success of Mercado's month-long advertising campaign became apparent when the Cheetah opened to a line of patrons that extended down the sidewalk and around the corner. Mercado remembers patrons "jam packed" in the nightclub, standing up against the stage, with everyone "sweatin' and having a good time."[26] The large crowd eased the anxiety of All-Star Cheo Feliciano, who recalls that his heart "jumped a few times" when he saw the throng of people and heard fans call his name. Having recently returned to the Latin music scene, Feliciano had been anxious about how fans would receive him. The welcoming shouts from patrons as he made his way through the crowd calmed his fears: "I felt my blood rush and I heard [fans] yelling, 'Cheo Cheo.' I knew I was home. I guess that feeling was what gave me the incentive to sing so well that night. It may be the night I've sung the best in my whole life."[27] The Fania All-Stars performed two sets that night that lasted about ninety minutes each to a crowd of approximately four thousand people, twice the Cheetah's official capacity.[28]

Pacheco and Valentín wrote out at least some of the riffs for the vocalists.[29] Nevertheless, Pete "El Conde" recalls that the competition between himself and other singers to display their improvisational chops made it one of his favorite performances, as seen during "Quítate tú" (Move). Of the concert that night, he said, "There was a lot of improvisation, there was competition. If you said something, I answered to see who sang the best improvisation. Everybody was up to it. I was trying to make the other guys a little bit mad, 'Hey man, this guy came out with a nice inspiration. Let me see if I can counter that.' To me, it was one of the best performances ever and it was a lot of fun."[30] Pacheco even roasted Mercado, for whom the going back and forth between the singers when they began *inspirando* (literally, inspiring; here, improvising) stood out among the "great memories" of the evening.[31] The audience responded to the energy, creativity, affection, and competition among the All-Stars with their cheers, dancing, and rapt attention. A typical pan of the crowd shows eighteen-year-old Nydia Ocasio on the dance floor. She grew up in Red Hook, Brooklyn, with Mercado and had been sneaking into nightclubs that featured Latin music since she was sixteen. During a solo by *bongocero* Roberto Roena, we see her watching the All-Stars, "in this daze, just staring at the band," as she recalled in our conversation.[32]

The choice of bandleaders, vocalists, and sidemen has been criticized for not featuring the more seasoned or talented musicians in the Fania stable. Rondón contends that Roena was chosen because he was the only bongocero who also led his own band, not because he was the most talented bongocero available.[33] But Roena's musicality, creativity, and absolute ferocity during his solo at the Cheetah blew away audiences, who cheered and roared as he performed. As Ocasio is transfixed by Roena's performance, her experience during this moment in the film shows how, as musician and cultural critic Marco Katz reminds us, "if . . . good music makes people move, great music can make them still. The best memories of good players usually involve those moments of intense listening by a crowd absorbed in the music."[34] The proximity of the audience to the performers, the dancing, and the sounds of cheering even when the camera focuses on the stage all add to the looseness felt by those who saw the film, whether they had been at the Cheetah or not. To Pacheco, the audience's fervor reflected salsa's cultural significance for the largely Puerto Rican audiences. Now, he explained during our phone interview, Latinas/os "had something that was ours"—an insight, certainly, into the source of the title of the documentary.

*Timbalero* (timbales player, masculine) Jimmy Delgado went to see *Our Latin Thing* as a teenager when he was still an aspiring musician. Percussionists Barretto, Orestes Vilató, and Roena "blew away" the young timbalero. The power of their performance washed over Delgado, who likened the experience to listening to Jimi Hendrix for the first time. The intensity of Barretto, Vilató, and Roena "got into his soul" just like Hendrix's guitar playing. The rawness Delgado described certainly benefited from bringing together bandleaders and vocalists unaccustomed to playing together, some of whom had learned to play by ear while others had received formal musical training; the lack of extensive rehearsals; and, of course, Pacheco's musical direction. The decision not to smooth out the edges in favor of a more professional, or cleaner, sound was also essential. Fania Records chose not to clean up the sound recording with overdubbing. Doing so would have removed the rawness Delgado remembers with a joy and admiration that lit up his face as he talked with me about the film almost thirty years after its premiere. Delgado played with Barretto for the first time just a few years after the premiere of *Our Latin Thing*, at the age of eighteen. In 1985, the timbalero would join the Fania All-Stars during their eleventh annual concert at Madison Square Garden. When Masucci called him in search of a timbalero to play that night, Delgado jumped at the opportunity to play with the acclaimed ensemble band whose looseness, sound, and energy had thrilled him almost fifteen years earlier. Ultimately, the rhythm felt good to the performers, the audience, and the viewers for whom the film has become a cult classic.

The idea to film the concert came from Harlow, one of the first artists signed to Fania Records, and Gast, a professional photographer who wanted to "do a film about the [Latin music] scene."[35] Harlow—who played oboe, flute, violin, bass, and piano—was a third-generation musician from Brooklyn who commuted to Manhattan to attend Music and Art High School on West 135th Street near Amsterdam Avenue.[36] While the budding musician studied classical traditions within the school's walls, the sounds of Latin music emanating from the mom-and-pop record shops in the neighborhood invigorated him, and he decided to continue his musical studies in Cuba.[37] As Harlow noted during our interview in his New York apartment, the entry of a Jewish bandleader into Latin music still raises an eyebrow for those unfamiliar with New York's geography and musical histories. But he would be the second artist signed to Fania Records, the musical director for Fania and its related labels, and one of its most illustrious producers.

Gast, whom Harlow recommended to film the concert, had worked as a photographer for *Esquire*, *Vogue*, and *Harper's Bazaar*. He had also shot various album covers for Fania, including the All-Stars' *Live at the Red Garter*, vol. 1, and Joe Bataan's *Riot*. Although Gast worked in the making of commercials, he had no significant experience when Masucci agreed to film the concert. The decision launched Gast's career as a documentary filmmaker as well as a relationship with the Fania All-Stars that would earn him an Academy Award.[38] For Gast, the city's Latina/o communities formed an integral part of the film's narrative, and he set about making a film that included "the emerging Latino culture and music scene in New York City."[39] In addition to the concert at the Cheetah and the rehearsal earlier that day, Gast filmed various vignettes with musicians, including one in which Masucci appears. Ismael Miranda took Gast to a cockfight seen in the film, and Harlow encouraged the director to film Santería practitioners. Except for a block party hosted by Fania and a couple of brief skits, the scenes filmed on the Lower East Side were not staged. Gast claims that he walked around the neighborhood with the film crew and recorded scenes from everyday life.[40]

Gast's aesthetic decisions served Masucci's commercial aspirations, even as the budget ballooned from an initial $15,000 to $100,000. Gast com-

**1.2**  Closing credits, *Our Latin Thing* (1972)

pleted the postproduction work at Good Vibrations. Co-owned by Gast, the New York recording studio boasted state-of-the-art facilities and cut most of Fania's records at the time.[41] Weaving concert footage with scenes featuring the "Spanish speaking people of New York City," as the film credits list local residents who appear in the film, Gast made extensive use of jump cuts between the rehearsal, the concert, and scenes filmed outside the nightclub. The transitions expressed the symbiotic relationship between salsa and the streets of Latin New York that Gast wanted to convey. The use of cinema verité and the lack of any identifying information for artists appearing on-screen heightened the film's affective relationship to viewers familiar with the Latin music scene and helped solidify Fania's branding as a grassroots independent label committed first and foremost to musicians and the music. The short filming period, like the harried days Pacheco and Valentín spent in the hotel composing the music, and the minimal rehearsal time likewise contributed to the authenticity suggested by using direct filming. While the decision not to employ a narrator may have contributed to the "tedium" the *New York Times* reviewer Roger Greenspun experienced in watching the film, the lack of a voice-over implies unmediated access to the communities and music featured on-screen.[42]

Fania Records released a two-volume recording of the concert in 1972 alongside the documentary *Our Latin Thing*, which debuted in New York that July, less than a year after the concert at the Cheetah. The *Billboard* review by Jim Melanson praised the "rich collage of 'salsa' rhythms" that was immune to the "fragmented and quite repetitive" editing of the film.[43] In the August 1972 issue of *New York Magazine*, devoted to "The City's Latin Soul," *Our Latin Thing* was billed as a "film about the Spanish-speaking community of New York, its music, its mores, and lifestyle, and the everyday life of the barrio." *Billboard* columnist Richard Goldstein described it as "a pretty solid intro to Latin music."[44] The "tedium" Greenspun cited notwithstanding, he expressed relief at seeing "a film about a pop concert that makes no serious claims to be sociology or world history." To him, the scenes of "domino games, shaved-ice vending, [and] cockfighting" were "interesting" but "gratuitous," apparently "dedicated to solving the problem of how to alleviate the tedium involved in photographing a musical performance."[45] Rondón, however, praised scenes filmed outside the Cheetah. They provided, he explained, a window into the material context that became the music's primary source of signification. The film resonated, he continued, with Latin American and Caribbean audiences that saw in Latin New York similar social and economic conditions to those found in urban centers like San Juan, Puerto Rico; Santo Domingo, Dominican Republic; and Caracas, Venezuela.[46] Writing for *Record World*, one of the music industry's main trade magazines (alongside *Billboard* and *Cashbox*), Tomás Fundora expressed surprise that the film's rhythms engaged the audience for the entire film.[47] *Rolling Stone* critic Vince Aletti also praised the film, describing it as one of only two decent documentaries since *Woodstock* (the other being *Gimme Shelter*). He also applauded the "glimpse of Latin culture" in *Our Latin Thing*.[48] Unlike most reviews, Aletti's did note the film's limited success in representing "Latin life" in New York, a topic "more complex than Gast's direction indicates."[49] Masucci and his brother, Alex, who presided over the newly formed A&R Distribution, capitalized on these reviews in arranging runs of *Our Latin Thing* in major US cities like Miami and Chicago. After return engagements in Chicago and New York, the film screened abroad in both Spanish- and non-Spanish-speaking countries such as Puerto Rico, the Dominican Republic, Venezuela, Holland, and the Benelux Union.

The only review to substantively address the intersection among the representation of New York's Puerto Rican communities, salsa, and the music's commercial aspirations appeared in the Young Lords' newsletter *Palante*. Minister of communication Pablo "Yoruba" Guzmán, who praised the "magnetic" music and the emphasis on its roots, enjoyed seeing Puerto Ricans on-screen in something other than the racist representations characteristic of films like *West Side Story*, *The Young Savages*, and *The Possession of Joe Delaney*. Guzmán, however, condemned the commercial aspirations of the film and the absence of the music's sociopolitical context. *Our Latin Thing*, he explained, excluded the struggles faced by "the majority of us, millions of working people, who make or enjoy music from Friday night to Sunday afternoon, to be in better shape come Monday so that, our children can eat, the rent is paid, the bills are paid."[50] Rather than represent the broader material context that informed the conditions of the Lower East Side shown on-screen, argued Guzmán, the film suggests that "as long as we make music, everything's gonna be all right. As long as we're making music in the parks, the movie makes ghettoes like the [L]ower [E]ast [S]ide look good."[51] Certainly the physical landscape of the opening scene is overdetermined by ruin—overflowing garbage, rubble, and abandoned buildings become a synecdoche for the city's Puerto Rican communities even as Gast attempts to capture how music pervaded everyday life in Latin New York. Guzmán suggests that *Our Latin Thing* and Fania Records are essentially "poverty pimping," spectacularizing Puerto Rican poverty for commercial gain.

The scenes filmed on the Lower East Side that "objectified, commodified, and iconicized" daily life featured one of New York's oldest Puerto Rican communities.[52] Various summaries of the film have erroneously reported that the scenes were set in the city's most iconic Puerto Rican neighborhood, El Barrio.[53] While El Barrio became the imagined home of the Puerto Rican diaspora in the United States, the scenes on the Lower East Side gesture at how salsa formed an integral part of everyday life throughout Latin New York. The Lower East Side, or *Loisaida*, had been home to Puerto Ricans arriving to New York since the turn of the twentieth century when cigar makers established themselves in the neighborhood.[54] In the 1960s and 1970s, the neighborhood became a locus of Puerto Rican activism and the Nuyorican Arts Movement. Loisaida's vibrant cultural and political history remains beyond the camera's frame in *Our Latin Thing*, which threatens to merely spectacularize abject poverty.[55]

### Salsa's Latin New York

Across Latin New York, music formed a part of everyday practices in Puerto Rican communities for aspiring musicians, many of whom began their journeys not by pursuing formal training but by playing music in their homes and neighborhoods. The streets, parks, schools, and tenement buildings brought together musicians who established relationships via the music itself. For Miranda, one of the lead singers in *Our Latin Thing*, Hell's Kitchen provided the first of many stages. As he told the newspaper *Primera Hora*, he joined a group playing congas on the sidewalk outside his building within a week of moving there from Puerto Rico:

> El primer sábado que vivimos allí, a las once de la mañana yo vi por la ventana a los tipos acomodándose para tocar. Pedí permiso, bajé y me colé entre ellos y cuando tuve un break toqué la conguita. Cogí confianza y ya la próxima semana era parte del grupo.[56]
>
> [The first Saturday that we lived there, at eleven in the morning I looked through the window and saw the guys getting ready to play. I asked permission, went down, and made my way into the group, and when I got a break, I played the small conga. I built up my confidence and the following week I was part of the group.]

Although Miranda took singing lessons at a young age, he learned to play congas in his neighborhood. Delgado, in turn, began playing timbales in his bedroom. Across the street, fellow aspiring musician Papo Cocote (Antonio Rivera Pereira) would join in from his first-floor apartment, and the sounds of the timbales floated out their windows and into the neighborhood. Delgado remembers, "He's practicing, making a racket over there, right across the street, and I'm making a racket in my house. And that's all you heard in that neighborhood, timbales and congas and bongos."[57] These experiences, replicated by aspiring musicians across the city, underscore how space, music, and social relations became mutually constituted.

Aspiring and up-and-coming musicians also leveraged relationships with local community institutions. The former PS 52 (now MS 52) public school in the Banana Kelly neighborhood of the South Bronx remains one of the most significant spaces in the development of Latin music in New York. Pianist and bandleader Eddie Palmieri received access to the school's basement to practice in return for playing at school dances.[58] Other musicians who graduated from PS 52 include Barretto, Charlie Palmieri, and Orlando Marín. Eddie Montalvo, a conguero who played with Héctor LaVoe and other salsa pioneers before pursuing a solo career, began playing in the Bronx as a teenager with so-called street bands. The band rehearsed in various spaces, including PS 130, where the custodian would open a room for them to rehearse, and the basement of a tenement building on Trinity Avenue.[59] Some of Montalvo's first professional gigs were in restaurants and afterhours clubs, spaces that gave young musicians the opportunity to develop their craft and gain exposure. Colón's professional trajectory similarly began on a sidewalk outside a bar in the Bronx with his band the Dandies, who would pass the hat around to any passersby who stopped to listen.[60] And then there were Orchard Beach in the Bronx and Central Park. At Orchard Beach, where jazz and R&B also filled the air, *salseros* and *salseras* (salsa fans) danced to live bands. At Bethesda Fountain, one of several places in Central Park where *rumberos* and salsa fans gathered, live percussion sounded alongside the radio as Felipe Luciano, a member of the Young Lords, mixed politics and salsa during his weekly Sunday show on WBLS, the home of DJ Frankie Crocker.[61]

### Everynight Life: The Cuchifrito Circuit

For up-and-coming musicians, the cuchifrito circuit provided the opportunity to play alongside legends, who themselves benefited from the expanded popularity of Latin music. The circuit of nightclubs where musicians performed extended far beyond the glitz of the Cheetah Lounge and other prestigious clubs. The cuchifrito circuit, much like the African American chitlin circuit, encompassed nightclubs, afterhours, and other performance spaces. Unlike the broadly multistate chitlin circuit, it was largely concentrated in the New York–New Jersey–Connecticut tristate area.[62] The cuchifrito circuit grew as venues added or switched to Latin music in the mid to late 1960s and 1970s. From the Chico East and Barney Google's in Manhattan to the Bronx Casino and the Hippo Campo in the Bronx; from the Colgate Gardens, Chez Sensual, Club Ochenta, and the Cork n Bottle; from the famed Hunts Point Palace in the Bronx, El Palladium Chiquito in Harlem, and the legendary Corso; to afterhours like the Tropicoro, Royals (I and II), and Christopher's, the sounds of salsa wafted through the air and allowed musicians to devote themselves to their music full-time.[63] Promoters organized dances at social halls and larger venues like the Manhattan Center and Riverside Plaza in Manhattan, the Hotel St. George in Brooklyn, and nightclubs in other parts of the tristate areas, like the Wagon Wheel (later the Crystal Ballroom) in Bridgeport, Connecticut. Musicians also played in nearby resort areas in New York's Hudson Valley like Las Villas, a group of hotels popular among Puerto Rican, Cuban, Dominican, and Spanish immigrants. Despite the proliferation of Latin nightclubs in New York, the cuchifrito circuit limited the earning

**1.3**   *Latin N.Y.* ad for the Corso and Barney Google's,
1976 (personal archive of Glenn Jacobs)

potential of musicians. In a 1976 interview for *Billboard*, Barretto stated,
"If we keep doing what we have been doing we are not going to get out of
the 'cuchifrito circuit' and we'll still be playing the small clubs on weekend
dates for a few hundred dollars a week."[64]

Fania Records identified emerging talent like Bobby Valentín and established musicians like Harlow, two of the earliest artists Pacheco brought
to the label, in the nightclubs, restaurants, and afterhours that formed part
of the cuchifrito circuit.[65] Though absent from *Our Latin Thing*, afterhours
formed an integral part of salsa's everynight life. Afterhours opened in just
about every available space, like a storefront or basement, in predominantly

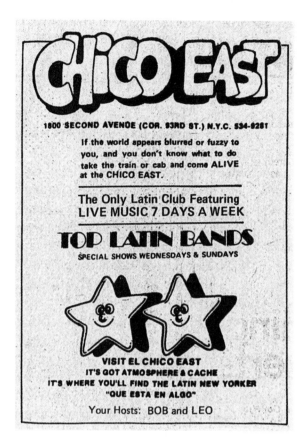

**1.4** *Latin N.Y.* ad for Chico East, 1976 (personal archive of Glenn Jacobs)

Puerto Rican communities. They did not have the fixedness that permanent physical space imparts; nevertheless, they benefited from the flexibility to move to different locations and reinvent themselves as necessary. In fact, afterhours thrived precisely because they accommodated themselves to the immediate circumstances of the economy. Operating without licenses, they existed outside the formal economy. Some afterhours, like Pozo's in El Barrio, became hangouts for musicians, who often joined in when a band performed. Some were run by salseros like Luis "Máquina" Flores, who danced at the nightclubs until closing, then went to his own afterhours, opened for business, and remained there until the last customer left—at whatever time that might happen to be.[66] Other afterhours were taxpaying nightclubs or social clubs that closed their front doors at two or three in the morning and then retreated to a back room for the rest of the night.[67] The dual role of some afterhours as both legal and illicit establishments blurred the line between the formal and informal economies even as they benefited from both. Due to their extralegal status, however, afterhours remained precarious business ventures. They were vulnerable to police raids, even if their managers paid bribes to the appropriate people.[68] The continuity of afterhours, which existed long before and long after the salsa boom, exceeded the regulation of the formal economy into which most Puerto Ricans were funneled after World War II, particularly the manufacturing sector, which was already in its initial stages of decline by the 1950s.

Side musicians, supporting musicians in a band, as well as those who were hired to perform on a record but did not form part of the group cutting an album, were the lifeblood of the cuchifrito circuit. While *Our Latin Thing* featured lead singers and bandleaders from multiple *orquestas* (bands), it was side musicians who filled out their bands on a daily basis. These musicians were highly susceptible to corrupt business practices and informal arrangements not bound by a contract. Many earned a flat fee for a recording, with no access to future royalties. As bongocero José Mangual Jr. noted, "When you're twenty, you don't care," but then "when you get older and have no social security, there's nothing."[69] Considering these issues, Montalvo kept a day job with the New York electrical company Con Edison throughout his career because "when you have a day job you know you'll have food in the house on Friday."[70] He was still working for the power company when I interviewed him in 2003, despite great successes in his career with orquestas led by some of salsa's biggest legends, like Colón, LaVoe, and Rubén Blades. The insecurity all musicians faced included gigs canceled without notice and payments unreasonably withheld by club owners, dance promoters, and unscrupulous managers who engaged in *double bidding*. This referred to a common practice whereby managers routinely lied to their clients about the fees paid by promoters and club owners in order to pocket the difference along with their acknowledged percentage.[71]

Side musicians contributed to the unique sound of each orquesta for which they played over the course of their careers. Some side musicians played with the same band for an extended period. Mangual, for example, joined Colón's band for the recording of *Cosa nuestra* (Our thing, 1969) and stayed with the group when the bandleader left to pursue other ventures. But club owners, promoters, and the like still wanted to book the band. LaVoe, however, knew nothing about being a bandleader. So he asked Mangual to manage the band. Mangual, in turn, could continue to support his family without a day job by playing eight to twelve gigs a week.[72] Most side musicians played for multiple bands over time, and some subbed in to orquestas as needed. Barretto's lead singer and several musicians defected in 1972 and formed the famed Típica 73 as a cooperative where all the band members shared the profits. A few years later, several of these artists would form another band, Los Kimbos. The familiarity with the structures and musical practices of playing—and providing backup vocals—with different bands allowed side musicians to develop their craft. Musicians like Montalvo, Mangual, and Delgado also developed their own sound and released their own recordings. Hence, the cuchifrito circuit provided an important source of experience and income as well as a site of creativity for musicians, even while it limited them to the periphery of the music industry.

Fania did not always live up to Pacheco's original vision of treating musicians as more than commodities. One particular scene in *Our Latin Thing* captures the idealized relationship between the label and artists under contract. A seamless transition between a performance of "Anacaona" at the Cheetah and the recording studio where the singers are laying down the track for the same song obscures the structural conditions that artists navigated. Salsa historian and musician Aurora Flores, who was a columnist for *Billboard* and *Latin N.Y.* during the salsa boom, once described these conditions as "the brutal and exploitive paths that must be taken by many Latin musicians before they can achieve any semblance of fame and respect."[73] The film, unsurprisingly, emphasizes the collectivity, musicality, and creativity of artists as part of the Fania formula. Harlow described another aspect of the formula to me as "get them in, knock them out, and send them home."[74]

Artists who signed with Fania managed creative disagreements, competition among each other, and economic exploitation. Fania's business practices, which were not unlike those of other recording labels of the time, contributed to the exploitation of artists and the unequal distribution of benefits within creative economies.[75] Masucci leveraged his legal background and Fania's increasing control of New York's Latin music industry to the label's benefit. Mercado and Mangual have stated that Masucci was the force behind the contractual terms given to artists and preyed on musicians who lacked legal representation and agents.[76] Certainly, Fania's contractual right to pick up options, or extensions, on a contract fostered unequal power relationships as well as competition among artists.[77] Contracts that required artists to repay expenses incurred during the recording and promotion of an album protected the label but fostered perilous economic circumstances for artists. If a record did not sell well, artists might ultimately owe the label money. Artists were known to ask Fania to pick up their option and record another album because they could leverage it for gigs, an important income source. This, in turn, encouraged artists to take on new debt for the subsequent album despite the prospect of remaining in debt to Fania.

While a handful of artists eventually negotiated contracts with more favorable terms, Fania's growth and acquisition of existing labels left artists with few choices. Many landed under the Fania umbrella because Masucci obtained their contracts when he bought out their label. Masucci leveraged Fania's complex network of business holdings and his legal background to "tie these guys up pretty good."[78] Fania, for example, persuaded songwriters to transfer their rights to the company's publishing arms as part of their recording deals, a topic discussed in chapters 5 and 6. Several artists have also surmised that the addition of the manufacturing plant in 1976 expanded Fania's ability to exploit artists. Harlow, who hired an accountant in the mid-1970s to provide an accurate count of album sales, contends that Fania manipulated the numbers to reduce royalty payments to songwriters and recording artists, including himself.[79] Just as Pacheco's disgust with Alegre led to the creation of Fania Records, musicians like Luis "Perico" Ortiz and Valentín began their own recording companies in the late 1970s. Other artists signed with competing labels when their contracts with Fania expired.

Fania could offer unfavorable terms in part because artists depended on bookings at nightclubs for income, and nightclubs preferred to sign artists with new albums.[80] The decision to film *Our Latin Thing* at the Cheetah is indicative of the importance of nightclubs and other performance venues to Fania. Masucci wanted the Cheetah for the Fania All-Stars concert largely because the spacious nightclub had a great dance floor.[81] The dancers, both in the nightclub and on the streets in the outdoor scenes, take center stage in the film alongside the performers: a couple dances while the All-Stars rehearse, the audience at the Cheetah dances throughout the concert, children dance under the scaffolding, and festivalgoers dance while Orchestra Harlow performs on the steps of a church in Hell's Kitchen. The camera often lingers on dancers in each of these spaces, stressing the importance of dancers on the cuchifrito circuit. One scene begins with an older gentleman sitting on a stoop singing and creating a rhythm by slapping the crate he sits on and tapping his foot on the concrete. As he sings, a younger man on the sidewalk dances by himself with outstretched arms, as if he were dancing with a partner. Others watch along the sidewalk as a woman lighting her cigarette walks by him. He takes her free hand, and the two begin dancing in a movement so fluid that the viewer cannot determine whether the action occurred spontaneously or if Gast choreographed it for the film.[82] The man on the crate keeps singing, and the couple on the sidewalk dances on as music from the Cheetah begins to play in the background. The camera then cuts from the sidewalk to the dance floor at the Cheetah. The continuity created when the viewer hears the concert music in the background before returning to the Cheetah connects the dancers on the street to those at the concert.

Those who went to nightclubs on a regular basis became part of a social network bound by the music, the musicians, and the dancers who faithfully attended. Fans who participated in the nightclub scene remember it as part of their everyday lives. "To dance is to live," commented Melba, who started dancing at nightclubs after her divorce in 1970. When I interviewed her, she talked with great fondness about dancing and seeing people she knew at the clubs, saying that the memories would be enough to sustain her if she did nothing ever again. Fans, like musicians, participated in a social network produced at the intersection of daily lived experience and affective bonds that translated into networks among dancers. She remembered Luis "Máquina" as an extraordinary dancer, and showed me a picture of his son dancing at an event held at the Corso. The first time Luis "Máquina" asked Melba to dance, she knew she had reached the highest echelons of dancers at the Corso.[83]

Amid all the places for performing, a few stand out in the memories of the salseras and salseros as the anchors of their social network. The Hunts Point Palace in the Bronx, with a 2,500-person capacity, was a favorite. It hosted various ethnoracial communities over its six decades before featuring Latin music. For its historic "battles of the bands," multiple orquestas were hired for the same night, with each successive group stepping up its game in order to win over the public.[84] The Hunts Point Palace, like the Park Palace (El Palladium Chiquito) and El Club Obrero Español in Harlem, was among those nightclubs that featured Latin music long before the salsa boom, as early as the 1930s and 1940s. Yet their role in the history of Latin music in New York and the "mambo madness" of the 1950s has largely remained outside the dominant narratives of that period. These narratives focus almost exclusively on the famed Palladium, idealizing it as a democratic, multiracial space despite the ambivalence of dancers toward each other and the racialized dynamics of the dance floor.[85] After the Palladium closed in 1966, these and other clubs located throughout New York continued to host Latin music.

The Chez José, located at Seventy-Seventh Street and Columbus Avenue, across the street from the Museum of Natural History, became the

Palladium's heir apparent. Known for featuring both established musicians and emerging artists, the Chez José attracted patrons who eagerly waited to learn who would play there on any given night. The club's practice of not announcing the bands helped create a mystique around the Chez, as patrons called it. According to manager Arnie Segarra, just the possibility of seeing timbalero Tito Puente or Pacheco kept patrons coming. The marketing strategy made the Chez an ideal stage to showcase new artists, who might be scheduled to play in between sets of the more well-known musicians.[86] Located on the Upper West Side, it gained a reputation as an "exclusive" nightclub with a strict admissions policy that required men to wear a jacket and tie. The nightclub routinely turned away the so-called sneaker crowd, or *títeres*, who dressed in jeans. Segarra kept a few ties in the club for patrons to use as needed.[87] In my interview with Harlow, however, he suggested that employees at the door turned away Latinas/os who were "too dark" and African Americans.[88]

Patrons who frequented the Chez enjoyed an exciting atmosphere. Antonio, who was underage during the height of the Chez's popularity, let his mustache grow to look older and forged his name onto the draft card of an eighteen-year-old to get through the door of the Upper West Side club. Antonio had begun listening to Latin music during "Canteen Nights" at St. Cecilia's in East Harlem, when the church would invite young people in to dance. It was there where he first saw Colón play. Antonio frequented various clubs across the city playing a variety of Latin music, including the Broadway Casino and the Caborrojeño, as well as larger venues like the Riverside Hotel. The Chez, however, remained his favorite. Antonio enjoyed the "privilege" of attending an "elegant" club and would start getting excited while he was still in line waiting to get in and the music wafted out the front door of the Chez.[89]

Another patron, José, would cross Central Park from El Barrio to get to the Chez. The night was more affordable than it might have been because he and his friends could bring their own alcohol; the Chez only sold set-ups of glasses, ice, and soda. Sometimes, the savings allowed them to take a taxi home at the end of the night rather than walk through Central Park. José, who worked with Segarra on the East Harlem Tenant Council, would get a heads-up about the performers. One week, José watched Eddie Palmieri and vibraphone player Cal Tjader on back-to-back nights; the venue featured various styles of music and catered to audiences accustomed to the city's heterogeneous musical traditions. The Chez showcased established headliners from mambo and charanga to boogaloo and salsa during its five-year run from 1965 to 1970. Leading orchestras like those of Palmieri, Pacheco, Harlow, Machito (born Francisco Gutiérrez Grillo), and Puente performed there. A young Willie Colón created a buzz when he performed at the Chez early in his career, foreshadowing the impact he would have as a chronicler of life in Latin New York.[90]

By the early 1970s, the popularity of the Chez gave way to the Corso, a two-floor nightclub located just off Third Avenue and East Eighty-Sixth Street. Luis "Máquina" Flores became one of the most well-known dancers at the club, as he had been at the Palladium years earlier. In high school, he would leave class to go practice new moves in front of the bathroom mirror. During a ride through his old haunts in El Barrio, Luis "Máquina" shared the story behind the Corso's decision to begin featuring Latin music.

> Let me tell you the story of the Corso. Era de un americano [it belonged to this American]. Había un tipo [There was this guy], Pete Bonet, a singer. He said, "I guarantee you that I can bring you 300–400 people here." . . . The owner told him, "If you bring me 200, we got a deal." When Pete put the word out, the place got filled . . . como en el '68 [sometime around '68]. . . . So now, Pete Bonet got the place running. Everybody started going to the Corso. Louie Ramírez had a band that Pete Bonet played with and from there everybody came. La Broadway. Everybody. Ray Barretto, Tito Puente, even Machito. All the bands. All the bands que tocaban en el [that played in the] Palladium.[91]

Bonet's success in filling the Corso paved the way for the rise in the club's popularity. Featuring the bands that initially performed at the Palladium certainly played a part in creating a loyal following, but the Corso also hosted all the up-and-coming stars of the salsa scene.

The Corso quickly acquired a reputation as a dancers' club and became a favorite among fans and musicians. It became known as a nightclub where the creativity and dexterity of dancers matched the musicality and innovation onstage. Melba, who danced six nights a week, stayed home on Tuesday nights so she could rest and gear up to dance at the Corso on Wednesdays. She stated, "The only day I slept was Tuesday. . . . I would just come home from work and just get knocked out completely, sleep to the next day. And then, start again on Wednesday, because the Corso was [the place to be on] Wednesdays."[92] The Corso hired the best bands and had the best dancers, she said, a common recollection among fans. Even artists went to the Corso after finishing their own gigs elsewhere. Although many fans might know the musicians as friends, in-laws, family members, and the like, performers remained veritable stars in these New York Puerto Rican communities and represented, as Aurora Flores described them, "royalty" to whom fans felt it was "an honor to talk." They were "gods who came down from the mountaintop to mingle with the people."[93]

Nightclub dance floors became spaces for reenacting social and cultural practices. Felipe Luciano describes nightclubs as places where "a pauper [could] be a king" regardless of their social and economic status outside the club. And neither wealth nor status outside the nightclub protected bad dancers. The clubs also became a space where, as Luciano recalled, "a wealthy person without social graces and who couldn't dance was on the social standing of a welfare person because he couldn't rap."[94] Salsero Antonio, in his late teens during this time, remembers a particular evening at the Chez when he was not yet a good dancer: "It was a horrible experience. I would step on toes. . . . I remember I got up to dance one time and I didn't do very well, and I think the young lady realized that but she was patient with me."[95] His recollection demonstrates how the hierarchies on the dance floor could prove difficult to navigate for those with less dexterity and experience.

The distinctions on the dance floor also mapped New York's social and physical geography. For salsera Lisa, dance styles mapped onto New York's boroughs: "Guys from Manhattan danced one way, guys from the Bronx danced another way, guys from Brooklyn danced this other way, and I always liked the Brooklyn guys better. They had more—Brooklyn guys could dance on the left and switch you over to the right very easily. Bronx guys and Manhattan guys stayed on the right all the time. Some guys do one step y te marean [they make you dizzy]. Brooklyn guys would improvise more."[96] The reciprocal relationship between style and skill also distinguished those who had been born in New York or who had lived there for a significant period from recent arrivals from Puerto Rico and other parts of Latin America and the Caribbean. Luciano explained it as follows: "Sometimes those who did not dance as well, mainly from other Latin American countries, would venture to the dance floor at early hours. No one would go at 9 p.m., although [they] opened at that hour. You went to the Corso at 11 p.m., midnight. That was when bands were smoking, when the groove was on. It was wonderful. . . . Even if someone was taking up a lot of room on the dance floor, even if they didn't dance well, dancers would move to the periphery."[97] Luciano's depiction of immigrants signals tensions among the different communities that shared the dance floor.

Other interviewees referred to recent Puerto Rican immigrants, in contrast to their Nuyorican counterparts, as *jíbaros* (Puerto Rican peasant, masculine) or "Marín Tallas." *Jíbaros*, or "hicks," in this context connotes recently arrived Puerto Ricans unaccustomed to life in New York and unfamiliar with social expectations, current fashion, and the like. Marín Tallas was a derogatory calque of *Marine Tiger*, a World War II naval ship that carried passengers from Puerto Rico to New York in the mid to late 1940s. Both terms allude to the divisions within the Puerto Rican community that filled the dance floor.[98] While these tensions played out in contexts other than salsa clubs, the ways dancers navigated these relationships suggest that the choreographies of power and belonging on the dance floor extended to the rearticulation of social, ethnonational hierarchies. These experiences that speak to the development of a New York style highlight the influence of place, not only on the music, but on the dancing that accompanied it. Dancing marked Nuyorican audiences as distinct from their Puerto Rico counterparts and recent Latin American and Caribbean immigrants, both of whom arrived at the clubs to encounter familiar dances that were nonetheless significantly different from those they already knew.[99]

The performance of the Fania All-Stars featured in *Our Latin Thing* represented the nightclub as a site of horizontal relationships, reproducing a heteronormative male gaze within the film. In one scene, an overhead view shows a braless woman in a tube top. Miranda, *inspirando* (riffing, improvising) onstage during "Quítate tú," simultaneously sings about a woman who slapped him because he grabbed this "thing, presumably the woman's breast." One of the most electric performances in *Our Latin Thing*, this and other moments in the film affirm heteronormativity as they accentuate the creativity, collectivity, and competition among vocalists showing off their improvisational chops. In another scene, the camera follows a couple on the dance floor as the All-Stars rehearse for the concert. The camera eventually settles on the woman, guiding the viewer's gaze to her butt until the camera begins to pull away and amplify the shot of the nightclub.

The presence of women within salsa, whether as artists, executives, or reporters, goes far beyond the film's masculinist narrative.[100] Ocasio's professional trajectory exemplifies how women's histories remain largely outside the film's frame. For Ocasio, the unexpected cameo in the film "proves [she] was there" during a watershed moment in the collective memory of salsa. Two years later, she was a professional dancer, performing with the All-Stars at Madison Square Garden and Yankee Stadium. She recalled watching from the dugout and preparing to perform with the All-Stars in 1974 when thousands of fans filled the arena while police turned away another three thousand at the door.[101] Ocasio would eventually become a professional dance instructor.

Through access to the public spaces of the salsa scene, salseras not only articulated a New York Puerto Rican identity in the public sphere but also transgressed the boundaries of the domestic space to assert their autonomy. Once women arrived at the clubs, they confronted a male gaze that attempted to situate them within prescriptive gender roles. Luciano describes the dance floor as a space where "courtesy, manners, civility and pride in who you were" resulted in an "incredible courtship" where men seduced women on the dance floor, even as chaperones watched.[102] Women, however, could also be viewed as the paradigmatic temptresses. One fan, who described himself as an "average dancer," recalled, "One time I asked this lady to dance and she wiggled and jiggled and [started] shaking. . . . I'm not really into that, I didn't know how to deal with it, so we sat down." The anxiety he felt about her dance style and suggestions of promiscuity, like Luciano's recollection, accentuate how heteropatriarchal recuperations of the dance floor fail to consider the ways women navigated the club space.

The recollections of Lisa, who preferred to dance with guys from Brooklyn but clearly spent some time dancing with men she found mediocre, highlight women's agency in the cuchifrito circuit. As she recalled, sometimes "you went to hide in the bathroom" if an "ugly guy was coming over, and you were afraid he's going to ask you to dance" so as not to feel the need to accept or navigate rejecting him.[103] Lisa described sitting at a bar in the back of one nightclub with friends so they could observe the dancers and decide with whom they would like to dance and who they should avoid. Female homosocial relations did not necessarily, as Cindy García argues with regard to the present-day salsa scene in Los Angeles, seek to overturn the heteropatriarchal social relations with the club. Women did, however, establish relationships with other women that allowed them to "smooth their way through them with disruptions as they go."[104]

Nightclubs' reputation as places where extralegal activities took place, like drug use, as well as the belief that women who went dancing were promiscuous, meant that some salseras confronted restrictions that made it difficult, if not impossible, to go dancing. Younger women living with their parents and married women whose husbands did not allow them to go dancing needed to find alternate ways to remain part of the scene. Mildred "from the Boogie Down Bronx" loved to dance but married a man who refused to let her patronize nightclubs. For Mildred, her girlfriends and the salsa records she bought allowed her to stay in the know. Her children remember their mother singing and dancing with a broomstick as she cleaned the apartment.[105] Lisa, who began dancing at the Palladium as a teenager, recalled, "I got married and all that [dancing in clubs] ceased" until after her divorce. So she bought salsa records and threw house parties. Efraín decided not to marry a woman he loved because, unlike her, he did not dance. Knowing that after they married he would want her to stop going to nightclubs, he decided to end their relationship. Such recollections provide a counterdiscourse to romanticized memories of the cuchifrito circuit.[106]

Women such as Mildred, Lisa, and Melba reclaimed their freedom on the dance floor after their respective divorces. As Lisa shared when we spoke in her apartment, "Then came the separation and that's when I broke out and started going to the Corso. . . . It was just fun. You gotta remember, I'm a divorced woman now. And I'm getting freedom like I never had before." Her independence manifested itself in various ways within the club. "Sometimes," she shared, "I'd leave with my boyfriend, sometimes my girlfriend. Sometimes I'd tell everybody to go to hell and take a cab home."[107] For her, the cuchifrito circuit itself embodied this renewed freedom, and she began to frequent many of the nightclubs on the salsa circuit with her girlfriends. For Lisa and other women, the centrality of the salsa scene to the social life of New York Puerto Rican communities encouraged them to transgress the spatial boundaries that restrict the mobility of women, reify patriarchal authority, and reproduce unequal status.[108]

The assumptions women faced in nightclubs mirrors perceptions of *rumberas* in places like Central Park. Yeyito Flores rarely took his sister Aurora, a budding musician herself, to the rumbas in Central Park. As Yeyito explained it to me, "It wasn't the kind of place a guy brought his girlfriend" because of the dominant attitudes about women who did participate. Many believed that women who went to the rumbas were sexually promiscuous.[109] The Latin music scene was widely viewed as an inappropriate place for women to find themselves. In fact, Aurora's instrument mysteriously disappeared (at the hands of a parent, she assumes) after she began showing interest in the Latin music scene.[110] Aurora, however, established her own place as a journalist and, later, as a musician in her own right. These structural conditions do not, as Frances Aparicio's study of how women listen to salsa has shown and the experiences of women who participated in New York's Latin music scene during the 1960s and 1970s confirm, determine how salseras participated in the boom or their potential for rewriting culture.[111]

*Our Latin Thing's* celebration of an ideal hypermasculine, heteronormative subject is cemented during the performance by bongocero Roena, who provides one of the most exhilarating yet androcentric performances during the number "Ponte duro" (Get hard). The number is preceded by shots of a cockfight; Miranda took Gast to the event and encouraged the director to include it in the film.[112] In a basement with low ceilings, exposed pipes, and brick walls, the roosters' owners explain the importance of breeding to an interviewer who remains off-camera as the animals are weighed, groomed, fitted with a metal claw, and then placed into a pit surrounded by men. The men place their bets, and those immediately surrounding the pit lean over the barrier, pound it passionately to encourage the roosters, and yell as the animals claw at each other. Recurring shots show an owner inside the pit being physically restrained from interfering. The yelling increases dramatically, the roosters become frenetic, and various men are prevented from climbing over the low wall separating spectators from the pit. The fight over, the music from the Cheetah overlaps with the scene as the men at the cockfight embrace and congratulate each other. The camera then cuts to the Cheetah, where the All-Stars perform "Ponte duro."

Camera angles like those used during the cockfight and moving between the cockfight and the Cheetah establish parallels between the two events. Like the spectators at the cockfight, the audience at the Cheetah watches, cheers, and becomes increasingly excited. Parallel editing and the use of similar camera angles suggest the commonalities between the All-Stars' performance at the Cheetah and the cockfight as the camera cuts back and forth between the two events. At one point the camera returns to the cockfight, where a man provides commentary on a rooster's quality and performance and expresses satisfaction with the results.[113] Back at the nightclub, fellow musicians and the audience encourage Roena as he begins his bongo solo. The rest of the All-Stars repeat "Ponte duro bongó / ponte duro" (Get hard bongo / get hard), and fans likewise respond to the music. The audience urges Roena on with cheers and dancing as the bongocero, with the bongos between his thighs organizing the phallocentric imagery, "gets hard." The tempo accelerates, and Roena's hands blur on-screen, energizing the crowd and his colleagues onstage, echoing the earlier frenzy of the cockfight as the solo reaches its climax. The parallel development of the cockfight and the concert emphasizes the corresponding configurations of the pit and the stage, the enthusiastic response and participation of spectators at each event, and the collegiality among men in both settings. In this way, the director's aesthetic decisions conflate the social worlds of men on and off the stage and connect sexual prowess—defined through physical stamina, aggression, and mastery—with aesthetic expression. The mise-en-scène, diegetic sounds, and blur effect come together in a powerful representation of pleasure and excitement integral to the film's iconic status.

Our Latin Thing reproduces the conflation of spaces and meanings in a scene that constitutes Santería and salsa as coextensive. An Afro-Caribbean creolized religious practice, Santería is composed "from a range of religious traditions and worldviews, including but not limited to indigenous rites and practices, rituals and spiritual entities that travelled with enslaved peoples transported from Africa to the Caribbean, and Catholic and Protestant practices and traditions."[114] The process of creolization with Catholicism includes the association between orishas (deities) and Catholic saints, or santos. The religious ceremony represented in Our Latin Thing features Black men, women, and children participating in a religious ceremony in honor of the orisha Shangó.[115] Multiple musical and visual signifiers convey the ceremony's meanings for viewers familiar with Santería, including the repetition of the orisha's name and the preponderance of red and white, colors associated with Shangó. Shangó, the deity of thunder and lightning, symbolizes virile masculinity, passion, and strength. He is patron of music, drumming, and dancing and master of the sacred batá drums.[116] An altar has a statue of Santa Bárbara, the orisha's syncretic figure within Catholicism's pantheon of saints.

The religious ceremony in Our Latin Thing operates as a fingerpost to the popular exposure of Santería's musical practices through Latin music in New York, illuminating a tension between the sacred and its spectacularization in secular and religious recordings and performances by artists like Mongo Santamaría.[117] The representation of a Santería community within Our Latin Thing, however, does not produce, and here I draw on Fred Moten, the double movement that "disrupts and resists certain formations of identity and interpretation by challenging the reducibility of phonic matter to verbal meaning or conventional musical form."[118] The film does not confront the disparaging representations of Santería within Puerto Rican and other Caribbean communities. The camera's focus on the corporeality of ritual, such as in moments when the camera stylizes the movement of Black women's bodies, including that of a female practitioner through whose body the orisha becomes manifest, mobilizes Santería and Black Caribbean diasporic religious practices as access to the sublime. That is, Our Latin Thing constitutes Santería as that which inspires extreme ambivalence, even as it is subject to aesthetic judgment.[119]

During a skit filmed for *Our Latin Thing* in a *botánica*, an establishment that sells medicinal herbs, candles, and other religous items, Ismael Miranda stands at the counter when a Latino customer enters the shop.[120] Hoping to find something that will enhance his virility, he also needs protection from aggressive women who want to trap men. The woman he is currently dating, Miranda informs the customer, "es una potencia" (is a power). While *potencia* means "power" in English, within the context of Santería it also refers to one of *las 7 potencias*, the seven orishas, or divinities, within Santería. The woman, Miranda suggests, is powerful and threatens men's free will. The banter between Miranda and the customer, both of whom are white, recurs to narratives of Black female hypersexuality through the scene's inclusion with the ritual portrayed on-screen. The scene's fetishization perpetuates the tropicalization of Blackness within the Caribbean and its diaspora as well as among audiences unfamiliar with Santería.[121] Rather than marshaling Black Caribbean diasporic musical, religious, and embodied practices as radical expressions of freedom, the film reinscribes racist and masculinist colonial imaginaries that reduce Santería to a bodily excess separated from the aesthetic, sacred, and historical legacies that inform entanglements with salsa.[122] *Our Latin Thing* capitalizes on the ways Santería informed Afro-Caribbean musical performance in New York and structured relationships among artists who were practitioners but ultimately recurs to representations of Blackness as primordial.[123]

While women appear in the scenes depicting Santería, on the dance floor at the Cheetah, and in the streets of Latin New York, they do not appear onstage in *Our Latin Thing*. The one young conguera who plays on the scaffolding with her fellow male percussionists in the opening scene faces away from the camera. In contrast to the young boy who morphs into Barretto, she receives no promise of an opportunity to become a professional musician. The only female singer in the film who is audibly present is an aging woman who sings as she sits on a stoop next to a man playing a guitar. Both figures participate in the very improvisation and everyday practices with which Fania sought to identify but failed to fully represent. Their presence exceeds the film's representation of musical practices as exclusively male and signals the experiences of women for whom, like their male counterparts, salsa provided a "refuge . . . after work and on weekends, at home and in dance halls, offering liberation of the body and mind through the experience of danc[ing]," singing, and listening in ways that force us to reimagine salsa's histories.[124]

The women who worked at Fania Records during the salsa boom have likewise remained largely anonymous. Eve Charlack, who managed the production of all albums, singles, and tapes released by Fania, also selected the music for a three-hour radio show five days per week. Carol Polizzi, along with her husband, helped Masucci distribute Fania Records releases to local stores in New York in the label's earliest days, when the company's "warehouse" was the home of Pacheco's brother. Gertrude Fredd had so many roles at Fania that, when interviewed as part of a thirty-page special section in the trade publication *Record World* celebrating Fania's tenth anniversary, she explained, "There is no title for my position." Hired initially as a bookkeeper, she was primarily responsible for recordkeeping for all contracts, royalty statements, and licensing agreements—which by 1975 included three hundred albums from Fania Records and its six subsidiaries.[125] Journalist Carmen Mirabal joined Fania Records as a publicist when she was just a teenager and later worked for Tico Records while it remained under the ownership of Morris Levy. In addition to Aurora Flores, Anne Saxon, Nayda Román, Adela López, Mary B. Hoffman, and Mercedes Acosta were among the women who wrote for *Latin N.Y.* In their embodiment of salsa's musical and social modalities, these women transmit an alternative genealogy obscured by salsa's dominant narratives and a majoritarian public culture that suppresses female and queer histories.[126]

## After the Cheetah

The success of *Our Latin Thing* in connecting with audiences contributed to its success at the box office. The film grossed $700,000 and catapulted the Fania All-Stars into stardom.[127] It was an outcome no one could have predicted. Less than three weeks after the film's debut, *New York Magazine* dedicated an issue to the "Latin impact on New York Style." In November, *Billboard* magazine published a special supplement on the "Latin Explosion" that featured salsa heavily and inaugurated increased coverage of salsa. It also included coverage of regional Latin music markets in Texas, Miami, Los Angeles, New York, and Puerto Rico; emerging markets along the Eastern Seaboard and in the Midwest; and mainstream artists like José Feliciano, Trini López, and Vicki Carr. Latin music labels (a term *Billboard* applied to a broad swath of music from salsa to La Onda Chicana), recording studios, and major mainstream labels bought ad space to congratulate *Billboard* on the launch of its Latin music coverage and to market their artists. The Cheetah, announcing itself as "the new home of Latin music," saluted the magazine "for its insight and awareness of the Latin music explosion."[128]

Continuous coverage of the New York salsa scene could be found in the magazine *Latin N.Y.* With financial support from Fania Records, in 1973 editor Izzy Sanabria resurrected what had been a short-lived magazine and began to chronicle the salsa scene alongside other forms of expressive culture across Latin New York.[129] Within a year, the magazine became "the most important place in which new salsa albums were advertised, reviewed, and otherwise brought to the attention of recorder buyers" and helped pressure "industry leaders to recognize the power of Latina/o consumers."[130] In 1974, Sanabria wrote an article for *Billboard* on the artistry of salsa's album covers.[131] In 1975, he hosted the first Latin Music Awards show from the Cheetah and debuted the short-lived variety show *Salsa* on a local Spanish-language network. When *Billboard* decided to print another special supplement on the "Salsa explosion" in 1976, it referred to *Latin N.Y.* as a "bible" for salsa fans. Coco Records took out two full-page ads in this same *Billboard* issue. On one page, they included a list of artists signed to the label who were nominated for music awards sponsored by *Latin N.Y.* The second full-page ad was devoted to Palmieri. In addition to celebrating Palmieri's Grammy, the label listed all the awards he received at both the 1975 and 1976 Latin Music Awards.[132]

By the time *Billboard* published the 1976 supplement, Masucci's distribution networks in the United States extended throughout the Northeast as well as Chicago, Philadelphia, Los Angeles, Miami, Baltimore, and Texas. On the West Coast alone, Fania reported a 150 percent increase in record and cassette sales in 1975.[133] Masucci also expanded markets outside the United States. Despite the initial lackluster response in Puerto Rico, the Fania All-Stars sold out their 1973 performance at the newly inaugurated Roberto Clemente Coliseum in San Juan, where Celia Cruz made her debut as the first and only woman to form part of the Fania All-Stars, and kicked off their first Latin American tour.

Puerto Rico had already become an "exciting record market" with more than a hundred radio stations, ten record labels, four pressing plants, and seven recording studios.[134] By 1977, Puerto Rico comprised 40 percent of Fania's market, second only to New York.[135] In the Dominican Republic, Fania's success stemmed from the perception of salsa as an urban, Afro-diasporic, pan-Caribbean musical form that shared various characteristics with Dominican merengue; from salsa's danceability; and from Pacheco's well-known role in the music's development. Fania's success also depended, as Deborah Pacini Hernández outlines, on the label's ability to—as one DJ described it—"shut down" merengue. Fania secured "powerful backers able to finance massive public relations and promotion campaigns" that facilitated the use of payola in exchange for radio and TV access.[136] Salsa became "an expression of Pan-Caribbean identity" that, when "confronted with merengue . . . became foreign and hostile," revealing the economic and ideological factors at play in the music's circulation—a reality that cannot be separated from US imperialism in the Caribbean.[137]

In South America, Fania benefited from historical distribution networks through which Latin "tropical" music had long circulated. In 1974, the label opened a sales and distribution center in Panama to increase access to these markets. In Venezuela and Colombia, salsa expressed an "urban reality in a way that individual local styles—each associated with a distinct town or region—could not" amid structural shifts in each country's economy that propelled massive migration from the countryside to urban centers and the growth of the working class. The music's cosmopolitan meanings, as ethnomusicologist Lise Waxer shows, "became strongly localized in these countries, a style with deep affective power that Venezuelans and Colombians consider to be 'legítimamente *nuestra*, ni más ni menos' (legitimately *ours*, no more, no less)."[138] Venezuela quickly became one of salsa's most profitable markets and remained so until the country's economic crisis in 1983.[139]

Fania's expansion in Europe took place alongside its increasing domestic, Latin American, and Caribbean expansion. In Europe, Fania created relationships with distributors in Spain, the Netherlands, and the Benelux Union by the mid-1970s, while the ever-expanding list of places where the Fania All-Stars performed solidified salsa's viability as a global commodity.[140] In September 1974, the group electrified audiences at the music festival that preceded the heavyweight bout between George Foreman and Muhammad Ali in Kinshasa, Zaire, featured in the 2008 documentary *Soul Power*, directed by Jeff Levy-Hinte. Within two years, the All-Stars had also performed in Tokyo, London, and Cannes. In 1977, Stevie Wonder jammed with the Fania All-Stars at the Hollywood Palladium and Barretto, along with Delgado and "Little" Ray Romero, visited Sesame Street to teach the neighborhood about bongos, congas, timbales, and *clave*, the 3–2/2–3 beat that organizes salsa's rhythms.

Fania's success increased attention within mainstream markets and encouraged the label and other music executives to pursue crossover dreams domestically. Ideas bubbled among music executives about how to move beyond the so-called ethnic niche to attract mainstream audiences. In a statement highlighting how conversations about expanding market shares often focused on expanding among white listeners, longtime music reporter Agustín Gurza sums up the period: "'Spanish was the problem,' said some. 'Simplify the lyrics or put them in English,' they advocated. 'Distribution was the key,' others argued. 'Put the music in the hands of the powerful American labels and let their promotion muscle do the work.' And so it went. The rhythm was too African, the melody too Spanish, the image too ethnic. Artists tinkered with variations. Label executives hustled new deals. All was fusion, polish, and fanfare."[141] Harvey Averne, Fania Records producer and vice president of the subsidiary Vaya Records, questioned salsa's crossover potential in a 1976 interview for *Billboard*. In the same article, Barretto notes that "the few singles which have crossed over have been flukes or fads" but reasserts the importance of establishing a permanent crossover audience for musicians to develop their musical potential and find financial security.[142]

Fania explicitly marketed to Black audiences with the short-lived Fania subsidiary Uptite Records, the Latin-funk-soul label that released approximately twenty-five singles between 1968 and 1970. The label drew on the success of Latin soul pioneer Joe Bataan, who was African American and Filipino and grew up in Harlem around the city's Puerto Rican communities, with recordings like the 1969 release "Young, Gifted, and Brown." Drawing on African American playwright Lorraine Hansberry's 1964 address, the single emphasizes the social, cultural, and musical convergences within Bataan's personal and professional trajectories.[143] First released on the Fania Records label, it was rereleased as a single by Uptite Records. Singles released on Uptite records, whether by Fania artists like Bataan, Ralfi Pagán, and Harvey Averne or those signed directly to Uptite like soul singers Billy Hamlin, Ray Mayberry, and Dean Parrish, were not distributed through Fania's usual networks in order to court African American audiences and crossover success on the US pop charts.[144] Fania also courted Black radio stations by capitalizing on historical musical collaborations that had already created inroads into African American communities for Latin music.[145] A report Columbia Records commissioned in 1972 may have encouraged the move. It showed that 30 percent of Top 40 songs originated on the soul music charts and identified Black listeners as the key to reaching the Top 40 audience.[146]

The increasing visibility of Latin music beyond Fania's largely Puerto Rican and broader Latina/o and Latin American markets appeared to reach a tipping point by 1975. The international arm of Columbia Records, CBS Records, had already agreed to distribute Caytronics's Latin catalog in 1972 to get ahead of competitors in reaching mainstream markets and to establish distribution networks within Latin markets.[147] Fania's crossover dreams seemed within reach when it struck a distribution deal with Columbia Records/CBS Records in 1975 for three Fania All-Stars albums that would be distributed internationally. But Masucci's previous statements linking salsa to poor and working-class New York Puerto Rican communities no longer benefited Fania's crossover dreams. By mid-decade, he worried that the racialized urban aesthetic might alienate mainstream audiences. He turned instead toward an origins narrative of salsa's Afro-Cuban roots to reproduce the mainstream fascination with Latin music that had soared at different times since the 1920s and 1930s.[148] Masucci hired Gast to direct a new documentary that would promote a new origins narrative.

Four years after the tremendous success of *Our Latin Thing*, Masucci and Gast released the musical documentary *Salsa* (1976). The film included footage of the Fania All-Stars performing in front of an estimated twenty thousand fans at the (in)famous Yankee Stadium concert in 1973, where exuberant fans rushed the stage, and the Roberto Clemente Coliseum in Puerto Rico that same year. Similarly to its predecessor, *Salsa* includes additional scenes that provided an origins narrative for the music and its commercialization. Gone, however, are the streets of the Lower East Side and its largely Puerto Rican Latina/o residents. Instead, *Salsa* inserts black-and-white film clips of Hollywood films that resort to racialized regimes of representation wherein the African continent is signified to the viewer through images of "primitive" peoples playing drums in the "wild."

Speaking directly to the viewer as the images appear on-screen, narrator Geraldo Rivera explains that salsa's polyrhythmic structures can be traced to African musical practices transported to the Caribbean via the transatlantic slave trade. Once in the Caribbean, he continues, they were transformed in Cuba through contact with Spanish and "North American" jazz. In this new account, Cuba becomes a space for an interplay between African primitivism, European modernity, and US tourism. Africa is rendered as a "source for diasporic populations and practice but not an active participant."[149] In other words, Africa remains the cradle of the music's Afro-diasporic rhythms but not a constitutive locus for salsa. The Hollywood clip of largely white *vedettes* in a Cuban nightclub, likely catering to US tourists, renders US imperialism palatable. Jazz, in turn, becomes deterritorialized from African American musical traditions. And Cuba's insertion into modernity is reduced to the circulation of "people, texts, images, desires, and attachments in the service of dominant market logics."[150]

Despite the rising star of Fania's ensemble band, *Salsa* did not translate into a desired crossover success with English-speaking audiences in the United States. Nor did the agreement between Fania and CBS Records. The albums did not increase the number of units sold for Fania, perhaps because Columbia did not know how to market them, or perhaps the attempt to create a sound that would draw a larger audience backfired. Music historian Rondón's overview of the albums produced under the agreement with CBS highlights the intersection of aesthetics, commercial priorities, and artists' attempts to navigate Fania's demands. The first of these albums, which included Traffic's British guitarist Steve Winwood to create a crossover sound, distanced itself from salsa's Nuyorican aesthetic and failed to excite either salsa's core audiences or the coveted crossover market.[151] In an interview with Rondón, Roena described the frustration of musicians in recording the album:

> They brought us (the six musicians from the rhythm section) together in New York to record this. . . . Then they took the tape and added everything else—the U.S. drums, the electric guitar, and the brass. . . . None of us liked what they were taping, but what could we do, you know? They're the ones in power. . . . Still, in those jam sessions, while we were recording that garbage, we did some jamming and that was really, really good, heavy. . . . I don't know. Jerry said maybe they would include that jamming in a record. . . . But what came out was really bad. It reminds me of supermarket music, that music they play while housewives do their grocery shopping and it is totally useless because those ladies don't even pay attention to it. . . . It was really, really bad music.[152]

Roena's comments highlight the creative failings and limited input of artists in these recordings. This flop and other less-than-stellar releases by labels seeking to capitalize on salsa's popularity showed that it was necessary to maintain the music's ethnic base while seeking crossover success.[153]

The inclusion of "Juan Pachanga" (Party boy Juan) on *Rhythm Machine* (1977), the next album released under the CBS deal, illustrates how music executives attempted to find a formula that would appeal to salsa's established fans and the coveted crossover audiences. For Rondón, the sonority of this "real" salsa song, written and performed by the incomparable Rubén Blades, provided an example of the successful fusion of different expressive modalities. The instrumentation included a large orchestra hired for the recording, a sign in and of itself of the financial investment in the album. Rondón considers that the decision to have the violin section perform a melodic, rather than rhythmic, role complemented Blades's acoustic guitar, itself a departure from salsa's usual instrumentation. The collaboration between percussionist Louie Ramírez and songwriter Jay Chattaway on the track augmented what the musical historian describes as "a distinctive and attractive new sonority."[154] While *Rhythm Machine* made it onto *Billboard's* Hot Latin LPs chart for New York, the album was panned by critics and musicians alike.

## "Fuego en el 23"

The music's social life beyond the dance floor, particularly with regard to how its soundscape formed part of a Nuyorican imaginary, cannot be accommodated within *Our Latin Thing*. There is, however, a brief moment when the music's meanings within Nuyorican liberatory praxis make themselves visible. While the camera pans the audience during Orchestra Harlow's performance in Hell's Kitchen, we see a man with a raised fist. The image provides a signpost of the way salsa remained intertwined with broader cultural and political movements of the mid to late 1960s and 1970s.

Evelyn, a community activist during the 1970s, used salsa during political rallies to transmit social messages because she recognized the music's significance for mobilizing residents in her neighborhood. Songs acquired multiple and overlapping meanings as she incorporated them into rallies. The refrain "Te conozco bacalao aunque vengas disfrazaó" (I recognize you despite your getup) from "Te conozco" (I know you, 1969) warned residents about politicians considered wolves in sheep's clothing, lobbying for votes despite a dismal record of supporting local racialized communities. Evelyn also listened to Young Lord Felipe Luciano on his weekly radio show, which combined discussions of salsa's cultural meanings with social commentary on, "basically, anything on the front page" of newspapers.[155]

The Youngs Lords newsletter *Palante* explored the connection between expressive culture and politics in a 1971 essay that applauded artists like Barretto, whose revolutionary spirit extended from their music to their support for the organization. Barretto became one of the first well-known musicians to reach out to the Young Lords, playing a benefit for them on 110th Street in East Harlem.[156] Barretto also invited Luciano to write the liner notes for, and to emcee with Guzmán, Barretto's 1976 performance at New York's Beacon Theatre, released on Atlantic Records as *Tomorrow: Barretto Live*. A friend of Young Lord Miguel "Mickey" Meléndez, Palmieri offered to help raise funds to cover the fines of Young Lords members arrested during their occupation of the Statue of Liberty in 1977.[157] In his important essay on culture and politics in salsa, Karl Hagstrom Miller suggests that Fania Records was well aware of the intersection of Puerto Rican nationalism, politics, and record sales.[158] The decision to hire Guzmán as publicity director for the label shortly after his departure from the Young Lords certainly suggests that possibility.

In the studio, musicians like Palmieri and Barretto recorded songs of social justice while Colón, who alongside LaVoe narrated life in El Barrio, likewise contributed to a sonic imaginary that reflected and informed emerging Nuyorican subjectivities. I turn here to a song, "Fuego en el 23" (Fire in number 23), recorded by La Sonora Ponceña in 1969, to underscore how the music sounded social relations within Puerto Rican communities in ways that exceeded Fania's representations of salsa. "Fuego en el 23," written by Lucía Martínez, was inspired by an actual fire. The fire erupted in a building at 23 West Sixty-Fifth Street, where Cuban songwriter and bandleader Arsenio Rodríguez, who was blind, lived. Residents, unaware that Rodríguez was already outside, called out for someone to help him. The original 1957 recording of "Fuego en el 23" by Rodríguez clearly places the fire at "twenty-three West de la sixty fifth" (west of Sixty-Fifth Street) and includes an important detail that would not make it onto the subsequent recording: that Luis "Wito" Kortright, a singer in Rodríguez's band, had led him out of the apartment to safety.

The 1969 recording by La Sonora Ponceña moves the fire to 23 110th Street, in the heart of El Barrio:

> En el 23 de la 110
> no se puede estar tranquilo
> te diré por qué.
>
> A veces a las doce del día, a la una o las tres
> A veces de madrugada lo mismo al amanecer
> Se forma un rebambaramba que se juntan cuatro, cinco, siete,
>     ocho, nueve o diez
> Y salen gritando,
> "¡Avísale al súper
> que nos estamos quemando
> y no se sabe el fuego en dónde es!"

Una mañana dormía y corriendo me tiré.
Por un grito que decía "¡Hay fuego en el 23!
¡Que se prendió la bombilla y no se sabe cómo fue!"

Yo lo sé
Fuego! . . .

Que lo pegaron con gasolina[159]

[In number 23 on 110th street
You can't be at peace
I'll tell you why

Sometimes at noon at one or at three
Sometimes in the middle of the night, sometimes at dawn
A commotion forms where four, five, seven, eight, nine, or ten
Get together and they come out screaming,
"Tell the super that we're burning,
and we don't know where the fire is!"

One morning I was sleeping and I left running
Because of a scream that said,
"There's a fire in number 23!
The light bulb caught fire and we don't know how it happened."

I know
Fire! . . .

They started it with gasoline]

The song's relocation of the fire invokes the rampant arson in 1960s and 1970s New York that ravaged Black and Puerto Rican communities amid the city's disinvestment in these "unsalvageable" communities. Landlords' abandonment of aged, overcrowded, and deteriorating buildings during this time certainly allowed for the possibility of an electrical fire, as suggested by one resident within the song. However, firehouse closures in 1972 that formed part of New York's planned shrinkage also increased the vulnerability of Black and Puerto Rican residents in areas of Manhattan, Queens, and the South Bronx. Within the confines of the song "Fuego en el 23," the possibility of arson also becomes clear when the lyrical subject confirms that gasoline was used to ignite the fire, declaring:

Yo lo sé . . .
lo pegaron con gasolina.

[I know . . .
they set it with gasoline]

The song further suggests arson when someone accuses "Jacobo" of setting the fire—whether he is the landlord, a resident, or another person remains unclear within the song. Unable to confirm this detail, the lyrical subject quickly notes, "pero eso yo no lo sé" (but that I don't know), reflecting the challenges faced in identifying culprits and prosecuting these cases in the rare instances when insurance companies pursued the possibility that the blaze might have been arson.[160]

The references within "Fuego en el 23" to the real fire and its painful consequences, as well as to the joyful rhythms of the song and descargas that are often referred to as "being on fire," highlight the relationship between the music and the material context in which it circulated. The song's *coro* (chorus) functions as a collective town crier informing residents about the fire with the repetition of the song's title. The improvisational utterances during instrumental sections also contribute by making residents aware of the fire and warning them "que te quemas" (you're burning) and that "tienes fuego bajo tus pies" (you've got fire beneath your feet) signifying the fire and ecstatic dancing. The sounds of fire engines and police radios that recur throughout the song serve a similar purpose, becoming progressively louder and eventually forming part of the music itself. Not merely reflecting the actual events that inspired the song, "Fuego en el 23" participates in the production of a public discourse surrounding these fires that acquires additional meanings over time. It allows New York Puerto Rican communities to question, challenge, and indict with an authority not available to them through institutional mechanisms that abandoned Black and Puerto Rican residents and then largely failed to prosecute landlords. The literal fire of "Fuego en el 23" thus becomes a floating signifier that becomes trapped in the real—the fires pervasive in the city at the time, a reality missed by those who did not share in, or have forgotten, that particular experience. The meanings of "Fuego en el 23" transgressed the parameters of the song and make apparent how the soundscapes created by the music became ensconced in the material context of New York Puerto Ricans' daily lives in ways that exceeded the understanding of Fania Records and the label's ability to fully organize the spaces, cultural practices, and discourses of salsa.

## Conclusion

Using *Our Latin Thing* as a jumping-off point for discussions of the spectacularization of Puerto Ricanness, this chapter has explored the ambivalent relationship between Fania Records and New York's Puerto Rican communities as both navigated the music's cultural and commercial meanings. I examine the ways in which Fania Records initially identified salsa with Latin New York; the ways New York Puerto Ricans both participated in and exceeded Fania's representations of salsa; and the contradictions that emerge through the process of commodification and commercialization. Yet the importance of the film cannot be underestimated at a time when a shifting economy increasingly looked to the cultural products of racialized communities— indeed, relied on their very identities—to negotiate the impact of social movements challenging hegemonic constructions of Americanness. While the musicians chosen for the Cheetah concert may not have been, as salsa historian Rondón contends, the most accomplished musicians, the music exceeds the individual performers. The film's significance lies as much in the performance itself as the affective experience of the All-Stars, the audience in attendance that night, and fans who saw the film on the big screen. In *Our Latin Thing*, the "foreign" sounds of Latin New York that mark the unassimilability of Puerto Ricans are the aural manifestations of a Nuyorican subjectivity sounded through salsa's aesthetics.

Ultimately, the reciprocal relationship between Fania Records and New York's Puerto Rican communities reveals one of the ways Nuyorican subjects navigated their political, cultural, and economic identities as salsa entered a global political economy. While Fania Records entered a system of collective exchange, the manifestations of a New York Puerto Rican identity in multiple spaces across the city created an excess that Fania remained unable to absorb. Even the nightclubs created the opportunity for fans and musicians to traverse the city and transform spaces both within and outside Puerto Rican communities into sites for the expression of a Nuyorican subjectivity. Puerto Rican communities simultaneously exploited and resisted the commercialization of salsa to maintain their own authority over these spaces and the cultural practices and discourses enacted within them, in the process enabling salsa's role as a viable cultural signifier.

# "Los Malotes de la Salsa"

## SALSA DONS AND THE PERFORMANCE
## OF SUBJECTHOOD

**2**

This chapter examines the performance of racialized masculinity by Willie Colón and Héctor LaVoe, who mined the potentiality of Afro-Caribbean musical practices, the streets of Latin New York, and Nuyorican aesthetics in their performance of subjecthood. The boastfulness, aggression, and competition embraced by los malotes de la salsa (salsa's bad boys or gangsters) in their songs mirrored their performative bravado on- and off-stage. Album covers, liner notes, and publicity materials for their earliest recordings drew on images in popular culture to build their reputation as gangsters who hustled for gigs and murdered competitors with a musical ferocity that left fans dancing themselves to death. The racialized masculinity expressed through Colón and LaVoe's gangster doubles reveled in an affective economy of pleasure and excess that defied orthodox musical practices as well as emerging neoliberal discourses of the productive citizen subject. Colón and LaVoe's music and embodied performances revolted against the status of Puerto Ricans as national abjects, both in the United States and in Puerto Rico.

Colón signed with Fania Records at the age of sixteen, five years before the Cheetah concert.[1] He appears only briefly in *Our Latin Thing*, playing third trombone during the 1971 Cheetah concert behind the incomparable Barry Rogers, who had formed part of Eddie Palmieri's band La Perfecta, and Reynaldo Jorge, a recent arrival to the New York Latin music scene. Just twenty-one years old at the time, Colón may not have possessed the artistic range of either of these more experienced musicians, but his *sonoridad* (musicality) evoked the ethnoracial, linguistic, and cultural heterogeneity within which New York's Puerto Rican communities had developed. Salsa's audiences had already made him a fan favorite; he didn't need significant screen time in *Our Latin Thing* to command a following. LaVoe, one of the seven vocalists in the film, also received limited screen time but no less than most other singers. Only Ismael Miranda, who provided lead vocals for Larry Harlow's band during the festival filmed in Hell's Kitchen, featured prominently in the film. By the Cheetah concert, Colón and LaVoe had already become two of Fania's most sought-after and bankable artists.

Colón's music grew out of distinctly antihegemonic listening practices that suited the image of the outlaw. Born in 1950, he gained an informal musical education from the rich musical history of the Bronx, which continued to evolve with the racial demographic shifts taking place after World War II. His family was part of the transformation of the neighborhood as African Americans and Puerto Ricans arrived to the Bronx at midcentury. The Bronx was two-thirds white in 1950. Within a decade, Black and Latina/o residents became two-thirds of the population. The population shift reflected the settlement patterns of African American and Puerto Rican migrants to New York as well as a pattern of white flight that made the Bronx, as a front-page story in the *New York Times* announced, the first borough with a Black and Puerto Rican majority.[2] Colón's musical influences reflected the ethnic and racial hybridity of the Bronx. He grew up listening to Puerto Rican, Latin American, and US popular music, including African American musical traditions such as jazz and soul. It also included the Puerto Rican *música típica* (folkloric music) that the old-timers played outside a bodega by his home, and that wafted out of the bar next to the lingerie store where his mother worked, and that his family listened to in Puerto Rico.[3]

For Colón, jam sessions in the Bronx with Dominican, Cuban, Puerto Rican, and African American musicians highlighted the musical possibilities of bringing together various traditions. As Wilson Valentín-Escobar notes in his overview of salsa's New York sound, "The attitude to experiment with tradition often created eagerness to modify musical paradigms. In this process, the new tradition that emerged—in varying degrees—was a reformulation and resemanticization of musical texts and boundaries. . . . Many salsa arrangements incorporated the heterogenous urban spatial economy of the city, reflecting and articulating the transnational consciousness of many musicians and consumers."[4] The listening practices that Colón cultivated meant, for example, that his exposure to the Beatles expanded his musical repertoire without replacing the influence of Puerto Rican music.[5]

In liner notes written in 2021 for a rerelease of his music online, Colón recalled the significance of those jam sessions in the 1960s. His comments highlight that his musical education on the streets of the Bronx took place within the context of local, national, and global events:

> The jam sessions in the schoolyards and parks are more developed now [meaning in the early 1960s]. They are well attended, with all kinds of amateur musicians showing up to play, including myself. I'm around 12 years old. Most of the conga drummers are Puerto Rican. Papín is Cuban and brings a full bass. Fernando is Dominican. He brings his violin. Tijoe is African American; he and I play the trumpet. Guaguancó, bomba, plena. The music represents our spirit and identity. Most of the older guys are gone. Drafted to Vietnam or in jail, mostly for drugs, or dead from one of the two. As the American Apartheid is in its death throes, we watch Martin Luther King marching through Selma on black and white TV. While hostile racist police . . . sweeps our jam sessions for "Illegal Assembly" or "Disturbing the Peace," we feel part of the movement. We return the following day if the weather and conditions are right. This is our little piece of civil disobedience, in solidarity with the cause.[6]

The jam sessions that sounded the possibilities created by integrating different rhythms took place within the context of the Vietnam War, the Civil Rights Movement in the United States, and the criminalization of Black and Puerto Rican New Yorkers. Making music in public spaces during this period often drew noise complaints in the increasingly Black and Puerto Rican neighborhood and brought police to break up the music. The confrontations with New York Police Department (NYPD) officers, who Colón remembers sometimes took an instrument with them or used it to knock somebody on their head, as he describes it, crystallize how racial tensions were projected onto the city's musical soundscape.[7]

Colón's diverse musical background fostered an eagerness to experiment with musical practices that were less ethnocentric. He freely juxtaposed and synthesized jazz, R&B, Cuban, and Puerto Rican musical traditions.[8] Like most of his contemporaries, he would increasingly turn toward placing Latin American and Caribbean rhythms in the forefront while Black US musical styles receded into the background. This musical tactic reflected the same cultural nationalist impetus that led artists to insist on Spanish-language lyrics. This latter expectation necessitated lead vocalists comfortable singing in Spanish or, as in the case of Colón, becoming fluent over time. His debut album, *El Malo* (literally, The Bad One; figuratively, The Gangster), which would become Colón's nickname, included English- and Spanish-language songs and incorporated musical rhythms such as boogaloo, jazz, *guaguancó*, and bomba. The shift in rhythms within a single song, in particular, defied established musical practices within Latin music. In a 2018 interview, Colón describes his process of arranging: "I just heard those sounds in my head. I enjoyed writing some of the lines one step away, so they had to just grate against each other. I did that a lot. I didn't know what I was doing, though; I just liked the way it sounded."[9] Colón's instinct for what "sounded good," his openness to working on arrangements with other musicians, and what he has described as a "reconciliation" of various musical traditions drove his artistic development and made him a foundational figure in salsa.

Trained "por el oído y no por el conservatorio" (by ear and not in a conservatory), Colón's "unpolished image" contributed to his irreverent persona.[10] Established musicians criticized Colón's "kiddie band" for his refusal to adhere to stylistic boundaries, the inability to keep time with the clave, and a general lack of musicality. In fact, the moniker El Malo may be an appropriation of the criticism leveled against him by older musicians, who, according to some, may have created the nickname to mock Colón's musicianship. However, as Valentín-Escobar explains, the faster 3–2 and 2–3 clave Colón used marshaled the pace of urban life, effectively sounding the spaces of the city.[11] The disregard for established clave time, like the synthesis of styles, should therefore be understood not as an aesthetic shortcoming but as a refusal to adhere to formal structures that delimited creative possibilities. Similarly, we should consider the departure from Black US musical styles as an aesthetic and political decision that did not fully encompass the Nuyorican imaginary expressed through Colón's music. Salsa, like Colón's musical experimentation, conveyed a Nuyorican imaginary but not its totality.

Colón tried his hand at leading a big band, but as he put it, he lacked "the chops" for it and transitioned instead to two trombones and a rhythm section. Inspired to play the trombone when he heard a "ripping and roaring" solo by Barry Rogers on the song "Dolores," released in 1963 by Joe Cotto, Colón developed a distinctive sound distinguished by trombone-led arrangements and a musical ear that thrived on dissonance.[12] The placement of trombones at the forefront can be traced to the nineteenth century when wind instruments camouflaged polyphonous meanings in *danzas*. In Puerto Rican music,

Afro–Puerto Rican musicians Mon and Efraín Rivera introduced the use of trombone into Puerto Rican plenas in the 1950s. In New York, Eddie Palmieri's arrangements were the first to give a prominent placement to trombones. His decision to substitute a trombone for a trumpet pioneered a "deeper and rougher sonority" that resonated with the sounds of New York. A decade later, Palmieri replaced the violins in his charanga big band with trombones, producing his distinctive *trombanga* sound. This shift invoked the brash, loud, and fast pace of urban life in New York, which became identified with salsa.[13]

What remains distinctive about Colón, who cites Mon Rivera among his influences, particularly in his earliest recordings with Fania, is the expansive, distinctive sound the trombones produced. His use of harmonic structures with intervals of fourths and fifths amplified the adventurous sonority of the trombones. The use of the piano to double the bass rather than play melody provided an additional punch to the band's expressivity. The band had a sheer volume that belied the use of just two trombones. When this combined with the use of dissonant chords and minor keys, Colón's band produced a distinctive, loud, bold, and aggressive sound that proclaimed his musical defiance, a boldness to which fans responded on the dance floors.[14] In a conversation with songwriter and bass player Gui Duvignau, with whom I spoke extensively about Colón's recordings, Duvignau commented on the length and centrality of the instrumental parts of songs. It seems, Duvignau remarked, that sometimes the verses are the vehicle for getting back to the instrumental section. Indeed, Colón's arrangements reverberated and intertwined with the lyrics and performance of lead vocalist Héctor LaVoe.

Héctor LaVoe, born Héctor Juan Pérez Martínez, joined the band as lead vocalist for Colón's debut album, *El Malo*, released in 1967. LaVoe arrived in New York from Puerto Rico in 1963 as a lanky seventeen-year-old determined to make a living as a professional singer. A native of Ponce, LaVoe had wide musical influences, like Colón. As Valentín-Escobar describes, LaVoe "grew up listening [to] and studying the music of Puerto Rico's most famous folklore and popular musicians and singers, such as Ramito, Chuito el de Bayamon, Odilio González, and Daniel Santos. He also admired and was influenced by salsa, bomba, and plena singers Cheo Feliciano and Ismael Rivera."[15] LaVoe had dropped out of school in 1960 to sing with local bands before going to New York. Once there, he sang with several bands, including the New Yorkers, Kako and His All-Stars, and the Tito Puente Orchestra, before becoming lead vocalist for Colón at the behest of Johnny Pacheco. LaVoe earned a reputation as one of the preeminent *soneros* of his generation, a title reserved for vocalists with extraordinary rhythm, improvisational skills, and capacity to move across musical genres. LaVoe was recognized as much for the quality of his voice as for his exquisite timing, phrasing (*fraseo*), timbre, expressivity, improvisational acumen, and command of multiple musical traditions. His expansive musical background and willingness to experiment resonated with Colón's approach to making music. The sonero's vocals and Colón's juxtaposition and synthesis of musical rhythms and trombone-driven arrangements expanded and transformed musical possibilities.[16] In "El Malo," for example, Valentín-Escobar notes how Colón's "trombone arrangements punctuated Lavoe's jíbaro twang as well as the young salsero's [Colón's] barrio philosophy."[17] The resignification of traditional and experimental musical modalities in salsa that Colón and LaVoe's collaborations sounded became more pronounced over time as the two developed as artists.[18]

As Colón gained experience as a bandleader and arranger and LaVoe's voice matured, their musical collaborations became increasingly complex, as seen in *El Juicio* (The trial), released in 1972. Music critic Aurora Flores has described the album as one in which "Colón stretches his wings . . . by smoothly mixing musical genres," including Brazilian samba, Afro-Cuban rhythms, and Puerto Rican bomba and danza. As she noted, by "harmonizing clusters of dissonant chords for the trombones, Colón's mature musical vision outpace[d] his young ears and developing skills."[19] Nowhere was the collaboration between Colón and LaVoe more evident than in a song's *montuno*, as in "El Malo," on Colón's eponymous album, and "Sonero mayor" (The greatest sonero), released on *Cosa nuestra* (Our thing, 1969).[20] These songs highlight how exchanges between the chorus, LaVoe's soneos (riffs), musicians' solos, and Colón's arrangements came together with a faster rhythmic syncopation to produce a raw, intense, and immensely danceable sound. The irreverent sonoridad helped define the "New York sound" that became a trademark of Fania Records and that Latin music recording executives at other labels began to covet by the early 1970s.[21] Both Colón and LaVoe initially resisted Pacheco's musical instincts to bring the two artists together. But as the story goes, after their first recording each was convinced of the other's prodigious artistic talent.

### The New York That Salsa Wrought

Though songs produced in New York during earlier periods in Latin music referred to El Barrio, this area developed fully as the imagined home of diasporic Puerto Ricans with the emergence of salsa. Alongside the sonoridad of the New York sound, song lyrics explicitly situated salsa in New York. The song lyrics of the title track to *El Malo* narrate men's attempts to establish their place in the social hierarchy of the streets. On 110th Street, a pretender to the title of El Malo, the object of the singing subject's contempt, gets slapped: "El malo de aquí so yo" (I'm the bad one here), sings LaVoe, where the song's "here" is El Barrio. The title track of Colón's 1969 album, *Guisando/Doing a Job*, similarly situates listeners in East Harlem. The song tells the story of Vicente, a thief whose body police find in a trash can at 110th Street and Lexington Avenue, the latter being the principal north-south thoroughfare that runs through East Harlem. References to New York landmarks, like the subway in "Chonqui," reinforce the music's "here" as New York.[22] These discursive references to New York proliferated throughout recordings from the period, sometimes in the album titles. The Fania All-Stars' *Live at Yankee Stadium*, vols. 1 and 2 (1975), and Eddie Palmieri and Harlem River Drive's *Live at Sing Sing*, vols. 1 and 2 (1972), referred, respectively, to one of the country's most famous ballparks and prisons, both located in New York.

Album covers became intertwined within salsa's representational strategies to reinforce the place of New York within the music. The album cover for Johnny Pacheco's 1964 release of *Cañonazo* (Cannon shot), the first released by Fania Records, featured the bandleader and label cofounder with a set of timbales, placed next to a cannon in Riverside Park in New York's Upper West Side. The cover and album title announced the label's "explosion" onto the Latin music scene. Subsequent album covers for Fania artists such as Joe Bataan, who would leave the label to found Ghetto Records and, later SalSoul, found their inspiration in public spaces that Puerto Ricans fought—often quite literally—to claim as their own in areas where older, more established European ethnic whites resented their presence. The photograph used for *Mr. New York and the East Side Kids* in 1971 put Bataan and his band in the middle of a street in front of public housing. The title and photograph constitute music as part of the everyday lives of poor and working-class Black and Puerto Rican communities of New York.

The album cover for Bataan's 1969 release of *Poor Boy* is particularly significant for the ways it hints at broader signifying practices within Latin soul and salsa during the mid to late 1960s and early 1970s. Bataan stands next to a garbage can amid the rubble of a collapsed building with his hands extended above a trash bin with a low fire. Bataan leans away from the smoke that billows toward the picture's background while looking at the camera. His palms face down, appearing suspended in a natural concave

**2.1** Album cover for Johnny Pacheco's *Cañonazo* (1964)

position over the lip of the tall, circular, and slim metal trash can. The shape of the trash can evokes a conga, and Bataan's hands appear to have been captured by the camera as they descend to play. The photography for each of these album covers symbolically reclaimed the streets of Latin New York for Puerto Rican bodies routinely displaced from public spaces. By featuring the same places from which city officials and residents wanted to remove Puerto Ricans, album covers linked the city's geography with demands for racial justice at a time when a predominantly white establishment portrayed community members who sought to increase their political power as "jeering Puerto Rican militants" to be blamed for the city's economic crisis.[23]

The predominance of Spanish within salsa can easily lead to a cursory analysis that ignores the significance of English. The insistence of artists on using Spanish in songs defended the rights of Puerto Ricans to maintain

**2.2**    Album cover for Joe Bataan's *Poor Boy* (1969)

or, in some cases, recover their heritage language. This insistence, however, did not reflect the lived realities of most artists. For many New York Puerto Ricans, bilingualism became a natural part of their existence as English remained the dominant language across various domains. As Ana Celia Zentella argues, for New York Puerto Ricans it is actually "more accurate to speak of a bilingual/multidialectal repertoire, that is, a spectrum of linguistic codes that range from standard to non-standard dialects in Spanish and English, one of which an individual may speak the best and others of which s/he may speak with specific interlocutors or for specific purposes."[24] Album titles like Colón's *The Hustler* (1968) and *The Big Break—La gran fuga* (1970), Barretto's *Rican/Struction* (1979), and Palmieri's *The Sun of Latin Music* (1973) reflected the predominance of English in musicians' everyday lives even as most songs remained in Spanish. This is particularly true for liner notes, where English remained common, as seen on *El Malo, The Hustler,*

**2.3** Album cover for Joe Bataan's *Mr. New York and the East Side Kids* (1971)

and *Cosa nuestra*, to name just a few albums. The use of English highlights the aesthetic and sociopolitical significance of language within Nuyorican communities, particularly when the music expresses affiliation with other racialized communities, such as Palmieri's "Everything Is Everything."

Despite Colón's own declarations regarding the sanctity of the relationship between Spanish and salsa, English appeared on his earliest albums. Released at the height of the boogaloo era, *El Malo* contained two songs completely in English. In "Willie Whopper," the singing subject narrates the life of a man by that name "who's nobody's fool" and walks around like "he owns the town." In "Skinny Papa," the eponymous singing subject invites listeners to "come on and do the boogaloo." "Willie Baby" moves between English and Spanish. The declaration that "I'm not getting out of hand it's just something you gotta understand . . . the way you dance makes me crazy . . .

the way you boogaloo" transitions into Spanish as the chorus sings "Ella tiene bugalú" (She's got boogaloo). Using English in these recordings played a significant role in establishing Colón and LaVoe as up-and-coming musicians with whom young Nuyorican audiences identified musically, socially, culturally, and linguistically.

Musicians did not unilaterally shift away from English-language lyrics. Barretto's "Right On," a track on *Barretto Power* (1971), celebrates New York's Black and Latina/o communities with English lyrics and arrangements that, as Bobby Sanabria explains, feature an explosive combination of funk and Latin rhythms that "exudes Nuyorcan Soul."[25] Palmieri's "Everything Is Everything" was released on *Justicia* (Justice) in 1972, an album that characteristically combines Afro-Caribbean rhythms with other Black diasporic traditions, including African American swing, funk, and jazz. Palmieri talks back to the idea that "everything is everything about justice," insisting on the continued and "persistent injustice" faced by racialized communities despite, perhaps, the gains of the racial and social justice movements in the previous decade. On the album *Live from Sing Sing*, vol. 1, the prisoners' raucous excitement and response to the music provide a glimpse into how Black and Puerto Rican audiences received Palmieri's music, whether in English or Spanish.

English provided LaVoe with a rhetorical device to exploit in lyrics and soneos, particularly with single-word code-switching and calques that tropicalized English.[26] LaVoe often code-switched during his performances to add emphasis or distinction. In "Popurri Navideño" (Salsa medley), the singing subject expresses a desire to return to Puerto Rico. He sings:

> Allá yo ando en camiseta
> y aquí yo ando con coat
> Borinquen me está llamando
> y mañana me voy yo.
>
> [Over there I'm in a T-shirt
> and here I'm wearing a coat
> Borinquen is calling me
> and tomorrow I'm leaving.]

"Coat" is pronounced with Spanish phonetics as "ko." It emphasizes the contrast between Puerto Rico's tropical climate and New York's frigid winter and, perhaps, also contrasts the singing subject's emotional relationship to each place.[27] Other instances of code alternation with Spanish phonetics include "show" in "El Cantante," "Mother flower," and *"tro"* for "truck." "Mother flower," a comedic take on "mother fucker," is a common expression among many Spanish-speaking Puerto Ricans, including my family.[28] The significance of linguistic variations like "show" and "tro" lies in the morphological changes that occur in their use, even in instances where the shift functions as a stylistic device used for comedic effect. By conforming these English words to Spanish phonology, LaVoe succeeds in asserting difference through pronunciation. In "Mr. Brownie" (1979), LaVoe mocks nonnative speakers of Spanish with Anglicized pronunciations of the lyrics.

One of the fundamental characteristics of salsa was precisely its ability to engage a generation of bilingual Puerto Ricans born in New York, some of whom were English dominant, for whom salsa played a significant role in their identity as members of bilingual/multidialectal, multicultural, and multiracial communities. As Zentella argues, a focus on the code choices of a community demonstrates how bilinguals employ language to "construct and display multiple identities, to understand their historic position, and to respond to relations of domination between groups."[29] The insistence on Spanish in salsa lyrics, while exceeding the bilingual spectrum of some English-dominant artists, undermined prescriptivist language views in the United States, according to which a normative variety of English was coextensive with Americanness. The moments where English rises to the surface reflect not only a form of joking around, *vacilón*, as might be presumed by listening to LaVoe outside the sociolinguistic context of the music, but the linguistic and social terrain inhabited by Nuyoricans.

### The Making of Salsa's Musical Dons

The musical, visual, and discursive imaginary of Colón's early recordings with LaVoe expresses a Nuyorican aesthetic that embraces the streets of Latin New York as a space of Puerto Rican performative practice. The recordings released during their initial eight-year collaboration disavowed normative Americanness and rejected previous generational claims to social justice that called on the rights of liberal citizenship.[30] The cover of Colón's *El Malo* pictured him on a fire escape gazing soulfully away from the camera. A second, smaller photo in the upper-right quadrant appears as a double exposure, one in which the seventeen-year-old Colón sits on the fire escape looking defiantly at the camera. Colón's short black hair, red shirt, and black blazer create a visual intertextuality with *West Side Story.*

In the opening scene of the 1961 film, Bernardo, the leader of the Puerto Rican Sharks, wears his black hair in a DA and sports a black undershirt and partially opened button-down red shirt. Both the Broadway play (1957) and film (1961) became the a priori referent for Puerto Ricans in New York, "project[ing] how the Puerto Rican migration to New York City in the 1940s and 1950s not only usurp[ed] the order and the semiotic spatial organization of Anglo-Americans, but how it also constitute[d] a threat to the assumed coherent and monolithic identity of the Anglo-American subject."[31] The album cover, like the title song, foreshadows the centrality of normative manhood to the self-actualization of salsa's ideal subject. At a time when the white, monolingual English-speaking, heteropatriarchal suburban family became the symbolic site for reproducing Americanness, "El Malo" marshaled the narrative of Puerto Ricans as failed citizen subjects in the name of racialized masculinity.

While the 1961 film cemented the representation of Puerto Ricans in New York, "El Malo" exploits the racialized regime of representation. The lyrics and arrangements of the title track characterize El Malo as a man with enough "heart" to assert his place in the social hierarchies of El Barrio and Latin music, whether with "un puño regala'o" (a free fist) or his trombone. The use of the trombone as a possible weapon informs the listener that Colón is, in fact, El Malo. Lead vocalist LaVoe simultaneously embodies the "I" of the song who proclaims that "el malo de aquí soy yo" (I'm the bad one here). Although the liner notes by Pete Rodríguez name Colón as the song's referent for "El Malo," the album cover's designer placed pictures of both Colón and LaVoe on the back cover. Together, these malotes de la salsa rebuke anybody who doubts their veracity or just cannot dance:

> Échate pa'llá
> que tú no estás en na'
> si no sabes bailar
>
> [Get out of here
> Because you aren't about anything
> If you can't dance]

Whether in the streets of El Barrio or on its stages, los malotes de la salsa draw on a masculine swagger earned as much through violence as sonoridad.

According to Colón, his gangster persona found its inspiration in the television series *The Untouchables*, which aired from 1959 to 1963 and chronicled

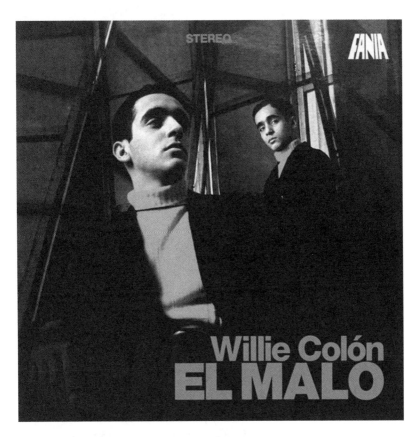

**2.4**    Album cover for Willie Colón's *El Malo* (1967)

the FBI's pursuit of Al Capone during Prohibition.[32] The cover for his sophomore album, *The Hustler*, updates the gangster image with a modern suit as
Colón, a cigar hanging from unsmiling lips, sits on the ledge of a pool table.
With his side musicians surrounding him, some looking at the table and
others at the camera, some with money in their hands, Colón holds a pool
stick and prepares to take his shot. Marty Topp, who also photographed Joe
Bataan for the cover of *Subway Joe* (1968), took the picture of the band at a
pool hall, and Izzy Sanabria designed the cover. The sepia tones and vintage-
style typography used for the title disassociate the photograph from black-
and-white newspaper images of Puerto Rican criminality in the mainstream
press and colorful costumes used in *West Side Story*. The album title and
cover art instead draw on the 1961 film *The Hustler*, starring Robert Redford
in the title role. Redford plays an up-and-coming professional pool hustler
who longs to unseat the king of them all, Minnesota Fats, played by Jackie

**2.5** George Chakiris (*center front*) as Bernardo in *West Side Story* (1962)

Gleason. The dialogue between the film and the cover art allows the album to further contest dominant stereotypes of Puerto Ricanness in New York.

The image of Colón as a hustler with his crew (band) supports an equivocation between musical endeavors and illicit activities that became the foundation from which the bandleader's image as El Malo continued to evolve. The album cover and title identify Colón and his band with extralegal economies. The instrumental title track arranged by Colón identifies him as "The Hustler," much like "El Malo." The track, particularly the trombone descarga (extended solo), layers multiple and overlapping imaginaries. Hustling parodies capitalist and consumer relations by duplicating them within an alternative economy.[33] Afterhours, "running numbers," and other similar hustles formed part of an informal economy that helped sustain New York Puerto Ricans as structural changes in the economy raised unemployment levels. The term also insinuates the need for a young, up-and-coming band like Colón's to work hard, or hustle, to land gigs and unseat the gatekeepers of Latin music. This hustle occurs primarily within the political economy of the cuchifrito circuit, where Colón's band left audiences in a "trance" that "lifted everyone off their feet."[34]

**2.6**    Album cover for Willie Colón's *The Hustler* (1968)

The covers of the 1969 release *Guisando/Doing a Job* and the 1972 anthology *Crime Pays* reinforced the image of salsa's gangsters as heads of a musical crime family. Whether the metaphor refers to the band, to Fania, or to Latin music in New York may be unclear, but the social meanings are not. *Guisando* features Colón and LaVoe leaning against the open door of a safe they appear to rob. Colón holds his now-ubiquitous cigar in his mouth and points a gun toward the camera/spectator intruding on the job. LaVoe, who appears with Colón for the first time on this album cover, counts the money while looking at the camera. The cover art of *Guisando*, released a year after *The Hustler*, reflects how the fledgling crew of the previous album had graduated from hustles to regular jobs, guisando, or doing jobs, on the cuchifrito circuit. The artwork for *Crime Pays* suggests as much, as LaVoe and Colón, wearing long wool coats and fedoras, pose next to a luxury car.

**2.7**    Album cover for Willie Colón's *Guisando / Doing a Job* (1969)

The association between the job of a musician and the presumed criminality of Puerto Ricans in public spaces disrupts white paternal stewardship of the city.[35]

As Wilson Valentín-Escobar's important essay makes clear, the ambiguity suggested on the cover of *The Hustler* quickly develops into signifying dominant masculinist mythologies within the US national imaginary. Images that became prominent on the Colón albums released between the mid-1960s and 1975 draw on images of the Wild West as a stand-in for urban street gangs, organized crime, and ethnic rivalry.[36] The album cover for *Cosa nuestra*, a play on the Italian "Cosa Nostra" (the mafia), drew heavily on public culture representations of Italian organized crime. Colón, featured here without LaVoe, occupies the primary position in the picture as his cigar organizes the phallocentric imagery on the cover. Photographed at the Fulton Fish Market in Brooklyn, which was popularly identified with organized crime in New York through the 1980s, Colón stands over a corpse while still holding the trombone case, within which lies the instrument used to execute the hit.[37] *The Good, the Bad, the Ugly* (1975), in turn, was inspired by the Clint Eastwood western by the same name and uses photographs of Colón, LaVoe, and cuatro player Yomo Toro dressed as revolutionaries to recontextualize the title to signify the Mexican Revolution. In so doing, the cover art draws on a history of Latin American revolutionary movements while symbolically collapsing boundaries between outlaw and revolutionary. The album cover simultaneously suggests the transnational musical communities that Colón grew up in and the increasing global reach of salsa by the mid-1970s.

The themes depicted on albums like *The Hustler*; *The Good, the Bad, the Ugly*; and *Cosa nuestra* demonstrate how the construction of masculinity rested on an intertextuality with cinematic and popular culture representations of extralegal activities, violent struggles against oppression by subaltern communities, and organized crime.[38] To this end, the series of album covers show how both musical and nonmusical practices became imbricated in the political economy of salsa. As bell hooks observes, "Photography has been, and is, central to that aspect of decolonization that calls us back to the past and offers a way to reclaim and renew old-affirming bonds. Using these images, we connect ourselves to a recuperative, redemptive memory that enables us to construct radial identities, images of ourselves that transcend the limits of the colonizing eye."[39] These album covers became sites for a performance of hypermasculinity, where excess, liminality, and satire emerge as tactics in forging a decolonial praxis through embodied performance.

The performance of subjecthood threatened to create slippages between the representation of extralegal practices and actual criminal activity. The album cover for Colón's *The Big Break—La gran fuga* declared the bandleader and his accomplice LaVoe to be fugitives pursued by the *Freaks Bureau of Investigation* in the Bronx. Released during a period of heightened political activism in New York, the album mined national references for meaning as well as local conflicts between the FBI and Black activists. On the album cover, the "fugitives," seen escaping a police escort in a poster packaged as part of the album, are accused of "kill[ing] people with little provocation with their exciting rhythm without a moment's notice." They are responsible for multiple hit records, including "Che che colé," the hit single that transformed Colón and LaVoe into superstars, as well as "Guisando," "Oíga señor" (Listen up, sir), "Juana Peña," and "I Wish I Had

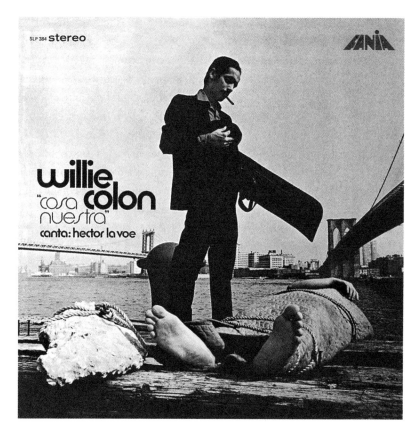

**2.8**    Album cover for Willie Colón's *Cosa nuestra* (1969)

a Watermelon," and the public is warned that "these men . . . are capable of starting riots [because] people immediately start to dance" when they perform.[40] Colón, who uses the aliases El Malo and The Hustler, is said to be "armed with a trombone and considered dangerous." The public is also warned about LaVoe's "smooth style of singing" that will leave unsuspecting victims "dancing a HOLE in [their] last pair of Shoes." Despite these "dangers," the FBI instructs the public that, should the whereabouts of Colón and LaVoe become known, the agency should *not* be notified. Instead, J. Edgar *González*, director of the Freaks Bureau of Investigation, instructs the dancing public to go directly to where the fugitives are performing.

Izzy Sanabria, who designed numerous covers and publicity posters for Fania, replicated FBI wanted posters for Black nationalists from the late 1960s and early 1970s for the cover of *The Big Break*. Sanabria placed the tagline "Wanted by FBI" across the top of the cover. He also included

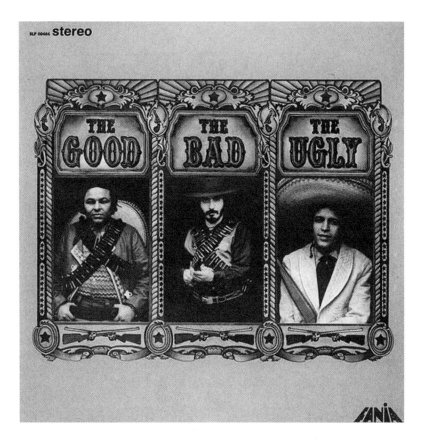

**2.9**    Album cover for Willie Colón's *The Good, the Bad, the Ugly* (1975)

Colón's "mug shot" and fingerprints. The urban lore that surrounds *The Big Break* reveals the slippages between the symbolic and the real. Fania Records reprinted the album cover as a publicity poster plastered around the city. According to Sanabria, Colón's grandmother "almost" suffered a heart attack when people began telling her that Colón was a fugitive from the FBI.[41] Both he and Colón have stated that various people called the FBI "to report Willie's whereabouts" and ask about a reward. Reportedly, the FBI instructed Fania to remove the tagline from all future releases and to direct record stores to display only the back of the original album cover.[42] This reported intervention by the FBI underscores how Colón and LaVoe's presumed fugitive status on *The Big Break* cannot be separated from the political economy of New York.[43] Surveillance of Puerto Rican nationalists in both Puerto Rico and the United States by the FBI through the program

**2.10** Front album cover for Willie Colón's *The Big Break* (1970)

called COINTELPRO began as early as 1961, and while the program officially ended a decade later, the strategies employed continued.[44] The album cover resemanticized narratives of Black and Puerto Rican nationalism and anti-colonial movements presented as a threat to the nation-state. Their musical and visual repertoire links salsa with the everyday cultural practices through which New York Puerto Ricans claimed public space in New York City. The songs, album titles, album covers and publicity projected, as Valentín-Escobar makes clear, "a collective, violent, male subjectivity articulated in opposition of and resistance to colonial and social oppression."[45]

Colón and LaVoe are not the ethnic outlaws who appeared in the movies of the 1930s, who "dress the best, drive the nicest cars, and eat in posh restaurants" but ultimately meet a violent death, the latter a product of censors concerned with the glorification of criminals during the 1930s.[46]

**2.11** Back album cover for Willie Colón's *The Big Break* (1970)

The anthology *Crime Pays* propose that these Nuyorican gangsters thrived and prospered by hustling for gigs and combining a formal wage economy with informal economic practices. This reading suggests the possibility of a double meaning. The first is that the crime of violating orthodox musical practices and hierarchies has paid off. The second is that clubs and labels criminally exploit musicians, who must then hustle and become gangsters themselves. Colón appears before a jury of his musical peers on the cover of *El Juicio*. But then the dons continue their "criminal" musical exploits on *Lo mato (si no compra este LP)* (I'll kill him [if he doesn't buy this LP], 1973), *Asalto Navideño*, vol. 1 (Christmas assault, 1970), and *The Good, the Bad, the Ugly*. The visual and discursive trajectory of salsa's bad boys suggests a racialized difference between them and the ethnic outlaw from popular culture on which their album covers draw. Whether the gangster was marked

# WANTED BY FBI
## For: THE BIG BREAK – La Gran Fuga
# WILLIE COLON
### Alias: EL MALO · THE HUSTLER

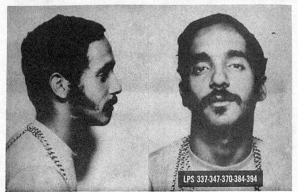

LPS 337-347-370-384-394

**ARMED WITH TROMBONE AND CONSIDERED DANGEROUS**

WILLIE COLON was last seen in New York City, he may be accompanied by one, HECTOR LaVOE, occupation "singer", also a very dangerous man with his voice.

**HECTOR LaVOE:**  **WILLIE COLON BEING APPREHENDED**

From left to right: Louie "Timbalito" Romero, Jose "Professor Joe" Torres, Willie Colon, Jose Mangual, Willie "Sweet" Campbell, Milton "Tito" Cardona, & Santi "Choflomo" Gonzalez.

## CRIMINAL RECORDS

These men are wanted by the dancing public. They are responsible for hit records such as: Che Che Cole, Guisando, Oiga Senor, Juana Pena, Jazzy and I Wish I Had A Watermelon.

## CAUTION

Willie Colon and Hector LaVoe have been known to kill people with little provocation with their exciting rhythm without a moments notice.

A word to the wise: These men are highly dangerous in a crowd and are capable of starting riots, people immediately start to dance, SO DO NOT, I repeat DO NOT let Hector LaVoe fool you with his smooth style of singing. If you do, you will find yourself dancing a HOLE in your last pair of Shoes.

If anyone knows the whereabouts of Willie Colon and his gang do not notify us. Go immediately to where they are and enjoy yourself.

WILLIE COLON EXCLUSIVE RECORDING STAR OF
FANIA RECORDS · 850 7th AVE. N.Y.C.

*J. Edgar Gonzalez*
J. Edgar Gonzalez
Director F.B.I.
Freaks Bureau of Investigation
Bronx, New York

Poster Idea & Design by Izzy Sanabria

**2.12** Poster advertising Willie Colón's *The Big Break*, included in album packaging as Jewish or Italian, ultimately the narrative of the outlaw leads to either assimilation or death. For Colón and LaVoe, however, death never arrives. Their performance of subjecthood as salsa's dons, as visually communicated on the cover art for these albums, rejects death in favor of Nuyorican excess performed as process and pleasure.

The album cover for *El Juicio* shows bandleader Willie Colón in a witness chair in the foreground. Lead lines created by a black-and-white checkered floor and the length of a jury box along the left side of the cover create the illusion of depth and guide the viewer's eye from Colón to the jury, composed of his band members. With a concerned look on his face, and his hands partially raised in a pleading gesture, Colón looks at the jury/band over his right shoulder. One member gives Colón the OK sign with his fingers, another is sleeping, and a third is laughing. The remaining members of the jury look on dispassionately. Jerry Masucci, the court stenographer, sits at a stenotype in front of the jury box. The judge's bench occupies the back wall, where Héctor LaVoe sits in a robe. A tall flagpole with the American flag is located to his right. The lettering "EL JUICIO" appears, barely visible, on the wood-paneled wall behind him, just below the figure of an eagle carved into the wood. While it is unclear what role Colón plays—whether witness, plaintiff, or defendant—reading this cover in light of previous album covers suggests he is the defendant. The back cover of *El Juicio*, a sketch of "Jury Room Section II" with a sign stating "Court in session," provides clarity. There we see a bewildered judge and a police officer sitting with their hands tied behind their backs. Joining them in the jury room are three additional men and two women, also immobilized. Colón, it seems, need not be worried because the fix is in. LaVoe presides over the case, Masucci forges the court record, and a jury of Colón's peers, his band members, delivers a verdict. The use of both the front and back of the album cover for this tongue-in-cheek take on the legal system comes to a head on *Lo mato (si no compra este LP)*. On the front cover, Colón holds a gun to the head of a man who looks warily at the bandleader as he considers his options. The tables are turned on the back of the album, however, where Colón lies on the floor while the erstwhile victim sits on top of him and points a gun at the bandleader's head, all the while looking at the camera and smiling.

The album covers examined here construct Colón and LaVoe's artistic personas at the nexus of extralegality and relajo, or humor, which revealed the self-reflexive aspect of the images and mobilized abjection for the performance of subjecthood.[47] The disidentificatory difference produced through Colón and LaVoe's gangster doubles mined the potentiality of

**2.13**  Front album cover for Willie Colón's *El Juicio* (1972)

New York's streets as a stage for Nuyorican aesthetics that disassociated them from hegemonic Americanness and Puerto Ricanness, both of which defined heteropatriarchal whiteness as integral to subjecthood.[48] Songs, album covers, publicity posters, and performances on- and offstage exploited, rather than recoiled from, representations of Puerto Ricans as a waste population. Excess, liminality, and satire expressed a racialized virile masculinity that reveled in abjection.

Colón has commented on the ways the outlaw persona he began to develop in his South Bronx neighborhood some years before he signed with Fania at times overdetermined him as an artist. Men in his audiences antagonized him and LaVoe "to test El Malo out."[49] A conversation about Colón with my father, who admittedly preferred merengue and *rancheras* to salsa, provides additional insight into how the bad-boy reputation circulated. My

**2.14** Back album cover for Willie Colón's *El Juicio* (1972)

father disliked Colón vehemently because of the singer's statements at a concert in my hometown of Bridgeport, Connecticut, in the 1970s. Colón reportedly referred to Puerto Rican men in the audience using a homophobic epithet. The lights went out "suddenly," and insulted members of the audience "le dieron una pela" (they beat the hell out of him). While it is unclear to what extent my father's version reflects events that took place, the story he recounted underscores the centrality of normative masculinity for the bad-boy image as well as the slippages between the artistic persona and Colón himself.

LaVoe was similarly understood through this image during his partnership with Colón. Latin music historian Max Salazar, who first interviewed LaVoe in 1976 for *Latin N.Y.*, was "startled" by LaVoe's "warm, soft voice," having "believed Colón and LaVoe to be two thugs who loved to hear their knuckles crunch against jaws for the hell of it. This belief was furthered by the reported fistfights at their dances, by Colón's being hospitalized on one occasion, and by LaVoe's surly look while wearing a black, wide-brimmed gangster hat, a cigar protruding from his mouth, on the cover of the album *Crime Pays*. I was waiting to hear LaVoe speak from the side of his mouth like Bogart."[50]

The collapse between their artistic persona and life beyond the stage culminated in the recording of one of the duo's most celebrated songs. In an interview, Colón has shared that he wrote "Calle Luna, Calle Sol" (Moon Street, Sun Street) for the album *Lo mato* after a fight in Puerto Rico. LaVoe kept aggravating the bouncer, Colón got blamed, and both got "a real good bucket of whoop ass" outside the bar. The incident inspired "Calle Luna, Calle Sol," which Colón intended to be a "scary" cautionary tale about life in a neighborhood where every man is a tough guy and violence becomes quotidian.[51] The bravado embedded within the evolving discourse and representations in Colón's early repertoire with LaVoe becomes exemplary of how male homosocial relationships within salsa developed through competition in a space where masculine aggression is valued and reified in the performance of abjection and a hypermasculinity amid homosociality.[52]

By August 1973, almost ten years after signing with Fania Records and mobilizing the image of the gangster, Colón began to reconsider his use of the image. As Colón told *Latin N.Y.* magazine that year, "Too many people really believe it and at times I myself have believed it."[53] Young Lord and DJ Luciano published an article that month in *Latin N.Y.* that asked, "Is the Gangster Image Good for Willie Colón?" Luciano criticized Colón for reproducing stereotypes of Puerto Ricans as criminals, which were ubiquitous in the media at the time. If crime pays, Luciano asked, why are so many Puerto Rican men in jail? Because "crime doesn't pay, *we do*. Crime only pays for those who are free, white and rich. And this country doesn't consider you to be any of the three." Moreover, he continued, as artists who " liv[e] off Puerto Ricans' hard earned money," Colón and LaVoe have a responsibility not to reify images of Puerto Rican criminality or suggest that "it's cool to be a gangster." Luciano, whose criticism fails to content itself with the satire of these images, focuses on what he suggests is an inherent celebration of illegality. Showing how los malotes were vulnerable to critiques aimed at their gangster personas, Luciano also indicts Fania Records for packaging the music and *Latin N.Y.* editor Izzy Sanabria, who designed several of Colón's covers, for participating in the imagery. Luciano insists that Fania Records and Sanabria, like Colón, have a responsibility to shift public discourse rather than exploit it for commercial success.[54]

Sanabria took his prerogative as editor to respond to Luciano's article with a rebuttal on the next page. He punctuated the use of exaggeration and irony in the depictions of Colón and LaVoe as gangsters. This marketing tool, he pointed out, was simply used to create a "personality." He criticized his "good friend" Luciano for not having a sense of humor, a deficit attributed to the latter's "revolutionary background."[55]

Sanabria refused to engage in a substantive conversation with Luciano's critiques, which spoke to the slippages inherent to a gangster imaginary whose playful satire is mobilized for consumption even as it unsettled racialized and colonial narratives of Puerto Rican abjection. Instead, Sanabria grounded his rebuttal by invoking Colón's past as a "skinny baby-faced kid" trying to make music with his trombone while bigger dudes threatened to steal his trombone and "kick [his] ass." Colón, who described himself as "a little skinny kid with a big mouth" who learned "to be a hustler" and "never run away from a fight," sold Kool-Aid for three cents a glass by the age of eight and by twelve played his trumpet on a street corner in the Bronx for nickels and dimes. According to multiple interviews Colón has given since the 1970s, he learned to fight because people tried to steal his trumpet.[56]

Like Colón during the height of the bad-boy image, LaVoe resorted to actual events to ground the veracity of the persona, and stories abound among fans in which the sonero is characterized as quick to fight. When *Latin N.Y.* asked LaVoe whether the gangster image worked well for the duo, he answered with characteristic self-deprecation and humor: "Good . . . it's been good for us. . . . Muchos golpes pero lo [*sic*] ha dejado mucho [Lots of bruises but it's given us a lot] . . . and I got a broken jaw because of it." In the same interview, LaVoe explained that Colón was "like a brother" and he would "always defend him"—like he did in France when "this big guy was fighting with Willie, and I came up behind him and punched him in the head. Nothing happened but I broke my pinkey." Asked if he and Colón would continue to use the gangster image on their next album, LaVoe suggested they dress as priests so fans would give them money.[57] LaVoe's humorous response highlights the duo's use of satire while simultaneously reinforcing their image as los malotes.

If the album covers resemanticized images of Puerto Rican excess on the streets and stages of Latin New York, the songs provided the soundscape where these themes were fully developed. Songs like "Sonero mayor," where LaVoe sung his own praises as a sonero, conflated masculine swagger and aesthetic prowess.[58] When LaVoe calls out to Colón during a trombone solo or encourages him with "*Guapea*, Willie Colón" during the song

"Soñando despierto" (Dreaming awake), the social meanings of *guapear*—to be brave, boastful, arrogant, to "represent"—become markers of an irreverent racialized masculinity. LaVoe also embodied the singing subject of "El Titán" (The Titan) on *Guisando*. Like LaVoe, "El Titán" came from Ponce and muscled his way into New York's Latin music scene through exceptional vocal skills. Nobody, he informs an unnamed "shark" with "sixty years of experience," will be able to dethrone him. The men as musicians in "El Malo," "The Hustler," "Sonero mayor," and "El Titán" aggressively swindled "victims," or audiences, away from other bands with their musicality.

### A Jíbaro in New York

Nowhere is the combination of traditional musical forms and salsa's experimental modalities more apparent than in Colón's Christmas albums *Asalto Navideño*, vols. 1 and 2, which fuse salsa with folkloric Puerto Rican musical traditions. These albums best demonstrate the process through which Colón and LaVoe's music becomes a vehicle for signifying New York as part of Puerto Rico and a place for the production of Puerto Ricanness.[59] The title of the two volumes riffs on the Puerto Rican tradition of the *parranda*, where Christmas carolers "assault" households, not unlike the implied threat of "trick or treat" on Halloween. Those who live there are expected to provide carolers with food and (often alcoholic) drinks before the group moves on to the next house, their most recent victims in tow. The title's assault also complemented Colón and LaVoe's gangster imagery; the album cover for the first volume features the duo apparently stealing Christmas gifts—Colón has explained they are actually putting the gifts *into* the bag—and the second shows them jumping a gas attendant while Santa Claus stands by and laughs.[60] The challenging tenor of the album's title foreshadows how salsa insinuates itself into the tradition of *música Navideña* (Christmas music).

*Asalto Navideño* consists of *música típica* (folkloric music), also referred to as *música jíbara* (peasant music), associated with the jíbaro (Puerto Rican peasant). The Hispanophile (white) image of the jíbaro celebrates Puerto Rico's racial mestizaje and demarcates *el campo* (the countryside), a space imagined as existing primarily within Puerto Rico's interior (i.e., not the coast), as the quintessential Puerto Rican landscape. This spatial-geographic demarcation of the interior with the figure of the jíbaro and their presumed whiteness functions as part of what Hilda Lloréns calls "geographic blackness," wherein "certain geographic locations are deployed as simply being 'Puerto Rican,' to signify Creole and/or white, while others are marked as exclusively inhabited by blacks."[61] As the music identified with this imagined countryside, música jíbara is likewise imagined as "simply Puerto Rican."

It was Colón who decided to record the albums, which brought together salsa and the música jíbara associated with the Puerto Rican countryside and the Christmas season in Puerto Rico. Colón worked with Marty Sheller on sketches for one of the medleys and charged LaVoe with selecting original Puerto Rican folkloric songs for the recording.[62] Released three years apart, the albums were designed to capitalize on a string of hits by Colón and LaVoe for Fania Records and to showcase LaVoe's voice, which moved seamlessly between salsa's New York sound and música típica. The album "mixed and blended, salsa-style, with a wide range of other rhythms, starting, of course, with Cuban guaguancó and African-American jazz, but ranging to Brazilian samba, Panamanian murga, Dominican merengue, and others."[63] The recording linked the duo's racialized masculinity to the iconic image of the Puerto Rican peasant as a figure of cultural authenticity within cultural nationalist narratives on the archipelago since the 1950s while still incorporating other Latin American influences.

Amid US economic development and the transition to the status of Estado Libre Asociado (ELA, Free Associated State) in 1952, the populist government of Luis Muñoz Marín circulated an image of the jíbaro, here referring specifically to the male Puerto Rican peasant, as the embodiment of Puerto Rico's cultural and spiritual character. The governor's populist narratives eschewed what he characterized as US materialism and superficiality that threatened Puerto Rico's essence. Operation Serenity sought to preserve this cultural identity amid social and economic transformations resulting from the country's entrance into modernity. The Hispanophile (white) and Catholic (heteropatriarchal) image of the Puerto Rican peasant foregrounded a relationship to land. Being born and residing in Puerto Rico became the sine qua non of Puerto Ricanness and relegated diasporic Puerto Ricans to an aberration of colonialism. The construction of cultural nationalism in Puerto Rico in the 1950s and its relevance to salsa's meanings is examined in chapter 4 but is relevant here insofar as Colón and LaVoe's recuperation of folkloric music and the image of the Puerto Rican jíbaro challenge official and popular representations of nationhood that exclude diasporic Puerto Ricans.

The role of salsa in constituting New York as a Puerto Rican space reaches its apex in the first volume, released in 1970. Invited to share the role of the brass in the front line of the orchestra is the cuatro, an eight- or ten-string guitar-like instrument in the lute family whose origins have been traced to the Spanish colonial period. Colón brought on cuatro player Toro, who along with LaVoe provided the authenticity the album marshalled to create música típica outside the geographic boundaries of Puerto Rico. The interplay between the trombone and the cuatro, an instrument that epitomizes the sound of música típica, characterizes Colón's approach to linking a Nuyorican aesthetic with Puerto Rican folkloric traditions that drew on the vibrant soundscape in New York City and other cities where Puerto Rican migrants settled (such as Chicago) and in places far from the migratory epicenter of New York (such as Hawai'i)."[64] Unlike the trombone-led arrangements of previous albums, on *Asalto Navideño* the trombone shares its privileged position with the cuatro, which plays harmonies, solos, and other roles usually taken on by a piano.

In "Canto a Borinquen" (Song for Borinquen, or I sing to Borinquen), the trombone leads the listener into the song but is joined by the cuatro. The trombones are also more subdued, played more softly and using harmonic progressions that create a more melodious sound than in previous albums. The back-and-forth between the two instruments, in turn, produces a call-and-response that sounds the dialogue and exchange between the various musical traditions incorporated into the recordings. In "Traigo la salsa" (I bring salsa), which more closely resembles the instrumentation in Colón's earlier songs, the cuatro can still be heard riffing alongside LaVoe's vocals. The modifications to the arrangements and musical texture of salsa's New York sound reveals an intention to highlight Puerto Rican folkloric musical traditions while re-semanticizing, or "assaulting," them with a Nuyorican aesthetic that proposes an alternative relationship between Puerto Rico and its diaspora. The performance of a diasporic Puerto Rican imaginary transcends the symbolic and geographic boundaries of Puerto Ricanness to incorporate a Nuyorican imaginary.

Like Juan Flores, I suggest that the musical modality produced through *Asalto Navideño* represents an attempt to script a Nuyorican aesthetic into ideas about Puerto Rican national identity that would otherwise exclude the diaspora. Colón tailored, but did not subsume, a Nuyorican aesthetic to the folkloric musical practices the album engaged. Once they have established *Asalto Navideño* as a bona fide Christmas recording in the tradition of música jíbara, as much with the privileged role of the cuatro as the "jíbaro quality" of LaVoe's vocals, in the fourth track a salsa texture predominates.[65] Unlike previous songs on the album, "Traigo la salsa" features a mambo section characteristic of Colón's earlier recordings. The song's arrangements and vocal aesthetics complement lyrics in which the musical persona "brings salsa" to an unnamed interlocutor initially hailed with the singular pronoun form "usted" (you) that implies social distance, but thereafter addressed with the more intimate form "tú" (you), which suggests social familiarity. The rhetorical shift suggests a change in the relationship between the song's narrator and his interlocutor. It seems that salsa itself diminishes the social distance between the diaspora and its ancestral homeland. While the English-dominant Colón experienced "a sense of pride to watch them as they eloquently challenged each other in verse" with "fancy words, quick wit," he could not express himself similarly, and certainly not in Spanish. LaVoe's Spanish dominance, including the various markers of Puerto Rican Spanish, and formation within Puerto Rican folkloric musical traditions enabled Colón, who "loved listening to the old timers sitting on milk crates in front of David's . . . Bodega singing 'décimas and aguinaldos,'" to fuse his adventurous innovations in salsa with Puerto Rico's música típica, or música jíbara.[66]

For Yeyito Flores, who began learning to play percussion in the 1970s, *Asalto Navideño* fostered an admiration for música típica as something more than "música de jíbaros"—as something more than "hick" or "country" music.[67] Colón himself spoke to this issue in an interview, noting how LaVoe's embodiment of the jíbaro became a touchstone for Puerto Ricans. "Suddenly a jíbaro [LaVoe] arrives who is mischievous," explains Colón, a jíbaro who has style, and suddenly "it wasn't so bad to be a jíbaro."[68] As Yeyito explained, the insertion of música típica into salsa reinvigorated the meaning of the music for a generation of Puerto Ricans born in New York and infused it with local significance. The album's stylistic elements and cultural meanings coalesce around the iconic figure of the jíbaro and the cuatro to Rican/Struct New York in an act of colonial and diasporic resistance. The *Asalto Navideño* album represents more than a nostalgic adulation for an Edenic space or an opportunistic exploitation of the cuatro.

The mutable meanings of jíbaro become clear in Felipe Luciano's poem "Jíbaro, My Pretty Nigger." Luciano has spoken at length about salsa's role in the recuperation of Afro-diasporic rhythms and its significance for him as a Black man.[69] In the poem, included on Palmieri's album *Live in Sing Sing*, Luciano begins by addressing and identifying with the "jíbaro, mi negro lindo" (my pretty Black man). The identification with/as jíbaro recurs to the image of land as central to Puerto Ricanness. However, the exaltation of the "earth of my people . . . the earth brown of my skin" expresses a racial pride that confronts the presumed whiteness of the jíbaro. As Patricia Herrera explains, the poem "traces his African, Taíno, and Puerto Rican lineages . . . [and] invites community members with similar histories to create alliances for future resistance." Yet, as Herrera goes on to note, Luciano's racial solidarity is framed within a masculinist agenda. "His poem directly speaks to men as he proclaims that the land is the 'Father of [his] yearning for the soil.' The few times that he mentions Black women in his poem, he portrays them as dancing bodies or sexual instruments, as when he says, 'The calves of your woman dancing' and 'I make crazy love to your daughter.'"[70] The masculinist ethos notwithstanding, Luciano's translation of "jíbaro, mi negro lindo" into the title of the poem constructs Black Puerto Rican histories as part of the African diaspora. References to land, sugar, soil, and "thoughts of freedom" likewise connect the history of slavery and liberation with 1970s movements for racial justice and liberation from colonialism. This jíbaro is Black and Nuyorican, speaks English as well as Spanish, and seeks an end to US imperialism.[71]

While *Asalto Navideño* expanded Puerto Rico's sonic boundaries, this process began before this particular album and continued in subsequent recordings. In "Timbalero" (Timbales player, masculine), LaVoe boldly declares:

> Ésta es la mejor salsa
> que ha dáo Puerto Rico
> Y que lo diga la gente
>
> [This is the best salsa
> That Puerto Rico has produced
> And people better recognize]

Singing from New York, LaVoe's cultural capital allows the singing subject to collapse the distance between New York and Puerto Rico. LaVoe once again disrupted the opposition between Puerto Rico and New York in his solo debut album, *La Voz* (The Voice, 1975), which cemented his reputation as a sonero and continued to extend his popularity among fans, who increasingly considered him one of their own. With LaVoe's solo debut, the image of salsa's gangsters disappeared from both the songs and the album cover. Reflecting not only Colón's departure but a shifting emphasis away from the entire band to the lead vocalist, the cover features a medium headshot of LaVoe's smiling face as he adjusts a large red bow tie. The first album produced by Colón, *La Voz* includes the previously released "Mi gente" as well as a series of hits that included "Rompe saragüey" (Yerba mate plant), "El Todopoderoso" (The Al-

**2.15** Album cover for Héctor LaVoe's *La Voz* (1975)

mighty), and "Paraíso de dulzura" (Sweet paradise). In the latter, LaVoe, the songwriter and presumed singing subject, declares himself the ambassador of "la sabrosura rica y sandunguera que Puerto Rico puede dar" (the rich and *sandunguera* flavor that Puerto Rico can produce) in "Paraíso de dulzura." Singing from New York, the "here" of the song, the lyrics challenge the status of Puerto Rico as the singular locus of Puerto Rican identity.

In a 2001 essay published in the journal *Diálogo*, published by the University of Puerto Rico, Río Piedras, cultural critic Miriam Jiménez Román began by proudly declaring, "Soy producto de la migración puertorriqueña, miembro de la otra mitad de la nación. Lo digo con orgullo, conciente de que para muchos es una condición desgraciada" (I am a product of the Puerto Rican migration, member of the other half of the nation. I say it with pride, conscious that for many it is a disgraced condition). She then chronicles her experience when she arrived in Puerto Rico with her parents in the 1970s, as someone "de allá" (from over there, i.e., the United States).[72] During the 1970s, Puerto Rican migration to the United States decreased dramatically. The net in-migration to Puerto Rico, which first rose significantly during the 1960s, remained steady.[73] Painting a picture of how diasporic Puerto Ricans were received, Jiménez Román draws parallels between dominant attitudes in the United States about diasporic Puerto Ricans and those she encountered after arriving in Puerto Rico. During that time in Puerto Rico, "to be de allá would seem to represent only failure: beyond the island's inability to provide a viable homeland for more than half of its people is the equally painful reality that the majority of the diaspora community lives in poverty, stigmatized as a racialized minority and expressing perspectives wrought from that experience." At a time when Puerto Rico remained at the verge of economic collapse, as detailed in chapter 4, it seemed as if "Puerto Rico was being invaded by a seeming horde of return migrants, and the children of the diaspora were beginning to be perceived as a problem, one that taxed the island's already scarce resources."[74] These return migrants, purportedly "'infected' with las ideas de allá" (ideas from over there), brought "apparent obsessions with race and racism and, most particularly, their identification with African Americans." This positionality challenged dominant racial attitudes in Puerto Rico that construct the archipelago as a racial utopia, which augmented the rejection of diasporic Puerto Ricans.[75] The insistence on Puerto Rico as a racial utopia persisted, Jiménez Román reminds readers, twenty-five years after cultural critic and philosopher Isabelo Zenón Cruz published his foundational scholarship on race and racism in Puerto Rico.[76] A Black Puerto Rican woman and founding figure in Afro-Latina/o studies, Jiménez Román weaves together an analysis of race, gender, class, and nationalist cultural politics that illustrates how Nuyorican difference was racialized and constructed as a problem de allá.

In his essay on diasporic Puerto Ricanness as a liminal space, Alberto Sandoval Sánchez remembers references during his childhood to those living outside Puerto Rico as beyond its geopolitical boundaries, indicated by the phrase *allá fuera* (out there). The phrase itself continues to be used in reference to the United States. As Sandoval Sánchez explains:

> Growing up in San Juan, I always hear relatives and friends saying, "Mi primo se va p'allá fuera" . . . "Mi hermana viene de fuera el domingo" . . . "Mi hijo estudia allá fuera." Fuera meant New York, New Jersey, Philadelphia, Florida, Illinois, California. Fuera became a synonym for the United States. Fuera was and still is a euphemism

for migration. Fuera is that space at a distance from the speaker, that location outside, away from the island that is always conducive to spatio-geographical demarcations such as *Allá and Acá*, "over there" and "over here."[77]

The spatialization of national belonging, where Puerto Rico remains the "over here," privileges the speaking subject by othering diasporic Puerto Ricans. Uses of "afuera" stand in for a difference interpreted as an inability to understand the social, political, and economic context of Puerto Rican life on the archipelago. As a diasporic Puerto Rican born and raised in the United States, where I continue to reside, I am often told, "Es que tú eres de afuera" (That's because you are from out there [the diaspora]) when I am in Puerto Rico. I have witnessed or experienced the flexibility of the phrase, mobilized to signify a broad terrain, from the mundane, like an order for a twenty-four-ounce coffee deemed too large to be appropriate and indicative of US commercialism; to the everyday frustration of a parent having to wake at 5 a.m. to join a queue to visit the doctor rather than having a fixed appointment; to the catastrophic lack of access to a family member's doctors while they were in the hospital. The claim to insider status does not imply an acceptance of structural forces that impact quality of life or a lack of agency in navigating these conditions. Rather, the phrase often suggests a lack of understanding of local realities that Puerto Ricans navigate. In each instance, the phrase symbolically displaces diasporic Puerto Ricans and DiaspoRican subjectivities, which insist on the diaspora as a site of identity formation, as always already outside the national boundaries of belonging, understanding, and even the right to an opinion on any and all aspects of life in Puerto Rico.[78]

The singing subject of "Paraíso de dulzura" subverts the poles of "over here" and "over there." The song begins with the singing subject asking themselves two questions:

¿Qué de adónde vengo?
¿Que pa' dónde voy?

[Where am I coming from,
And where am I going?]

The answer to the first is Puerto Rico: "De Borinquén vengo yo" (I come from Borinquen). He comes from Borinquen, a reference to the precolonial name of Puerto Rico, the "paraíso de la dulzura" from which the LaVoe brings "salsa, sabor y control" (salsa, *sabor*, and control). Salsa stands in for not only the music itself but the sabor (flavor), or sonoridad, that requires mastery. This sonoridad originates in the land of "la rica *plena*," of the "rich and melodic" sounds of plena like "El rico bombón de Elena" (Elena's delicious candy), one of the most popular plenas recorded by Afro–Puerto Rican musicians Rafael Cortijo and Ismael Rivera. Plena is a working-class Afro–Puerto Rican musical form that emerged along the southern coast of Puerto Rico and spread throughout the archipelago in the early twentieth century. By the 1930s, the plena's popularity extended, as Juan Flores chronicles, into the salons and ballrooms of the cultural elite and the Puerto Rican diaspora, where it flourished.

The European, Afro–Puerto Rican, and Afro-Caribbean musical traditions syncretized in plenas underscore global structures of colonialism and slavery in addition to Black migration to Puerto Rico from the British Caribbean.[79] Although the music's commercialization initially distanced plenas from its popular roots, by the 1950s Afro–Puerto Rican musicians Mon Rivera, Cortijo, and Rivera recovered its working-class and Afro-Caribbean bomba rhythms. As Flores describes it, they brought plenas "back to the streets and among the poor workers and unemployed masses from which it had sprung."[80] Cortijo's 1950s show *La taberna India*, which created a "*visual* presence of blacks on television," disrupted the whiteness of Puerto Rico's televisual space.[81] Plena's use of improvisation, its narratives of everyday life, and its identification with LaVoe's hometown of Ponce likely encourage him to credit the music with "la sabrosura rica y sandungera" of Puerto Rico. While LaVoe immediately answers the question about where he is coming from, what remains unasked and unanswered is "¿Adónde estoy?"—"Where am I?"

New York can remain unnamed in the song precisely because of its identification as the capital of salsa by the mid-1970s. This was fitting, as there was wide agreement that New York was salsa's main stage. *New York Magazine*'s special issue on the city's "Latin soul" in 1972 had already described salsa as a "music born in New York for young Puerto Ricans."[82] A special section on Latin music in July 1974 similarly identified New York with salsa's emergence, albeit by reifying cultural hierarchies that place the music's origins in Cuba.[83] In *Billboard*'s second special issue on salsa in 1977, Aurora Flores described New York as "salsa's unofficial capital."[84] Salsa transformed the city into a site of both colonial and *diasporic* resistance.

The arrangements, instrumentation, and phrasings in "Paraíso de dulzura" confirm salsa's site of enunciation as New York. Within the song, New York becomes a "here," an extension of Puerto Rico and its musical histories. Salsa's emergence "afuera" might render it foreign for some in Puerto Rico, as discussed in chapter 4. But for LaVoe, it is precisely the characteristics that salsa shares with the plena that give his salsa "sabrosura." To display "salsa, sabor y control" requires Afro-Caribbean and Afro–Puerto Rican rhythms, skillful improvisation, and resonance with the listening public. In "Paraíso de dulzura," salsa's foundational characteristics extend the cultural and symbolic boundaries of Puerto Ricanness beyond Puerto Rico.[85]

There are certainly images of Puerto Rico as an Edenic homeland throughout the corpus. In "Paraíso de dulzura," "Borinquen" also becomes

> La tierra del Edén
> la que el gran Gautier
> llamó la "Perla de los Mares
>
> [The Edenic land
> The one the great Gautier
> Named the "Pearl of the Seas"][86]

The reference to José Gautier Benítez, a nineteenth-century Puerto Rican Romantic poet, invokes his poem "A Puerto Rico (Regreso)" (To Puerto Rico, return). Using nature as the framework for describing Puerto Rico and its beauty, Gautier's poetic voice extols the virtues of his homeland in the tradition of lyric poetry. For LaVoe, who wrote "Paraíso de dulzura," Puerto Rico presents a still lush, natural Edenic possibility. In "Pescao (Potpourri sambao)" (Fish, samba medley), the singing subject urges his friends to let a fire burn despite the threat to their harvest:

> Si se quema el monte
> dejalo quemar
> Siempre mi cosecha
> da' pa' guardar
>
> [If the mountain burns
> Let it burn
> My harvest always
> Yields more than enough]

Puerto Rico's natural landscape remains full of promise despite the fire. It will regenerate in time, and the bountiful harvest will sustain the singing subject until that time. His primary concern is for his livestock. He sings:

> Que no se queme
> la vaca ni el buey
>
> [Don't let burn
> The cow or ox]

They are market commodities, literally stock, or investments for the future that do not regenerate like the land even as they rely on it for food. The song reminds us how, as Valentín-Escobar explains, "space, geography, and land are ingredients essential to traditional constructions of nationalism" even as salsa expanded "discussions of the nation via the diaspora."[87] It is therefore the land, the essence of Puerto Ricanness, not the market, that protects the iconic Puerto Rican jíbaro's future. The mobilization of this imagery in this and other songs threatens to reinforce official narratives of Puerto Ricanness wherein US economic development during the mid-twentieth century provides an entrance into modernity but cannot replace a Puerto Rican essence rooted in the image of the jíbaro. This soundscape, however, is not merely a deterritorialized and nostalgic recuperation of a national Puerto Rican imaginary.[88] Reducing Colón and LaVoe's resemanticization of Puerto Ricanness to such would fail to consider how these musical practices and the embodiment of Colón, a third-generation Nuyorican, and LaVoe, who by the end of his life had lived longer in the United States than in Puerto Rico, disrupt the a priori oppositions between Puerto Ricans "de aquí y de allá" (from here and there).

"Calle Luna, Calle Sol" leaves behind any romanticized illusions about Puerto Rico. It does not offer the mythical view that Efraín Barradas identifies in certain Nuyorican poetry.[89] Nor do the imagery and lyrics play the role, as Raymond Williams might suggest, of "a myth functioning as a memory" through which diasporic Puerto Rican subjects, in their repeated expulsion from public space, might express their aspirations.[90] Rather, the song obliterates the opposition between the Puerto Rico's idyllic countryside and the presumably morally deviant streets of Puerto Rican New York that presented constitute an impediment to modernity in both Puerto Rico and the United States. In "Calle Luna, Calle Sol," los malotes de ls salsa warn the listening public about the neighborhood La Perla in Puerto Rico:

Mete la mano en el bolsillo
Saca y abre tu cuchillo
y ten cuidaʼo.
Pónganme oído
en este barrio
muchos guapos lo han mataʼo.

. . . . . . . . . . . . . . . . . . . . . . . .

Saca las bolsillos
Tú estaʼ arrancaʼo.
Diles que fuiste paʼ La Perla
y pelaʼo te han dejaʼo

[Put your hand in your pocket
Take out and open your switchblade
And be careful
Listen to me
In this neighborhood
Lots of tough guys have been killed

. . . . . . . . . . . . . . . . . . . . . . . . . . . .

Pull out your pockets
You're broke
Tell them that you went to La Perla
And they didn't leave you a dime]

"Calle Luna, Calle Sol" places the listener in La Perla, a racially and economically marginalized community at the geographic and symbolic margins of Viejo San Juan.[91] The song reinforces the dichotomy between a rural paradise and urban malaise—ironicized by the community's name and its reference to Gautier's poem. Yet it also challenges official representations and idealized notions of Puerto Rico as a horizontally structured society.

Released amid Puerto Rico's economic crisis in the 1970s, the song undermines the opposition between Puerto Ricans and Nuyoricans by making the difference *between* them—the idyllic colonized space versus the morally corrupt metropolis—one *within* Puerto Rico itself. "Calle Luna, Calle Sol" was released on *Lo mato* in 1973. By this time, the failures of US economic development policies in Puerto Rico, which I discuss in chapter 4, had become increasingly apparent. By the mid-1970s, economic stagnation and decreasing labor force participation would underscore these failures; public debt grew by an average of 22 percent between 1972 and 1976.[92] I propose that "Calle Luna, Calle Sol" exposes poverty, marginalization, and violence that are not supposed to exist in Puerto Rican modernity. Here, I extend, and perhaps play with, Homi Bhabha's description of the ambivalence of mimicry that is both resemblance and menace. I propose that the "problem" of racial and economic marginality that makes Nuyoricans not quite the same as Puerto Ricans is not quite so different from that within Puerto Rico itself.[93]

By the song's release in 1973, salsa sales in Puerto Rico had already begun to take off. Just a year later, *Billboard* reported that the increased sales were accompanied by a downturn in US rock sales in Puerto Rico. Charles Tarrab, head of Fania International until 1975 and founder of the Puerto Rican record distribution company Allied Wholesale Company of Puerto Rico, attributed the rise in salsa sales to Puerto Rican cultural nationalism. The identification of salsa fans in Puerto Rico during this period with salsa as an autochthonous musical form, discussed in chapter 4, would certainly bear out Tarrab's assertion. Karl Hagstrom Miller, however, adds another dimension to salsa's increasing popularity: salsa fans in Puerto Rico "found in the clave rhythms of New York salsa evidence of a shared social reality."[94] The clave, he suggests, undermines the opposition between the "nation" and the diaspora, between Puerto Rico and what has been constructed as its abject other. This convergence challenges official and popular representations of Puerto Rico that propose a national identity culturally distinct from that of the United States.

## Conclusion

In NuYoRico, that place without a "here" or "there," Nuyorican subjects claim rights and a place as part of the performance of sovereignty amid colonial abjection.[95] In their embodiment as criminals overtaking the streets—and stages—of New York, the musical and nonmusical practices of salsa's bad boys turned representations of Puerto Rican abjection on their head. Colón and LaVoe's recordings, performances, and representational practices exceeded the geographic, political, and symbolic boundaries that constituted Puerto Ricans as a surplus population in both the American and Puerto Rican imaginaries. The songs highlighted in this chapter form part of an imaginary wherein Nuyorican and Puerto Rican are coextensive identities that repudiate normative belonging. Whether moving through the rhythms of bomba and guaguancó in "El Malo" or looking to Latin American musical genres in *Asalto Navideño* while "assaulting"

Puerto Rican traditions, salsa—the music, artists, performances, and visual iconography—drew on popular representations of virile masculinity on the periphery of the US economy to perform subjecthood. This imaginary marshaled artistic mastery, masculine swagger, and Afro-diasporic musical traditions in the construction of salsa's ideal subject.

# Salsa's Dirty Secret

## LIBERATED WOMEN, HAIRY HIPPIES, AND THE END OF THE WORLD

In the opening scene of *Our Latin Thing*, a young woman plays congas alongside her male counterparts on the scaffolding. She faces away from the camera as it closes in on her, and her laughter cannot be heard over the music, but viewers see the joy that radiates from her body and feel the self-confidence she exudes. Yet while the conguero on the scaffolding morphs into Ray Barretto at the Cheetah, where the Fania All-Stars rehearse for their concert, suggesting continuity in the scene, the young conguera simply disappears. The only woman singing audibly is an unidentified elderly woman who sings as she sits on a stoop next to a man playing guitar in a scene filmed outside the Cheetah. Unlike the guitarist, she repeatedly looks away from the camera, rejecting its spectacularization. When the camera closes in on the guitar player, it leaves the woman outside the shot altogether. Her voice falters momentarily as she struggles to recall the lyrics. Her voice returns forcefully as the song concludes, producing an aural presence that defies her physical absence from the frame. Another scene features a woman dancing with a male partner on an otherwise empty dance floor as the All-Stars rehearse for the concert. The scene refutes the invisibility of women on stage at the Cheetah. The scene lasts almost a minute and a half as the camera tracks their movement across a largely dark dance floor. At times lingering on the woman's torso and backside, the tracking shot draws the viewer's eye to her. Since the club's lighting is centered on the stage, the powder-blue hot pants she wears stand out against the darkened backdrop, accentuating bodily kinesthetics more complex and creative than that of her male partner. Each of these "performances"—by the conguera on the scaffolding, the singer on the stoop, and the dancer at the Cheetah—challenge the film's representation of salsa as an exclusively male performative space.

There are no female vocalists or musicians onstage at the Cheetah. Vocalist Celia Cruz would not join the Fania All-Stars until two years after the concert, and La Lupe, the only woman signed to Fania Records at the time, had already been marginalized by both the label and the Latin music scene generally.[1] Both Cruz and La Lupe form part of a broader cadre of women in the Latin music scene, whether as artists, music industry personnel, or journalists, during the 1960s and 1970s. In addition to the women included in chapter 1, women in the salsa scene include vocalists Ada Chabrier and Nancy O'Neill as well as percussionists Mydia Matos, Susan Hadjopoulos, and Annette López, who formed the first all-female salsa group in New York, Latin Fever; Vivian Velázquez, who shared operations responsibilities for the promotion agency Musically Yours; and "Cookie" Pacheco and Frances Rodríguez, the wives and managers of the late Johnny Pacheco and Pete "El Conde" Rodríguez, respectively. An executive at Montuno Records, Orquidia "Orchid" Santiago was also a DJ at nightclubs and afterhours like Christopher's, Hippocampo, 310½, the Chez Sensual, and Casablanca. Aurora Flores interviewed Orchid for *Billboard* in 1977. In the interview, Orchid explained that as the daughter of Alegre Records founder and music historian Al Santiago, she "was in the front line of the business [and] learned, at an early age, where the industry meets the public . . . what records were sellers, the varying musical tastes of music buyers, and . . . was in constant contact with the wide assortment of musicians who always visited [Santiago's] record shop [Casa Alegre]."[2] Similarly to the queer and feminist histories of the Nuyorican Poets Café and Nuyorican Arts Movement more broadly, the histories of women such as these carry the potential to transmit an alternative genealogy obscured by salsa's dominant narratives and a majoritarian public culture that suppresses female and queer histories.[3]

The previous chapter explored how salsa's streets, stages, and recording studios became spaces for performances of racialized virile masculinity. In this chapter, I continue my analysis of Willie Colón and Héctor LaVoe's corpus of songs recorded between 1965 and 1978 to examine the symbolic representation of women in the performance of subjecthood by salsa's bad boys. In what follows, I draw on the work of Vanita Reddy and use an analytic of intimacy to triangulate representations, heteronormative desire,

**3.1**    Still from *Our Latin Thing* (1972)

and racial solidarity in Colón and LaVoe's performance of subjecthood.[4] In other words, as my analysis shifts largely to song lyrics in this chapter, with some notable attention to musical arrangements, I explore the imbrication of social, political, and economic histories in which Colón and LaVoe's music acquired meaning.[5] This chapter has three distinct but related parts. In the first section, I trace the accumulation and exchange of women by the male singing subjects from one song to another, and one album to the next. Underscoring the symbolic role of women as screens for male homosocial relations, I then draw on the work of Frances Aparicio to explore the double-edged meanings of sentimentality. Focusing on a close reading of lyrics, I show that expressions of heteronormative desire also threaten racialized citizenship grounded on normative masculinity. In the final section, I turn to the queer surplus of *sucias*, of women who refuse the project of racial citizenship within this representational system wherein women who talk too much, spend too much time in the street, or betray the sexual contract of dual-heteronormative romantic love are subsequently expelled from salsa's symbolic spaces. By challenging the capitalist imperative of dual partnership and monogamy, these women threaten to reinscribe abjection as the status of salsa's gangsters.[6]

**3.2**   Still from *Our Latin Thing* (1972)

## ¡Qué linda estás!

Contrary to songs about heterosexual relationships, competition, and musicality, songs that map women's bodies onto the geography of Latin America constitute virile masculinity as coextensive with the expansion of salsa's markets in the Spanish-speaking Americas. This continental geography of male desire that Frances Aparicio traces in *Listening to Salsa* reveals a traffic in women that parallels the expansion of Fania's markets. "Panameña" (Panamanian woman) is one of two songs on *The Big Break—La gran fuga* (1970) that highlight salsa's increasing Latin American and Caribbean audiences. The male singing subject invites the "Panameña" to dance and have a good time before inviting the "Dominicana" (Dominican woman) to do the same.

The first two-thirds of the song use a repetitive chord progression, sparse arrangements, and a more active rhythmic and harmonic structure than previous Colón recordings. As the singing subject turns his attention to the "Borinqueña" (Puerto Rican woman), the song transforms. As musician, songwriter, and producer Bobby Marín aptly describes, "All hell breaks loose, thanks to Colón's roaring trombone and the jerky piano lines by the maestro, Professor Joe Torres."[7] The music pauses for a moment, allowing LaVoe to introduce "la salsa de Puerto Rico, el aguinaldo" (Puerto Rico's salsa, the *aguinaldo*), a folkloric musical form. Reminiscent of *Asalto Navideño* in the way Colón combines salsa's rhythmic practices with música típica, the break in the arrangements signals the serenade to come. LaVoe, as the singing subject, sings to the aguinaldo and la Borinqueña, which translates to "Puerto Rican woman" but is also the title of the unofficial national anthem. Together, la Borinqueña and the aguinaldo, the woman and the music, represent Puerto Rico. Using the language of sentimentality, the singing subject declares his love and loyalty to la Borinqueña, as if Puerto Rico itself is the object of love. While LaVoe's vocals easily adapt to singing Latin American rhythms, the singing subject assures the listener that he never forgets Puerto Rico—the imaginary within the song composed of the country itself, its folkloric music, and its women. In fact, without the Borinqueña, the singing subject declares he "would die."

Puerto Rico remains exceptional within the song even as it celebrates salsa's reception by Latin American audiences and the music's global flows, both mapped onto heterosexual male desire for women's bodies. Aligning male sexual conquest with the formalization of salsa's Latin American markets, these songs link masculinity to sexual mastery, aesthetic prowess, and expanding markets, including the geographic mobility produced through Fania's distribution networks.

In "Pa' Colombia" (To Colombia), the singing subject celebrates the popularity of salsa there and the presumed availability of women in each of the cities visited by the singing subject. The Colombian cities of Baranquilla, Cartagena, Medellín, Bogotá, and the "lovely Cali" are also five women:

> Las cinco novias que
> yo tengo allá en Colombia
>
> [The five girlfriends that
> I have there in Colombia]

As in "Panameña," the desire of the singing subject remains, as Luce Irigaray might argue, to accumulate women, to count off his conquests publicly, "sequentially and cumulatively, as a measure of standards."[8] By mapping the geography of Fania's markets onto women's bodies, the song renders desire and exchange interchangeable, revealing accumulation as the ultimate purpose of masculine capitalist desire. This commodification of male heteronormative desire also links masculinity and commerce while simultaneously distancing men from the process of commodification.

The growing infrastructure that Fania Records created physically distanced salsa and its musicians from the microlocal urban spaces where the music emerged. In so doing, salsa's (trans)national flows threatened to symbolically remove the salseros from their site of enunciation. I turn here to Nelson George's concern regarding rap's development as a transnational cultural product to elucidate my point. George concluded his 1989 tribute to rap by decrying the commercialization that left rap increasingly "vulnerable" "to cultural emasculation" as corporations wrested control of it from what he called "its street corner constituency."[9] This separation of a "masculine" and "authentic" product from a "feminine" and "commodified" one, which reinscribes nineteenth-century discourses of mass culture, illuminates a similar anxiety within salsa.[10] The potential disarticulation of salseros from the streets of New York and their identification with processes of commodification, while signaling salsa's increasing global popularity, threaten to emasculate salsa's ideal subject by suggesting that male musicians, like women, are to be consumed. Following Shoshana Felman, I argue that the accumulation of women functions within the Colón–LaVoe corpus as a screen that separates the relationship between (male) musicians from processes of (feminine) commodification, thus placing salsa's ideal subject beyond the process of exchange.[11] The symbolic role of women within the corpus illuminates how, as Faye Harrison argues, "the profitability, capital mobility, and structural power constitutive of globalization are fundamentally gendered phenomena marked by a masculinist logic."[12] Insofar as salsa's development as a cultural product and its expanding markets are framed by heteronormative desire, the music's transnational networks pose no contradictions for a male singing subject symbolically and aesthetically constituted in relation to the streets of New York. By mapping the geography of Fania's markets onto women's bodies, the songs describe desire and loss, like accumulation and exchange, as contiguous, revealing accumulation as the ultimate purpose of masculine capitalist desire.[13]

The contradictions illuminated here do not negate the aesthetic meanings of "Panameña" and "Pa' Colombia" in the production of Latinidad within salsa. These songs, like others that name Latin American and Caribbean listeners through lyrics or musical arrangements, forged a space that reflects salsa's local and transnational communities. When asked about the significance of "el barrio" in his musical formation, Colón responded by referring to the multiple Latin American cultural influences around which he was raised and their impact on his development as an artist:

> Mira, yo nací en el South Bronx, hijo de dos latinos también nacidos en Nueva York y nieto de una puertorriqueña que salió de la isla en 1923 y todavía hoy no habla inglés. La señora que me cuidaba cuando niño era panameña y en el bloque en que vivíamos había también cubanos, dominicanos, venezolanos, chicanos, gente de todo el Caribe y todo lo que se oía era música en español.[14]

> [Look, I was born in the South Bronx, child of two Latinos also born in New York and grandson of a Puerto Rican woman who left the island in 1923 and still today does not speak English. The woman who took care of me as a child was Panamanian, and on the block where we lived there were also Cubans, Dominicans, Venezuelans, Chicanos, people from all the Caribbean and all that you heard was music in Spanish.]

This description of the block on which Colón grew up speaks to the continuous migration and diasporicity of Latin(a/o) American communities in New York that informed Colón's musical formation. This dimension of Colón's background reflects, not a facile fabrication of markets, but the ways that Latin(a/o) American communities in New York and their converging musical histories and everyday lives within the United States impacted the aesthetic and material context of salsa.[15]

In fact, the very participation of countries like Venezuela and Colombia in the production, reproduction, and consumption of salsa speaks to salsa's significance as a marker of a pan-Latina/o and Latin American subjectivities. Venezuela became one of Fania's largest markets by the end of the 1970s, and groups like Dimensión Latina and Sonero Clásico del Caribe sound salsa's Venezuelan meanings. And yet these very global flows of salsa could threaten to displace local musical forms and capital. The establishment in the mid-1970s of a Fania Records office in the Dominican Republic created a direct competition with merengue, a competition that moved beyond control of the marketplace to a struggle over the meanings of music and national identity.[16] The different trajectories of salsa in Latin America speak to the proliferation of multiple "salsas," a term Rondón used, in each of these spaces and both the possibilities and contradictions created at the intersection of culture, politics, and economic relations.

Colón and LaVoe's musical collaboration constituted aggression, competition, and sonoridad as male spheres of authority. Even as the image of salsa's bad boys repudiated narratives of Puerto Ricans as a disposable surplus population, their artistic persona reified nonnormative gender practices as aberrations that threaten virile manhood. Songs like "Timbalero" (Timbales player), "The Hustler," and "Oíga señor" (Listen up, sir) celebrated musical ferocity and insisted on the masculinity of the singing subject by deriding other men. In "Señora Lola" (Ms. Lola), the woman of the title serves as an intermediary between the singing subject and a husband derided as weak. LaVoe, as the male singing subject, advises Señora Lola to convey a message to her husband: he should stop talking smack and pretending to be a big man. Otherwise, he'll get his head knocked off. For while the husband shows up to a fight with a machete, the song goes, LaVoe brings an automatic rifle to the fight. The conflation of musical and social practices detailed in the previous chapter suggests that the automatic rifle symbolizes LaVoe's voice, Colón's trombone, and the band's sonoridad. LaVoe asserts himself as the real man and derides Señora Lola's husband's pretensions to normative masculinity. Finally, the song deploys metaphors of domesticity that reassert the singing subject's patriarchal authority. LaVoe tells the husband (through Señora Lola) to go put on a housecoat, presumably his wife's, since it is she who faces the singing subject. Presumably hiding behind his wife's skirts (to carry the metaphor through to its conclusion), the husband does not even rule his own home. Thus, the husband's claims to manhood and musicianship are rebuked.

Metaphors of domesticity emerge again in one of LaVoe's signature songs, "El Cantante." Released on the album *Comedia* (Comedy, 1978), LaVoe's riff announces:

> Algunos cantan con faldas
> Yo canto con pantalones
>
> [Some sing while wearing skirts
> I sing with pants on]

Once again virile masculinity and sonoridad are mutually reinforcing categories buttressed by rebuking nonnormative manhood. The riff, like the admonitions in "Señora Lola," illustrates how, as Lawrence La Fountain-Stokes argues, effeminate men are necessary for the performance of normative Puerto Rican masculinity. Effeminate men, like male-to-female transvestites and masculine women, he explains,

> are ubiquitous in all Puerto Rican towns and diasporic neighborhoods, yet they are also the frequent object of derision and even attacks. Prescriptions against male effeminacy and female masculinity do not work to simply eliminate gender-variance or trans practices and identities, but rather stigmatize this behavior and give it a specific meaning. . . . In this configuration, the social performance of effeminate manhood is *necessary* for other men's successful enactment of virile masculinity to work, as it is performed in perfect counterpoint. To put it simply, in this relation system, there can be no *macho* if there is no *loca* or *maricón*.[17]

The performance of los malotes de la salsa (salsa's gangsters or bad boys) as they dispensed with male rivals, whether musicians or sexual competitors, routinely exalts in the emasculation of other men—men who cannot dance, innovate musically, or fight, or who, as in the case of Ramón Puntilla in the song "Qué lío" (What a mess), resort to practices diminished as feminine.

While Colón and LaVoe embrace abjection, they do so as a masculinist heteronormative possibility that depends on both the performance and expulsion of nonnormative sexualities. The song "Qué lío" begins with the lamentations of Ramón Puntilla, a man who discovers that the woman he loves is also seeing another man, his friend. Puntilla pours his heart out to his mother, despairing at the possibility of never finding a woman who "will love him right" and call him "papi" (daddy, baby). Puntilla screams in agony, goes to church to plead with God to help him forget the faithless Mariana, and lights candles as part of his supplication. The coro (chorus) expresses sympathy for Puntilla, singing:

> Que problema con Mariana
> el que se encontró mi pana

> [What a problem with Mariana
> My boy has found]

However, the song quickly deteriorates into derision and mockery as the perspective shifts from Puntilla to the singing subject, who routinely "enjoyed"

Mariana "all night long." Presumably the friend to whom Puntilla refers, the singing subject also mocks him for pleading with God and lighting "little" candles, *velitas*. The ritual is presented as a feminine practice that further diminishes Puntilla. Ridiculing Puntilla, the singing subject proclaims sexual mastery over both him and Mariana. Employing the figure of Mariana to express sexual pleasure, LaVoe projects sentimental love onto Puntilla, disassociating himself from what are considered sentimental, read feminine, practices. This rhetorical strategy serves a similar function to the tirade leveled at Señora Lola so that she may pass it on to her husband. Both Señora Lola and Mariana sustain and mediate the relationship between two men, functioning as screens for male homosocial relations and the consolidation of subjecthood.[18]

Desire and exchange become interchangeable, revealing accumulation as the ultimate purpose of masculine capitalist desire.[19] In "Recomendación" (Recommendation), the lyrical subject needs a woman who understands him so he asks for recommendations from a woman's grandmother, brother-in-law, and, last, her former husband. He needs their assurance that she will be good to him. Since the song appears on the album *Asalto Navideño*, vol. 2 (Christmas assault, 1973), perhaps she will be his Christmas gift. No longer married, the female object of desire has, after all, once again entered the market. As such, she may have been ruined by liberated women in the public sphere. Structured around a male-female-male triangle, this song once again elucidates how "men's heterosexual relationships have as their raison d'être an ultimate bonding between men; and that this bonding, if successfully achieved, is not detrimental to 'masculinity' but definitive of it."[20]

Whereas women's presence in men's lives facilitates sonorous expressions of male superiority over other men, songs of unrequited love provide a space for the articulation of the very sentimentality derided in "Qué lío." [21] Aparicio shows that, as objects of "unquenchable desire" in these songs, women are "never actualized into sexual or erotic pleasure." Instead, and here Aparicio draws on the work of Iris Zavala, "woman" is constituted as "an ideal, a divine being," who is "evoked and discursively present through the male voice of the interpreter . . . through the act of singing, and through the bolero as performative act."[22] The influence of the bolero can be found throughout LaVoe's songs, as both lead vocalist for Colón and soloist. In "Ausencia" (Absence), coincidentally the title of one of the most well-known boleros by Puerto Rican composer Rafael Hernández, LaVoe expresses a sentimentality uncharacteristic of salsa's ideal subject. Despite his best attempts to forget a woman, he continues to pray for her return. LaVoe's expressivity conveys a depth of sentimentality that appears to surprise even the singing subject, as he confesses:

Yo vi llorar a un hombre ante un espejo
por un amor que le negara el cielo
Y asombrado me dio un escalofrío
al ver en el espejo el rostro mío

[I saw a man cry in front of a mirror
For a love that heaven had denied
And surprised I got goose bumps
To see in the mirror my own face]

The reflection in the mirror of a man denied love by God himself, a sentiment like that of Ramón Puntilla in "Qué lío," frightens the male subject, giving him goose bumps when he realizes that the man in the mirror is, in fact, himself. The willingness to die for love; expressions of anguish, desperation, and melancholy over a lost love; and the insistence on waiting for the return of the lover all situate the singing subject, as Aparicio has shown, in what has traditionally been considered the feminine sphere of emotion and sentimentality. Similar to the gendered abjection theorized by Michelle Cho in South Korean film comedy, "gender transgression, made pleasurable as abject spectacle, signals both the endurance and the instability of patriarchal gender norms."[23]

In "Ausencia," the absence of the woman that propels expressions of heterosexual desire also threatens the masculinity of salsa's singing subject, underscoring the dual signification of gendered abjection. While the accumulation of women provides access to racialized masculinity, their absence threatens the project of subjecthood. In "Sigue feliz" (Stay happy), sentimentality once again threatens the masculinity of the male singing subject, who loved a woman with the innocence of a child. She, in turn, provided merely an illusion of what sentimental love might offer. She stole his heart and then betrayed him, leaving him inconsolable. Thus, while the singing subject depends precisely on gender difference for the representation of his authority, he finds himself at the mercy of a woman whose absence motivates expressions of abject sentimentality. So, while "yesterday he cried," today he laughs and sends the woman, who attempts to return to him, on her way. This moment reveals a "male egocentric subject location that precludes any possibility for emotional reciprocity or communion" with women.[24]

Sentimental love threatens the masculinity of salsa's ideal subject because it leaves him vulnerable to liberated women, "dirty" women who are full of treachery and deceit. In "Se acaba este mundo" (The world is ending), released in 1968 on *The Hustler*, the instrumental sections assert normative masculinity through musicality and become the symbolic foil for "liberated" women and other harbingers of the apocalypse referred to in the song: hairy (male) hippies and dirty, miniskirt-wearing women who "don't even want to bathe." As RosaLinda Fregoso suggests in relation to Chicana urban identities, the streets constitute a "site of danger, where young girls become *pachucas* and callejeras."[25]

### Salsa's Femme Fatales

The 1975 interview in *Latin N.Y.* with a "liberated man and woman" formed part of a series of pieces featured in the magazine about relationships between women and men. In this particular piece, Marc Sangria interviews Maria, a "beautiful 21-year-old sensual Latin woman . . . the kind of woman that men stare at and desire." He prefaces the interview with a summary of failed relationships with men that motivated Maria to return to high school, graduate, and then enter college. He concludes the introduction by stating that "her attitudes toward life and men . . . changed as she acquired self-confidence and knowledge," making her "a strong advocate of the women's lib movement [who] picks the men she wants when she wants to with no further involvement." Maria also believes all men are "chauvinists" who "hide it" and use women's lib "as a rap" once they know a woman is "liberated." Choosing to focus on her responsibilities to her studies, home, and daughter, Maria freely expresses her desire for men while expressly rejecting marriage. Most men, however, "usually can't cope" with her frankness. Her liberated ideology stems, Sangria suggests, from being unable to succeed at sentimental love.[26]

The interviewer repeatedly attempts to reveal the hypocrisy of liberated women. He questions her rejection of "being treated as a sex object" by questioning Maria's attempts to "dress up and look sexy" and "provoke men's stares," and her decision to "go . . . braless." She challenges his interrogation and the presumption of women's availability for male consumption by explaining that she dresses to please *herself*. She continues, "I can't help the way I walk and I go bra-less because it's comfortable. I just don't like bras, and if men find that sexy . . . that's their problem. What if men were turned on by painted toenails, should I hide my toes?" The interview ends with Sangria asking Maria whether she ever pays the bill on a date. She tells him she will occasionally buy a drink, but "I never have any money anyway, so I would say the man pays." When she does have money, however, she goes out with her girls and they "share expenses and have a great time goofing and partying and coming home alone."[27] The interview attempts to characterize Maria as a woman who herself objectifies men, and the questions themselves signify an anxiety about women's economic and sexual freedom.

For Puerto Rican women in New York, access to public space included not only the ability to enjoy the salsa boom but the right to become active participants in it and the Nuyorican Arts Movement as well as leaders in their communities and ongoing social movements. Like other women of color active in social justice movements during the 1960s and 1970s, Puerto Rican women navigated historical legacies of colonialism and, for Afro–Puerto Rican women, slavery. Puerto Rican women simultaneously navigated "women's issues" via caregiving activities and daily interactions within organizations that formed within the public sphere of their communities.[28] Cultural nationalism in diasporic Puerto Rican communities prompted collective action to effect structural changes, contest dominant narratives of criminality, and advocate for both racial liberation and Puerto Rico's independence. Yet the gendered assumptions of cultural nationalism reproduced hegemonic gender norms, subjugating women's struggles in the name of a collective national identity.

The nationalist discourse that emphasized a collective Puerto Rican identity within the Young Lords Party in New York reproduced gendered hierarchies that relegated women to what former Young Lord Denise Oliver described as status as "second class citizens."[29] In fact, the Young Lords' 1970 Thirteen Point Program and Platform affirmed the need for "revolutionary" machismo that "support[ed] their women in their fight for economic and social equality, and must recognize that our women are equals in every way within the revolutionary ranks."[30] The Women's Caucus within the organization, which met weekly to discuss writings by women in the feminist movement, including other women of color with whom they developed coalitions, rejected the assumption that the cultural framework of machismo could be untethered from patriarchal authority over women. As Oliver described this period in the organization, "We march[ed] together with our brothers as equals" and demanded that they "struggle against their machismo and not turn it into some bullshit about it being revolutionary."[31]

The Young Lords' Position Paper on Women, issued in September 1970 by the Women's Caucus, rejected the conflation of women with "traditions" and discourses of cultural nationalism framed within heteropatriarchal imperatives that marginalized nonnormative sexualities. The position paper emphasized women's reproductive rights and denounced the control of their sexuality as a mechanism of both misogyny and US imperialism.[32] Under the new leadership of the Young Lords that emerged at the insistence of the Women's Caucus in 1970, Oliver became minister of finance, and both a men's caucus and a gay and lesbian caucus emerged. Notably, Sylvia Rivera, a Puerto Rican and Venezuelan foundational figure in the fight for gay liberation and transgender rights who cofounded Street Transvestite Action Revolutionaries (STAR) with Marsha Johnson, joined the Young Lords after meeting several members at a protest against police repression. However, lesbian, gay, bisexual, and trans* members of the Young Lords remained excluded from leadership positions. In 1971, the Young Lords' Central Committee issued a report concluding that feminism and nationalism were irreconcilable. The report coincided with what former Young Lord Iris Morales has described as the organization's "narrowing nationalist" framework, wherein the decision to establish a chapter in Puerto Rico questioned the authenticity of Puerto Ricans who did not support the move and the role of non–Puerto Rican members of the Young Lords, including African Americans.[33] Within the radical politics of the Young Lords, patriarchy remained dominant, if differentiated from the racial and capitalist logic of the United States.

The outreach of the Women's Caucus to other women of color highlights the breadth of diasporic Puerto Rican women's activism in New York as they created an alternative public sphere incommensurate with hegemonic Americanness, the heteronormative and patriarchal contours of cultural nationalism, and the women's liberation movement. Women in the Young Lords connected with women in other Puerto Rican organizations such El Movimiento Pro-Independencia (the Pro-Independence Movement) and El Comité (the Committee). Their solidarity with other Third World women in the Black Panther Party, the Black Women's Alliance, the Brown Berets, and I Wor Kuen marked the "revolution with the revolution."[34] New York Puerto Rican activist Daisy DeJesús was a founding member of Third World Gay Wimmin, an organization of Black women, including Latinas, broadly known as the Salsa Soul Sisters, founded in New York in 1974.[35] While DeJesús supported independence for Puerto Rico, she rejected the ideology that framed homosexuality as a product of US imperialism in the organizational meetings for a socialist pro-independence group in New York.[36] These contradictions demonstrate both the potential and limits of nationalist cultural politics within diasporic Puerto Rican communities and the ways Puerto Rican and other women of color repudiated and transgressed its limits through their own appropriation of New York's streets.

For Puerto Rican women in the salsa scene, taking it to the streets, nightclubs, afterhours, and parks of salsa shifted the locus of emancipatory hope, to draw on Delgado and Muñoz, from the everyday to everynight life.[37] The songs introduced in this chapter, however, show how Colón and LaVoe's songs reanimated the belief in women's proper social space as the private world of the family, where they, as sexual property, can be guarded; where sexuality can be policed; and where women respect the men who love them.[38] In contrast, women who "behave" are rewarded with affection ("Recomendación"). Even then, the singing subject threatens:

> Que no me coja de bobo
> porque yo no soy bobito
>
> [She better not play me
> Because I'm not a fool]

That is, she should not make a fool out of him because a fool he is not. This warning also surfaces in the song "No me den candela" (Don't give me heat), where the singing subject pleads for freedom from the envy and gossip that surround him and advises one woman in particular:

> Óyeme bien Micaela
> Con los santos no se juega
> Y conmigo tampoco vas a jugar
>
> [Listen to me, Micaela
> You don't mess with the *santos*
> And you're not going to play with me either][39]

In these and similar songs, "good" treatment is a reward for performing normative gender. These songs provide insight into male anxieties about women who transgressed gendered notions of ethnic community, wherein they are "constructed as private citizens responsible for providing spiritual values and moral guidance to the families and refueling kinship networks."[40]

Drawing on Tricia Rose's analysis of rap, I see within LaVoe and Colón's repertoire a male anxiety about women's newfound sexual freedom combined with fears of vulnerability that recast already existing ideologies regarding identity, community, and gender difference.[41]

While expressions of sentimental love surface throughout Colón and LaVoe's recordings, in songs like "Ausencia" and "Si la ves," the actual reunions with departed lovers provide an opportunity for the male subject to reproach and humiliate women for their betrayal. In "No cambiaré" (I won't change), a woman returns to the male singing subject asking for forgiveness, insisting that her departure was a mistake. Yet her apparent desire to make amends becomes a source of frustration for the male singing subject. Though he continues to love her, he refuses to forgive her. His desire to distance himself from the affective language and practices associated with romantic love is expressed through time. The sentimental expressions of "yesterday" must be refused in favor of admonishing the woman upon her return "today." What he will not change, as the title foretells, is his mind. Attempts at reunion are futile. "No, no te humilles" (Don't humiliate yourself), he tells her, "ahora te toca a ti perder" (now it's your turn to lose). In these and other songs of sentimental love, "woman" becomes "a treacherous signifier, a slippery, shifting sign impossible to decode, a social and discursive image that permeates men's perceptions of women."[42]

Love, LaVoe's songs suggest, is a game with multiple rounds, where fortune determines the winner and loser from one day to the next. In this game, love poses a threat to subjecthood. Such is the case within the lyrics of "Juana Peña" and "Mentira" (Lie), released on the albums *Cosa nuestra* (Our thing, 1969) and *De ti depende* (It depends on you, 1976), respectively. Here, women are vilified as unrelenting sources of betrayal. Juana Peña deceived many men, including the singing subject, until a man came along who betrayed her instead. Unlike the woman in "Ausencia," whose tears provide evidence of remorse, Juana Peña's tears reveal evidence of her previous infidelities. Similarly, "Mentira," an old Cuban *son* by Ignacio Piñeiro, tells the tale of Salomé, a woman who becomes the object of a discursive attack by the singing subject. Like the biblical figure by the same name, she is dishonest and deceitful, motivated by malice and greed:

> Mujer falacia, impostora de caricias
> Tu beso es virus que al alma envenena
> Sobre tus ansias un corazón de piedra
> con las maldades que encierra la codicia

[Dishonest woman, deceitful caresses
Your kiss is a virus that poisons the soul
A heart of stone upon your longings
With the evil that greed encompasses]

Her tears, like those of the biblical Salomé, are treacherous. At the end, the chorus sings "Mentira" over and over again during a conga solo. Both the chorus and instrumentation function as a Greek chorus that summarizes the song in one phrase. Salomé is a liar.

Similar to the act of name-calling in rap examined by Rose, the symbolic violence renders women and alternative masculinities as a threat to salsa's male subject.[43] In "Bandolera" (Rogue, or Villain), a song released in 1978 as part of LaVoe's album *Comedia*, the absent woman is described by the singing subject as a tenacious liar whose innate character drives her desire to destroy their "dulce hogar" (sweet home). Her selfishness and lack of respect fuel the singing subject's solipsistic declaration:

Yo creo en mí
Yo sé de mí
Yo sé vivir

[I believe in me
I know me
I know how to live]

But if he "throws her out the window she'll come back up the stairs." The song's arrangements and use of onomatopoeia function as counterparts to the verbal assault that follows. The use of "pau, pau, pau" mimics the way Spanish-speaking parents might warn misbehaving children to behave or receive a spanking (as in "Behave, or I'm going to give you *pau pau*"). The sound mimics the sound of a spanking while infantilizing the object of his violence. The use for comedic effect naturalizes and disavows the violence of gendered abjection fundamental to the representation of women within late capitalist modernity.[44] The rhythm and rapid repetition of "te voy a pegar" (I'm going to hit you) provides an auditory flash-forward to the physical violence to come, which the unnamed "bandolera" is told to "suck up." At approximately 9:28 minutes, LaVoe's vocal performance, the chorus, and grandiose musical arrangements with an expanded brass section, consisting of two trumpets in addition to the usual two trombones, work together to produce the sounds of violence within intimacy. While the complementary relationship between vocals and instrumentation is not in and of itself remarkable, the placement and the symbolic role of the instruments in the violence stand out.

"Bandolera" begins and ends with instrumental sections, with another three placed throughout the song. The first instrumental section follows the song's initial lyrics that proclaim the treachery and warn of the violence to come. When LaVoe begins singing again almost a minute later, the singing subject declares:

Pau, pau, pau
Te vuelvo a dar pa' que aprendas

[Pau, pau, pau
I hit you again so you'll learn]

The use of "again" signals that the threatened violence manifested itself during the instrumental, suggesting that the interlude itself becomes the soundscape of intimate partner violence. It is in this second section of lyrics where LaVoe riffs, "Te voy a pegar," "Te voy a pegar," "Te voy a pegar," "Te voy a pegar," "Te voy a pegar" over a repeating chorus of "aléjate bandolera" (stay away villain). The section ends with "pau, pau, pau." The instrumental section that follows lasts approximately three minutes and thirty seconds, most of which consists of a virtuosic piano solo. The instrumental section sounds an individual and collective response to the woman's failure to accede to normative gender roles. The trumpets emphasize this message later in the song by reflecting back the way LaVoe extends his notes. The singing subject ends the lyrics with the assurance:

Si yo no te quiero
Anda tranquila
Ya no te quiero
Vive tu vida

[I don't love you anymore
Don't worry
I don't love you anymore
Live your life]

A thirty-second instrumental section follows with both piano and trumpet solos that become a prelude to the song's final revelation. The "bandolera" rifled through his pockets and stole his wallet. And that, according to the singing subject, is why—as the chorus of "aléjate bandolera" continues between each riff—the singing subject is going to literally "throw her out," as announced earlier in the song. As the song concludes, he provides final instructions: "Calm yourself and don't give me any problems."

When the woman in "Bandolera" gets caught rifling through the male singing subject's pockets, she destroys their "dulce hogar" by laying bare a material and economic context for their relationship. Her actions indict an affective economy of pleasure based on the idealization of sentimental love, the objectification of women, and the marginalization of nonnormative gender identities. The woman's representation in "Bandolera" draws on the image of the gold digger, one of the figures that has often emerged in popular culture during periods of economic transition, alongside that of the "lost woman." Aparicio explains a similar process in relation to the bolero. The genre's popularity throughout Latin America during the early and mid-twentieth century coincided with various periods of modernization, migration, and urbanization that increasingly brought women into the public sphere. Aparicio's reading of the silences created by the masculinist perspectives in salsa underscores how the motif of the "absent woman" reveals male anxieties about patriarchal power amid women's increasing presence outside the domestic sphere at different historical moments. In the Colón–LaVoe repertoire, salsa songs became a symbolic space for negotiating gendered conflicts between men and women through the language of sentimental love, physical violence, and name-calling.[45]

While unrequited love in boleros drives the singing subject to expressions of sentimentality, its betrayal transforms women into objects of derision. The "very basic speech act of name-calling, of insults and vituperative language, what we may deem as discursive terrorism or violence through words" dominates lyrics where women transgress gendered boundaries.[46] The track "Un amor de la calle" (A love from the street), a bolero written by Orlando Brito and released in 1975 on LaVoe's album *La Voz*, centers the archetypal theme of *la mujer de la calle* (the street woman) and *la mujer perdida* (the lost woman), both of which function as euphemisms for whore and sex worker and are pervasive within the bolero tradition. He claims that he can find the love of *una cualquiera* (an anybody) in the street, a term that implies sexual promiscuity. By describing the woman of "Un amor de la calle" as just another cualquiera that played with his life and his heart, the singing subject identifies her with all those in the corpus who betrayed him. Retroactively defining them all as *mujeres perdidas* (literally, lost women), he projects abandonment, sexual promiscuity, and betrayal as threats to subjecthood.

Women who transgress the boundaries of romantic love threaten the ability of salsa's ideal subject to access and remain within the realm of subjecthood. The female figure in "Periódico de ayer" ("Yesterday's newspaper"), tossed into the street like "garbage" or "yesterday's newspaper," symbolizes the remains of a relationship. Having "had" her, he now belongs to the ranks of those who have "read" her "sensational" headlines to ultimately discover that, like yesterday's newspaper, she is "worthless." A gossiping, sexually promiscuous, and false woman, she belongs in the street with the trash. In the song, released on the album *Comedia* at the height of Colón and LaVoe's relationship with Fania Records, the use of strings and a bigger horn section sounds not only the grandiose instrumentation of orchestral soul trends in the 1970s but the expressivity of LaVoe's vocals. The double meaning of *querer*—to desire, to love—amplifies the derision when LaVoe sings, "te quise, te tuve, te mantuve y ahora no te quiero" (I loved you, desired you, I had you, I financially supported you and now I don't love/want you), while demonstrating impeccable control of timing and rhythm that contributes to the song's emphasis on power. The songs underscore the persistent belief that women's sexuality remains the property of men and must be surveilled. Unlike objects of unconsummated desire and male longing in songs that extol sentimental love, the women in "Bandolera" and "Periódico de ayer" are cast as unfaithful thieves, traitors, liars, gossips, gold diggers, and whores.[47] What Faye Harrison has described as the "misogynous symbolic assault against women" underlies the racialized and masculinist subjecthood of salsa's singing subject.[48]

The desire to be free from sucias in these songs is most clearly expressed in songs that recur to the countryside as the site of idyllic sentimental love. In "Guajira ven" (Guajira come; feminine), released in 1973 on *Lo mato (si no compra este LP)* (I'll kill him [if he doesn't buy this LP]), the male singing subject sings the virtues of the land, nature, and even his dog to convince his "guajira" to join him there.[49]

Nunca se nota tristeza
ay, en mi bella campiña
donde la caña y la piña
a la tierra dan riqueza

Allí la naturaleza
regó toda su hermosura
y todo el que lo ve jura
que allí el paraíso empieza

[There is never sadness
Oh, in my beautiful countryside
Where the sugarcane and pineapple
Make the soil rich

There, nature
Spread all her beauty
And everyone who sees it swears
That paradise begins there]

This idealized landscape offers serenity, joy, and repose. The presumed jíbaro rests easily under the canopy of resplendent trees that protect him from the sun's heat while his loyal dog protects the harvest. The song "Vo so" (You are), released on the same album, is loosely based on arrangements of, along with some lyrics from, the Brazilian song "Maracangalha," by Dorival Caymmi. In "Vo so," the male singing subject punishes his female companion because she refused to accompany him on a previous night for a piragua (shaved ice). So tonight, he leaves her behind when he goes to a rumba. If New York offers women mobility through their access to the public sphere, the campo (countryside) comes to represent a space where women may be more easily restricted within traditional gender roles, rural isolation, and (in many cases) lack of public transportation.

The spatialization of desire and performance in these songs recurs to images of the countryside to reestablish normative gender roles. The countryside's Edenic natural state, underscored by the references to landscapes and harvests, stands in contrast to the moral corruption of cities with liberated women. The urban-rural dichotomy within these songs aligns with the similar premise in Puerto Rico's literary canon, wherein urban melancholy leads to the moral corruption of women and the alienation of Puerto Rican men.[50] Yet it is precisely in the streets of Latin New York where the reputation of salsa's bad boys coheres around the accumulation of women. The acquisition and expulsion of women makes salsa's racialized masculinity possible and symbolically places it outside processes of exchange.[51]

An analysis of the gendered self-representation of Colón and LaVoe and the symbolic function of women within that narrative must address how

La Lupe signified the very liberated woman, or mujer perdida, that threat-ened salsa's ideal subject. LaVoe's personal trials, drug addiction, and char-acter flaws did not prevent him from being "canonized and integrated into the masculine genealogy of Puerto Rican national musical forms. La Lupe's irreverence, unlike that of her male counterpart, was characterized as dis-respectful and disorderly." In their essay on the memorialization of LaVoe and La Lupe by audiences, musicians, and critics, Aparicio and Wilson Valentín-Escobar describe performances that were "excessive in their anger, violence, and sensuality." Her self-eroticization and performativity, however, provoked revulsion and controversy even as she—like LaVoe—reveled in ex-cess.[52] With a performative style that rejected middle-class respectability, she defied, as Muñoz argues, the constraints demanded of the "good immigrant" by both the dominant American culture and recent Cuban exiles. La Lupe's *chillona* (screeching) singing style and other performative gestures of erotic excess included stripping off clothes, jewelry, and shoes as well as moments of spiritual possession or sexual ecstasy. Her chusmería, or performance of racialized and gendered abjection, defied the reactionary aspects of Latini-dad that demanded Latinas/os, as Muñoz reminds us, "not be too black, too poor, too sexual, too loud, too emotional, or too theatrical."[53] La Lupe's "an-tics" were simply "too much," and she became, in the words of one reporter, "the ultimate representation of the image the Cubans were trying to dispel."[54] The intersection of drama and performance produced a disidentificatory self-fashioning that rejected, as Carmelita Tropicana's homage to La Lupe stresses, Hispanophile middle-class codes of conduct in favor of a racialized, gendered, sexual, and national difference.[55] Whether relegating La Lupe to the affective realm of the feminine through descriptions of her "energy" and "madness" or reducing her to an "entertainer" who used her sexuality to attract audiences, disparaging descriptions deny her agency as an artist and Black woman. Within salsa's masculinist histories, La Lupe effectively became "La Tirana" (the tyrant) of her eponymously titled song, "la mala" (the bad one), "la vampiresa" (the femme fatale) reduced to the "venenosos comentarios" (venomous commentary) of her male counterparts.[56]

La Lupe's gender nonconformity signified disrespect because she threat-ened the symbolic order and real hierarchies within salsa.[57] Her first re-cording after her departure from the Tito Puente Orchestra accused the renowned bandleader of "booting her," a declaration that challenged any interpretations that blamed her for the rift. La Lupe also called out Fania Records, which failed to invite her to form part of the Fania All-Stars or to promote her records despite brisk sales of earlier recordings—sales having often been the marker by which Fania determined which options were picked up by the label. The song, like her performative aesthetics, "reclaimed the centrality, ownership, and authority" denied to her by the music industry.[58] La Lupe's performative desperation, longing, and irreverent *desorden* (chaos) reclaim an individual authority while simultaneously asserting the right of female performers and their voices to be heard alongside their male counterparts and paid accordingly.[59]

La Lupe, the Cuban-born "Queen of Latin Soul," provoked both pleasure and panic. There were families that kept their children from watching her "vulgar, cheap, and offensive" television appearances. Fans, however, embraced what has been characterized as La Lupe's "unbound passion, feeling, anger, madness, and sexuality."[60] Her chusmería provided a glimpse of a present futurity wherein her gendered and racialized subjecthood repudiates the heteronormative and patriarchal subjecthood of salsa's bad boys. Whereas the irreverence and bad-boy image of LaVoe and Colón helped catapult them to the upper echelons of Fania Records and salsa, La Lupe embodied a menacing transgressive potential that became a symbolic referent for the threat posed by sucias. La Lupe's racialized and gendered queer sublimity exceeded the limits of salsa's masculinist capitalist priorities and disrupted salsa's masculinist histories to defy the erasure of women's histories and queerness.[61]

## Conclusion

Whether the object of affection or the recipient of scorn, women become the boundary that separates abjection and subjecthood. Just as the repudiation of effeminate manhood and the accumulation of women's bodies are necessary for the performance of virile masculinity, so too is the disposal of women who exceed the limits of patriarchal intimacy. The self-reflexive artistic personas of salsa's bad boys constituted their own masculinity and that of the music through a series of aesthetic and representational practices that emerged in relation to the colonial, diasporic, and racialized political economy of Puerto Ricans in New York during the mid to late 1960s and 1970s. This performance of difference produced a collective and violent subjectivity that depended on the reification of heteropatriarchal structures.[62] Women who defy the male singing subject are constituted as mujeres perdidas rather than collaborators in the performance of Nuyorican imaginaries.

Male anxiety about women's newfound sexual freedom combines with fears of a racialized vulnerability to recast already existing ideas about identity, community, and gender difference, much as is done in rap.[63] These songs thus illuminate the contradictions posed by salsa's male singing subject. Though women can be discarded, violated, and replaced, they cannot be killed. The presence (through absence) of these "problem" women is required in the process of male bonding and subjecthood formation. Their absence would threaten to reveal the status of (male) salseros as objects of exchange. This is not the performance within marketing studies of a "sexy man" whose physical attractiveness and muscular build inspire desirability for cisgender heterosexual men.[64] Rather, it is the performance of racialized subjecthood—which also sells records. Triangulating the political economy of intimacy, the aesthetic and cultural politics of patriarchal nationalism, and liberatory movements shows how the representation of women as commodities to be circulated, consumed, and discarded both consolidates and threatens the performance of subjecthood.

PART II

# After the Boom Is Gone, 1980–2000s

# Puerto Rico's (Un)Freedom

## THE SOUNDSCAPE OF NATION BRANDING

**4**

La proyección de Puerto Rico más allá de nuestros linderos insulares fue una visión que guió muchas de mis decisiones.

[Puerto Rico's visibility beyond our insular boundaries was a vision that guided many of my decisions.]

**Rafael Hernández Colón,** former governor of Puerto Rico (ca. 2023)

During a visit to Puerto Rico in 1987, Spanish monarch Juan Carlos I extended a formal invitation to Governor Rafael Hernández Colón to participate in the 1992 Universal Expo in Seville, Spain.[1] Eager to celebrate Puerto Rico's Hispanic heritage and increase foreign investment from Europe, the governor accepted the invitation. He repeatedly trumpeted the invitation in speeches and press releases as an opportunity for Puerto Rico to host its first individual exhibit at a world's fair, independent of the United States, as befit a "nation among nations." Over the next several years, the Puerto Rican government invested approximately $31 million in Expo '92 for the design, construction, administration, programming, and upkeep of a permanent structure on the island of Cartuja in Seville.[2] At home, the governor forged ahead with cultural initiatives designed to foster a Hispanophile cultural renaissance that commemorated the "encounter" between Spain and the Americas. The governor had already established the Commission for the Celebration of the Quincentennial. By 1990, as organizers for the Puerto Rico pavilion at Expo '92 oversaw the plans for the exhibit, the commission began sponsoring conferences, exhibits, artisanal fairs, and other events celebrating Christopher Columbus's arrival to the Americas in 1492 and to Puerto Rico a year later. Waterfront development anticipated an increase in cruise ships docking at the San Juan harbor as well as the arrival of the Columbus Grand Regatta. More than two hundred ships docked in San Juan for ten days in 1992, drawing visitors who packed the waterfront to tour the ships and enjoy the multitude of concerts, exhibits, festivals, and fireworks. Additional initiatives included the renovation of Viejo San Juan and other municipalities with Spanish colonial architecture, an effort supported in part by funding from the Spanish government.[3] The Expo, however, remained at the center of the governor's plan to marry a Hispanophile cultural revival with Puerto Rico's economic recovery. This chapter focuses on the use of salsa as part of Puerto Rico's nation branding campaign at Expo '92 that sought to promote Puerto Rico as a potential trade partner, tourist destination, and nexus of internationalized capital for foreign investors in new and emerging European markets. Mobilized as a repository of Puerto Rico's cultural exceptionalism and economic aspirations, salsa became the soundscape for the governor's plan to establish a sphere of economic and political autonomy within the colonial context, or the performance of "(un) freedom."[4]

Hernández Colón considered the reunification of Germany, the dissolution of the Soviet Union, and the impending integration of the European Economic Community (EEC) into a single market as unprecedented opportunities to attract revenue that would ensure Puerto Rico's vibrant economic future. The governor hoped that by reorienting Puerto Rico's economy toward Europe, he would reproduce the gains of the 1950s, a period of social and economic advances described as the "Puerto Rican miracle." Obfuscating structural inequalities and all that the state owed its most vulnerable communities, the governor presented Puerto Rico as a horizontally structured society whose social and economic stability investors could rely on. Puerto Rico's cosmopolitan labor force and the political and economic stability afforded by the country's relationship to the United States topped the list of incentives for foreign investors. The performance of nationhood and a dual loyalty to Hispanophile culturalist narratives of whiteness and to US empire became the lynchpin to the nation branding campaign that linked the cultural politics of whiteness, public policy, and corporate marketing strategies.[5]

In January 1992, three months before the world's fair was scheduled to begin, the director of programming for the Puerto Rico pavilion announced the concert "Puerto Rico es salsa" (Puerto Rico is salsa). The star-studded concert would be the culminating event of Puerto Rico's "national day" at the Expo. The concert marshaled salsa's status as a global commodity and created an accompanying soundscape for the campaign to develop commercial links with Europe and reduce economic dependence on the United States.[6] The decision, which elevated salsa to the status of cultural patrimony, met a vociferous backlash from elected officials, artists, intellectuals, and private figures in Puerto Rico. It was hotly debated for weeks after the announcement, and sporadic coverage in the press lasted months. Program organizers rebuffed alternate suggestions and proceeded with the concert and plans to feature salsa nightly at the Puerto Rico pavilion. On Puerto Rico's national day, Alex D'Castro, Tony Vega, Ismael Miranda, and Andy Montañez preceded the evening's main performance by El Gran Combo de Puerto Rico on the Expo's main stage.

"Puerto Rico es salsa" celebrated the narrative of cosmopolitanism and cultural particularity produced through a "glorious" racial mixture of Hispanic, African, and Indigenous roots. Both nationalists and annexationists have repeatedly turned to the lie of racial democracy to disentangle Puerto Rico's cultural identity from that of the United States.[7] This time, the myth of a racial utopia served to buttress a nation branding campaign that touted Puerto Rico's economic autonomy and cultural exceptionalism while emphasizing loyalty to the United States.[8] Salsa's Afro-Caribbean rhythms became a resource to be operationalized in the performance of Puerto Rico's cosmopolitan cultural particularity for potential European tourists. The music's Spanish-language lyrics, however, represented the legacy of Puerto Rico's Spanish (i.e., European and white) colonial past. Salsa's global flows represented Puerto Rico's openness to internationalized capital. Salsa's soundscape of Afro-diasporic musical practices and diasporic origins, however, threatened official and popular investment in whiteness and the structures that support it.

### The Political Economy of Crisis

Hernández Colón's plan to insert Puerto Rico into global flows of culture and capital drew on a long history of operationalizing discourses of cultural nationalism and racial democracy while relying on foreign investment to revitalize the economy. In the 1940s and 1950s, US economic development policies created rapid social and economic transformation that propelled investments in education, infrastructure development, and home building. The post–World War II economic development plan Manos a la Obra (Operation Bootstrap) oriented Puerto Rico's shift toward an export economy reliant on the archipelago's colonial relationship to ensure openness to foreign (mainly US) investment and the free movement of consumer goods, capital, and power. From 1950 to 1970, federal tax incentives and the promise of low-wage labor encouraged manufacturing corporations like RCA, Westinghouse, General Electric, Ford Motor Company, Coca-Cola, Goya, Sun Oil, and Union Carbide to establish subsidiaries in Puerto Rico, which became the principal supplier of clothes and textiles to the United States.[9] The transformation from an agricultural to an urban-centered manufacturing economy, however labor intensive, was unable to absorb the massive displacement of agricultural laborers.[10] The migration of almost half a million largely rural and working-class Puerto Ricans during the 1950s made possible Puerto Rico's economic transformation. Nevertheless, as Eileen Suárez Findlay has shown, official discourses "incessantly" promoted the changes in Puerto Rico's economy and geography as the only way to ensure economic and political stability while retaining the country's spiritual dignity. "Denying the [manufacturing] machine," the government insisted, "meant missing the path of progress. And lingering in History is deterioration, is backwardness, is decadence, and is a sin paid in hunger and pain." Accordingly, the government dismissed alternative economic possibilities such as land redistribution and the creation of both individually and collectively owned small-scale farming communities.[11]

The populist narrative articulated by then governor Luis Muñoz Marín proposed modernity itself as enabling futurity. He went so far as to assert that the "democratic capitalism" that shaped industrial development provided an alternative to dangerous and violent anti-colonial movements that led to sovereignty. An architect of Puerto Rico's political status as an Estado Libre Asociado (ELA, Free Associated State, or Commonwealth), initiated in 1952, he assured both his supporters and his critics that ELA provided a countermodel to anti-colonial movements that threatened rather than promoted democracy.[12] The ideology of *muñocismo* (from Muñoz Marín) was expressed through a series of foundational myths about "development, industrialization, political self-determination, global centers of economic and political power, and a national identity articulated through racial and social harmony."[13] These pillars of modernity would translate into a campaign organized around economic and social progress punctuated by a discourse of racial, class, and gender equality.

The disdain for the "narrow nationalisms" of decolonial movements aligned with US Cold War anxieties, particularly after the Cuban Revolution, and earned praise from abroad.[14] According to Muñoz Marín and the Partido Popular Democrático (PPD, Popular Democratic Party), Puerto Rico's status as a "free-associated state" under ELA was exceptional among ongoing decolonial movements. It would ensure "jobs . . . homes . . . [and] abundant consumer goods" and bring forth "a liberating age of progress, development, and modernity."[15] For Muñoz Marín, his inauguration in 1949 as Puerto Rico's first popularly elected governor "was not a step toward self-determination that would eventually lead toward political independence: it was its substitute, its replacement, and its transcendence. Colonial governmentality had reached its maturity. Democracy was the rejection of autonomy. Freedom was antithetical to the (independent) state."[16] Accordingly, the PPD lauded what it saw as the advantages of ELA: increased local autonomy, the right to democratically elect a governor, and continued US citizenship. Puerto Rico's political status under ELA would usher in a liberating age of modernity characterized by social progress and economic development without the drawbacks of political nationalism.

Tourism became central to the vision of social and economic progress under national submission, what Richard Rosa describes as the performance of "(un)freedom."[17] Puerto Rico had first turned its attention toward tourism in the 1930s to offset losses in a declining sugar industry, a process that accelerated in the 1940s as tourism and its need for the beautiful sceneries of the beaches displaced coastal communities. Muñoz Marín's inauguration as governor also saw the opening of the Caribe Hilton in San Juan. As Rosa explains, US journalists and Hollywood celebrities invited to Puerto Rico by Conrad Hilton for the opening became ambassadors in a publicity campaign designed to promote US Cold War values. Conrad Hilton presented the property, his company's first outside the continental United States, as the symbolic and concrete terrain of his desire "to promote capitalism's virtues and show its material gratifications."[18] The governor and the PPD took it as an opportunity to counter persistent images of Puerto Rico as poor, overpopulated, and racially inferior with a performance of Puerto Rican cosmopolitanism.

The spectacularization of Puerto Rico's entrance into modernity became, as Rosa argues, an expression of economic autonomy that actually increased dependence on the United States by relying on US tourists.[19] When Cuba's tourism industry deteriorated after the Cuban Revolution, the PPD capitalized on Puerto Rico's representation as a tropical and alluring, but modernized, tourist destination.[20] This narrative of Puerto Rican modernity necessitated an ongoing purposeful silence around histories of colonial violence under both the United States and Spain, the mass expulsion of Puerto Rican laborers to the United States, the expansion of the US military apparatus in Puerto Rico, and scientific experimentation. It ignored not only the persistence of racial, gendered, and sexual hierarchies and inequalities but ongoing radical organizing, such as the Black internationalist and Black Power anti-colonial politics of the Movimiento Pro Independencia (Pro-Independence Movement).[21]

While *Time* magazine celebrated "Democracy's Lab in Latin America," President John F. Kennedy looked to Puerto Rico as a model for additional US-backed modernization projects. Economic fluctuations, however, threatened to derail the country's image as a showcase for Caribbean and Latin American economic development during the Cold War.[22] Manos a la Obra failed to stimulate the growth of local businesses and instead fostered dependence on export-oriented US corporations. The social and economic gains of the 1950s and 1960s became increasingly difficult to sustain as a shift away from labor-intensive manufacturing gave way to an increasing number of companies in capital-intensive industries. By the mid-1970s, economic stagnation and decreasing labor force participation underscored the limits of US economic development. Unemployment rates reached double digits by the end of the 1970s and increased during the 1981–82 US recession, reaching 20 percent overall and as high as 38 percent in rural areas, which initiated a resurgence of migration to the United States during the 1980s.[23]

The United States' investment in sustaining Puerto Rico's economy led to increased federal subsidies. Federal tax incentives prevented complete economic collapse in the 1970s but intensified structural changes in the economy. Infrastructure developments in high-tech manufacturing, finance, trade, and commerce by US companies increasingly tied Puerto Rico's economy to periods of economic prosperity in the United States. Moreover, nonresidents earned an increasing percentage of income in the form of profits to US corporations.[24] Puerto Rico also faced increasing competition for US investment as the latter entered into multinational agreements with newly industrialized economies and "developing" nations.[25] Structural shifts in the economy, the widespread recession of the mid-1970s, and the economic downturns of the US economy in the 1980s not only revealed the limits of US economic development but also put an end to Puerto Rico's historic economic growth.[26]

By the time Governor Hernández Colón took office for a second, nonconsecutive term in 1984, the US Congress was intent on balancing the federal budget, and it threatened to eliminate federal tax incentives for US compa-

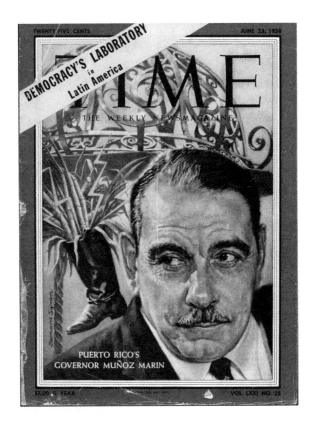

**4.1**    *Time* magazine cover for June 23, 1958

nies with operations in Puerto Rico. The governor successfully argued that eliminating these enticements would devastate Puerto Rico's efforts to attract US investment and reinvigorate the economy. In return for the continuation of the incentives, the governor agreed to use some of the resulting revenue to support the newly started Caribbean Basin Initiative.[27] The use of these funds to support the creation of manufacturing plants in other parts of the Caribbean with a complementary, or "twin," counterpart in Puerto Rico actually added to competition for US investments. As important, the approach reproduced an export-substitution model of economic development in other Caribbean countries that had led to Puerto Rico's own financial crisis.[28]

Having secured federal tax incentives for US corporations in Puerto Rico, Hernández Colón looked to foreign investment from countries other than the United States to invigorate the economy.[29] Forty years after the passage of ELA, Expo '92 provided an opportunity to showcase Puerto Rico's productive capabilities and technological advancements on a global stage. In a 1990 press release where Hernández Colón promoted the Puerto Rico exhibit, he also emphasized the prospect of decreasing dependence on trade with the United States:

> Aunque tradicionalmente hemos enfatizado el mercado norteamericano, estamos redoblando esfuerzos para lograr una penetración efectiva de nuestros productos en . . . Europa. Como medida de promoción estaremos participando prominentemente en la Feria Internacional de Sevilla en 1992, encaminada a promover la venta de productos hechos en Puerto Rico, así como la promoción turística e industrial de empresas europeas en Puerto Rico.[30]

> [Although we have traditionally emphasized the North American market, we are doubling our efforts to achieve an effective infiltration of our products in . . . Europe. As a promotional measure, we will be participating prominently in the World Expo in Seville in 1992 with the goal of promoting the sale of products made in Puerto Rico as well as the promotion of tourism and European corporations in Puerto Rico.]

The Puerto Rico pavilion at Expo '92 thus became the principal site through which the government, corporate representatives, and various public figures assigned to this project asserted the need to look beyond the US economic sphere. It became a way of shaming the United States for failing to sufficiently aid in Puerto Rico's economic recovery. Hernández Colón looked instead to its former imperial power, Spain, as an entrance into the European Union (EU) market:

> España, país integrante del mercado común europeo, ha estado presente en Puerto Rico por más de una década a través de tres de sus bancos comerciales más prestigiosos. La convivencia de esas instituciones en Puerto Rico ha sido magnífica, reflejándose en un mutuo beneficio que esperamos se solidifique aún más en el porvenir inmediato.[31]

> [Spain, a member country of the common European market, has been present in Puerto Rico for more than a decade through three of its most prestigious commercial banks. The coexistence of these institutions in Puerto Rico has been magnificent, reflecting a mutually beneficial relationship we hope to solidify even more in the immediate future.]

The complementary ambitions of Spanish and Puerto Rican officials dramatized a symbiotic relationship between the two countries. Both sought a foothold in the European economic markets through advertising campaigns designed to shed images of themselves as underdeveloped, and, in the case of Spain, nondemocratic, nations. Hernández Colón routinely described the Expo as a "unique" opportunity to shed Puerto Rico's image as a developing country mired in debates about its political status and paralyzed by partisan deadlock that thwarted attempts at economic progress. These latter concerns appear to have overstated Puerto Rico's role in the global imaginary. While most visitors to the pavilion who were interviewed for newscasts, newspapers, and other mediums commented on their own ignorance about Puerto Rico—one even mentioned *West Side Story* as her only reference—they appeared to have no sense of Puerto Rico's ongoing political and economic climate.[32]

Puerto Rico's self-representation as both familiar and exotic reproduced dominant images circulated by the United States as part of other world's fairs during the early twentieth century. The 1901 and 1904 world's fairs in Buffalo, New York, and St. Louis, Missouri, respectively, provided the United States an opportunity to legitimize imperial expansion after Spain ceded Cuba, Puerto Rico, and the Philippines in 1898. These official depictions of Puerto Rico emphasized the country's natural, agricultural, and industrial opportunities. The portrayal of Puerto Rico as culturally and racially other dominated popular representations in 1901. A narrative of Puerto Rico as increasingly "receptive to civilization and progress" in 1904 produced more benevolent (and still racist) representations of Puerto Ricans, a strategy designed to differentiate them from unassimilable Filipinos.[33] The Puerto Rico exhibit in St. Louis, for example, emphasized American "progress" in education on the archipelago.[34] This narrative of Puerto Rico's progress amid US colonialism anchored the rise of Muñoz Marín and the PPD at mid-century and became a central tenet of speeches given by Hernández Colón in relation to Expo '92. The representation of Puerto Rico as a modern state formed an important prong to the tourism goals that promoted Puerto Rico at the Expo as a place of natural beauty, adventure, and a unique cultural heritage.

Hernández Colón assigned oversight of the Expo exhibit to the Puerto Rico Industrial Development Company (PRIDCO). Established in 1942, PRIDCO was created to oversee the development of low-rent sites where US manufacturing companies could establish subsidiaries. For the Expo, the governor tasked PRIDCO with marketing Puerto Rico as a lucrative investment site for internationalized capital. He designated Alfredo Salazar, president of PRIDCO, to head a commission of eight private-sector representatives, two government officials, and the governor himself to implement plans for the Puerto Rico exhibit.[35] The commission oversaw the construction and administration of the pavilion as well as displays, programming, commercial activity (e.g., a restaurant), and staffing for the six-month duration of the Expo.[36] The appointment of Elías López Sobá, the former head of the Instituto de Cultura Puertorriqueña (ICP, Institute of Puerto Rican Culture), as commissioner general and liaison to Expo organizers in Spain underscores the symbolic role of culture in the governor's branding campaign. Indeed, culture lay at the heart of PRIDCO's campaign to brand the archipelago as a cosmopolitan yet ethnospecific culture and gateway to Latin American markets, uniquely positioned for transnational investments related to capital-intensive technologies.

But Puerto Rico was in the grips of a recession that had challenged the government's ability to meet residents' basic needs for more than a decade, which raised concerns about the costs associated with the Expo.[37] As the government of Puerto Rico authorized the construction of a $13.5 million permanent structure in Seville and an estimated $16.5 million for the building's administration and maintenance, 60 percent of Puerto Rico's residents lived in poverty.[38] An April 1992 letter to the editor of the daily newspaper *El Nuevo Día* responded to the publication of a story wherein Hernández Colón exalted the pavilion. The reader lambasted the governor for contributing to Puerto Rico's national deficit instead of its national identity.[39] In an editorial by Richard Agrait published in *El Nuevo Día* that same day, the poet, playwright, and journalist insisted that the pavilion would not support one teacher or "cure even one hospitalized child."[40] A letter to the editor of the weekly publication *Claridad* in August of the same year similarly criticized Hernández Colón's desire to develop patriotism vis-à-vis the Expo while disregarding growing social problems in Puerto Rico and persistent racial inequality. As the bureaucratic apparatus for the pavilion expanded, detractors criticized Hernández Colón for contributing to the growth of a public sector that, by the late 1980s, employed almost one-quarter of Puerto Rico's population.[41]

The April letter printed by *El Nuevo Día* also derided Hernández Colón for hypocrisy, highlighting the contradictions of attempting to consolidate a national identity at the Expo while simultaneously seeking out the political benefits of ELA.[42] This sentiment intersected with that of the Partido Nuevo Progresista (PNP, New Progressive Party), which advocates for Puerto Rico's annexation to the United States. Detractors in the PNP opposed the idea of a stand-alone Puerto Rico exhibit and criticized the governor and his political party for performing a national identity in the public sphere consistent with that of a sovereign nation-state—and doing so while touting the political and economic stability credited to ELA. The PPD replied by asserting that ELA provided the economic and political autonomy to pursue European capital without statehood. Hernández Colón went so far as to criticize the "narrow views" of PNP critics for failing to see the logic of his bold move.[43] Participation in Expo '92 as an individual exhibitor became a way to pursue a project of nation branding predicated on discourses of economic productivity that transcended submission to the United States under ELA.

Hernández Colón insisted that the Expo offered a rare chance to attract European foreign investment and tourism. The importance of Puerto Rico's tourist economy, in fact, had been at the center of a 1990 five-week series of actions by the Latina/o Caucus of New York's AIDS Coalition to Unleash Power (ACT UP/NY) and ACT UP/Puerto Rico against Hernández Colón. Activists charged the governor and his administration with minimizing the AIDS epidemic in Puerto Rico. They accused him of failing to advocate for additional federal funds that would allow residents to access life-sustaining HIV medications—one of which was produced by pharmaceutical companies *in* Puerto Rico but remained too expensive to be accessible to residents. Activists also asserted that the governor actively distanced Puerto Rico from the AIDS epidemic, concerned not with those who were sick but with the "health crisis alienating potential tourists." Indeed, as René Esparza notes, "when a local television report on AIDS aired, the official response came not from medical experts but from the tourism department."[44] Pointing to the financial investments of both the governor and the Catholic Church in Puerto Rico, ACT UP's decolonial queer praxis centered the colonial and neoliberal conditions that informed the AIDS epidemic and the governor's response to it.[45] A year later, Puerto Rican AIDS and transgender rights activist and Stonewall veteran Christina Hayworth led the first Pride parade in Puerto Rico.

### A "Nation among Nations"

As an individual exhibitor at the Seville Expo, formally separate from the United States, Puerto Rico broke with the historically antinationalist practices of Hernández Colón's political party. The PPD had promoted an ideology of cultural nationalism throughout the 1950s, 1960s, and 1970s while refusing to engage in expressions of political and economic sovereignty. Hernández Colón maintained the party line in his first term, 1973–77. But when he took office again in 1985, the PPD considered expressions of nationalism beyond the cultural sphere a political necessity. Between Hernández Colón's two terms, the pro-annexation PNP had succeeded in increasing the popularity of US statehood as a resolution of the country's political status among Puerto Rico's voters.[46] When Hernández Colón and the PPD returned to power, they sought to reconsolidate its pro-ELA political position by emphasizing Puerto Rico's cultural, political, and economic autonomy amid the colonial context. The decisions to make Spanish the official language of Puerto Rico and to participate as an independent exhibitor in the 1992 Universal Expo as a "nation among nations" asserted a political will that ran counter to the national submission to the United States codified through ELA.

Pavilion organizers responded to public and political criticism by embarking on a campaign designed to increase public awareness of the Expo's benefits. A static exhibit at the shopping mall Plaza las Américas near San Juan hoped to increase support of the government's investment in the project. Plaza, built on the former site of a sugarcane estate, was the first indoor mall in Puerto Rico and the symbol par excellence of the country's social and economic progress.[47] The largest indoor mall in the Caribbean, Plaza opened in 1968 with seventy-two retailers, including the first JCPenney outside the fifty US states and Washington, DC. A symbol of Puerto Rico's entrance into modernity, Plaza was also anchored by Puerto Rican–owned retailers González Padín and Velasco, and a multilevel Sears was added during the mall's renovation in 1979.[48] By 1992, the shopping mall had developed into a space that, already a site for investment and speculation for largely North American–owned businesses like Sears and JCPenney, could motivate investment in the nation itself.[49]

The presentation at Plaza offered those who went to the mall the opportunity to interact with a narrative that set local and global consumer culture as a locus for national identity. Shopping malls are "predicated on notions of openness and consumer citizenship that demand special consideration insofar as they directly interpellate middling groups as participants in global consumer culture and modernity."[50] Plaza's location in Hato Rey puts it at the center of Puerto Rico's most densely populated area and the intersection of the country's two main highways, providing easy access from various sectors, including the San Juan financial district. The mall's central location, popularity, and accessibility provided an opportunity for exhibit organizers to reach a broad spectrum of the public despite limiting the presentation to the metropolitan area that surrounds San Juan. As a site for various types of activities other than consumption, and one that brought an economically diverse cross section of residents to the location, the mall provided an ideal opportunity for the government to receive feedback.[51]

Visitors' comments revealed mixed reactions. Some exalted the Puerto Rico pavilion as a "marvelous idea" that encouraged national pride in Puerto Rico's cultural heritage. Others expressed dismay at "a waste of money" that should have been directed to addressing homelessness, health care, and the overall well-being of the Puerto Rican people. Underscoring the role of shopping malls as spaces "where equity and citizenship rights are consistently contested," the presentation's signature book recorded a dialogue among the vastly differing viewpoints.[52] For example, one of the lengthier comments read:

> Como vamos a enseñar una fachada bella cuando la casa está revuelta. Este gobierno vive de fantasías. Este pabellón en contra de muchos, se hizo a la cañona. He trabajado en el gobierno y conozco la fantasía, la falta de realidad de estos ejecutivos. Todo lo hacen por encimita, nada en profundidad. Debo felicitar a los publicistas que son malabaristas de la realidad puertorriqueña.[53]

> [How are we going to show a beautiful facade when the house is a mess. This government lives off fantasies. Against the will of many, this pavilion was shoved down our throats. I have worked in the government and recognize the fantasy, these executives' lack of reality. Everything is superficial, nothing is well developed. I should congratulate the publicists, experts at manipulation who use dizzying spectacles to obscure Puerto Rican reality.]

Another visitor responded to this statement by writing directly below it, "Así pensaban los que objetaban que la reina Isabel financiara 'la locura' de Cristobal Colón" (Those who objected to "the madness" of Queen Isabel financing Christopher Columbus thought the same thing).[54] The implication was that the presentation was a positive sign of modernization and that critics were akin to those who would have cautioned the Spanish Crown against investing in a venture that ultimately made its empire possible. Public support remained thin, however.

The governor responded to continued criticism by framing Puerto Rico's participation in Expo '92 within the neoliberal rhetoric of fiscal responsibility.[55] The world's fair, he explained, offered an unparalleled opportunity to showcase Puerto Rico's productive capabilities to an anticipated two million visitors, and it would be far more expensive to execute an equivalent campaign without the exposure provided by the Expo.[56] Hernández Colón assured critics that Spanish developers would purchase the pavilion at the conclusion of the Expo, producing significant direct return on investment. This claim was based on Spain's plans to use the Expo to jumpstart development on Cartuja.[57]

The governor's desire to attract internationalized capital motivated public policy designed to anticipate an increase in foreign investments after Expo '92. Two years after Hernández Colón accepted the invitation to the world's fair, he passed a law to regulate the "organization, incorporation, operation, and regulation" of multinational banking institutions with the express purpose of transforming Puerto Rico into a center for global finance.[58] The desire to establish European subsidiaries in Puerto Rico echoed the financial trajectory of the 1950s that failed to develop a local economy and led to the financial crisis in Puerto Rico. According to Hernández Colón, however, European investors recruited at Expo '92 would position Puerto Rico as a crossroads for European capital and Latin American and Caribbean development. The governor pointed to the current increase in exports to Europe and the success of European subsidiaries already in Puerto Rico as evidence of the potential economic growth.[59] He touted the success of three of Spain's most prestigious banks with subsidiaries in Puerto Rico, which "magnificent[ly]" "reflect[ed] a mutually beneficial relationship we hope to solidify even more in the immediate future."[60] But Banco Santander's expansion largely resulted from acquiring Puerto Rican financial institutions. These acquisition increased foreign ownership of local institutions rather than bolstering the local economy. Hernández Colón nonetheless looked to banking as a lucrative avenue for a revenue stream not dependent on the United States.[61]

### La noble hidalguía de la madre España

At home and in Spain, Hernández Colón promoted the belief that Expo '92 would serve as the site of a symbolic reunion between Spain and Puerto Rico, one that would prove as "transcendental" as Columbus's arrival in the New World.[62] During an official visit to Spain in May 1988, he stressed the cultural affinities between Puerto Rico and the so-called *madre patria* (mother country) by emphasizing colonialism's Hispanophile legacy. The daily Spanish newspaper *ABC Sevilla* published the talk he gave in Madrid, titled "La Españolidad de Puerto Rico" (Puerto Rico's Spanishness). In it, the governor stated that Indigenous cultures in Puerto Rico had been "practically erased from the population and the Africans who followed were assimilated almost completely by the dominant [Spanish] culture." Therefore, "whatever may be the color of our skin . . . our culture . . . is essentially Spanish."[63] The same article appeared a month later in *El Nuevo Día*. Facing accusations of racism, Hernández Colón responded by explaining that his comments had been misunderstood. He was simply referring to "the racial integration of our people around its Hispanic roots."[64]

To quell criticism, the PPD used one of its candidates for a local office to propose that the Palace of Fine Arts be renamed after Afro–Puerto Rican musician Rafael Cortijo, one of Puerto Rico's most celebrated artists, whose success in the 1950s reintroduced Afro–Puerto Rican popular musical practices into the national imaginary. As Juan Flores explains in his essay about reactions to the proposal, objections came fast and furious from across the political and social order, particularly from those who positioned themselves as arbiters of culture. Critics complained about the cost of the endeavor and described financial support for popular music as the purview of private businesses. Criticism coalesced around the presumably ridiculous idea of naming a space for fine arts after a musician who played popular music, and the need to preserve spaces for high culture. Cortijo's "vulgar" music, one well-known folklorist contended, did not uplift Black Puerto Ricans; it degraded them. A constitutional lawyer charged that Cortijo's drug use set a bad example for society. Although the debate lasted less than a week and never reached the House floor, the message was clear. As Flores states, it remained unimaginable for the arbiters of culture to open the national patrimony to an unlettered, untutored Black musician of Afro–Puerto Rican popular culture and recognize the Afro-diasporic roots of Puerto Rican national culture.[65] Four years later, the backlash against "Puerto Rico es salsa" would once again bring to the fore racialized arguments about the contours of Puerto Rican national identity expressed through attitudes about Afro-diasporic popular music.

Popular and official disdain for salsa and its right to be considered part of Puerto Rico's cultural patrimony converged in the press around the Puerto Rico pavilion at Expo '92. Various critics initially misunderstood the January 1992 announcement of the concert "Puerto Rico es salsa" and assumed that the pavilion would host no other music but salsa during the six months of the Expo. Director of entertainment Jean Pierre Santoni clarified that various folkloric musical traditions—including tríos (trios), cuartetos (quartets), *conjuntos* (ensembles), and *pleneros* (plena musicians)—would perform on the pavilion's two stages in the late afternoons and early to mid-evenings. Salsa would, however, dominate. Pavilion director Eira Piñeiro reassured critics that financial sponsorships were being sought for other types of music groups as well, but Santoni admitted that most entertainment sponsors only wanted to underwrite salsa.[66] The response of the pavilion oversight committee to the controversy highlighted the nexus of culture and capital for those who decried "Puerto Rico es salsa." Implicitly acknowledging the accusation that they were capitulating to Spanish commercial interests, they defended the decision to host the concert by pointing to the music's popularity in Europe and its importance as a marketing tool for the pavilion.

Salsa's popularity had increased in Puerto Rico during the mid to late 1970s, during which self-proclaimed *cocolos* identified the music as part of the country's autochthonous cultural heritage. The term, previously a pejorative used to refer generally to Afro-Caribbean communities in Puerto Rico, became resemanticized to signify the racialized and class contours of what were largely Black, working-class, and poor fans of salsa.[67] The schism between official and popular narratives of Puerto Ricanness and salsa's development as an urban, Black diasporic musical form became increasingly projected onto the listening practices of cocolos by the 1980s. Characterized by "historically specific ideological processes that fostered a variety of racial, political, cultural and social meanings," ideologies about Puerto Rico's racial identity were expressed through musical tastes.[68] Cocolos were distinguished from their "light-skinned" or white middle- and upper-class counterparts, *rockeros*, who favored rock and heavy metal.

Interviews with both groups for Ana García's documentary *Cocolos y rockeros* (1992) show that largely racialized, gendered, and class attitudes about musical "taste" were coded in discussions of "cultural," and therefore "national," identity. Rockeros often identified salsa fans as part of a jobless "lower class," racialized as Black by both public officials and the media, that formed part of an extralegal economy and participated in illicit activities. Illustrating the persistence of these attitudes during the late 1980s and early 1990s, an organizer for an ICP-backed festival refused to include salsa in order to avoid "'disarray in a family type setting, because it [salsa] attracts cocolos that have no respect for anything' and would only lead to disarray, disorder, and lack of control."[69] The racialized symbolic meanings of salsa were also intertwined with broader social tendencies. Sensationalist media and government policy targeted racially and economically marginalized urban poor neighborhoods, particularly public housing developments (*caseríos*), imagined as sites of violence and criminal activity in need of police surveillance. Amid the criminalization of largely Black populations in the name of protecting "decent" Puerto Ricans, the dissonance between cocolos and rockeros became a stand-in for conversations about race and class mediated through salsa and other forms of Black expressive culture.[70]

The attitudes about salsa began to shift in the mid to late 1980s as the music became increasingly separated from Black and diasporic Puerto Rican communities. Politicians, for example, recognized the political value of incorporating salsa jingles into their campaign ads.[71] In a late 1980s interview conducted by a local news station at a salsa concert in Puerto Rico, Hernández Colón told the reporter that "la salsa viene del corazón del pueblo de Puerto Rico, del alma de Puerto Rico. Y es una expresión propia, nuestra, *universal*, que nos ha llevao a todas partes del mundo" (salsa comes from the heart of the Puerto Rican people, from the soul of Puerto Rico. And it is an expression of us, ours, *universal*, that has taken us to every part of the world).[72] When asked about rock, the governor deftly maneuvered his own apparent desire to identify with salsa by emphasizing that many in Puerto Rico enjoyed rock. He went on to note, however, that "el rock es un fenómeno que nos llega de afuera . . . que es bueno también, pero que no es una expresión propia de lo que sale del corazón de este pueblo" (rock is a phenomenon that comes from outside [the island]. . . . It's also good, but it's not our expression of what's in the heart of the people). The governor repeated his comments almost verbatim at the inauguration of the Plaza de los Salseros in Santurce, Puerto Rico, in 1988. The ICP, on the other hand, continued to exclude salsa from official programming. The ICP had been founded in the 1950s to preserve and disseminate an "authentic" Puerto Rican popular culture devoid of its relationship to marronage and resistance. Programming centered on either "universal" high culture or folkloric practices that reinforced narratives of a utopian Hispanophile past.[73] The general public included salsa in their familial and community-based activities, including local festivals with corporate sponsors with no such reticence as to what constituted "authentic" or "foreign" cultural influences.[74]

The intermingling of musical rhythms within salsa, including folkloric musical traditions like plena (and, of course, Spanish lyrics), facilitated the music's appropriation. Just three months before the governor's 1988 visit to

Spain during which the governor reduced Puerto Rico's Black communities and cultural practices to an "adscription," Hernández Colón allotted $500,000 for the creation of a plaza in the Villa Palmera neighborhood of San Juan to honor some of salsa's greatest artists. In his announcement, the governor extolled salsa as part of Puerto Rico's cultural heritage, as something "con lo que todos nacemos y que ha traído reconocimiento internacional a Puerto Rico" (with which we are all born and that has brought international recognition to Puerto Rico). Salsa, Hernández Colón added, "ha estado, está y estará presente siempre en la médula de nuestra puertorriqueñidad" (has been, is, and always will be present in the marrow of our Puerto Ricanness).[75] That October, the governor dedicated La Placita de los Salseros, telling the assembled crowd, "Ésta es una ocasión memorable para nosotros los preocupados por la vigencia de nuestra cultura puertorriqueña, a la que pertenece la música popular en sus diferentes manifestaciones pasadas y presentes" (This is a memorable occasion for those of us concerned with the validity of our Puerto Rican culture, to which various manifestations of popular music of the past and present belong). Salsa, he added, "sang to the dreams and aspirations of the Puerto Rican people." Lauding the music as the birthright of every Puerto Rican, he celebrated salsa as an emblem of Puerto Rico's racial democracy, a product of a "glorious" mestizaje (racial mixture) that led to the "ancestral chorus" created by salsa musicians.[76]

Despite the reluctance of the ICP, salsa's representation as a "Puerto Rican" phenomenon bolstered a collective national identity aligned with insular narratives of Puerto Rican national belonging. It illuminates what sociologist Mimi Sheller describes as a universal process of creolization in which "*any* encounter of mixing between dislocated cultures" can creolize anyone, a deterritorialization intensified by processes of globalization.[77] The shifting attitudes toward salsa align with the PPD's hope of undermining annexationist discourses that had predominated under the PNP in the earlier part of the decade. Salsa's increasing appeal was also intertwined with a desire to celebrate the music in the face of merengue's rising popularity in Puerto Rico. Criticized as an "inferior" musical form, merengue faced similar racialized concerns about its increasing appeal while Dominicans faced discrimination in Puerto Rico.[78]

Public debate about the selection of appropriate music for the Puerto Rico exhibit at Expo '92 stood in for broader debates about national identity, race, and diaspora during a period when official narratives of Puerto Ricanness as a "glorious" mixture of Spanish, African, and Indigenous roots that resulted in a racial democracy were becoming increasingly destabilized. The emergence of rap in Puerto Rico during the 1980s and its emphasis on racial, class, and generational identities provides one of the most significant examples of counternarratives that threatened the hold of national culture.[79] Puerto Ricans in New York played an integral role in Hip Hop's emergence and development in the 1970s as rappers, emcees, graffiti artists, b-boys, and b-girls. Its origins within Black communities within the United States, however, renders rap as external to dominant narratives of what constitutes Puerto Ricanness.[80] Identified in Puerto Rico as the music of Black, poor, and urban communities already considered threats to the state, rap became conflated with a panic over juvenile delinquency and immorality overtaking socially and economically marginalized young people. Insofar as race and social class are intricately bound in Puerto Rico, the state demonization of rap and the underground youth culture in which it flourished primarily targeted poor Black communities already seen as the main perpetrators of crime and social disorder.[81] The "Mano Dura Contra el Crimen" (Iron Fist against Crime) neoliberal policing policies of the early 1990s targeted the very communities from which rap's artists and audiences came, an example of how neoliberal policies intensify racial and class difference by increasingly criminalizing vulnerable communities.[82] Rap questioned racial and class inequality, connecting social and economic development to repressive policing of poor urban communities, especially public housing residents.[83]

Even as attitudes about salsa began to shift and anti-Black attitudes were increasingly mapped onto rap, salsa's privileged place as a signifier of Puerto Ricanness at the Expo provoked an uproar. Letters to the editor and news reports in *El Nuevo Día* almost exclusively derided the decision to highlight salsa. These rebukes often paralleled the backlash against the possibility of renaming the Palace of Fine Arts after Cortijo. Critics rejected salsa as an appropriate representation of Puerto Rico's vast cultural heritage. An op-ed that appeared in *El Nuevo Día* from a reader in Río Piedras questioned the music's decency. The reader's letter asked rhetorically, "¿Es ésa la cultura que pretendían defender a través del referéndum?" (Is that the culture that the referendum purportedly sought to defend?).[84] This was a reference to a referendum on the status of Puerto Rico concluded two months earlier, which had affirmed the right to protect "nuestra cultura, idioma e identidad propia" (our culture, language, and identity), regardless of Puerto Rico's relationship to the United States.[85] The letter went on to criticize the politicians heading each of the Committees on Culture in the Puerto Rico Senate and House of Representatives, who "remained mute" on the matter rather than publicly opposing the concert.[86] Another letter to the editor that ran in *El Nuevo Día* rejected salsa in favor of a "more representative" cultural icon such as the "elegant" opera singer Margarita Alberty, who would not "shame" Puerto Rico, presumably by being Black, poor, or working class. The debate illuminates how, as Raquel Rivera states, when it comes to cultural nationalism, "what looks like a 'virtue' to one person can appear as a 'vice' to another."[87]

The public outcry against salsa's official use at the Puerto Rico pavilion did not openly acknowledge contempt for the music and its fans but rather resorted to a variety of rhetorical strategies to insist that organizers represent the complexity of Puerto Rico's cultural patrimony. Patronizing disclaimers assured the public that "no es que haya nada malo con la salsa" (it's not that there's anything wrong with salsa) but rather the exhibit should seek "balance" among the musical traditions of "today and yesterday" to provide a more accurate representation of Puerto Rico's multifaceted cultural spectrum.[88] After all, one critic reminded the public, "Puerto Rico es mucho muchísimo más" (Puerto Rico is much, much more) than salsa.[89] It would make as much sense, a letter to the editor of *El Nuevo Día* argued, to claim that "Puerto Rico is tango," given the music's popularity in Puerto Rico.[90]

Critiques of salsa's commercial nature rested on the opposition between market and culture at the heart of populist narratives of the 1950s. Tony D'Astro, founder of the National Folkloric Ballet of Puerto Rico, argued that salsa was too commercial to convey Puerto Rican culture. He objected to the commercialization of Puerto Rico proposed by the concert, comparing it to the way tourism initiatives capitalized on hegemonic tropicalizations of the Caribbean. Appearing in both *El Nuevo Día* and *Claridad*, his article equated the promotion of salsa to commercials run in the United States by the Puerto Rico Tourism Company, "where sun bathers provocatively promote Puerto Rico as a paradise of tropical sex."[91] D'Astro's criticism, however, constitutes salsa itself as antithetical to a Puerto Rican essence. He was one of several critics who questioned the right of pavilion organizers to arbitrate Puerto Rican culture. If representatives of such institutions as the government's Institute for Puerto Rican Culture, the Puerto Rican Athenaeum (a guardian of Puerto Rican music, letters, and arts founded in 1876), and the Fine Arts Center had been involved in the decision to host "Puerto Rico es salsa," he wrote, the pavilion would have provided an expansive view of Puerto Rico's broad cultural opus rather than a tropicalized tourist gaze produced through salsa.

Juan Albors, then president of the board of directors for the Corporación de las Artes Musicales (Corporation for the Musical Arts), explained that salsa was nothing more than a passing fad in Europe and called on the planners of the Puerto Rico exhibit to choose a "universal" musical expression more suitable for a world's fair. Moreover, salsa's broad popular appeal guaranteed its global diffusion. The government should support musical genres in greater need of assistance.[92] In February, shortly after the announcement of "Puerto Rico es salsa," Albors pointed out that Puerto Rico's Symphonic Orchestra remained unable to raise the $500,000 necessary to send eighty-five musicians to Seville to perform. Maestro Odón Alonso, who had recently resigned as conductor of the Symphonic Orchestra, told *El Nuevo Día* in March, "Popular music is easy to please. We do not need to help salsa, which helps itself. The music of the spirit is the one that needs help. Helping the righteous, you find more of the righteous."[93] The racially coded language bolstered the affective value of the Symphonic Orchestra as essential to Puerto Rico's cultural identity.[94]

Arguments about the commercial viability of salsa also led critics to erroneous assumptions about the remuneration offered to salsa musicians invited to perform. In fact, the honorariums offered to salsa performers by Puerto Rico exhibit organizers reflected similar attitudes to those espoused by Albors and Odón Alonso. In an interview with *Claridad*, bandleader and vocalist Gilberto Santa Rosa explained that he declined to perform at the Expo because the honorarium amounted to a salary of approximately $60 to $70 per day for each of his sixteen musicians.[95] Like Santa Rosa, vocalist and Fania All-Star Cheo Feliciano rejected an invitation to perform twenty-one shows in seven days for a mere $7,000.[96] Pavilion organizers appeared dismissive of Santa Rosa and Feliciano. Piñeiro condemned Feliciano publicly, criticizing him for being unwilling to make a financial sacrifice. Santoni, for his part, dismissed criticism by framing performances at the Expo as advertising campaigns that would reap financial rewards later.[97] He emphasized the commercial possibilities of performing at the Expo for groups such as El Gran Combo, who would experience increased popularity in Spain's emerging market and benefit from the opportunity to play before record executives and producers from both Andalucía and the rest of Spain.[98]

Salsa's detractors participated in a long tradition of objecting to commercially successful music as unable to represent *el pueblo* (the people), reproducing a presumed opposition between market and culture even as fans increasingly identified salsa as an autochthonous cultural expression. Among critics, "Puerto Rico es salsa" reanimated the late nineteenth-century trope of *la gran familia puertorriqueña* (the grand Puerto Rican

family). This imagined gran familia puertorriqueña privileges a Hispanophile (white) Catholic (heteronormative and patriarchal) subject reproduced
through a nuclear and extended family based on blood and marital ties.
Black Puerto Ricans and other gendered and sexual marginalized groups
remained outside the boundaries of national (be)longing.[99] As anthropologist Hilda Lloréns Torres has demonstrated, the representational economy of
la gran familia puertorriqueña persisted throughout the twentieth century
despite its transformations over time. In the 1924 elections, the hacendados,
the bourgeoise, and the professional class adopted "La Borinqueña" (1870)
as the unofficial hymn of Puerto Rico. Based on the poem by the same name
by Lola Rodríguez de Tió, it became their rallying cry against the working
class and the Socialist Party. During the 1930s, as artists in Puerto Rico began
to include Black Puerto Ricans in their paintings, paternalist discourses reanimated representations of a Puerto Rican essence that opposed itself to a
US identity and its presumed superficiality.[100]

*Insularismo*, by Antonio Pedreira, emerged as the classic text within
the paternalist canon, conceptualizing Puerto Rico as ill and infantilized
by colonialism. Puerto Rico, overrun by a "túpida cantidad de afemina-
dos" (overflowing number of effeminates), is conceived as a feminized and
impotent state threatened by racial hybridity.[101] Informed by the Chicago
School sociologists who explained social disorganization as a product of
racial mixing and its production of an indeterminate subject, Pedreira's
discourse of racial hybridity reads as "a battle between racial strands" that
would determine Puerto Rico's future.[102] Pedreira's call for Puerto Rico to
realize its virile "manhood" and, in so doing, sovereignty reverberates in
official policies of the late 1940s and 1950s.

Already in the late 1940s, as Muñoz Marín advocated for economic
and political autonomy under US colonialism rather than sovereignty, he
expressed his desire for Puerto Rico's self-actualization through a racialized paternalist discourse. Puerto Ricans, he maintained, deserved to be
treated not as "children under the tutelage and protection" of the United
States but as men with the rights and dignity afforded with manhood.[103]
Like Pedreira, Muñoz Marín recast Puerto Rico's political maturation in
terms of normative, racially unmarked (white) manhood. Unlike Pedreira,
he characterized this process as antithetical to sovereignty. As Suárez Findlay
explains, Muñoz Marín and the PPD "continually sought . . . to recast the US-
Puerto Rican relationship as familial rather than colonial. The more powerful
of the two partners would serve as a father, generously dispensing resources
to his loving son, now a fully grown man with goals and plans of his own.

The son's plans, however, were always formed in consultation with his father. Each man would recognize both the enduring ties between them and the right of the other to masculine honor and respect."[104] The right to maintain a distinct Puerto Rican "spirituality" within this relationship projected nationalism onto the realm of the cultural. The intellectual elite enthusiastically collaborated, reinvigorating nineteenth-century discourses to contrast a national cultural identity predicated on Puerto Rico's Hispanic European and Catholic past with that of an Anglo and Protestant United States.[105]

Opposition to salsa's privileged role at the Puerto Rico pavilion reanimated modernist discourses of nationhood that relied on a cultural distinction from the United States. Rafael Aponte Ledee, one of Puerto Rico's foremost classical musicians and composers, was among those who dismissed salsa as a "commercial product that began in New York." In an article published by *El Nuevo Día* on February 22, 1992, titled "Desafinada la selección musical del pabellón Boricua en Sevilla" (The musical selection for the Seville exhibit is out of tune), Ledee also pointed to the prominence of Celia Cruz, who was Cuban and presumably precluded the music's Puerto Ricanness. The music's emergence among diasporic Puerto Ricans also rendered salsa ineligible for inclusion in Puerto Rico's cultural patrimony. Salsa represented a colonial import from the United States vis-à-vis New York and not an autochthonous form of expressive culture; attempts to "pretend" that salsa embodied Puerto Ricanness were, he noted, nothing more than exaggerated attempts to "cater to European markets" where the music remained enormously popular.[106]

The exception taken to salsa's emergence outside the territorial boundaries of Puerto Rico reveals the degree to which official, popular, and literary perceptions of Puerto Rican diasporicity remained embedded within the national imaginary. The novel *La mirada* (The gaze, 1975), by Puerto Rican author René Marqués, identifies homosexuality with colonialism and, by extension, the collective condition of Puerto Ricans that prevents the infantilized country from reaching manhood.[107] Within this paternalist discourse that resonates with that of Pedreira in *Insularismo*, migration to the United States is conceived as a (feminine) betrayal of Puerto Rico and its national project for independence. With regard to the United States, where the colonial status and racialized subjectivity of Puerto Ricans prevent access to paternal power, the nation is narrated through the emasculation of the Puerto Rican male subject within the metropolis.

A cartoon in *El Vocero* (The spokesperson) by satirical cartoonist Tomás Yépez, titled "Romería incompleta" (Incomplete pilgrimage), captured the racialized and class dimensions of the debate surrounding "Puerto Rico es salsa" in ways that the media skirted. The cartoon features a woman wearing a high-collared, floor-length dress with leg-o'-mutton sleeves, a fitted bodice, and a bustle silhouette that draws the viewer to identify her with the Spanish colonial period. Coiffed, but without a hat or stole, she holds a Spanish fan in her left hand while a purse dangles from her right wrist. Her elegance is reinforced as she stands tall beside a short, stout jíbaro identified by the *pava* (straw hat) and guiro, an instrument believed to have originated with the archipelago's Indigenous inhabitants. The jíbaro's white-buttoned shirt, tied at the front, exposes a large stomach neatly tucked inside his rolled-up pants, signaling his socially and economically humble background. The cartoon draws on the image of the jíbaro consolidated in early twentieth-century visual culture wherein the Puerto Rican peasant stands as the symbolic container of Puerto Rico's cultural dissonance with the United States. While the jíbaro stands in for authentic musical traditions, the woman beside him symbolizes the universality of European and high culture.

The cartoon includes a tent that stands in for the pavilion and, inside it, a band of racially ambiguous curly-haired men play their instruments below the word "SALSA" as musical notes float above their heads. A sign outside the pavilion reads, "No pase. Sólo cocolos" (No admittance. Cocolos only). Outside the exhibit, the woman and jíbaro stand open-mouthed with a concerned look on their faces as they watch the musicians play. Their pilgrimage to Spain and the Expo incomplete without entering the pavilion, they wonder aloud whether they will be admitted. The anxiety of the couple in the cartoon is shared by Coquiyé, the *coquí* (arboreal frog) character created by Yépez that often accompanies his satirical drawings. Coquiyé appears in the lower left corner of the drawing and asks, "¿Y para mí no habrá un huequito allí?" (What about me? Will there be a little bit of space over there?). Native to Puerto Rico, the coquí is the quintessential symbol of Puerto Rican culture and authenticity. Two inches long and weighing about four ounces, with a mating call that belies its small size, the coquí and its song are presumably excluded, much like the danza and música típica—though both were informed by Afro-Caribbean musical practices. The cartoon nevertheless pits salsa against the presumably Hispanophile classical traditions of danza (in the form of the woman) and música típica (in the form of the jíbaro). Both figures rebuke salsa's Afro-diasporic musical practices, commercial origins, and global success—even as actual jíbaros were loathed, and "their music was never truly exalted and it was not institutionalized like the literate musical forms that became the backbone of musical education" in official cultural programs of the sort created through Operation Serenity.[108] If Puerto Rico's agricultural past, symbolized by the countryside and its presumed Hispanic (white) jíbaro, contains the cultural and spiritual nexus of el pueblo, salsa's urban, diasporic, and Black aesthetics present its opposite.

Héctor Rodríguez, a columnist for the weekly pro-independence newspaper *Claridad*, was one of the few in the press who supported "Puerto Rico es salsa" and came to the pavilion managers' defense. In a column that ran less than two weeks before Puerto Rico's national day at the Expo, he sidestepped concerns about whether salsa formed part of the cultural patrimony. What mattered, he insisted, was "que los pueblos se identifican con la salsa y que ésta adquiere una importancia para el ciudadano común que la convierte en su música" (that the people identify with salsa and that it acquires importance for the common citizen who transforms it into their music). He continued:

> ¿Qué es la salsa? La salsa la podemos definir como música de origen afrocubano que al pasar por el crisol de Nueva York adquiere armonías de jazz con toques brasileros, colombianos, venezolanos, panameños y del calypso del Caribe. La aportación de Puerto Rico a la salsa entre otras cosas, está en la forma de frasear los cantantes basados en una fuerte influencia de la bomba y la plena y en algunos casos en la música campesina. Esta aportación boricua lleva la salsa a su madurez musical.[109]

> [What is salsa? We can define salsa as an Afro-Cuban musical genre that, once it passes through the melting pot of New York, acquires jazz harmonies with a touch of Brazilian, Colombian, Venezuelan, Panamanian, and Caribbean calypso. Puerto Rico's contribution to salsa, among other things, is in the way of singing that is based on a strong influence of bomba, plena, and in some cases mountain music. This Boricua contribution brings salsa to its musical maturity.]

The essay highlighted the role of Puerto Rican musicians and salsa pioneers Willie Colón, Ismael Rivera, and El Gran Combo, the latter of which was formed in Puerto Rico during the 1950s, in salsa's development. Why, he asked, if people the world over identified Puerto Rico with not just salsa but the best of salsa, would Puerto Ricans attempt to deny its significance? The Symphonic Orchestra, on the other hand, failed to represent Puerto

Rican music and musicians because it did not typically play music by Puerto Rican composers.[110]

Gilberto Santa Rosa and Cheo Feliciano expressed similar sentiments in an interview with *Claridad*. Santa Rosa described Puerto Rico as the salsa music "capital."[111] Feliciano—one of the original members of the Fania All-Stars ensemble and a performer at the concert sponsored by Spanish Expo organizers to open the world's fair—explained it this way to an *El Nuevo Día* reporter:

> La salsa es el vehículo, el instrumento mundial que nos conecta, como gente con las demás gentes del mundo. Nos da la oportunidad de conocerlos. . . . Aunque Puerto Rico tiene otros géneros que no son salsa, es la salsa la que nos ha abierto las puertas a nivel mundial.[112]

> [Salsa is the vehicle; it is the worldwide instrument that connects us, as a people, with the rest of the world. It gives us the opportunity to know them. . . . Although Puerto Rico has other genres that are not salsa, it is salsa that has opened doors globally.]

The only voice that explicitly named the pathologization of Black Puerto Ricans as the root of opposition to salsa was that of salsa artist Alex D'Castro, who performed in Cartuja. He described the opposition to salsa as being born from "un profundo prejuicio hacia la salsa y los salseros" (a deep prejudice against salsa, salsa artists, and salsa fans) related to "visiones clasistas y racistas que consideran a los salseros 'tecatos'" (classist and racist visions that consider salsa fans drug addicts).[113] His criticism of elitist and racist attitudes that criminalized salsa fans and undergirded the controversy surrounding the pavilion drew attention to the racially coded language.

The identification of salsa with New York's Puerto Rican communities, like its association with poor and working-class Black Puerto Ricans on the archipelago, lay beneath overarching concern about popular versus high culture. The same issue of *Claridad* that questioned the terms of the debate included another article about the continued high level of poverty and unemployment among Puerto Ricans in the United States. The article describes the diaspora as a "reluctant spectator" rather than a participant in the US economy. The rejection of salsa in favor of a "more representative" culture and cultural icons exposes the racialized and class dimension of a desire to privilege "elegant" world-renowned artists who would not "shame" Puerto Rico. Elite or "high" culture remained within the sphere of authenticity through claims to universality. Ironically, salsa formed the soundscape for a nation branding campaign that Hernández Colón hoped would do away with any association between Puerto Rico and *West Side Story*.

Empirically, the music attracted Expo visitors to the pavilion. One of the guides recalled that visitors expressed a pleasant surprise at the quantity and variety of Puerto Rican exports, but "todo el mundo pregunta cuando tocan las orquestas de salsa" (everybody asks when the salsa bands play).[114] The answer was, essentially, every night. Salsa became the musical component that provided continuity among the various elements of the nation branding campaign spectacularized at the exhibit.[115] According to a news article in *El Nuevo Día*, the pavilion was one of the most visited over the six-month duration of Expo '92. Visitors and Expo workers alike congregated there in the evenings, wanting to dance salsa. Those who visited the pavilion for the musical performances in the evening may or may not have represented a significant swath of the demographic that Hernández Colón sought to attract as investors. At the very least, however, they were potential tourists and may have impressed potential investors.

### Designing the Puerto Rico Pavilion

The architecture of the Puerto Rico pavilion aligned the symbolic role of the exhibit with its functional capacity as a stage for the governor's promotional campaign, which illuminates the role of architecture in embodying not only the imagined national culture but also the national brand.[116] The lead architect of Puerto Rico's pavilion, Segundo Cardona, sought to fulfill both the symbolic and programmatic functions of the pavilion. The final design consisted of three purposefully disparate structures that each represented a phase in the narrative of Puerto Rico's transformation over time from a Spanish colony to a nation at the forefront of a global economy. The largest section invoked a Spanish colonial past with materials that resonated with the lines of the Spanish-era fort El Morro in Viejo San Juan and the general military architecture of that colonial period.[117]

The open-air middle structure represented a break with Puerto Rico's past as an insular, underdeveloped nation and its "turn toward modern political and economic models and toward modernity itself" under ELA.[118] Functioning as the entrance to the pavilion, the diaphanous middle structure celebrated the period of Puerto Rico's economic growth during the 1950s and 1960s, particularly the openness to external investment that US development policies favored. The use of clean lines and white texture purposefully recalled

**4.2**   Puerto Rico pavilion at the 1992 Universal Expo in Seville, Spain
(Archivo Histórico Fundación Rafael Hernández Colón)

how Puerto Rico's government used architecture, as seen in the design of the University of Puerto Rico, as an instrument of modernity in the 1960s.[119] The open corridor served as a viewing platform for the third and final section of the pavilion. Cardona used a cylindrical structure to represent contemporary Puerto Rico "as a highly developed society" and future Puerto Rico "as a link between the hemispheres." The architect chose modular copper panels and green etched glass to communicate Puerto Rico's position at the cutting edge of technological and manufacturing advances. This cylinder stood alongside "an undulating beach-like" plaza that represented Puerto Rico's beaches and tropical geography.[120] Two stages provided the setting for live performances and recorded music, including salsa.

Once at the pavilion, visitors from around the world could peruse exhibits about Puerto Rico's economic development and culture, attend various cultural events, and eat at a restaurant featuring Puerto Rican food. Visitors could also watch a film that highlighted Puerto Rico as an ideal tourist destination and emphasized the scientific, technological, and financial infrastructure for potential investors. By the early 1990s, as Arlene Dávila demonstrates, corporate interests were treated "not as forces contrary to the development of ideas of cultural distinctiveness, but rather as added players elaborating conceptions of Puerto Ricanness."[121] Presentations by corporate representatives reinforced Puerto Rico's openness to foreign investment while college students and recent graduates fluent in English, French, or Italian and se-lected from various universities in Puerto Rico, educated visitors to the pavilion about Puerto Rican history, economy, and culture.

A theater inside the pavilion ran the short film *Puerto Rico* at regular in-tervals. The fifteen-minute travelogue opens with scenes of lush landscapes and Indigenous carvings that signify pre-Hispanic origins.[122] It then trans-ports the viewer to the "Age of Discovery," the theme of Expo '92, initiated in the film by the arrival of Spanish colonizers on-screen. A Spanish car-tographer adds Puerto Rico to a world map, establishing its geographic and national boundaries within the Spanish empire. The film culminates with a representation of Puerto Rico as an ideal destination for both production and consumption—of natural resources, Afro–Puerto Rican and European culture, and a highly trained and capable workforce. Scenic panoramas and images of a vibrant nightlife, economic productivity, and workers appear one after the other on-screen, accompanied by the song "Puerto Rico," composed by Eddie Palmieri and Ismael Quintana with the latter provid-ing vocals. Released in 1973 on Palmieri's album *Sentido* (Feeling), the song provides the soundscape to the images of Puerto Rico as nation, culture, and commodity. The film's incorporation of Puerto Rican music complements the visual imagery on-screen to fuse Puerto Rico's national identity with salsa's commercial and cultural meanings. Salsa embodies the sum of a historical process culminating in this moment of late capi-talism, revealing how the nation became a branded space for performing global nationalism.

While the governor's sense of Puerto Rico within a global imaginary may have been exaggerated, the concern over hegemonic representations of the archipelago alongside diasporic Puerto Rican poverty and criminality underscores the racialized anxieties of critics who opposed "Puerto Rico es salsa." The Nuyorican imaginary embedded within salsa and its performance of abjection threatened the very message of cultural particularity promoted by Hernández Colón. Promoted primarily by Puerto Rican elites, the dis-course of racial democracy that upholds white supremacy "permeates every facet of Puerto Rican race relations and popular life" and, like Muñocismo, claimed a whiteness distinct from that of the United States.[123] Although Muñoz Marín framed entrance into modernity as a process of whitening, he maintained that Puerto Rico's transformation would eradicate racist structural barriers rooted in slavery that remained embedded within an agricultural economy.[124] Race became, as Licia Fiol-Matta underscores, "a construct of benevolence whose pernicious role in the symbolic chain is not exposed; its logic of segregation ranging from condescension to brutal exclusion and degradation [is] disguised."[125]

The refusal to acknowledge persistent racial and class inequalities in favor of a discourse of racial hybridity persisted even as the creation of factories and physical infrastructure in urban areas aggravated racial and class hierarchies. Urban development included the systematic razing of multiracial *arrabales* (squatter areas) where individuals and families who had migrated from the countryside looking for work had built homes and created dense familial and kinship ties.[126] Portrayed as incubators of moral corruption and disease, the arrabales failed to adhere to discursive and visible narratives of a modernity embodied by well-organized, "hygienic" urban residential areas, or *urbanizaciones*, with homes headed by the "new" (white and urban) virile Puerto Rican man as head of Puerto Rico's whitened domesticity and economic stability. Modernity in the urban landscape was thus predicated on the destruction of arrabales and the displacement of residents, who, deemed unfit for the "ultramodern" urbanizaciones, were forcibly relocated to new public housing projects.[127] Decades later, Hernández Colón continued to mobilize official narratives of racial democracy framed by scripts of Blackness that relegated Puerto Rico's Afro–Puerto Rican histories to a premodern past, during the "dead time" of history that predates the entrance into modernity under muñocismo.[128]

### Puerto Rico's National Day: Reconciling Broken Memories

"Puerto Rico es salsa" culminated Puerto Rico's day of honor on June 23 at the Expo. Scheduled to coincide with the Catholic feast day of St. John the Baptist, Puerto Rico's patron saint, the date symbolically reaffirmed the racialized and religious legacies of Spanish colonialism and became one more example of the archipelago's affinities with Spain. The official ceremony to kick off the day took place that morning at the open-air palenque, where eight hundred elementary school children holding Puerto Rican flags joined Hernández Colón and other Puerto Rican and Spanish public officials. As what the governor called "the most noble and inspiring wealth of [Puerto Rico's] future," these children had been brought to Spain by Puerto Rico's Office of Youth Affairs to symbolize the archipelago's potential and human capital.[129] Puerto Rico's Symphonic Orchestra, possibly in response to the vociferous outcries of its musical director when "Puerto Rico es salsa" was announced, initiated the day's musical events, while the Expo's commissioner general complimented Puerto Rico on its pavilion.

Emilio Cassinello, the commissioner of the Expo and the Spanish minister of education and science, highlighted the cultural ties between the two countries that led Spaniards like Juan Ramón Jiménez, Pedro Salinas, and Pablo Casals to seek refuge in Puerto Rico and to "find in the 'Island of Enchantment' much more than a place to live and create"—an entrance point to the Caribbean. As such, Puerto Rico's participation represented "un regalo de vuelta, de regreso, es el vivo retrato enriquecido de nosotros mismos" (a homecoming, a return, it is the living rejuvenated picture of ourselves).[130] The comments reflected a speech Hernández Colón had delivered a year earlier, in 1991, at the University of Granada, wherein he described Puerto Rico as one of Spain's "most favored colonies" prior to the Spanish-American War and affirmed the country's Hispanic affiliations.

Having organized the Expo around the theme "The Age of Discovery," Spain sought to demonstrate how its imperialist expansion provided the foundation for human development and the cultural, scientific, technical, and economic advances that followed in the Western Hemisphere.[131] Expo '92, like the rebranding campaign Spain launched in the late 1980s, provided the Spanish government with an opportunity to market an image of a modern post–Francisco Franco society with the human capital and technological infrastructure necessary to compete with the strongest economies in the European community.[132] The nostalgic recuperation of Spain's Golden Age was designed, in part, to "show the new Spain to the world."[133] Like Puerto Rico, the Spanish government hoped to use the world's fair to launch economic development in the Seville region and increase Spain's standing in the EEC after the end of the Franco dictatorship.

As Indigenous peoples across the Americas and protestors in Spain condemned the celebration and the willful amnesia about the genocide, slavery, and theft initiated by Columbus's arrival in the Americas, Expo organizers forged ahead with the controversial hope that Expo '92 would bring a reconciliation between Spain and its former colonial empire. Using the built environment to stage a symbolic reconciliation with its Latin American and Caribbean former colonies, Spain's Expo planners created a "Plaza de América" (American Plaza). The pavilion hosted all but four of the exhibits by former Latin American and Caribbean colonies and served as a symbolic space for claiming Hispanoamérica (Hispanic America) as a transoceanic community created through Spanish imperialism in the past and neocolonial flows of global capital in the present.[134] As an incentive to participate in this symbolic reconciliation, Spain provided $20 billion in aid across the Latin American countries that participated in

Expo '92, an amount that represented 31 percent of the European Community (now the European Union [EU]) investment in Latin America by 1992.[135] These efforts positioned Spain as a gateway to Latin American markets.[136] The emphasis on reconciliation as a step toward becoming a major player in the EU dramatized the way that, as Paul Julian Smith has argued, the Expo shifted from "a celebration of discovery to shop window for the New Spain."[137]

Across the Expo, the built environment embodied the idea of Spanish imperial expansion as the foundation for social, cultural, economic, and scientific developments across Western nations.[138] Pavilions related to the Expo's theme, "Age of Discovery," stood at the pinnacle of a layout that resembled a right triangle.[139] The Sony jumbotron, positioned on the end of the Expo grounds opposite the themed pavilions, broadcast both Spain's technological prowess and Sony's worldwide expansion.[140] Just beyond the area devoted to Spain, Expo organizers placed the pavilion of Retinis, a Spanish telecommunications company; the International Olympic Committee pavilion, a reminder that the 1992 Olympics were hosted by Barcelona; and, finally, the "Pavilion of the Future," a symbol of Spain's "jump" toward modernity.[141] The spatial planning of the campus claimed Spain's past, present, and future impact on global human development.[142] The atrocities of the Spanish colonial government and its agents in Puerto Rico; the violent imposition of colonial authority vis-à-vis Catholicism on Indigenous peoples and the topography; the atrocities of the transatlantic slave trade; the failure to situate the exile of Spaniards in the 1930s within the context of the Spanish Civil War and the Franco dictatorship; and the gendered, heteronormative, and racialized hierarchies that form part of the legacy of Hispanic and Catholic imperialism all had to be willfully excised to make possible the alliance celebrated at Expo '92.

The concert crowned Hernández Colón's attempts to establish a sphere of economic and political autonomy within Puerto Rico's colonial context. The narrative of Puerto Rico as a "nation among nations" allowed him to distance Puerto Rico culturally from the colonial gaze of the United States. No longer would Puerto Rico's modernity be predicated solely on the ascendancy of the PPD in the 1940s and the culmination of its political aspirations with the passage of ELA.[143] The governor's campaign and "Puerto Rico es salsa" promised to initiate a new stage of Puerto Rican modernity. Like those of his predecessor, Hernández Colón's policies reproduced the symbolic and real violence against Black Puerto Ricans, women, economically marginalized and queer communities (which, of course, are not mutually exclusive groups).

## The Concert

The concert at the open-air palenque was shown on the outdoor stage's Sony jumbotron. Meanwhile, a second concert at the Lago de España featured another series of Puerto Rican performances that included Ballet Gíbaro, Antonio Cabán Vale ("El Topo"), Edwin Colón Zayas, Taller Campesino, and Chucho Avellanet. After midnight, a concert by Andy Montañez began as the multimedia and fireworks show featured "imágenes que reflejan el colorido de nuestra tierra" (images that reflect the color of our land).[144] Hernández Colón greeted the audience for "Puerto Rico es salsa," announcing:

> Le traemos un regalo de Puerto Rico, que es esta noche de salsa. Y esperamos que Uds. disfruten mucho, y al yo darme cuenta cuánto le gustaba la salsa a la juventud española y al público español la salsa, pensé que ese era el mejor regalo que les podríamos traer esta noche.[145]

> [We bring you a present from Puerto Rico, which is this night of salsa. And we hope that you enjoy it a lot, and when I noticed how much the Spanish youth and the Spanish public liked salsa, I thought this was the best present we could give you tonight.]

The rhetoric of the gift and the affective relationship to salsa frame the governor's welcome even as it once again confirmed critics' insistence that the concert represented a capitulation to Spain's Expo planners. The program began with a brief video that opened with an aerial view of Puerto Rico from its eastern coast with a voice-over describing the archipelago as "la perla de los mares" (the pearl of the seas), a reference to the poem "A Puerto Rico (Regreso)," discussed in chapter 2. The shot, emphasizing Puerto Rico's natural beauty and "warm" people, reanimated ideologies the United States had long perpetuated in order to legitimize holding Puerto Rico as a colony. The narrator described Puerto Rico as a racial democracy, a combination of three races and their instruments: the Indigenous maraca and guiro, the African conga, and the Spanish guitar.

The concert's teleology presents a musical trajectory wherein Afro-diasporic cultural expression is the foundational "adscription" of Puerto Rico's cultural particularity, one ultimately subsumed within a hemispheric musical trajectory that culminates onstage with salsa. The video began with an overview of Puerto Rican music as a series of dancers crossed the stage, each to a different rhythm presented as constitutive of salsa: Black Puerto Rican women dancing to bomba rhythms in nineteenth-century dresses once again relegated the contributions of African cultural expression to a folkloric past rather than a constitutive locus of Puerto Ricanness. Their entrance was followed by dancers of various skin tones, including a couple with locked arms who moved in sync, but not smoothly, to a bolero; women in dresses covered with brightly colored frills who appeared onstage as the orchestra played a cha-cha that ceded to Carlos Santana's rendition of "Oye como va" and its exaltation of the *mulata*; the performance of pleneros who crossed the stage wearing pavas (straw hats) to represent the iconic jíbaro; and, finally, the apex of the introduction, the dancers and the band moving to the rhythms of salsa. Deterritorialized from its Black, diasporic, poor, and working-class roots, salsa became a receptacle for Puerto Rico's global nationalism.

Despite the Puerto Rico exhibit organizers' attempts to resemanticize salsa's meanings, the music became an official vehicle for imagining an alternative relationship to US colonial power. On the one hand, in embracing salsa, Hernández Colón and the organizing committee exploited the music as a symbol of difference and pluralism to claim a cultural particularity and cosmopolitanism.[146] On the other hand, by equating salsa with the nation, they privileged diasporic Afro-Caribbean expressive culture. Criticisms of "Puerto Rico es salsa" showed the failures of the government's attempt to build support for the Expo '92 pavilion at home and the ways that branding not merely commodifies the nation but also extends nationalism and national identities.[147] To a normative "listening ear," the official embrace of salsa disrupted scripts of Blackness that relegate Afro-Caribbean cultural practices to a folkloric past.[148] The backlash showed that salsa could not be reduced to the government's commercial and political logics, nor could it be separated from its racialized, class, and diasporic meanings.

Spain was positioned as a way station to the European community at a moment when ELA had failed to make a return on its promise of long-term economic development, and Hernández Colón was concerned about a resulting backlash against his party. The nostalgia for a Hispanic past shows both the potential and the limits of cultural nationalism. Hernández Colón's desire to reinsert Puerto Rico into narratives of modernity by turning to Afro–Puerto Rican musical practices offered the possibility of enacting what Sheller describes as "a form of colonization in reverse," or a "spewing back of what Europe had emitted (and omitted)."[149] The nostalgia for a presumed Hispanic, rural past on which Hernández Colón drew, however, formed part a strategic move for renewed cultural, economic, and political ties with Spain.

**The Gambit**

Hernández Colón, who decided not to seek reelection, ended his final term as governor with the economic failure of his promotional gambit. In an Associated Press article that ran on July 15, 1993, the PNP, which assumed power after the election of Governor Pedro Rosselló the year before, stated that the pavilion had failed to stimulate any foreign investment in Puerto Rico despite the weekly info sessions that presented avenues for investment.[150] It is impossible to hold Hernández Colón entirely responsible for Puerto Rico's trouble; there were barriers to stimulating economic growth in Puerto Rico through European tourism, trade, and investment. For example, standing economic relationships between Europe and other Caribbean countries presented an obstacle to his aspirations to make Puerto Rico a bridge to regional markets.[151] In addition, even as Hernández Colón attempted to assert a sphere of sovereignty within ELA, the colonial relationship with the United States continued to limit the country's authority to enter into agreements with foreign governments; in 1986, the US State Department refuted Hernández Colón's right to enter into an economic agreement with Japan whereby Japanese corporations with subsidiaries in Puerto Rico would have received tax incentives similar to those US subsidiaries received on the archipelago.[152] The continued economic reliance on foreign investments and tax exemptions approved by Hernández Colón also threatened to reproduce, rather than end, Puerto Rico's dependence on the economies of other countries while failing to spur local economic development. At the end of his term, Puerto Rico had acquired an additional $5 billion in debt. The pavilion sold for only $4 million in 1993, dashing organizers' hopes to sell it for a profit.[153]

While the PNP had opposed the Puerto Rico exhibit, it continued the neoliberal discourse of privatization, free trade, and economic progress initiated by Hernández Colón and accelerated the neoliberal development agenda. It succeeded, in fact, in selling the government-owned Puerto Rico Telephone Company to a Spanish corporation, which Hernández Colón had attempted but failed to do. Rosselló's term also ushered in an era of economic policies that attracted sought-after capital but contributed another $12 billion to Puerto Rico's debt by the end of his term in 2001. The strategies used by each party to exploit global economic capital and increase tourism were thus very closely aligned to a political position around whether Puerto Rico should remain a Free Associated State or pursue statehood and what these positions offer to whom in the new global economy. The foregrounding of salsa at Expo '92 was yet another battlefield on which that fight raged.

Expo '92 had crowned Hernández Colón's vision of expanding Puerto Rico's visibility globally, an impetus that characterized his terms as governor. "Puerto Rico es salsa," like other moments when his administration supported the music's institutionalization, exploited salsa's Afro-Caribbean soundscape to convey a particular narrative of a Puerto Rican modernity predicated on a discourse of racial particularity buttressed by scripts of Blackness that relegate Afro-diasporic cultural practices and Afro-descended Puerto Ricans to the periphery of the nation. Afro–Puerto Ricans on the archipelago remained targets of police surveillance and suffered continued economic and social inequality even as salsa's mobilization at Expo '92 celebrated Afro-Caribbean musical practices informed by Afro–Puerto Rican lived experience and dynamic aesthetic practices.

## Conclusion

Even as salsa threatened dominant ideologies about Puerto Ricanness, salsa's mobilization as a sonic container of Puerto Rico's presumed racial and cultural exceptionalism promoted white supremacy—the same discourse upheld by the concert's detractors. Whether the history of Puerto Rico is put forth as a failed bildungsroman characterized by a colonialism that emasculates (Pedreira) or the need to avoid the anti-democratic impulse toward sovereignty (Muñoz Marín), the only "remedy" for the "illness" is instituting appropriate forms of masculinity and paternal authority. For Muñoz Marín, this process culminated with the electoral success of the PPD, symbolized by the new (white and urban) man and the heteropatriarchal family featured prominently in visual media and political discourses, and the passage of ELA.[154] At Expo '92, salsa's soundscape became the aural embodiment of contradictory narratives celebrating a Hispanophile and Catholic (read heteropatriarchal) grand Puerto Rican family as well as diasporic, urban, and Afro-Caribbean lives and musical practices. Like the exhibit, both the concert and the slogan "Puerto Rico es salsa" promoted a totalizing narrative of Puerto Rican modernity even as it challenged the same with discourses that emphasized pluralism.[155] The desire to tell a story that would motivate foreign investment, tourism, and an expanded market for Puerto Rico's exports relied on salsa's celebration of the masculinist subjecthood longed for by Pedreira (even if its Nuyorican imaginary would have activated his concerns about racial hybridity). That manhood/nationhood, or its approximation through the performance of (un)freedom, might arrive in the form of music that emerged within largely Black, poor, and working-class diasporic communities upends the opposition between the Puerto Rican "spirituality" and US culture on which an official Puerto Rican national identity has been predicated since the late 1940s.

Rather than attempt to recuperate Afro-diasporic histories as part of Puerto Rico's present, "Puerto Rico es salsa" reinscribed hegemonic narratives of Afro-diasporic cultural practices. The nation branding campaign, of which the concert and night performances formed part, separated the music's aesthetic contours from the everyday lives of Afro-descended Puerto Ricans and the music's diasporic meanings. The pavilion thus risked reifying hegemonic tropicalizations of the Caribbean as a site of pleasure and excess. Hegemonic representations of the Caribbean as a site of pleasure, as Sheller suggests in her criticisms of the appropriation of creolization, act to reproduce the subordination of the Global South.[156]

Hernández Colón challenged official narratives of Puerto Ricanness established by his own political party in the mid-twentieth century by tying nationalist ideology to the market at Expo '92. As part of quincentennial celebrations, "Puerto Rico es salsa" showcased an "inclusive and conciliatory" vision of the nation that is no longer homogeneous but rather plural.[157] Promoting globalization and plurality, Hernández Colón disrupted prevailing attitudes about race, class, and diasporic belonging. The decision to elevate salsa turned to Afro-Caribbean performative practices to assert an autonomous Puerto Rican national identity. Salsa's mobilization however, privileged Puerto Rico's colonial relationship to Spain, a Hispanophile whiteness operationalized to symbolically link the archipelago to Europe more broadly.[158] Salsa's soundscape, however, as demonstrated by its detractors, could not be separated from the diasporic communities in which it emerged or the everyday lives of Afro–Puerto Ricans in the archipelago, who claimed salsa as their own. The racial, class, and territorial anxiety inherent in objections to the music's representation as part of Puerto Rico's cultural patrimony shows that the process of nation branding cannot be reduced to the commodification of the nation.

"Puerto Rico es salsa" became the sonic embodiment of the intersection of culture, corporate advertising techniques, and the performance of sovereignty under colonial domination that both challenged and reified narratives of Puerto Rican modernity. The concerns about a globalized performance of Puerto Ricanness that centered Afro-diasporic rhythms reflects the significance of popular music and the ways global economies potentially contribute to alternative conceptualizations of belonging.[159] Salsa's Black diasporic musical traditions served to commercialize the archipelago's cultural particularity within an increasingly competitive market for internationalized capital. The backlash, however, brought the music's Black, diasporic, and urban Nuyorican imaginary to the fore. As Jossianna Arroyo asserts, "Representation[s] of race in Puerto Rico survive alongside a discourse of silence, mockery, and disavowal" embedded in ideologies of national belonging wherein "those who do not belong are seen as nonnational, racialized, foreign, and dangerous."[160] Ultimately, the opposition to "Puerto Rico es salsa," like the Puerto Rico exhibit itself, revealed the limits of attempting to mobilize culture from above even as the privileged status of salsa recontextualized the sonic boundaries of the nation. Hernández Colón's vision of the world's fair as a crucial opportunity to attract foreign investment, and salsa as a crucial tool to do so, sounded a long history of Puerto Rican dependence on foreign investment and a performance of (un)freedom through the disavowal of Black social, cultural, and musical practices alongside the violence and marginalization of those who remained outside the boundaries of heteropatriarchal white nationalism.

The backlash, against both the pavilion and the elevation of salsa to the status of cultural patrimony, revealed the limits of attempts by governments and corporations to manipulate culture for political and economic purposes. The attempt to resemanticize salsa as a product of "glorious mestizaje" reminds us, as Sheller states, that while the Caribbean was the original site of theorizing hybridity and creolization, the term continues to be appropriated for use in descriptions of deterritorialized cultural practices.[161] Erasing salsa's emergence among a largely Black, poor, and working-class diasporic Puerto Rican community was a way to erase racially and economically marginalized communities from the public performance of global nationalism.

Despite the limits of both the slogan and the concert, "Puerto Rico es salsa" created a space where salsa's Nuyorican aesthetics and Black diasporic musical practices disrupted hegemonic soundscapes of Puerto Ricanness. Salsa's Black, urban, and diasporic meanings exceeded the commercial and political logic of "Puerto Rico es salsa." This surplus of meanings prevails, even as the concert and the Puerto Rico exhibit itself leveraged the music's social and commercial meanings in a performance of global nationalism that ultimately reinvigorated mid-twentieth-century economic development policies and official narratives of national belonging that bolstered white, heteropatriarchal, and xenophobic nationalism. The recuperation of counternarratives that celebrated Black and diasporic music in ways that exceeded the intertwined cultural and market logic of the political establishment to appropriate salsa and the legacy of Rafael Cortijo, and which remain largely outside the historical record, is necessary to provide a deeper and richer understanding of this process of nation branding within this context—and to understand the ways racialized fear and disdain are entangled with the government's fascination with salsa.[162] I would argue that this is precisely why the decision to privilege salsa generated such a visceral response from opponents. For to privilege salsa is to privilege a history of Black, urban, poor, and diasporic musical expression, cultural remittances, and the lived experiences of racially and economically marginalized Puerto Ricans—in both Puerto Rico and the United States—who embraced and continued to embrace the music long before it became part of the "national" patrimony.

# Entre la Letra y la Nota

**5**

BECOMING "EL CANTANTE DE
LOS CANTANTES"

It had been two years since Héctor LaVoe had released his sophomore solo recording, *De ti depende* (It's up to you), in 1976. While LaVoe had been among Fania Records' most bankable artists, his failure to produce a new album and his increasingly erratic behavior were taking a toll on his professional life. At the same time, while the label controlled approximately two-thirds of the Latin music market domestically, in no small part by its radio presence and the number of albums Fania released every year, the company's growth seemed to have peaked. The 1975 agreement with CBS Records to produce and distribute three Fania All-Stars albums had not achieved the crossover success that Fania hoped would increase domestic sales beyond metropolitan areas with large Latina/o populations. By 1978, Jerry Masucci's goal of releasing a number 1 disco hit remained out of reach, the label had not been able to maintain its dominance of FM radio stations, and rumors spread of difficult contract negotiations with artists like Pete "El Conde" Rodríguez and Típica 73. A steep decline in sales in New York and Puerto Rico added to Fania's woes, as did the rate of piracy, the latter prompting Fania to collaborate with the FBI.[1] LaVoe remained a fan favorite, but the sonero had not recorded a new album in two years and had disappeared from the music scene for four months. Willie Colón, who had disbanded his own band but continued to support LaVoe's solo career, contacted the up-and-coming Panamanian singer-songwriter Rubén Blades to ask for a song that might help the sonero launch his comeback—and increase Fania's sales. Blades had already established himself as a gifted songwriter, and "El Cantante" (The Singer), the song he passed on to LaVoe, was released in 1978 on the album *Comedia*.

The album, including "El Cantante," earned critical and commercial acclaim. LaVoe himself became so identified with the song and the chasm between artistic prowess and tragedy it chronicled—between the public performance and the private struggles—that fans and artists alike endowed him with the moniker "El Cantante de los Cantantes" (The Singer's Singer). LaVoe's embodiment of both Nuyorican and jíbaro subjectivities had already generated an intimate relationship with New York Puerto Rican audiences by the time he recorded "El Cantante" in 1978. The conflation of LaVoe with "El Cantante"—both the song and the narrative subject—overdetermined his public persona and the collective memory of the sonero as an effigy of the salsa boom, its excesses, and its uncertainties. Dominant narratives of LaVoe's trajectory had already begun to emphasize the ill-fated destiny of a singer who would die penniless, exploited by the music industry, abandoned by his family and friends, and dependent on those who would exploit him for financial gain. This narrative interpellated LaVoe as a failed subject, reinscribing failed citizenship as the collective condition of Puerto Ricans. The reduction of LaVoe's trajectory to the dichotomy in "El Cantante" between professional success and personal tragedy ignores the very ways in which the sonero interrupted the affective economy of pity that enveloped him in death. "El Cantante"—both LaVoe and the singing subject—claims the very space where personal trials and performance come together as a privileged site of everyday life in NuYoRico.

LaVoe's death in June 1993 precipitated an understanding of his life as the consequence of corruption, exploitation, and betrayal at the hands of Fania Records, promoters and club owners, family, friends, and peers. "Héctor Juan Pérez," wrote Colón in the sonero's obituary, "transformed himself into a persona called Hector LaVoe to accomplish a mission that slowly changed from a pleasure cruise to a battle of life and death." While Colón recognized that "the good-looking country boy that drove all the women crazy also wanted to be a barrio badass," he also indicted those who failed LaVoe. Colón criticized fans who forgave LaVoe's every transgression, lamented his own lack of courage for not visiting the sonero during his illness, and condemned unnamed individuals whose "shady gifts [of drugs] became chains around [LaVoe's] neck." Colón reserved his most strident condemnation for the "record moguls who live[d] like Saudi princes selling

[LaVoe's] records . . . without paying royalties as LaVoe languished in poverty" and "promoters who . . . offer[ed] him crumbs so they might sell tickets to exhibit 'The Singer of Singers' in his agony." Colón ended with a plea for LaVoe's forgiveness, calling him the "hero of the poor, victim of the forces that are decimating our people, martyr of Salsa—the monster you helped create."[2] The obituary maps the trajectory of LaVoe's life onto the story elaborated within "El Cantante," underscoring the ways the sonero had already become a synecdoche for diasporic Puerto Ricanness, the salsa boom, and even Fania Records.

### "El Cantante": The Song and Its Inspiration

Blades had taken inspiration from Ruggero Leoncavallo's *Pagliacci* (1892), an opera that uses a play-within-a-play device to extraordinary effect. It begins with an aria sung by a deformed, brokenhearted clown who informs the audience that the play they are about to see deals with real life. He declares that the play's author has shared nothing less than the memories of his "innermost soul, and he has written them with real tears, and his sobs are marking the beat." "Therefore," he explains, "you will see love as real as human beings' love. You will see the sad fruit of hate. You will hear agonies of grief, cries of rage, and bitter laughter." The prologue reminds the audience that although the actors stage a performance, they remain actual people, with real emotions that the public should recognize as such. "So think then, not of our poor theatrical costumes," the clown implores, "but of our souls, for we are men of flesh and blood. Breathing the air of this lonely world just like you."[3] The prologue culminates as the clown calls for the opera to begin. In *Pagliacci*'s most famous scene, the character Tonio performs as the laughing clown Pagliaccio at the very moment his heart breaks from the knowledge that his wife loves another actor.

Like *Pagliacci*, "El Cantante" is a self-reflexive artistic text, one that articulates what it means to be a performer through the act of performance. Similarly to the opening aria of *Pagliacci*, the initial two stanzas of "El Cantante" written by Blades function as a prologue for the listening public, informing them that LaVoe, as El Cantante, sings to a life

> de risas y penas
> de momentos malos
> y de cosas buenas

[Of laughter and sorrows
Of bad moments
And good things]

The singer contrasts his iconic status onstage with the sorrows he experiences "cuando el show se acaba" (when the show ends), thereby entreating the audience to consider his humanity. Reflecting on the nature of fandom, LaVoe describes those fans who routinely approach him in public and presume that "estás hecho / siempre con hembras y en fiestas" (you've got it made / always with women and partying) but who fail to consider "si sufro, si lloro / si tengo una pena / que hiere muy hondo" (whether I suffer or cry / if I have a sorrow / that hurts deeply). Conceding that the members of the audience "vinieron a divertirse / y pagaron en la puerta" (came to have a good time / and paid at the door), El Cantante begins and ends the first two stanzas by "offering" his songs to those who will listen before calling for his own performance to begin.

**The Players**

LaVoe recorded "El Cantante" after a hiatus from the Latin music scene in 1977 that lasted several months and led to public speculation about his personal life. Rumors spread quickly about the hiatus and the possible causes that led to what some speculated was a "nervous breakdown." In July 1977, *Latin N.Y.* magazine reported on the "mystery" of LaVoe's "disappearance." Unable to obtain information from the singer's "family, personal friends, managers and record companies," the magazine openly admitted that it resorted to "bits and pieces of information, theories and hear-say." The reporter speculated that LaVoe had been admitted to a rehabilitation center in Puerto Rico or taken to a *santero*, a priest within Santería, for guidance and healing. "Whatever the truth is[,] whatever has happened to Hector, the world of salsa misses him and his talent," the article stated. A letter to the editor printed the following month highlights the degree to which rumor and conjecture fueled the speculation about LaVoe. A reader asked why, if LaVoe's last performance had been in April—as reported in the article about the vocalist's absence—had a *Latin N.Y.* reporter attended a June concert appearance? The magazine explained that "contradictory statements arise because we were dealing with hearsay" but failed to provide further explanation.[4]

LaVoe had already acknowledged his drug use in 1976 to *Latin N.Y.* writer and music historian Max Salazar. The latter did not mention it in the magazine because he felt it might damage LaVoe's career. In his 2002 collection of Latin music essays and artist profiles, Salazar wrote that LaVoe had showed a "complete lack of inhibition about his drug problem" and the "thousands of dollars" it cost him.[5] In an interview with publicist Carmen Mirabal published circa 1976, however, LaVoe denied allegations of drug addiction and expressed frustration with the persistent rumor. In response to a question that circled around the rumors of drug use, LaVoe replied:

> Ya sé por dónde vienes, ¿que si es cierto que soy teco? . . . Te diré que la gente siempre tiene que hablar de los que estamos en la música; los que no son homosexuales usamos drogas. . . . Si la gente dice por ahí que soy teco porque tengo amistades en el Barrio o en La Perla [en San Juan, Puerto Rico], o porque no he sabido escoger mis amistades, entonces no sé qué decir, porque yo soy de origen humilde y mis amigos también, no puedo negarlo, pero eso no quiere decir que sea drogadicto, ni que me meta estupefacientes de ningún tipo. Si soy un tipo medio loco y en los escenarios digo varios disparates, es para hacerle más amena la noche a la gente, no porque esté "enmota'o."[6]

> [I already know where you're going with this. If it's true that I'm a drug addict? . . . I'll tell you that people always have to talk about those of us in the music business; the ones who aren't homosexuals use drugs. . . . If people around the way say that I'm a drug addict because I have friends in El Barrio or in La Perla [in San Juan, Puerto Rico], or because I haven't known how to choose my friends, then I don't know what to say, because I come from humble origins and so do my friends, I can't deny it. But that doesn't mean that I'm a drug addict, or that I take drugs of any kind. If I'm kind of crazy and I talk nonsense onstage, it's to make the evening pleasant for the audience, not because I'm lit.]

LaVoe's reference to being accused of being homosexual is as close as that interview comes to acknowledging rumors about LaVoe's sexuality, but the understanding that the singer had same-sex sexual relations has received increased attention since the release of his biopic, *El Cantante*. In denying both this and his drug use, LaVoe criticized narratives of Puerto Rican abjection that draw on hegemonic representations of Puerto Rican communities in both New York and La Perla.

Whether Blades willingly ceded "El Cantante" to LaVoe or acquiesced in response to pressure from Colón and Fania Records has long been a topic of speculation. Blades had joined Fania in the mid-1970s and provided vocals for Ray Barretto and Colón. When Colón called Blades to ask for a song, their critically acclaimed joint album *Siembra* (Planting, 1978)—which would surpass all existing salsa sales and catapult Blades to international acclaim and the upper echelons of salsa—had yet to be released. Blades had, however, already released his album with Colón, *Metiendo mano*, in 1977. This album marked his transition from writing songs for other performers to recording his own compositions. Blades addressed this shift in a 1979 interview with *Latin N.Y.* "When I couldn't record my own songs, I gave them to other singers who were in a position to record them. Now that I'm established, I don't want to continue writing for everyone else."[7] The request from Colón comes precisely at this intermediate moment—*Metiendo mano* was out, and *Siembra* was still in production when Fania released *Comedia*.[8] Blades admits that he intended to record the song as his own signature piece. However, he also insists that he willingly passed "El Cantante" to LaVoe because the sonero "really needed it so I respected him enough to give it to him. And he sang the heck out of it."[9]

The 2006 LaVoe biopic *El Cantante* dramatizes Blades's statement. In the film, an emcee at the famed Corso nightclub in New York introduces a "surprise guest" to the audience, a young Blades played by singer Victor Manuel. As Blades prepares to perform "El Cantante" publicly for the first time, he announces that he is there "to give someone a present." The camera cuts to LaVoe, played by Marc Anthony, who stands at the bar with his back to the stage talking to percussionist Eddie Montalvo (played by himself). When LaVoe hears Blades tell the audience that he wrote a song for him, the sonero turns and looks at the stage in surprise. Meanwhile, Blades explains to the audience that LaVoe is "someone I really admired since I was a kid who wanted to be a singer, cuando [él] iba por allá por Panamá con Willie Colón [when he would go to Panama with Willie Colón]. After I sing it for you, it's his. It's called 'El Cantante.'" A chuckling Blades then adds, "Cualquier parecido con la vida real, Héctor, es pura coincidencia" (Any similarity to real life, Héctor, is purely coincidental). Blades begins to sing as LaVoe watches in awe, nodding his head briefly. Blades, who accompanies himself on the acoustic guitar, sings the first verse before the camera cuts to LaVoe laying down the track for "El Cantante" in a recording studio.

The representation of events within the film notwithstanding, the rumors that Fania—whether that be Colón or cofounder Jerry Masucci—forced

**5.1** Rubén Blades's handwritten lyrics for "El Cantante" on a napkin (1978; Rubén Blades Archive, Harvard University)

Blades to give up the song resurfaced in 2007 after the biopic premiered in theaters. The soundtrack featured Anthony covering LaVoe's songs and debuted at number 1 on the *Billboard* Latin music chart, where it remained for six weeks. Codigo, which had purchased the Fania catalog in 2005, also released a compilation of Héctor LaVoe's remastered recordings as part of the series *A Man and His Music*. The liner notes include an image of Blades's handwritten lyrics for the initial two verses of the song. On iTunes, which distributed *A Man and His Music* exclusively for one week, the recording reached number 3 on the digital provider's Latin music charts. It also rose to number 18 on the *Billboard* Latin music charts, where a second album released by Codigo for Walmart, *Cantante: The Originals*, reached number 3.[10] Codigo's success in capitalizing on LaVoe's legacy almost fifteen years after his death punctuates LaVoe's legacy as "El Cantante de los Cantantes," forever identified with the singing subject of his signature song.

El cantante – R. Blades
(1977)

I  Yo soy el cantante
que hoy han venido a escuchar:
lo mejor del repertorio
a ustedes voy a brindar.
Y canto ~~canciones~~ a la vida,
de risas y penas,
de momentos malos y de cosas buenas,
Yo soy el cantante
porque lo mío es cantar
y el público viene para poderme
(paga)              escuchar.
                         Je, Je,
                         Je, Je –

II  Me paran siempre en la calle,
mucha gente, que comenta,
Muchacho, usté está hecho,
siempre con hembras y en fiestas.
Y nadie pregunta, si sufro, si lloro.
Si tengo una pena que hiere muy hondo,
Vinieron a divertirse y pagaron en la puerta
no hay tiempo para tristezas,
vamos cantante comienza,  Je, Je,
                         Je, Je,

**5.2**  Rubén Blades's handwritten lyrics for "El Cantante" on lined paper
(1978; Rubén Blades Archive, Harvard University)

According to Paula Campbell, who was dating Blades in 1978, he initially balked at the idea of "giving up the song." An up-and-coming artist in New York's Latin music scene, he certainly could have been susceptible to pressure from Colón and Masucci. Blades, however, "doesn't remember hesitating" when Colón called to ask for a song LaVoe could record for his upcoming album. Blades also maintains that he never regretted passing on recording the song, which "fit [LaVoe's] reality more than mine at the time. I couldn't have possibly produced the authenticity he injected into it."[11] Blades reiterated his position during the August 2007 airing of his video webcast SDRB (*Show de Rubén Blades*; Rubén Blades's show) in response to viewer questions:

> Yo personalmente ni me acuerdo como fue el proceso. . . . Yo recuerdo que a mí me pidieron la canción [*pause*] para Héctor. Eso es lo que yo recuerdo. Porque estaba pasando por problemas. Estaba pasando por problemas porque las ventas estaban empezando a decaer. Eso es la memoria que yo tengo. . . . La gente se pone a hablar pendeja's . . . que si Héctor, que si [*cuts himself off*]. Si yo no le hubiera querido dar la canción, no la doy. Ni siquiera digo que la tengo escrita. Me vienen a preguntar por una canción [y digo]: "No, yo no tengo nada. Mi estilo no es el mismo." Y me hubiera queda'o calla'o.[12]

> [I personally don't even remember how the process went. . . . I remember that I was asked for the song [*pause*] for Héctor. That's what I remember. Because he was experiencing problems. He was experiencing problems because record sales were beginning to decline. That is the memory that I have. . . . People start talking shit . . . that Héctor this, that [*cuts himself off*]. If I didn't want to give him the song, I don't give it. I don't even say that I've written it. They come and ask for a song [and I say]: "No, I don't have anything. My style isn't the same." I would've kept it to myself.]

Blades acknowledged his own limited memory of events but disputed claims that he was forced to give up "El Cantante." He then criticized those speculating about the turn of events depicted in the film, reserving his strongest disapproval for individuals who did not participate in the process yet felt compelled to give their opinion. By the end of the webcast, Blades loses his patience and vehemently reaffirms that "si yo no le hubiera querido darle [*sic*] la canción yo no se la doy y punto" (if I did not want to give him the song, I wouldn't have given it to him, and that's that). Blades dismisses even the possibility that anyone could force him to surrender control of his creative labor, instead admonishing those who would continue to suggest otherwise. What matters, Blades suggests, is that he ultimately gave LaVoe a song that fit the late sonero's reality more than his own.

> Y en realidad la canción le quedaba mejor a Héctor que a mí porque la vida de Héctor le daba una autenticidad a la canción que yo no le hubiera podido dar en ese tiempo. Yo no tenía, ni ahora tampoco, mi vida no es una vida de escándalo. Yo no tengo problemas de drogas, ni ese tipo de problemas. Había un elemento trágico que le daba mucha autenticidad a la interpretación de Héctor entonces y yo dije bueno, si esto ojalá lo pueda ayudar, y por eso le di.[13]

> [And in reality, the song was better suited for Héctor than for me because Héctor's life gave an authenticity to the song that I would not have been able to provide at that time. I didn't have, nor do I now, my life was not a life of scandal. I don't have problems with drugs or those types of problems. There was a tragic element that gave Héctor's performance a lot of authenticity and so I said well, maybe this can help him, and that's why I gave it to him.]

As in previous interviews Blades had given, he lauded LaVoe's performance while simultaneously distancing himself from the sonero. The consistency in Blades's recollection of the events in question merits quoting the 1996 interview at length:

> I couldn't really get to Héctor because we had different lifestyles. I didn't do drugs, I never did do drugs. Never. I don't have any story of drugs, you know, to speak of. Never did drugs, never interested in drugs and then I wasn't interested in the people around the drugs. So that if anyone used drugs, I mean for me that was a turnoff and conversations couldn't go beyond a certain stage. So that I wasn't that friendly with Héctor, whose life revolved around drugs in many ways, and the people who were with him were also using drugs so . . . I got to spend time with him as a professional, I always respected him, and as a singer I think that he was just very,

very special. I gave him a tune called "El Cantante," which I was going to use for myself, after one of the worst episodes that he had because of his drug use and that song helped to bring him back. And Willie did the arrangement. And I wrote the song and I was going to use it as my signature but he really needed it so I respected him enough to give it to him. And he sang the heck out of it, but unfortunately there wasn't really that much closeness. . . . I always used to tell him, I said, "You know, why don't you move away from this?" And he really couldn't. I don't think he could. And, unfortunately, it ended up eating him.[14]

Blades deftly shifted the focus away from himself by referring to drugs and "scandals" in LaVoe's life, a rhetorical shift like the one he used in the *Los Angeles Times* article by Agustín Gurza when he denied Campbell's claim. Highlighting the very aspects of LaVoe's life that brought genuineness to his performance of "El Cantante," such statements serve to distinguish Blades from the sonero and his "tumultuous" life. Situated alongside Blades's desire to help LaVoe "after one of the worst episodes that [LaVoe] had because of his drug use," these comments also serve to dispel rumors about the circumstances under which LaVoe came to record the song.[15] Blades expressed compassion while distancing himself from the choices his colleague made. Instead of describing himself as a dispossessed artist who may not have been able to protect his creative labor, Blades presents himself as a colleague and friend, albeit one who could not save LaVoe.

Questions have continued to revolve around the exchange and how Blades would have had to navigate his priorities as an artist alongside concerns about future recording opportunities with Fania Records. As mentioned previously, Fania had sole discretion to determine whether to pick up the options on his contract, as was standard practice at the label.[16] LaVoe was not the only one who needed commercial success. Despite its control of the salsa market, the label needed the all-but-guaranteed sales of fan favorite LaVoe. But the acclaim Colón and Blades received for *Metiendo mano* also boded well for *Siembra*—though Fania could not have anticipated the revenue generated by the Colón-Blades collaboration. *Siembra* sold 600,000 copies its first year on the market.[17] LaVoe's return to the Latin music scene thus necessitated a strong comeback for Fania Records as well as the struggling sonero. Although LaVoe recorded his debut and sophomore efforts as a soloist in back-to-back years, he had not recorded another in more than a year.

## Between Relajo and Abjection

That LaVoe had difficulties is unquestionable. Critics blamed his drug use for his erratic behavior; the sonero repeatedly arrived late to rehearsals, recording sessions, and performances and sometimes failed to show up at all (even though sometimes he showed up early). LaVoe was so notorious for arriving late that Johnny Pacheco wrote "El Rey de la Puntualidad" (The King of Punctuality) for him to perform. The song begins with an instrumental prelude repeated several times, as if the band were actually waiting for the habitually late LaVoe to arrive. The two verses that follow feature the band, which addresses the audience and makes, if you will, their case: they are good colleagues, but their singer is late with such regularity that they have ironically crowned him the "King of Punctuality." LaVoe, who remained offstage during live performances while the band sang, would appear onstage to deliver the third verse. He, too, would address the audience, but not to refute the band's claims or defend himself. He begins by expressing his devotion to fans and hails them as "mi gente" (my people) a reference to his song by the same name. Considered by some a "Nuyorican anthem," "Mi gente" professes LaVoe's love, gratitude, and devotion to his fans.[18] By addressing the audience as such, he claims their loyalty.

"El Rey de la Puntualidad" proceeds with a call-and-response pattern that builds the musical and narrative tension within the song. This part of the song alternates between LaVoe's two-line fraseos (riffs, or semi-improvised lines) and the band's refrain, where they remind the vocalist that while

> Tu gente quiere
> oír tu voz sonora
> Nosotros sólo queremos
> que llegues a la hora
>
> [Your people want
> To hear your mellifluous voice
> We just want you
> To arrive on time]

These lyrics, of course, also invoke "Mi gente," suggesting that the audience's affection for the singer accounts for their failure to hold him accountable for his unprofessional behavior. For his part, LaVoe explains that, unlike the band, the audience appreciates what it takes to perform:

Ustedes me critican
con eso de llegar tarde
Pero mi gente se da cuenta
que yo vengo con bonito maquillaje

[You [the band] criticize me
For being late
But my people notice
that I show up looking good]

Rather than badger him, the audience appreciates what it takes for him to put on his face. LaVoe's use of irony and humor rejects productive time in favor of the worldmaking possibilities of relajo (boasting, play). His conversational tone exemplifies how LaVoe, as celebrated songwriter Tite Curet Alonso described it, "sang as if he were standing on the corner." He sang, Curet Alonso specified, "the way people talk," and the conversational tone allowed him to remain part of the audience even as he performed.[19]

Indeed, audiences embraced LaVoe as one of their own. They forgave him for arriving late (and sometimes not at all) and enthusiastically welcomed him to the stage time and again. The rumors of drug use did not deter fans, for whom LaVoe's personal failings accentuated his humanity, enhancing an artistic persona that oscillated between that of a tragic, Christlike figure beset by fate and a salsa badass. After his months-long disappearance, fans greeted LaVoe with chants of "Héctor, Héctor" as he joined the Fania All-Stars onstage for their annual performance at New York's Madison Square Garden in October 1977. The review of the concert in the *New York Daily News* likened his "thunderous" welcome to "the heralding of a political savior or an all-healing holy figure."[20]

LaVoe, known for his penchant for relajo, fully exploited "El Rey de la Puntualidad" for its comedic and ironic potential. When he "jura por su madre" (swears on his mother) that he will never be late again, the audience is in on the joke. The joke, of course, might not play as well if the song also referred to the times he did not show up at all to a gig. But it does not matter. The singer insists that the band forget that "nonsense" about him being late. Look at me, "yo soy estuche de monería" (I'm a good-looking bundle of relajo). Releasing himself and the listening public from censure, he reminds the band that he is a living, breathing, gorgeous embodiment of mischief. The band should not be so serious. He goes so far as to argue:

no es que yo llegue tarde
es que ustedes [the band and the audience] llegan muy temprano

[it's not that I'm late
it's that you arrive too early]

The problem is not LaVoe but the expectations of a wage economy to which the musicians choose to adhere. He rejects cultural narratives of a productive citizen subject within a wage economy that constituted Puerto Ricans as surplus, expendable labor. Amid the humor there is also a mild rebuke, given, according to LaVoe, like a brother: band members may have succumbed to the normative expectations of productive, or majoritarian, time, but they have no right to dampen his flow with their newly reformed ways. LaVoe's critique of straight time relies, and here I draw on Muñoz, on the sonero's self-consciousness and obliviousness of his relajo—a relajo that can still be heard in his response to the band and the laughter that exists still in the recording; a laughter that, like the cheers during live performances from fans who had sometimes waited hours for him to arrive, sounds an ecstatic disruption, a "different, joyously rebellious solidarity—that of the underdog"—that underpins LaVoe's performance.[21] He was, after all, known for *relajando* (joking around) offstage too. One day, as the story goes, he arrived at a rehearsal so late all he could say in his defense was that he had gotten not one but *four* flat tires! The sonic imaginary revels in his sonority and humanity, including his participation in a wage economy in which he operates but to which LaVoe refuses to remain subject. In the song, LaVoe suggests that his timing—that is, the time he arrives at the gig, like the timing that marks his success as a sonero—is as much a part of his performative persona as it is a part of his sonority. As at other moments when LaVoe turned to the audience, he expresses a solidarity with them through the performative act of relajo, implicating them in transgressive behavior.

### "El Cantante": The Song as Gift

"El Cantante" builds on LaVoe's relationship to his audience. The first half of the song establishes the schism between the performer and his personal life, which mirrors the relationship between El Cantante and the listening public. In the first three stanzas, El Cantante refers to the audience as "ustedes" (you, plural), a monolithic group that sees his talents and the benefits of fame but remains oblivious to his personal sorrows. The second half of the song shifts to the singular and more socially intimate "tú" (you) when El Cantante and the band use the chorus to dedicate LaVoe's best pregones to the audience: "hoy te dedico mis mejores pregones" (today I dedicate my best verses to you). The pregones that follow, two-line verses LaVoe wrote into the song, strengthen LaVoe's relationship with the listening public.

Historically, *pregones* refers to the centuries-old practice of making proclamations in the public squares or markets of large cities and small towns alike. Characterized by a poetic or laudatory character, street vendors and laborers incorporated everyday language and idioms, slang, or local patois into their pregones. Over time, pregones were also used to initiate public rites and popular celebrations, whether through oration or music. During the mid to late nineteenth century in Latin America, *pregones* came to refer to the popular music by the same name. Nineteenth-century Cuban composers added music to well-known pregones.[22] In Puerto Rico, the *pregón* was often used in alcohol and tobacco jingles. Early to mid-twentieth-century iterations by composers such as Manuel "Canario" Jiménez and Rafael Hernández often centered on humorous themes or life in the street. Pregones, as a musical practice, retain the characteristics of the original street vendor and laborer pregones while selling, not the goods or skills in the lyrics, but the musical value of the performer.[23]

The potential disjuncture of the economic transaction does not engender alienation between LaVoe and the listening public. LaVoe's pregones identify the sonero with the audience. He uses the first-person plural "nosotros" (we) when he sings to them:

> Yo soy El Cantante, vamos a celebrar
> no quiero tristezas, lo mío es cantar, cantar
>
> [I'm the singer, we're going to celebrate
> I don't want sadness, my thing is to sing, to sing]

The performance itself strengthens the intimacy between El Cantante and the audience, a relationship undiminished by the fact that they paid to hear him sing. The bond between LaVoe and the audience does not exist despite the commercial transaction but through it. By explicitly naming his music as both gift and commodity, LaVoe disavows the opposition between market and culture. He reconciles the tension between the public persona and the private tumult by exposing that tension in the act of performance. LaVoe presents the song to his fans as a gift and invites them to celebrate with him: "baila si quieres bailar, canta, si quieres cantar " (dance if you want to dance, sing if you want to sing). As with other systems of gift exchange, LaVoe's act of giving requires reciprocation. While LaVoe's performance demonstrates his status as a superior sonero worthy of his fans' devotion, the audience's dancing demonstrates their status as loyal fans worthy of the sonero. The instantaneous and continuous response between LaVoe and the audience not only subverts the temporal separation between the gift and the countergift but undermines the structural separation between performer and audience. LaVoe's pregones draw on his/El Cantante's shared experiences of "sorrows" and "pains" with the audience while the performance itself—both theirs and his—expresses a present futurity in NuYoRico.

LaVoe, as El Cantante, does not attempt to mask the expectation of reciprocity. The song's form requires it. The pregones that formed the second half of the song use a call-and-response pattern that relies on the exchanges among LaVoe, the chorus sung by band members, and the musical arrangements. The band plays continuously as the song alternates between the individual pregones and the chorus. Sometimes an instrumental interlude follows the chorus. At other times, it follows one of LaVoe's pregones. The alternating roles in the call-and-response among LaVoe, the chorus, the instrumental interludes, and, of course, the audience express an immediate and continuous reciprocity that builds throughout the more-than-ten-minute song.

LaVoe exploits the improvisational possibilities that the pregones offer, which often changed during live performances. Whether in the initial recording or subsequent performances, LaVoe's sonoridad is constituted in relation to normative masculinity. With assurances to the audience and his contemporaries that his pregones "son mejor que los de ayer" (are better than yesterday's), LaVoe defies his "criticones" (critics) to prove otherwise. A call-and-response between the chorus and the instrumental interludes explodes approximately halfway through the pregones and testifies to LaVoe's claim that "mientras algunos cantan con faldas, yo canto con pantalones" (although there are those who sing with skirts on, I sing with pants on). The lines also reminds us that, as discussed in chapter 3, of Lawrence La Fountain-Stokes's work, "there can be no *macho* if there is no *loca*."[24] LaVoe continues to exploit the improvisational possibilities of the song to define his own value as an artist—and not just any artist but "el sonero mayor" (the greatest sonero), a reference that aligns him with *the* sonero mayor, Ismael Rivera. Elevating himself, as Wilson Valentín-Escobar puts it, into the "male pantheon of pleneros . . . upholds and reproduces a masculine hegemony in Plena music while also accenting the gendered construction of public culture and the way in which masculinity shapes collective memory."[25]

"El Cantante" draws attention to LaVoe's participation in a system of competition that is typical of salsa but that also constitutes an important characteristic of the system of gift exchange. He makes a calculated exchange of his pregones for recognition as not just a talented sonero but the best.[26] LaVoe sends a *saludo*, or shoutout, to Celia Cruz, Cheo Feliciano, and Rivera as "grandes cantores" (great singers) who "cantan de verdad" (really sing) and "ponen a gozar la gente" (and make people have a good time). Doing so places LaVoe alongside renowned and beloved Afro-Caribbean vocalists—Cruz was from Cuba, Rivera and Feliciano from Puerto Rico—whose music linked the Caribbean with New York, and Afro-Caribbean musical practices with salsa's "way of making music."[27] A *blanquito* (white boy) from Ponce, LaVoe declares his place alongside three of the most renowned and talented soneros and sonera in the Puerto Rico–Cuba–New York nexus of Afro-Caribbean musical traditions.

The swagger of LaVoe's performance accompanies the unpretentiousness of someone who repeatedly described himself as a humble jíbaro. In various recorded performances, such as the one released on *Héctor LaVoe Live* (1997), LaVoe begins "El Cantante" by reminding the crowd that he loves them "for free" and asks them to remember that he is an everyman, a prologue similar to the one given by the clown from *Pagliacci*.[28] "Digan lo que digan, pase lo que pase, hablen de mí lo que hablen de mí, ustedes saben que yo los quiero de gratis. Que Dios los bendiga a todos. . . . Pero . . . ustedes recuérdense que yo sólo soy mísero" (Say what they may say, no matter what happens, say what they may about me, you know that I love you for free. May God bless you all. . . . But remember that I'm just a wretch). The prologue, like "El Cantante," builds on LaVoe's status as part of New York's Puerto Rican communities, an everyman beset by life's tragicomedy. The prologue reminds the audience of his devotion even as he draws attention to the commodity status of El Cantante—both the subject of the song and himself—thereby disrupting the commodity function of the performance.

LaVoe's recording of "El Cantante" challenges what Arjun Appadurai describes as the exaggerated distinction between gift exchange and market economies by instead revealing consumption to be a "social, relational act."[29] Here the gift is, as Ralph Waldo Emerson describes it, "a portion of thyself" that an artist gives to the public. For Emerson, a gift must convey that which properly belonged to one's character. "The only gift is a portion of thyself. Thou must bleed for me. Therefore the poet brings his poem; the shepherd, his lamb; the farmer, corn; the miner, a gem; the sailor, coral and shells; the painter, his picture"—a sentiment echoed in the prologue to *Pagliacci* as much as "El Cantante."[30] To "bleed" for his audience, to share his voice, El Cantante offers his pregones. El Cantante, that is, LaVoe, offered fans his voice and his love for them. An everyman, he expresses a social bond through the performance of shared abjection. LaVoe's love is "free" and exceeds the limits of his commodity status. It is based on his success as a talented sonero and "poor wretch" who gives himself to the public. The song develops within a coadaptive relationship between "El Cantante" (both LaVoe and the song) and his audience, the latter remaining part of, not something separate from, the performance and El Cantante.

LaVoe's sonority and the public nature of his private life only partially explain why the sonero became so closely identified with the figure of "El Cantante." LaVoe's timbre, phrasing, and overall dramatic rendering combined with Colón's arrangements for a performance through which the very figure of El Cantante was constituted for the listening public. The song's lush string arrangements provided a symphonic quality while the overall orchestration evoked the verismo style of *Pagliacci*. The timbre of the string instruments, which sometimes play the melody and at other times join the rhythm section, beautifully complemented the resonance of LaVoe's voice. When LaVoe sang the melody in harmony with the strings, the combination produced a rich chordal sound. LaVoe's dramatic rendering of the melody was deepened but not restricted. The reverberation of LaVoe's voice, heard as an echo on the final sound in "El le le le le," creates a wistful sound that sustains the song's narrative. The layered and complex orchestration successfully married the song's arrangements and LaVoe's vocal aesthetics.

Fania released the album with "El Cantante," *Comedia*, in 1978. The cover featured LaVoe dressed as Charlie Chaplin's Little Tramp; it proposed an image of the singer as an everyman beset by external forces that, as various songs on the album declare, would destroy him. Chaplin, the "London ragamuffin" immortalized for his representations of humans' "tragicomic conflicts with fate," became LaVoe's doppelgänger. An English comedy actor whose impersonations of mimes and clowns inspired future performers, Chaplin represented, as described in the *New York Times*, a "harassed but gallant Everyman . . . part clown, part social outcast, part philosopher." Chaplin had died the previous year after a series of personal tragedies. His experiences included his father's alcoholism, his mother's admission to an

**5.3**  Front album cover for Héctor LaVoe's *Comedia* (1978)

insane asylum, and various other events that audiences projected onto his characters. Like Chaplin, LaVoe used fashion as a site through which excess dramatized his public persona—large bow ties, loud plaid suits, and mismatched colors—and set him apart from his contemporaries. LaVoe sported Chaplin's signature outfit, "a comedic ensemble of baggy trousers, outsize shoes, and undersize derby redolent of decayed gentility, a frayed short cutaway and a sporty bamboo cane," for the front album cover for *Comedia*.[31] The pose features LaVoe standing alone in the middle of the photograph, his black ensemble stark against the translucent beige background. The solitary image of LaVoe, using makeup to complete the impersonation of Chaplin's Little Tramp, contrasts sharply with the one on the back cover. There LaVoe appears in the foreground while the album credits appear to recede. He is in the same costume, sitting on the floor now with his knees bent and roller skates on his feet. The pancake makeup and fake mustache

**5.4**   Back album cover for Héctor LaVoe's *Comedia* (1978)

are gone, however, and the cane rests on one knee. The camera angle provides a full-body view of LaVoe, accentuating his legs and the skates, which are featured prominently. The inscrutable expression on the front cover is now replaced by a jocular grin as LaVoe looks directly into the camera. It visually combines the look of Chaplin with LaVoe's musical persona, suggesting the sonero's wit and sense of humor and signifying the play of meanings and artifice implied in the visual imagery.

While the two images reinforce the meanings of El Cantante, the front album cover resonates with the melancholy title track. In "Comedia," LaVoe waxes poetic about life, fate, and disillusionment. The lyrics for "Comedia" complement the signification of LaVoe as a tragic figure whose personal suffering belied aesthetic creativity and professional accolades, a self-referential moment that evokes both Pagliacci and Chaplin's 1928 film *The Circus*. In life, "mucho has de llorar / poco has de reír" (you will cry plenty / you will laugh little). Happiness proves fleeting and exists primarily through its absence, while despair and earthly suffering dominate the musical persona's role as an "extra" in life's tragic comedy. As a bolero, the song's slow tempo and the somber lyrics combine with the expressivity of LaVoe's voice to create a sense of loss and despair. The circus melody that emerges in counterpoint to the dominant melody suggests the image of the clown on the cover. The melody of the circus mimics the "earthly suffering" performed by the musical persona for the amusement of fate. In the persona of Chaplin, the singing subject of LaVoe's corpus can express the sentimentality that previously threatened subjecthood.

*Comedia* quickly topped *Billboard* magazine's "Hot Latin LPs" in the New York and Chicago salsa charts. In Miami, the album claimed the number 2 spot behind the Celia Cruz–Willie Colón collaboration *Only They Could Have Made This Album* for each week in September. In fact, *Comedia* had already received popular acclaim before it went on sale because LaVoe performed songs from the album while on tour in Latin America just prior to the record's release.[32] In December 1979, *Billboard* ranked *Comedia* third among "Top Latin Salsa Albums" of the year.

### The After-Party: "El Cantante" in Death

I turn here briefly toward LaVoe's biography to provide some context for the extramusical aspects of his life that contributed to the cultural imaginary that developed over time and for which "El Cantante" became a type of origins narrative. LaVoe grew up in Puerto Rico. His brother moved to New York City before he did and died there of a drug overdose. Thus, LaVoe's father objected to having another son relocate to New York, but he went in 1963 without his father's blessing. As highlighted in a *Latin N.Y.* article, by 1978 public speculation about drug use, "nervous breakdowns," and "need for spiritual guidance" had long circulated among salsa fans. In 1987, Héctor LaVoe's son died from a gunshot wound, and his mother-in-law was murdered. A year later, LaVoe suffered multiple injuries after jumping through a window to escape a fire that destroyed his home. These public tragedies added layers of meaning to LaVoe's performance of "El Cantante."[33] When LaVoe fell from a hotel window in Puerto Rico in 1988, conflicting rumors—it was an accident, he was trying to commit suicide, someone pushed him—quickly surfaced as fans and musicians alike attempted to make sense of what happened. By the mid-1980s, his health and the clarity of his voice began to deteriorate. He struggled at times to recall lyrics, and the distinct articulation that fans remembered during my interviews began to fade. His physical mobility also declined. By the end of his life, he needed help with activities of daily living, including walking. Yet promoters continued to book LaVoe, who reportedly struggled financially, providing fans with a startling view of his condition.

The off-Broadway play ¿Quién mató a Héctor LaVoe? / Who Killed Héctor LaVoe?, like the 2006 biopic, pitted the singer's charisma and tremendous vocal talents against ill-fated personal choices and tragic events that transpired during the vocalist's life. The play debuted off-Broadway in 1999 and in Puerto Rico in 2000. It was written and directed by Pablo Cabrera and produced by Latin music promoter David Maldonado. In it, vocalist Domingo Quiñones played LaVoe; the soundtrack became the first cast recording to make the Billboard Latin 50 chart. After the play's 2000 performance in Puerto Rico, the publishing agencies Latin American Music Company (LAMCO) and the Association of Latin American Composers and Editors (ACEMLA, Asociación de Compositores y Editores de la Música) filed a copyright infringement lawsuit in the District Court of Puerto Rico (DPR) against the show's producer, CFDM Theatrical Productions (CFDM). They charged that CFDM failed to obtain licenses for the use of five songs authored or co-authored by LaVoe and included in the play: "Paraíso de dulzura" (Sweet paradise), "Periódico de ayer" (Yesterday's newspaper), "Piraña" (Piranha), "El Todopoderoso" (The Almighty), and "La fama" (Fame).[34] Accordingly, LAMCO and ACEMLA produced the copyright assignments purchased from LaVoe's son José Pérez after his father's death in 1993. Pérez had registered the copyrights to the vocalist's songs with the US Copyright Office and then transferred them to LAMCO and ACEMLA.[35] The producers of ¿Quién mató a Héctor LaVoe? in fact had obtained permission to use these songs—through Fania's successor Sonido. The producers presented the licenses to the court. It fell to the court to determine who owned the copyrights to LaVoe's composition: LAMCO and ACEMLA or Sonido. Sonido intervened on the side of CFDM to defend its right to license the songs in question.[36]

While the court in Puerto Rico deliberated, the beginnings of a separate legal fight over LaVoe's royalties began to brew in New York. David Lugo, a percussionist who played in LaVoe's band, claimed that the late sonero transferred all royalties to him before his death. LaVoe's heirs—his widow, Nilda Román Pérez; daughter, Leslie Pérez; and son, José Pérez—warned Sonido that the label should "not issue any money, property, interest, royalties and/or anything of value belonging to the deceased Héctor LaVoe to David Lugo." According to the estate, any contract that Lugo might produce with LaVoe's signature was fraudulent.[37] Lugo filed a lawsuit in 1999 against Sonido in New York to recover past royalties owed to LaVoe. Fearing that LaVoe's estate might sue for the same monies, Sonido petitioned the court to determine who actually owned LaVoe's royalties. These royalties included income from the sale of LaVoe's recordings as well as licensing fees paid by third parties to use the songs he wrote—as in the case of *¿Quién mató a Héctor LaVoe?* The court deferred its decision until the Puerto Rico case settled the question whether Sonido or LAMCO and ACEMLA owned the copyright to the songs written by LaVoe.

The case of *Latin American Music Co. and ACEMLA v. Cárdenas Fernández and Associates* in Puerto Rico came down to whether LaVoe's son or Sonido held the copyright to the sonero's songs after his death. Like most artists who signed with Fania Records and its subsidiaries, LaVoe had signed a standard songwriter's agreement (SSA) with Fania Publishing. The SSA transferred the copyright to all the songs LaVoe composed while under contract to Fania Records to the label's publishing arm, Fania Publishing. The SSA could not be terminated or amended without written consent from both LaVoe and Fania Publishing, or successors to the same. These successor rights were transferred to Valsyn when it purchased the Fania catalog, including assignments to Fania Publishing, in 1979. When Sonido signed a series of licensing agreements with Valsyn, it included the right to license LaVoe's compositions to third parties like CFDM. In 1999, CFDM licensed the songs from Sonido for *¿Quién mató a Héctor LaVoe?* The court in Puerto Rico found that this "standard songwriter's agreement between LaVoe and Fania did not expire upon LaVoe's death and, having not been terminated via mutual written agreement by LaVoe or his heirs, the copyrights continued to reside with Fania and its successors."[38] In other words, because neither Fania Publishing nor its successors Valsyn and Sonido agreed to transfer the rights to Pérez, the latter did not own the copyright to the songs LaVoe wrote after the sonero's death. Pérez did not have the right to license the songs or transfer the copyrights to LAMCO and ACEMLA. Only Sonido, having been granted licensing rights to LaVoe's songs by Valsyn, had the authority to license their use in *¿Quién mató a Héctor LaVoe?*

With the copyright question in Puerto Rico settled, the case in New York concerning LaVoe's royalties proceeded. Neither Lugo nor LaVoe's estate contested the validity of the SSAs LaVoe signed with Fania Publishing, their terms, or whether they remained in effect after his death. This failure to challenge the SSAs is no small matter. The SSAs assigned the copyrights to Fania Publishing and paid the artist royalties for the use of the songs he wrote. Because the agreement also stipulated that LaVoe could not transfer these royalties to a third party without the consent of Fania Publishing (or its successors), the royalties from songs LaVoe wrote while signed to Fania Records belonged to his estate.[39] Lugo could, however, sue for royalties from LaVoe's record sales. Unlike the songwriter royalties, those from record sales did not require authorization from Fania Publishing or its successors. The document LaVoe signed was sufficient to transfer the royalties to Lugo.

When reviewing the court papers, I came across two documents related to a transfer of rights from LaVoe to Lugo, at least one of which Lugo presented to the court as proof that LaVoe had transferred royalties to him before dying. The first was a one-sentence handwritten note on a sheet of paper wherein LaVoe transferred his royalties to Lugo for a nominal fee of ten dollars. The second document, a typed and signed letter dated six months before LaVoe's death, also transferred the royalties to Lugo but did not include any request for payment. It did include instructions for the division of LaVoe's royalties among his heirs and Lugo, with instructions that the latter should use some of the monies to create a nonprofit organization to provide education about AIDS and drug abuse.[40]

LaVoe's estate did not dispute the authenticity of his signature on the document. Instead, the estate presented evidence of LaVoe's drug addiction, deteriorating health, and mental incapacitation to challenge the validity of the letter transferring royalties to Lugo.[41] The family claimed that LaVoe's physical and psychological state was such that it was impossible for him to "comprehend [the] true nature and potential effect" of the assignment letter. Like Lugo, they argued that LaVoe needed help to bathe, complete bodily functions, and even smoke. They also asserted that, per rumors circulating toward the end of LaVoe's life, Lugo provided the vocalist with a steady supply of cocaine and heroin. This, they explained, allowed Lugo to exert undue influence over a physically and psychologically dependent LaVoe.[42] Sonido, in turn, claimed that Lugo did not establish the Hector LaVoe AIDS foundation for which he held fundraisers.[43]

Lugo vehemently denied Sonido's allegations and countered the accusations levied against him by LaVoe's estate. Lugo described himself as a faithful friend and caretaker who began caring for LaVoe in mid-1992 because no one else assumed responsibility for the singer's well-being. Lugo went so far as to accuse LaVoe's family of having abandoned the singer as he became increasingly ill due to drug use. In his affidavit, Lugo recounts finding LaVoe living in virtual "squalor" in the artist's Queens apartment in 1992, without utilities or food, so he assumed the role of caretaker who bathed, fed, and transported his friend to medical appointments. LaVoe was angry at his family for abandoning him, explained Lugo. He alone among LaVoe's family and friends, Lugo asserted, had acted as caregiver. And as caregiver, it was he who feared that the singer's wife, Nilda Román Pérez, would provide LaVoe with illicit drugs. Lugo then doubled down on his loyalty. According to Lugo, he "tried desperately to get her to be a good wife to her husband." As LaVoe's friend, it was also he who "persuaded" the sonero to assign a percentage of his royalties to his wife because "the family should have some share of his legacy."[44] And it was also he, not LaVoe's family, who transported the artist to a Florida medical center for treatment that summer.[45] Lugo's lawyer pointed to the psychological evaluation conducted during the intake process at the Florida treatment center to dispute the claim that LaVoe did not have the mental capacity to understand the nature of what he signed. In the evaluation, the doctor describes LaVoe as "appear[ing] organized, logical and goal directed . . . alert and oriented for time, place and person with [n]o significant memory impairment for recent and remote events."[46] Lugo also submitted a video recording of LaVoe's final televised interview in May 1992 as evidence of their friendship.

An unedited version of the interview was submitted as evidence of Lugo's relationship to LaVoe. Although the unedited Beta tape was absent from the court file, a partial transcript remains in the files. The program that aired, albeit in its edited form, was also available online for me to view in its entirety. Reporter Gloria Soltero conducted the interview with LaVoe, which took place a few months before he was admitted to the Florida treatment center in July 1992, for the investigative news show *Ocurrió así* (This is how it happened) that aired on the Telemundo network based out of Miami.[47] The segment begins with a teaser designed to whet the viewer's appetite with the promise of revealing LaVoe's journey "de la gloria al ocaso" (from glory to downfall). Contrasting images of LaVoe appear on-screen as the narrator informs the audience that "fue el mejor en la salsa pero la droga acabó con la carrera de Héctor LaVoe" (he was the best at salsa, but drugs ended Héctor LaVoe's career). The first still shows a robust LaVoe during a performance at the height of his career, while the second features a thin and frail image from the interview for *Ocurrió así.*

The segment begins by describing LaVoe as a prodigious talent who achieved overnight fame in New York but succumbed to the weight of life's tribulations. Brief interviews with Lugo and record promoter Ralph Mercado provide a now-familiar story about LaVoe's trajectory. Lugo confirms LaVoe's centrality for the viewer, while Mercado explains that LaVoe "no le hacía daño a nadie" (never hurt anyone) but had to be "pushed" because he would refuse to wake up and get dressed and he routinely arrived late to performances. What follows is a preview of the litany of calamities LaVoe endured. Now, the reporter informs viewers, LaVoe lives alone, subsumed by his solitude and memories. After these introductory comments by Lugo and Mercado, as well as Soltero, the video shows an unidentified child opening the door to LaVoe's apartment. Lugo, Soltero, and the television crew then enter the apartment. Establishing shots confirm the veracity of the interview's teaser. The camera pans the apartment, showing framed photographs with friends, family, media personalities, and musicians that line the walls, including the Gold Album for *Comedia*. The camera provides close-ups of various photographs and then continues to pan the space, settling on a long shot of a hallway with a small, round table in the far corner covered with a white tablecloth. The camera continues to present LaVoe's surroundings before he enters the living room, zooming in on the altar. The grainy close-up shows a Santería practitioner's altar with the statue of the Catholic figure Santa Bárbara, the double of the Santería deity Shangó, draped with Catholic prayer beads. Smaller statues, such as that of Christ and another of Saint Martín de Porres, a Black Catholic saint, as well as glasses of water and other items also sit atop the table. For viewers familiar with the murmurings about LaVoe's reported attempts to find spiritual and psychological healing within Santería, raised by Mercado in the opening segment of the show, the decision to linger on the altar reanimates narratives that link LaVoe's spiritual practices to an inability to cope with the deaths of family members, drug addiction, and, possibly, an AIDS diagnosis that Lugo denied during the interview.

The camera remains on the altar as voices can be heard in the background and LaVoe enters the field of view. Disheveled, he walks slowly into the living room wearing black-and-white pajama bottoms and a green T-shirt with "Music Makes People Beautiful" emblazoned in black letters across the front. He sits on the end of a navy couch, as directed by the crew, who proceed to put a plastic cape across his shoulders in preparation for makeup. Lugo then helps LaVoe put on a suit jacket that hangs loosely on his now-diminutive frame. LaVoe does not engage with the interviewer, Lugo, or the crew as they bustle about him. He looks into the distance and appears physically uncomfortable as the camera repeatedly frames him alongside photographs on the wall behind the couch where he sits. These shots emphasize the contrast between LaVoe's glorious past and his current state, producing an impression of two person(a)s that aligns with the segment's approach and reducing LaVoe, in both the interview and the courtroom, to the disjuncture between life on- and offstage.

The chasm is further highlighted as LaVoe sings along to "La fama," a song playing in the background, which he wrote and recorded for the album *Revento* (Exploded), released in 1985.[48] When the music begins to play, LaVoe becomes more animated. His speech regularly falters, but he continues to sing along with his recordings and even flirts with the female reporter. As in "El Cantante," the song's musical persona incorporates his status as both artist and commodity:

Yo soy la fama
soy tristeza y sonrisa pagada
que con dinero se puede obtener
Y escuchen por qué
Doy placer y en regreso yo no pido nada
Sí, es trabajo llegar a la fama
y a la fama saber mantener

[I am fame
I am sadness and a paid smile
That you can procure with money
And listen why:
I give pleasure and ask for nothing in return
Yes, it's hard work to obtain fame
And know how to keep it]

No tengo amigos
Y si un amor fácil lo consigo
así de fácil lo he de perder
Mi madre dijo:
No creas ser un gran tenorio
Pararás en un sanatorio
Y allí la fama tu has de perder

[I don't have friends
And if I find love easily
I lose it just as easily

My mother told me:
Don't be a Casanova
You'll end up in a sanatorium
And there, you'll lose your fame]

Whereas the figure of "El Cantante" (as well as "Mi gente" and "El Rey de la Puntualidad") finds pleasure in his relationship to the audience, LaVoe as the personification of fame remains alienated. Enduring love remains elusive and echoes a mother's warning about the dangers of fame, even for a great sonero. In hindsight, the song may seem eerily prescient of LaVoe's challenges in the last years of his life. LaVoe nevertheless revels in the pleasure of his own artistic prowess, a talent "que manda madre" (that's tight). He will remain legendary even in death so he does not say goodbye but rather "hasta siempre" (until forever).

Soltero begins the interview by asking LaVoe about a performance at the New York nightclub SOB's two weeks earlier, in what would turn out to be his last public appearance. She then pivots to LaVoe's living conditions and asks about Lugo's regular visits. LaVoe's thoughts appear unorganized during various parts of the interview, and sometimes his responses are unrelated to what he has been asked or told. Yet, while LaVoe's speech is impaired, he is lucid and assertive as he describes how much he values Lugo. LaVoe's expression changes when asked about his family, and he becomes more guarded. As to whether they visit, he gives a one-word answer: "Sometimes." The sentences that follow are largely inaudible but clearly convey reluctance to talk about his children or wife. Instead, he returns to Lugo, indicating his companion as he says, "He is my family, okay? . . . Right, papi. You're my family. . . . If something happens to him, forget it, I don't know what to do. Because he's the only one who's always there for me." Later in the interview, he refers to this statement and explains that Lugo has earned the right to be LaVoe's "everything"—"my brother, my father, my uncle, my family." The interview appears to confirm Lugo's claim that he became LaVoe's sole caretaker while the family remained largely outside of the picture.

Taking a cue from LaVoe's unwillingness to talk about his family, the interviewer asks about his quick ascent to fame. LaVoe challenges the implication that it was quick. He straightens himself on the couch, brows furrowed, and gives the interviewer the side-eye, saying, "Huh. Not easy, baby." The interviewer fails to hear him or to understand him, so LaVoe repeats himself. "Not easy." Rather than follow up on the answer, the interviewer responds by asking LaVoe to describe the traumas he faced during his life, asking what it is like to have "lost everything." LaVoe, however, challenges the premise of the question. "No he perdido todo" (I have not lost everything).

Lugo submitted the unedited recording as evidence of his "close friendship" with LaVoe but not the latter's state of mind. According to Lugo, "Hector's abilities to respond to questions and to articulate his thoughts were actually better" when the latter transferred his rights.[49] This statement notwithstanding, Lugo's lawyer highlights the singer's ability "to respond intelligently to the interviewer's questions." The lawyer also draws the court's attention to the relationship between LaVoe and Lugo. LaVoe, he states, "speaks glowingly" of Lugo. This, the lawyer goes on to argue, provides evidence of both the reason LaVoe assigned his royalties to Lugo and the intent to do so. It also supports LaVoe's decision to name Lugo as his health care proxy, which the estate did not challenge, as well as transfer a general power of attorney to Lugo in October 1992. The lawyer points to the absence of LaVoe's family from the interview as a further indication of their estrangement.[50]

The interview may have played a role in the settlement between the parties to the lawsuit, which divided LaVoe's artist royalties between Lugo and the sonero's estate. Ultimately, Sonido acknowledged that Fania owed $122,150 in past artist royalties and $85,600 in past songwriter royalties. The estate of Héctor LaVoe was awarded 100 percent of past and future songwriter royalties, 60 percent of past artist royalties, and 67.5 percent of future artist royalties.[51] Because the assignment of songwriter rights from LaVoe to Lugo was declared null and void, Lugo was not awarded any royalties from LaVoe's compositions. Lugo was awarded 40 percent of past artist royalties and 32.5 percent of future artist royalties.

In death, LaVoe remained unable to exercise his moral rights to the songs he composed in life, through a turn of events that reaffirmed the sonero's cultural authority over "El Cantante" even as it distorted LaVoe's performance of abjection and subjecthood. The master narratives about LaVoe reduce the sonero to an archetype devoid of the performative practices through which LaVoe manifested a trans-Boricua imaginary, transmitting the cultural memory and social history of New York's Puerto Rican communities.[52] Representations by Blades, Lugo, LaVoe's estate, *Ocurrió así*, and others are not interested in how the sonero's performativity destabilized the boundaries between subjecthood and abjection. The submission of LaVoe's psychological profile, the viewing of LaVoe's final televised interview, and the descriptions by both parties detailing his physical and psychological decline reproduced LaVoe's abjection as a racialized and colonial subject, while the performer himself illuminated the liberatory potential of performing abjection.

### *Archisme* as Archive

I return here to the *Ocurrió así* news segment to examine the discourse of illness that accompanies the narrative of LaVoe's life. The heavy makeup applied to LaVoe partially covers Kaposi's sarcoma lesions on his face. Rumors of LaVoe's AIDS diagnosis circulated widely by the early 1990s but were not confirmed publicly until after his death. Lugo denied these claims during his interview for *Ocurrió así*, which aired as part of the same segment: "No tiene SIDA. Lo que le pasa es un abuso de drogas. . . . No es SIDA porque no tiene SIDA" (It's not AIDS. What's wrong is that he abused drugs. . . . It's not AIDS because he doesn't have AIDS). While Lugo insisted that LaVoe's medical problems stemmed from intravenous drug use, LaVoe's sister, Nancy Pérez, remained less committal in her comments for the *Ocurrió así* segment. She expressed concern for her brother but hesitated to acknowledge the nature of his illness. Those who knew LaVoe, she explained, would tell her about the rumors. "Siempre hay gente" (There are always people), she said, who know she is LaVoe's sister and ask her about the rumors:

> A mí me ven [y piensan] "Contra. Su hermana, déjame preguntarle." A veces viene gente y dicen "Mira que tu hermano tiene aquello. . . . Mira que tu hermano . . ." desto y que esto. Tú sabes. Bueno, pues, yo no sé. No tiene na' porque, él no tiene, tú sabes como dicen, el SIDA o el desto o, si lo tiene, pues, pero no sé.

> [They see me [and think] "Damn. His sister, let me ask her." Sometimes people come up to me and say, "Listen, your brother has that thing. Listen, your brother" this and that. You know [how it is]. Well, that is, I don't know. He doesn't have anything because, he doesn't have, you know how they say, AIDS or the thing or, if he has it, well, I don't know.]

Her response evokes the description of fans in "El Cantante" who approach the musical persona on the street, once again underscoring the public nature of LaVoe's personal life and the role of gossip in discussions of the sonero's medical condition. The incomplete sentences and use of filler language ("you know") accentuate her equivocation, as does the reference to rumors that came to her attention ("this and that") and "the thing" about AIDS, to which she refers but which she leaves unnamed.

In New York, where Latinos made up more than one-quarter of reported AIDS cases in the 1980s and 1990s, Puerto Ricans constituted the overwhelming majority of these cases, with mortality rates among Puerto Rican men in New York twice as high as for whites, and 36 percent higher than for African Americans. While Puerto Rican men were disproportionately likely to have contracted HIV from intravenous drug use rather than sexual contact, only the latter was publicly named as fans, musicians, and journalists speculated about LaVoe's diagnosis.[53] The denials and equivocations surrounding AIDS in the late 1980s and 1990s within diasporic Puerto Rican communities must be situated within the stigmatization of male homosexual bodies, the conflation of disease and desire, and the moralistic frames through which Latina/o subjectivities are expressed, as Horacio Roque Ramírez argued.[54] In Puerto Rican communities, where family members may prefer to attribute an AIDS diagnosis of a male family member to intravenous drug use rather than same-sex relations with men, the denial and equivocations about LaVoe's AIDS diagnosis must be considered as attempts to defuse bochinche (gossip, rumor). I propose that the allegations made by Lugo and LaVoe's widow in court documents, like the statements made by LaVoe's sister, work to redirect any suggestion that the sonero engaged in sexual relations with men.

My interest in the framing of LaVoe's AIDS diagnosis arose during an interview I conducted in September 2002 with a Fania Records executive who continued to work for its successor Sonido. During the interview, he referred to the lawsuit filed by Lugo, which had been settled just a few months earlier. It was clear that the executive assumed I knew about both, but I did not, and he was surprised by my follow-up questions. His cautious replies marked a shift from the confidence and occasional arrogance he had projected up to that point during the interview. He explained that Lugo was a musician from LaVoe's band and his "compañero" (companion). The use of this term, which could be used to designate a friend, helper, or partner—the meaning of the latter itself dependent on context—drew my attention. Using a semiformal and semistructured approach to interviews, I encouraged him to elaborate on the lawsuit and tell me about Lugo, a name with which I was unfamiliar at the time. The tone of the interview immediately shifted, and he became guarded as he explained that Lugo "took care of" LaVoe toward the end of his life when no one else did. The executive spoke slowly and carefully, with obvious discomfort. He also trailed off momentarily while explaining that Lugo "andaba con él" (was with him), meaning LaVoe. An ambiguous phrase, it suggests that LaVoe and Lugo were close without clarifying the context of the relationship.[55] Although I wondered about the choice of language and the relationship itself, I eventually veered away from the topic.

The executive's evasion and discomfort at my questions, whether due to the topic itself or the recent lawsuit, dissuaded me. I was also unsure how to continue probing the relationship when the person with whom I was speaking remained reticent to elaborate on it. And, frankly, already an outsider to the salsa scene, I became concerned that should I proceed with additional questions despite his caginess, he might end the interview. Did I become complicit with salsa's masculinist gatekeeping? Certainly, the Fania executive presented himself, as Muñoz wrote in relation to queer memory, as "a gatekeeper, representing a straight present, who will labor to invalidate the historical fact of queer lives—present, past, and future."[56] Outside of salsa's masculinist narratives, the belief that LaVoe engaged in sex with other men is not uncommon. But as with comments about salsa duo singer Bobby Cruz and pianist Richie Ray, about whom allusions to a possible sexual relationship arose spontaneously during my interview with another music executive, the topic was treated as *chisme* (gossip) or bochinche, an inappropriate topic to pursue and irrelevant to the research. My desire for "evidence" in the form of further elaboration during an interview, however, would not resolve the questions raised. For queerness, as Muñoz reminds us, can only be "proven" by "suturing it to the concept of ephemera . . . a trace, the remains, the things that are left, hanging in the air like a rumor."[57] I decided to research the history of the lawsuit *Lugo v. Sonido*. Doing so led me not only to explore how LaVoe became a synecdoche for Nuyoricanness vis-à-vis the courts and public commentary but to question the narrative around the sonero's life and death.

Certainly, LaVoe's answer when asked about Lugo during the *Ocurrió así* interview contributes to the ambivalence. A contemplative LaVoe described their relationship as follows for the reporter:

> Él me cuida mucho [*inaudible*] yo lo aprecio mucho. El me ama [*LaVoe laughs*]. Me quiere mucho. Se portó muy bien [conmigo]. Él es el único que fue al hospital, right, papi? [*Glances at Lugo*] [*Inaudible*] Siempre estaba allí [*inaudible*]. Él vino todos los días a chequearme, a ver si necesitaba algo. Él estaba ahí. No lo amaba [*LaVoe chuckles*] pero me gustaba.

[He cares about me very much and I cherish him. He loves me [*La Voe laughs*]. I love him a lot. He was good [to me]. He is the only one who went to the hospital, right, papi? [*Glances at Lugo*] [*Inaudible*] He was always there [*inaudible*]. He came every day to check on me, to see if I needed anything. He was there. I didn't love him [*La Voe chuckles*] but I liked him.

LaVoe's penchant for relajo was evident even as he conveyed how much he depended on Lugo, to whom he refers as "papi," "lindo" (nice, beautiful), and "Calindo," terms of endearment that may suggest an intimacy between the two men that exceeds the public framing of Lugo as a friend or helper. In framing the use of these terms to the court, Lugo explained that LaVoe used "lindo" to "express how he felt about our friendship."[58] On the one hand, LaVoe earnestly described the daily care Lugo provided during a hospital stay when no one else visited or offered help, chuckling as he described their affective relationship. LaVoe distinguished between "cherishing" Lugo's support and the latter's "loving" him. The statement that he liked but did not love Lugo is nevertheless ambiguous because *querer* has multiple meanings—to like, to want or desire, to love—that are not mutually exclusive. LaVoe's chuckles, and his glances toward Lugo, suggest an inside joke to which neither the reporter nor the audience is privy.

It is not my goal to determine whether LaVoe and Lugo were sexual partners but rather to bring attention to the importance of ephemera in sifting through the "bundle of silences" that makes some narratives possible and silences others. For, as Michel-Rolph Trouillot argues, "what matters most are the process and conditions of production of such narratives."[59] I offer that the discomfort, repetition, pauses, trailing off, denial, equivocation, relajo, and bochinche themselves form an alternative archive of knowledge within salsa that prompts us to interrogate how heteronormative and patriarchal assumptions inform the collective memory around the life and death of LaVoe. I further suggest that this archive of enunciative acts, in that they do the work of knowledge production, illuminates the ambiguities inherent to the social process of meaning making around LaVoe's life. I rely here on the epistemological possibilities of a queer reading afforded, as Deborah Vargas insists, by "acknowledging hearsay, murmurs, and silent gestures . . . as another base of knowledge production," an *archive of chisme*, or *archisme*, composed of ephemeral, performative acts that transmit knowledge and disrupt the presumed legitimacy of the archive.[60] Insofar as LaVoe's artistic mastery was predicated as much on his vocal and improvisational abilities as the performance of virile masculinity, the interviews with LaVoe, Lugo, Nancy Pérez, and the music executive reveal the continued silences, more than thirty years after LaVoe's death, around how he came to be diagnosed with AIDS. In other words, I propose that Lugo's repetition that LaVoe did not, could not, have AIDS; Pérez's incomplete sentences and references to the unnamed "thing" that "you know"; and the executive's discomfort manifest desires to repudiate queerness that LaVoe's appearance on *Ocurrió así* refuses to repudiate.

My point here is to challenge the rhetoric of denial and deflection that reifies heteropatriarchal and colonial erasures of queerness.[61] Denying the possibility that LaVoe may have become HIV positive because of sex with other men pronounces queerness as that which must remain outside salsa's Nuyorican meanings. Alberto Sandoval Sánchez reminds us, AIDS is "'all about shit and blood,' mierda y sangre, about waste. How much more abject can you get when you are un (a) Latino maricón con SIDA (faggot with AIDS), all in one package? What does it mean to have the monster under your skin? How can you love your abject body when it betrays you? How do you feel in a society that expels the sick, the Latino, the queer, the migrant, the Other?"[62] As Karen Jaime might argue, while LaVoe's embodied performance may have resisted the "sanitizing impulse" of salsa's commercialization, the hegemonic framing of AIDS precludes the possibility of queer histories within salsa.[63] As we consider how LaVoe's life and decisions are narrated in the courtroom and public fear amid the AIDS crisis, we must consider not only the role of music in collective memory but what it means to challenge the narrative through which he, as an effigy of Nuyorican possibilities, is constituted. If politicizing abjection is, as Sandoval Sánchez argues and Vargas and Roque Ramírez also suggest, the keystone to disrupting the opposition between subject and abject, a Rican/Struction of LaVoe's embodied persona as El Cantante is essential to Rican/Structing the sonero as an effigy of Nuyorican belonging.

## Conclusion

The collective memory around LaVoe's life and death offers him up as a synecdoche of Fania Records and the salsa boom. But LaVoe's stirring performance of "El Cantante" (and "La fama," for that matter) cannot be encapsulated by such limits. Audiences embraced LaVoe for his ferocious talent as well as the ways his own life reflected the histories and everyday lives of diasporic Puerto Ricans. Salsa, like the Nuyorican Arts Movement, took form alongside movements for racial justice, women's rights, and gay liberation in which Puerto Ricans participated. The desire to disassociate LaVoe from the AIDS crisis perpetuates silence, discrimination, and stigma surrounding AIDS and queer Latinidad.

Almost fifteen years after LaVoe's death, reggaeton artist Gallego and the singer-songwriter-poet-actor La Bruja released tributes to the singer. In the "Intro" to *Tributo urbano a Héctor LaVoe*, released in 2007, Gallego emphasizes joy and life rather than tragedy and personal failures. Combining salsa and reggaeton, Gallego's introduction to the tribute album describes what others consider a life marked by tragedy as a life lived through the pleasure of performance. He celebrates LaVoe's commitment "to the death" to his music and "su gente" (his people), to Afro-Caribbean rhythms and Puerto Rico. Like LaVoe, Gallego embraces the performative possibilities of abjection. In so doing, he links LaVoe to a generation of reggaeton artists who reject the politics of respectability in favor of centering the everyday lives of Puerto Ricans who remain outside narratives of national belonging. More than a symbolic gesture, Gallego's insistence on pleasure underscores music as a site of futurity.

La Bruja, for her part, presents an unflinching portrait of LaVoe's failings that rivals the song's celebration of his talent on her rap "Revento" (Exploded), released on the album *Brujalicious* in 2006. A reference to LaVoe's eponymous album, she "blasts" the contrast between the "great sonero" and "the tragic decline."[64] She begins by recounting LaVoe's "combustible" musicality, instructing listeners to "take out their money, take our their gun" as the same line from "Calle Lune, Calle Sol" plays in the background. She pays tribute to the man who "would send shivers down your spine when a mic was in his hand," making music so hot it was "combustible," even when he was late. But when La Bruja brings up the "shit that blurs the vision," she underlines LaVoe's desires, agency, and efforts to fight off the "monster." In "Revento," the complicity of the public marks how "the adoring fans watched the struggle, gaining strength from his trouble," knowing that "no es fácil" (it's not easy). And still "nothing could hold him back." She ends by warning the listener to "take your move, because it could be your last shot. Plau!" A rap, "Revento" sounds salsa's continued relevance as well as salsa and Hip Hop's parallel histories in the 1970s. It reminds us that while Latin music played on the streets of the Bronx on any given night, Black and Puerto Rican emcees moved the crowd on the next. "Revento" refuses the trope of the tragic clown and shines a light on the importance of recuperating alternate and intersecting histories of NuYoRico.

# (Copy)Rights and Wrongs

## "EL CANTANTE" AND THE LEGISLATION OF CREATIVE LABOR

**6**

While Rubén Blades may also have arrived in New York unprepared for the challenges of the music industry, the trajectory of his life was quite different from Héctor LaVoe's, whom he first saw perform in Panama with Willie Colón. Blown away and inspired by their performance, Blades would make his way to New York and to Fania. Blades first traveled to the United States in 1969 during the temporary closure of the Universidad Nacional de Panamá (Panama National University), which he was attending. During this initial trip, he debuted as a vocalist on Pete Rodríguez's album *From Panama to New York* (1970) but returned to Panama when the university reopened. Blades returned to the United States in 1974 and famously worked in the Fania mailroom before signing a contract with Vaya Records. He recorded various songs for Ray Barretto on the bandleader's self-titled album and performed vocals for Colón alongside LaVoe on *The Good, the Bad, the Ugly* (1975). Blades then provided vocals for LaVoe's debut album, *La Voz* (The Voice, 1975). When LaVoe launched a solo career right after his last recording as lead vocalist for Colón, Blades's collaboration with Colón was just beginning. Blades renewed his contract with Vaya Records in 1976 and the following year released the first of four joint albums with Colón, *Metiendo mano* (Getting into it). The album established Blades as a talented songwriter whose songs, like the classic "Pablo Pueblo," where *pueblo* stands in for "the people," narrated the economic struggle and political disenfran-chisement found in the everyday lives of urban centers in Latin America.

Colón and Blades next collaborated on *Siembra* (Planting, 1978), which outperformed every Fania release before it. The album cemented Blades's rep-utation as a songwriter; he has since been compared to Bob Dylan.[1] Music critic Agustín Gurza, a regular columnist for *Billboard* and contributor to *Latin N.Y.*, praised the "the album's intellectual and poetic subjects . . . its subtle moods and impassioned messages." Suggesting that Colón's previous recordings lacked the narrative authority of *Siembra*, Gurza underscored the absence of "percussive power" and instrumental solos that made *Siembra* "an album for listening, and only for dancing secondarily, if at all."[2] Fans in the United States, Latin America, and the Hispanophone Caribbean re-sponded enthusiastically to the call to political consciousness in the title song. Other fan favorites on the album included "Pedro Navaja" (Switch-blade Pete). Inspired by "Mack the Knife," the song narrates the exploits of a thief preying on victims in an unspecified barrio of Latin America. As with "Pablo Pueblo," the song resonated with themes of everyday life, class struggle, and political solidarity across Latin America and its diaspora.

Blades recorded two additional albums with Colón and various solo recordings before signing with Elektra Records in 1984. That same year, Blades filed the first of three lawsuits he has brought against Fania Records, its various associated companies (e.g., Vaya Records, Vaya Publishing, and Vev Publishing), and its successors (e.g., Musica Latina International and Sonido). The settlement agreement for the first of these lawsuits, *Musica Latina International v. Ruben Blades*, awarded the artist ownership rights to all the songs he wrote while signed to Fania/Vaya Records. In 1988, Blades went back to court, charging that Fania failed to remit royalties to him ac-cording to the terms of the settlement agreement. In 2002, Blades sued Fania successor Sonido and various affiliated Fania corporations for violations of the initial settlement agreement and copyright violations that included the licensing of "El Cantante."

Blades claimed sole copyright to "El Cantante," which would entitle him to 100 percent of the songwriter royalties when Sonido licensed the song to third parties. Sonido, in turn, argued that the song was a joint work be-tween him and LaVoe, entitling Blades to just 50 percent of the licensing fees per a rider to the standard songwriter's agreement (SSA) concerning joint compositions.[3] While Blades acknowledged that the song would not have captured audiences in the same way had he recorded it rather than LaVoe, he maintained his claim to sole authorship as the primary contributor. He also noted that the song's popularity had more to do with LaVoe's personal challenges than the late sonero's prodigious talent.[4] The insistence on the success of LaVoe's recording serves to distinguish his performance of "El Cantante" from the song itself. This strategy reinforces the sonero's rights to the sound recording while reifying Blades's claim to sole authorship of the song in the form of the first two verses. In other words, LaVoe is positioned as the creator of the sound recording but not the co-songwriter.[5] The issue of authorship was set aside, however, by Sonido when executive Victor Gallo conceded sole authorship to Blades during a deposition:

Question: Who wrote El Cantante?

Answer: Ruben Blades.

Question: 100 percent author?

Answer: 100 percent.[6]

Sonido, doing business as Fania, thus dropped its pursuit of joint copyright for "El Cantante." When Blades and Sonido signed an undisclosed agreement that settled the lawsuit, "El Cantante" was included among the list of songs owned solely by the artist.

The competing claims to "El Cantante" underscore critical questions about intellectual property, voice, and creative labor. By reducing the song to its textual representation of the initial verses, Blades failed to acknowledge the multiple moments of production and performance that have taken place during the social life of the song. LaVoe's recording of "El Cantante" and subsequent performances transmitted not only what diasporic Puerto Rican audiences and broader Latin American listeners immediately interpreted as his own trajectory, but also the diasporic history of New York's Puerto Rican communities. LaVoe's reiterated behaviors, improvised from one performance to the next, made visible and audible the ways in which Nuyorican subjectivities encoded within salsa privileged New York and its Puerto Rican communities, even as Puerto Rico and the greater Caribbean and Latin America remained sources of cultural inspiration. The recognition of LaVoe's significance for diasporic Puerto Rican communities does not propose an origins narrative for salsa or a prescriptive reading of legal and social claims to "El Cantante." Rather, the social life of "El Cantante" (the song) illuminates how the repeated reenactments of this persona by LaVoe entered into the collective memory of salsa and became part of the intangible cultural heritage of Puerto Ricans, Latinas/os, and Hispanophone

Caribbean and Latin American audiences for whom the sonero remains "El Cantante de los Cantantes" (The Singer's Singer).

The trajectory of "El Cantante" underscores broader issues related to the rights of those who contribute to the development of cultural products, be they studio musicians who participate in the creation of work-for-hire, which leaves them without rights to their creative labor, or individual songwriters who transfer their rights to a publishing company. As legal scholar Peter Jaszi has argued, the courts need to reject "the grand narrative of authorship and 'authority' in favor of an approach that distributes attention and concern across the full range of participants in the processes of cultural production and consumption."[7] Yet, as Martha Woodmansee argued in the early 1990s, "It would [still] seem that as creative production becomes more corporate, collective, and collaborative, the law invokes the Romantic author all the more insistently."[8] The inability—if not unwillingness—of US courts to move away from the Romantic concept of original genius and embrace the plurality inherent in cultural expression risks marginalizing practices that song lyrics alone cannot capture.

### Fania and Its Discontents

By the late 1970s, the Fania formula faced multiple challenges that threatened the company's ability to flood the market with recordings and retain its dominance in Latin music. Major recording labels interested in tapping Fania's demographic continued to court the Latin market, expanded their Latin music catalogs, and prepared to increase their footprint in the United States and Latin America. Miami's ascendance in the US Latin music market and Latin American entertainment and media industries threatened not only Fania but also the status of New York as the epicenter of tropical music.[9] The increasing popularity of other Latin music genres among Fania's demographic and the success of Miami-based labels in reaching these consumers posed additional challenges. Declining record sales in Latin music overall and the economic decline that closed scores of nightclubs in the cuchifrito circuit also threatened Fania's longevity.[10] The departure of stars like Colón and Blades added to the difficulties confronting Fania. Jerry Masucci's investment in the feature film *The Last Fight* (1983), a "creative and financial fracas," likewise strained Fania's resources.[11]

Internally at Fania, Masucci reportedly became disgusted with artists who demanded an increasing share of the revenues produced from their creative labor and others who signed with competing labels once their Fania contracts expired. In 1979, Masucci sold all of Fania's assets to Valsyn, a company in Uruguay, including "copyrights, master recordings, publishing rights, manufacturing rights, distribution rights and rights to lease, sell, and exploit musical compositions from the catalogues."[12] Fania retained only the right to distribute its remaining inventory in the United States and Puerto Rico. That same year, Fania Records and all but one of its subsidiaries, Musica Latina, ceased operations. Masucci turned his attention to Musica Latina, which assumed the rights he had negotiated with Valsyn, and continued to release new recordings. In 1981, Masucci copyrighted the Fania name on behalf of Musica Latina, which became the first company after the sale of the catalog to do business as Fania.[13]

In 1986, Masucci created the label Sonido as the successor to Musica Latina and transferred the Fania trademark to this new label. Sonido began doing business as Fania and continued to market recordings from the legendary catalog as allowed by the Valsyn agreement previously administered by Musica Latina.[14] With Masucci as president of the company, Sonido negotiated a new licensing agreement that same year that gave the label the option of putting the licensing fees toward the $10 million cost of buying back the Fania catalog from Valsyn.[15] Sonido amended the Valsyn license in November 1997 to include all "masters, labels, publishing rights and recording contracts, including the worldwide rights to reproduce, manufacture, distribute and publish all of such works and all copyrights, trademarks and other property rights in such works, upon the consummation of this offering." Valsyn would continue to own the copyright until Sonido completed its payments.[16] In sum, once the $10 million payment was completed, the agreement would grant Sonido all the assets Masucci sold to Valsyn in 1979.

Less than a month after negotiating the amended license, Masucci, as president of Sonido, transferred the Fania trademark and all the label's assets to his new company Fania Entertainment Group (FEG). The company then filed paperwork with the Securities and Exchange Commission (SEC) in advance of an initial public offering (IPO) that would make it a publicly traded company. A portion of the proceeds from the IPO would be used to help Sonido pay the remaining $4 million balance for the acquisition of Fania's assets from Valsyn. Further, FEG intended to reimburse Sonido for the $6 million in payments it had already made. In return, Sonido's assets would be transferred to FEG, but Sonido would receive 65 percent of the common stock in the company. The deal would leave Masucci, the head of Sonido, as the majority stockholder in FEG after it went public.

The FEG documents submitted to the SEC suggest that Masucci sought to duplicate the success of the original label by exploiting the purchasing power of Latina/o markets. While the first $10 million raised during the IPO would be used to acquire Fania's assets, FEG intended to use part of the remaining monies to "exploit the Fania catalog, sign and record new artists, and expand geographic markets."[17] Like radio and television advertisers targeting the Hispanic market in the 1990s, FEG sought the loyalty of one of the fastest-growing ethnic markets in the United States. The IPO, however, would never take place. Masucci's death on December 21, 1997, occurred just two days after FEG filed with the SEC.[18] Shortly thereafter, FEG withdrew its NASDAQ registration. At the time, Sonido's final $4 million payment to Valsyn for the Fania catalog remained outstanding.[19] Two years later, Sonido negotiated an extension on the Valsyn license until 2004.[20] The Fania catalog would remain largely dormant until 2005.

In 2005, Emusica Entertainment purchased the catalog from Masucci's estate for an undisclosed price that has been estimated at approximately $10 million.[21] Shortly thereafter, Emusica staff identified a storage unit with three thousand pressed albums, not all of which had been previously released. They also located somewhere between 85 and 90 percent of the master tapes for the Fania catalog, in addition to other materials.[22] Emusica announced plans to reissue the catalog and released the first batch of remastered recordings the following spring. By June 2006, Jody Rosen of the *New York Times* heralded the "return of the record company [meaning Fania] that made salsa hot" even as critics lamented the "poor remastering and packaging materials."[23] Within three years, Codigo Group, an entertainment company funded by a private equity group in New York that had obtained the Westside Latino catalog in 2008, bought the Fania catalog from Emusica.[24] Like Musica Latina, Sonido, and Emusica before it, Codigo trademarked the name Fania and began to do business as such. As the latest successor to Fania, Codigo also trademarked the original label's multicolored logo, designed by Izzy Sanabria, for use on advertisements and merchandise. Codigo began digitizing the catalog and continued to release remastered recordings and new compilations, including remixes of Fania classics aimed at attracting a younger audience.[25] Within a year, Codigo established distributorship in Europe, Africa, and parts of Asia.[26] The entertainment group sold 250,000 albums in physical and digital form in 2013 before turning to an all-digital format the following year.[27]

Codigo responded to the decline of compact disc (CD) sales by capitalizing on the ability of social media to connect with fans of the original

**6.1**    Fania logo designed by Izzy Sanabria

Fania Records and help the company exploit the Fania catalog as well as that of Westside Latino. Codigo began by creating a website for Fania, followed by a Facebook page in November 2009. Within a month, the Facebook page received 20,000 likes. Codigo continued to expand its online presence over the next five years. By the end of 2014, the Facebook page exceeded 626,000 likes, and the Twitter feed boasted 26,500 followers. Fans also connected with each other while staying updated on Codigo's releases and other events related to Fania via a Tumblr feed. On the Fania website, fans could listen to music, watch videos, post photographs, download digital recordings, and purchase merchandise such as T-shirts, hats, posters, skateboards, and various other accessories. As part of the move to an all-digital format in 2014, Codigo created a subscription service for its music with Drip.fm and launched the "first ever Latin music app" with the digital music provider Spotify, where listeners could stream the entire catalog.[28]

That same year, the company celebrated Fania Records' fiftieth anniversary by hosting a Fania All-Stars concert in Puerto Rico with many of the remaining members of the ensemble band. Additional events commemorating the original Fania labels included a concert series in New York offered through a partnership with Summerstage, a program of the City Parks Foundation; "pop-up stores" in Miami and New York; the "Armada Fania" summer-long series of DJ and live music events in New York featuring songs from the expansive catalog; and a performance of original Fania All-Star Larry Harlow's *Hommy: A Latin Opera* at Lincoln Center. There was also a free public screening of *Our Latin Thing*.[29] Three years earlier, Codigo had released a limited-edition two-CD/DVD set of the film that marked the

**6.2**    Armada Fania flyer, New York City Summer
Series, 2014

fortieth anniversary of the concert at the Cheetah. Using a theater copy of
the original film it purchased through eBay, Codigo digitized and updated
the film to high-definition (HD) video and remastered the audio.[30] Both the
screening and the remastered version of *Our Latin Thing* capitalized on the
film's cult status among audiences, who had been forced to rely on bootleg
copies of the documentary for more than a decade. In 2018, Concord Music
Group (CMG, now Concord), a US-based music rights company with worldwide distribution, purchased the catalog from Codigo.[31] The vinyl reissue

**6.3**　Fania release bundle for *Live at the Cheetah*, vol. 1, Fania.com, 2022

of volumes 1 and 2 of *Live at the Cheetah* by Concord label Craft Recordings in 2022 and 2023, respectively, celebrated the "salsa-induced delirium" of the 1971 Fania All-Stars concert.[32]

### Blades versus Fania

Blades completed his contractual obligations with Musica Latina in 1983. Shortly thereafter, he ascertained the existence of record sales in Latin America for which no royalties had been paid. Blades contacted Musica Latina and threatened to sue to procure information about the purported sales. Musica Latina responded by suing Blades for the return of royalties. The label claimed that it had overpaid royalties to Blades for a song he cowrote with Willie Colón. Blades denied the claim and countersued Masucci, Fania Records, Vaya Records, Vaya Publishing, and Fania Publishing for unpaid artist and songwriter royalties. He also asked the court to nullify the songwriter's agreement he had signed with Vaya Publishing based on what he alleged to be Fania's willful and knowing deceit.[33] As lucrative as the recordings themselves, the SSA allowed Valsyn and its agents to license Blades's songs and collect the royalties assigned to the artist in the SSA on his behalf.

Blades and Musica Latina reached a settlement in 1985 that granted the artist sole ownership of the songs he wrote while under contract to Vaya Records, co-ownership of joint compositions, and unpaid royalties. The settlement restored Blades's ownership to classic recordings such as "Pedro Navaja" (1978) and "Siembra" (1978), songs that reflected Blades's extraordinary impact on the music. As part of the settlement agreement, Blades agreed to record three albums for Musica Latina. He titled one of them *Doble filo* (Double edge), a reference perhaps to the fact that while he was required to record the album, it was allowing him to sever all contractual ties with the label. The album included his own rendition of "El Cantante." Musica Latina retained certain publishing and mechanical rights to the songs, but it had to continue paying artist royalties to Blades for the albums he recorded for Vaya Records and Musica Latina, obligations it did not fulfill, according to the two additional lawsuits Blades filed against Fania successors.[34] The first of these, filed in 1988, focused exclusively on the failure of Musica Latina and its successor, Sonido, to provide regular and accurate royalty statements and payments in accordance with the previous lawsuit. The parties once again reached a settlement.

In 2002, Blades again filed suit against Sonido. He claimed that Sonido failed to provide the accurate and complete statements required by the 1985 settlement agreement and failed to pay appropriate royalties. Blades amended the original complaint against Sonido to include copyright infringement when, during the discovery process, he learned that the label licensed several of his most celebrated songs to third parties without his permission, in violation of the conditions of the 1985 settlement. The songs included "Cazanguero" (1975), "Plástico" (Plastic, 1978), "Pablo Pueblo" (1977), "Ligia Elena" (1981), and "El Cantante" (1978). Blades alleged that Sonido licensed "El Cantante" on three separate occasions: for a documentary film about Basque singer Manu Chao in 1997, to Sony Discos, and for use in the play *¿Quién mató a Héctor LaVoe? / Who Killed Héctor LaVoe?* in 1999.[35] Sonido denied that it illegally licensed any songs written by Blades and attempted, unsuccessfully, to have the copyright infringement claim thrown out. Sonido eventually conceded that it "inadvertently erred in licensing [the song]" but filed a motion to dismiss the copyright claim. Sonido alleged that Blades knew about the agreement with CFDM Theatrical Productions for the play, had been compensated appropriately, and failed to act within the statute of limitations.[36]

Sonido also challenged Blades's legal standing to bring a copyright infringement claim for "El Cantante" before the court. Sonido maintained that, unlike "Cazanguero," "Plástico," "Pablo Pueblo," and "Ligia Elena," which Blades wrote in their entirety, "El Cantante" was cowritten by LaVoe, who added his pregones—the series of two-line verses that followed the initial two verses—to the original recording, thus fixing them as required by copyright law. The company also cited a 1994 registration form, filed with the US Copyright Office by David Lugo a year after LaVoe's death, that listed both Blades and LaVoe as authors. Blades had already used this form to show he fulfilled the legal requirement that a work be registered with the US Copyright Office before a claimant can file copyright infringement charges.[37] Given that, Sonido made three arguments: first, that Blades could not now deny LaVoe's collaboration and the song's status as a joint work for the purpose of copyright; second, that since LaVoe had signed an SSA with Fania, Sonido could license the song without Blades's permission, per copyright law pertaining to joint works; and, third, that Blades could not initiate a copyright infringement suit without Lugo's consent (although *Lugo v. Sonido*, as discussed in chapter 5, would establish that Lugo did not have the legal right to make that claim). The recognition of LaVoe as coauthor would, of course, also entitle Sonido to a percentage of licensing fees for "El Cantante" under the SSA. Sonido thus protected its own legal and financial interests by protecting the late sonero's rights to the song. Blades, however, rested his claim to sole copyright on the argument that LaVoe's pregones did not constitute part of "El Cantante" for the purpose of copyright. This assertion rested on the argument that Blades gave LaVoe a completed song.

### Copyright and "El Cantante"

Under copyright law, Blades's insistence that he alone wrote "El Cantante" does not entail a wholesale denial of LaVoe's creative contributions to the recording, only that those contributions do not constitute a valid copyright claim. Creators of copyrightable work can, as Blades did in transferring ownership to Fania's publishing company, transfer exclusive rights to another party. In the case of "El Cantante," Blades's insistence on sole authorship reflects the way copyright law determines (1) what constitutes a copyrightable work and (2) under what circumstances contributions can constitute grounds for claiming a joint work. Blades argued he "was and is the sole creator and author" of the compositions in question, which were "wholly original works that are copyrightable subject matter under the laws of the United States, and are fixed in a tangible medium of expression."[38] This legal argument frames the claim within the terms established by the Copyright Act of 1976.

Renaissance and neoclassical conceptualizations defined an author primarily as a craftsperson who mastered the rules of rhetoric and poetics. In the rare instance when the author might exceed these expectations, he was considered to have been inspired by an external force. The concept of authorship as it relates to copyright emerged in Britain and Germany during the eighteenth century as writers who sought to make a living from their work began to reflect on the nature of their creative labor, driving a shift from perceptions of inspiration as an external force toward the idea of an "original genius" that emanated from within the writer. Supported by the belief in individualism and the trope of personality that accompanied it, the discourse of original genius found its raison d'être at the intersection of market forces and Romantic aesthetics that fetishized what the poet William Wordsworth described as a solitary process through which genius emerges in the form of an original work. A writer's work was to be considered a unique product and the property of the writer.[39] The origins of this approach can be traced to the 1774 landmark case *Donaldson v. Beckett*, which simultaneously upheld the proprietary rights of the author and laid the foundation for modern copyright law. Although Lord Chief Justice William de Grey mused over musical copyright in the decision, it remained outside English copyright statutes until 1777. *Bach v. Longman* (1777) established that published compositions were to be protected like "books and other writings" already protected by copyright law.[40] The court based its judgment on the argument that compositions, like books, were conveyed by "signs and symbols."[41]

The US Copyright Act of 1976 rests on the Romantic elaboration of the author that reifies the division between the initial moment in which a presumably solitary individual places their work onto a page and its performance. Copyright law stipulates that only content that is "fixed in a tangible medium," such as sheet music or a recording, and remains invariant is copyrightable.[42] The parameters for defining a collaboration for the purposes of copyright intensify the division between an initial moment of creation and performance. Under the 1976 Copyright Act, a joint work for the purpose of copyright is "prepared by two or more authors with the intention that their contributions be merged into inseparable or interdependent parts of a unitary whole." Since an author's right to prevent a work from being reproduced without permission begins at the moment the work is put into tangible forms (what the copyright statute denotes as "visible signs"), these terms require, as Peter Jaszi explains, "the intention, *at the time the writing is done*, that the parts be absorbed or combined into an integrated unit."[43] The law requires the intention not merely to work together but to become joint authors. It requires an explicit, finite period in the creative process during which the decision to collaborate takes place and the process to produce a copyrightable joint work begins. Prior to the 1976 law, collaboration was defined more broadly and did not require the synchronous, limited moment. As a result, lyrics could be added to previously finished song lyrics. The Copyright Act of 1976, however, "narrow[ed] the range of circumstances in which what might be termed a 'collaboration' in the lay sense is recognized as a 'joint work' in the legal one." [44] Lyrics added to what is determined to have been a completed song do not produce a joint work in the legal sense.

*Childress v. Taylor* (1991), one of the most cited cases for its elaboration of the conditions necessary for determining coauthorship, illuminates the serpentine construction of copyright law and the reductive interpretation of the court. The case centered on whether or not actress Clarice Taylor's research and ideas constituted joint authorship of the play *Moms*, based on the life of comedian Jackie "Moms" Mobley. Taylor hired Alice Childress to write the play in 1986. When Childress and Taylor failed to arrive at an agreement regarding ownership, the latter hired another playwright to develop a script based on Mobley's life and staged that play. Childress filed suit alleging violations of the Copyright Act, a claim predicated on the assertion that she maintained sole authorship of the original play on which Taylor's subsequent version drew.[45]

The court considered whether *each* party's contributions to a work had to be copyrightable or "whether the combined result of both of the authors must be copyrightable" in order for the play be considered a joint work.[46] This prerequisite refers to the unchanging, tangible expression of a theatrical production in a script or, in the case of a song, the sheet music or recording. The court decided that each contribution had to be copyrightable in order to prevent "spurious claims of joint authorship" and that Taylor's "research and ideas" were not copyrightable.[47] As important, the court determined that insofar as the Copyright Act "clearly requires that each author intend their respective contributions be merged into a unitary whole," Taylor's collaboration in and of itself was not sufficient to establish a joint work.[48] This centered on two points. First, the two parties did not come to an agreement when Taylor first approached Childress to write the play. Second, Childress refused to accept Taylor's draft agreement for co-ownership, which is why the latter developed the second play. The ruling also expressed a preference to err by failing to recognize multiple authors rather than risk mistakenly denying sole copyright to a single author.[49] Ultimately, *Childress v. Taylor* upheld the majority view in case law as to what constitutes copyrightable work and what the parameters are for establishing a joint work for the purpose of copyright.[50]

The desire to protect a single original genius, like attempts to reduce music to those aspects that can be conveyed by the first to verses of "El Cantante," fails to account for the ways that the song acquired meaning through its sound recording and subsequent performances by LaVoe. By the late 1970s, when LaVoe recorded "El Cantante," the collaboration among producers, musicians, and vocalists in recording studios increasingly undermined the role of the score as the primary referent for popular music.[51] The emergence of multitracking, together with the creation of melody, harmony, and rhythm in the recording studio, only added to the ways that sound recordings formed part of the creative process. Indeed, in some countries, the artist who records a composition may be considered the author of the resulting sound recording, but US law does not recognize this category of authorship. In fact, US courts have invoked the discourse of the author even more insistently as new technologies have emerged.[52]

As a result, primary contributors to a song (e.g., Blades with regard to the first two verses of "El Cantante") increasingly benefit from how the courts limit the rights of secondary contributors (e.g., LaVoe's pregones for "El Cantante") to the sound recording, which does not grant ownership of the underlying song. Moreover, an artist's creative contributions are not enough to establish their recording as a new category of work for purposes of determining their rights as a creator (e.g., of lyrics to "El Cantante").[53] This aspect of US law codifies not only the original moment of creation but also the opposition between embodied performance, which may change over time, and creative labor that remains fixed (such as original sheet music). The additional insistence within US copyright law that a work remain unchanging fails to consider the role of improvisation in creative expression on the part of an artist like LaVoe, a sonero whose cultural capital as a vocalist was based in no small part on his extraordinary improvisational acumen. LaVoe was renowned for his ability to improvise from one recording to the next and one performance to another. Thus, even if "El Cantante" were not considered a completed song before LaVoe added the pregones—and the latter were thus included as part of the copyrighted musical work, resulting from a process of creation that extends beyond the original moment—his repertoire of improvisational practices might mean his contributions were not copyrightable.

The issues of improvisation and copyright are not new or particular to Latin music. Jazz musicians have navigated the legal terrain of authorial contribution since the early twentieth century. The 1917 lawsuit where multiple parties claimed the copyright to the sheet music for the instrumental blues recording "Livery Stable Blues," first released by the Original Dixieland Jass Band, highlights the legal conflict that results from musical practices that privilege "communal, inclusive musical processes over single-authored, exclusive products."[54] Approximately thirty-five witnesses testified about the song's origins, which was part of a popular blues repertoire during the time. As Katherine Leo describes, witness testimony "unearthed a network of at least ten musicians seemingly eligible for legal authorial claims, many of whom had played in a band together, and at least two closely related instrumental compositions." The case, Leo goes on to explain, "was ultimately dismissed on the ground that the composition lacked originality, such that no musician could claim legal ownership." While the lawsuit has often been highlighted in discussions on the limits of copyright law, Katherine Leo turns to the lawsuit to argue for a model of "distributive authorship" that aligns with creative processes in blues and jazz. Rather than attempting to identify discrete ownership by a single person or group of musicians, Leo argues for a model of public authorship that emphasizes social, collaborative, creative practices over time. Antithetical to the emphasis on a discrete, individual author, a turn toward social authorship would recognize each adaptation of a composition as a copyrightable work.[55]

Since the mid-1980s, intellectual property scholars have begun to draw on literary and cultural criticism as well as media studies to challenge the Romantic assumptions of copyright law and the ways in which the author-function reproduced systems of power while delimiting the potential meanings of a text. By the early 2000s, court rulings expanding what constitutes a transformative work (which does not, therefore, infringe copyright) signaled an opening to undermine the grand narrative of original genius and expand who the court would consider to be a creator. But the rhetoric of the individual creator as author remained persistent. The division between songwriter, on one side, and performers, on the other, continues to preclude the latter from being recognized under US law as creators of the works. The reticence of courts, particularly as new technologies continue to transform the process of musical creation, has prevented a shift toward framing questions of copyright within a process of dialogue and exchange that takes place over a continuum of music making.

### Entre la Letra y la Nota

Music creation takes place within a web of social relations, one that, in the case of "El Cantante," was marked by unequal power relations between Blades and La Voe in the courts, and by the opposition between the rational and the corporeal embedded within the public and legal imaginary. Blades's well-deserved accolades build on the social capital he accumulated early in his career as a *canta-autor* (singer-author, or author who sings) and public intellectual. From his debut album with Pete Rodríguez to his collaborations with Colón and eventual solo career, Blades emerged as a superb storyteller whose songs extended salsa's saliency for Latin American audiences through lyrics that engaged current political events, shining a light on structural inequalities and advocating for social justice. He often created musical figures through which he documented the "realities from the urban cities of Latin America," as seen in "Pablo Pueblo," "Juan Pachanga," and "Ligia Elena."[56] The latter, for example, describes a woman from the upper class who runs away with a trumpet player. His album *Agua de luna* (Moon water, 1987), based on the short stories of Gabriel García Márquez, lent further authority to his status as a canta-autor. The inspiration from Latin America's literary canon challenged the opposition between literature and music, demonstrating how popular music, as cultural critic Jean Franco has noted, can serve as "a privileged vehicle for the exploration of Latin American identity and the nature of modernity." On the other hand, his elaboration of musical protagonists similar to those found in Latin American literary works was influenced by the privilege accorded to the very lettered city with which he collaborated.[57]

Blades's songs reflected his political aspirations. As he has said, his political activities have been "about changing the conditions I am denouncing in my songs, [which] can only be done through political work."[58] A founder of the Papa Egró political party in Panama, he ran for president as the party's candidate in the 1994 election on a platform that promised economic reform and an end to corruption. Blades lost the election but retained significant political clout, and his endorsement of Martín Torrijos Espino in 2004 may have played a role in the latter's election to the presidency.

Torrijos Espino appointed Blades to a five-year term as Panama's minister of tourism, during which he focused on "a national plan for Panama to grow its tourism industry."[59] Blades's return to salsa in 2009 began with a performance at the Latin Grammys with Calle 13, a Puerto Rican reggaeton group whose songs highlight their own political awareness. In an interview that provides an example of Blades's tremendous and continuing influence across multiple generations, Calle 13 member René Pérez noted, "In musical terms, it's like he's the teacher and we are his students. I've listened to his music since I was little and have learned from him not just how to write but also political awareness. We believe in his message."[60]

In 1987, Blades released a lackluster recording of "El Cantante" for the album *Doble filo*, which he recorded to fulfill his legal obligations under the first lawsuit against Fania successor Musica Latina. While he undoubtedly loathed recording an album for Fania, doing so allowed him to finally extricate himself from the label while emphasizing his legal and symbolic claim to the song, if not the experience it narrates. The approximation of and increasing departure from the original 1978 recording in terms of musical arrangements, vocal aesthetics, pregones, and the musical figure's perspective separate Blades's rendition from LaVoe's. The song's opening creates a musical echo of Colón's arrangements for LaVoe's 1978 recording without being overdetermined by the original melody. However, only a trumpet plays the opening notes for Blades's recording. The symphonic arrangements for the 1978 recording included trumpets, piano, and strings that each play the opening melody in overlapping succession before converging, while the percussion delivers a rich and complex rhythmic texture. Blades's rendition of the first two verses sticks to the original lyrics as he wrote them. The melody, however, repeatedly approaches and diverges from LaVoe's. Blades's musical phrasing also distinguishes his recording from LaVoe's, and over the course of the song, he increasingly departs from the original melody. Overall, Blades's performance lacks the operatic quality produced through the combination of Colón's arrangements and LaVoe's emotive performance.

The textual and sonic intertextuality creates a counterpoint between Blades's and LaVoe's recorded renditions that actually reinforces the 1978 recording as the primary referent for "El Cantante." Like LaVoe, Blades's use of a Romantic "I" reinforces the narrative of original genius and authority over the song and the experience it conveys. The first person also emphasizes Blades's rights to the song and his positionality as El Cantante as distinct from LaVoe's. However, at the moment when Blades reaches the lines where fans in the audience would traditionally call out "Oye, Héctor" (Hey,

Héctor) when LaVoe performed, Blades mimics the voice of a drunken fan singing, "Vaya, hombre, brother, oof" (Hey man, brother, oof) rather than inserting his own name.

In the final stanza before the pregones, Blades changes a line. His original handwritten lyrics stated, as LaVoe sang it:

> Yo soy el cantante
> y mi negocio es cantar
>
> [I'm the singer
> And singing is my business]

Blades changes the line slightly:

> Yo soy el cantante
> y lo mío es cantar
>
> [I'm the singer
> And singing is my thing]

The original lyrics explicitly emphasize the performer as both artist and commodity, while Blades's change downplays the second part. Both versions, however, complete the line with

> Y el público paga
> para poderme escuchar
>
> [And the audience pays
> To hear me sing]

LaVoe's self-reflexivity is part of what creates an intimacy with the audience that figures their dancing as the counterpart to his performance. This combination undermines the mythology of original genius even as LaVoe's pregones mark him as a genius alongside other great soneras/os he calls out to in the recording. In Blades's rendition, the same transaction—the patrons pay to hear El Cantante—produces a sense of alienation between the musical figure and the audience. He also mimics the voices of apparently drunk audience members talking and grousing while El Cantante (Blades) performs, separating the singer from the audience through derision.

The difference in the relationship with listeners develops most fully in each performer's improvisational verses. Blades sacrifices the specificity of the local in favor of a pan-Latin American audience, identifying with "todos los barrios de cualquier ciudad" (all the neighborhoods in any city). It presents a strong contrast with LaVoe's identification with an immediate audience through a shared experience signaled through a shift from "I" to "us" in the pregones. Whereas the audience for LaVoe becomes part of the song, in Blades's version they are listeners with whom the lyrical subject empathizes but from whom he remains separate:

> Mi sentimiento es el tuyo
> Tuyas son mis emociones
>
> [I share your feelings,
> And my emotions belong to you]

LaVoe's performance resonated with an "irreverente y callejero" (irreverent and street-based) Nuyorican aesthetic that identified the sonero with New York's Puerto Rican audiences and the very streets he sang about in the song.[61] Blades's performance lacks the emotive quality of LaVoe's recording, one produced at the intersection of the sonero's dramatic rendering and the circumstances in his own life that added layers of meaning to his performance. Blades certainly identified with the condition of "El Cantante," as he has previously shared. In fact, he had an ongoing relationship with the themes of "El Cantante," which appear in songs Blades wrote subsequently, like "Para ser rumbero" (To be a rumbero) and "Nadie sabe" (No one knows), recorded by Roberto Roena y su Apollo Sound. But he fails to achieve the "gusto 'e la calle" (street flavor) his pregones celebrate. Blades's recorded version affirmed his rights to "El Cantante" through the process of recording and releasing the song, but the rendition lacked the affective meanings of the initial recording.

Blades's "El Cantante" asserted an authority over the song's narrative positioned through his voice, the use of the Romantic "I," and the recording itself. LaVoe also deploys the discourse of original genius when he places his stamp on the song early on, at the moment he quotes fans on the street who call out to him, saying, "Oye, Héctor, tú estás hecho" (Hey, Héctor, you got it made), using the second-person form of "you," which highlights his intimacy with his audiences. LaVoe's insertion of his own name into the lyrics contributes to the conflation of identities between the singing subject and

LaVoe even as he asserts his individuality, one recognized when fellow artists, music critics, and fans all dubbed him "El Cantante de los Cantantes." His self-proclaimed status as "el sonero mayor" (the greatest sonero) and the recurring image within the corpus of the tragic jíbaro (Puerto Rican peasant) and Christlike figure betrayed by fame itself also contributed to this and granted LaVoe a cultural authority over the narrative of "El Cantante" that no other performer, including Blades, could reproduce.

I turn here to the work of Immanuel Kant and G. W. F. Hegel, whose writings on ethics and creative labor informed legal doctrine and continue to influence modern philosophy. If, as Kant and Hegel propose, creative work is the extension of the human self, granting spiritual rights to the creator, then it can be argued that LaVoe's performance of "El Cantante" vested the sonero with property rights to the song, as it contained his spiritual embodiment.[62] LaVoe displayed the "innate productive faculty of the artist," and the performance archived through the sound recording of 1978 and recorded live performances displays the originality that Kant argues must be the first property of genius.[63] Kant's focus in *Critique of Judgement* on intentionality, originality, and the contribution of genius to aesthetics, which influenced the Romantic conception of creative genius, provides an important element in advancing multiple claims of authorship to "El Cantante." My intent here is not to reify Romantic perceptions of the author. Instead, I hope to demonstrate how even within the rhetoric of the autonomous creator, the emphasis placed on creativity undermines the identification of popular music with an individual, discrete original genius. Blades's right to "El Cantante," to draw on Kant, means he may "own" it even when LaVoe performed it. But LaVoe's performances provide evidence of his creativity and labor.

Even among his fiercest competitors and critics, LaVoe's charismatic appeal stemmed from the confidence, focus, and emotive quality of his performances. If "one who speaks to the public in his own name is called the author," as Kant argues in *Metaphysics of Morals*, then LaVoe's performances, by assuming authority over "El Cantante" with the use of the solipsistic "I" and his own improvisational verses, signified the vocalist himself as the subject of the song.[64] Kant does not recognize the production of creative genius within the aesthetic and material context in which expressive culture emerges, but LaVoe's "El Cantante" exemplifies that this omission limits our understanding of expressive culture. LaVoe's ability to marshal salsa's aesthetic, cultural, and social possibilities in his performance of "El Cantante," particularly through his improvisational riffs, rests on his musical chops as well as his relationship to New York's Puerto Rican communities and their mutual position as racialized and colonial subjects as well as cultural agents.

Both Blades and LaVoe employ the symbolic power of language and performance to assert their legal, artistic, and cultural authority over the song. For both, the use of rhetorical strategies that reify the conflation of identities between the singer and the singing subject of the composition prove integral in this regard. The use of personal pronouns and possessive adjectives in the song exploits the self-reflexive nature of the lyrics and allows each artist to promote *himself*, emphasize *his* cultural authority, and highlight *his* own uniqueness. For LaVoe, however, the pregones underscore his individuality as he successfully places himself in a class beyond his peers. Blades, a gifted vocalist and performer, is not known as a sonero.

Blades's live performances of "El Cantante," unlike the 1985 recording, closely resemble Colón's arrangements that were used for LaVoe's 1978 recording. In Blades's 2013 performance of "El Cantante" during the Lincoln Center free summer concert series in New York, posted to YouTube, Blades introduced the song by both proclaiming his authorship and recognizing LaVoe's cultural authority.[65] Noting, "I don't mess with what Héctor did," he turned to the band to signal them to start playing. He then returned to the mic and said, "But since I wrote it . . ." and began to sing the song. Notably, he omitted "Oye, Héctor," which other artists typically sing at the appropriate moment in the second verse. I suggest that the ambivalence in the introductory comments reflects the tension between Blades's legal status as the song's creator and LaVoe's creative labor and status as "El Cantante de los Cantantes" among fans and musicians alike. Blades is the only performer of whom I am aware who has not deferred to this status by using "he" instead of "I" when singing "El Cantante," as a token that their rendition is only a tribute. Even Blades framed the 2013 performance as "in memory" of and a sign of "respect" for LaVoe.

In spite of using Colón's melody for "El Cantante," Blades placed his own stamp on the performance through stylistic differences that increase as the performance goes on. In the first stanza, these differences were largely limited to small changes in pitch and the length of notes. The most notable alteration is that in the lines "vinieron a divertirse / y pagaron en la puerta" (you came to have a good time / and you paid at the door), Blades replaced "paid at the door" with "passed through the door," pivoting away from the commodification of creative labor and commodity aspect of the relationship between audience and singer. The crowd sang along with Blades even as his phrasings increasingly departed from LaVoe's. In the second stanza, the performance began to conform to Blades's recording on *Doble filo*. Blades changed the inflection of entire lines, lingered over certain words, and shortened notes. The dissonance became audible in the audience, whose singing was mediated through their memory of LaVoe's performances and the 1978 recording. Some in the audience conformed to Blades's stylistic changes while others continued with LaVoe's interpretation.

While Blades usually performs his own pregones for the latter half of the song, for the concert in New York he invited Puerto Rican Bronx native Flaco Navaja (Osvaldo Rivera) to the stage to perform the pregones. Navaja, who is also a poet and actor, chose his stage name in tribute to Blades's classic song "Pedro Navaja" and has serious chops as a vocalist and improviser. The "new old school salsero" debuted on the New York scene in the mid-1990s as part of the Welfare Poets at the Nuyorican Poets Café.[66] The bio of Navaja on the Internet Movie Database (IMDb) reads, "If Héctor LaVoe boxed Rubén Blades and KRS-1 was the referee you'd get Flaco. A nostalgic old sound with brand new spoken word."[67] He brought to the Lincoln Center performance a vocal style that evoked the layered and complex orchestrations of 1970s salsa as well as the foundational artists of Hip Hop.[68] His phrasing and intonation, bodily gestures, and overall performance embodied LaVoe's corporeal aesthetics while reflecting his own performative practices. The audiences could not sing along with Navaja once he departed from LaVoe's recorded version of "El Cantante," but they signaled their approval in joining him for the chorus, repeating:

> Hoy te dedico
> mis mejores pregones
>
> [Today I dedicate
> My best verses to you]

Blades's and Navaja's performance onstage that evening engaged and transformed LaVoe's performance in a way no previous interpretation had achieved, largely due to Navaja's ability to function as an interlocutor between Blades and the New York audience. Blades's legal rights, LaVoe's cultural authority, and the audience's recognition of multiple and overlapping claims to "El Cantante" reproduced and exceeded the song's legal interpretation.

Blades, who included "El Cantante" on his greatest hits recording *The Best* in 1992, argued that Masucci and his successors had organized a financial conspiracy to defraud artists and composers signed to Fania Records and other companies owned or operated by the label's founder, such as Vaya Records. Unable to locate documents related to the sale of the catalog to Valsyn, Blades argued that Masucci organized the sale "as part of a complex and illegitimate series of transactions . . . intended to make it exceedingly difficult for the artists and composers who were providing recording and composing services . . . to obtain royalties and other payments to which they are contractually entitled."[69] The claim stemmed from the belief among musicians and industry personnel that Masucci orchestrated the sale to Valsyn to avoid paying corporate taxes in the United States.

Fania has faced multiple lawsuits in the United States and Puerto Rico for unpaid royalties, copyright infringement, and breach of contract. Questionable accounting practices, a preference for handwritten records, a complex network of recording labels and publishing companies, and the succession of companies doing business as Fania since the original label ceased operations have challenged artists' ability to assert their rights in court. Strong financial secrecy laws in Uruguay, where Valsyn was located, exacerbated these challenges. Banking and tax-reporting secrecy, as well as low tax rates, helped establish the country as a regional financial center in the 1980s. Valsyn potentially benefited from strong financial privacy laws that concealed company ownership and protected assets from lawsuits. Until 2010, corporations in Uruguay that conducted all their business offshore were subject to a tax rate of just 0.3 percent and paid no other corporate taxes.[70] If Masucci used the sale to create a tax shelter, the license he negotiated with Valsyn to distribute Fania's remaining inventory in the United States and Puerto Rico would ensure that Valsyn's income was generated outside Uruguay and would be exempt from additional corporate taxes. The continued distribution of Fania's catalog across the Americas during the 1980s and 1990s by distributors such as Palacio de la Música in Venezuela and Industrias Eléctricas y Musicales Peruanas (IEMPSA) in Peru would produce additional income in their respective countries not subject to corporate taxes in Uruguay. The privacy laws also made it difficult for those who sued Fania Records and its successors to trace the catalog's ownership while providing a foothold for Latin American markets.

Blades's allegations against Masucci individually and Fania generally were detailed across the various lawsuits. Masucci, Blades argued in 2002, "compelled" him to sign an SSA as an unwritten condition for being awarded a recording contract with Vaya Records.[71] This condition formed part and parcel of an organization that had "since developed a well-deserved reputation, for conducting business in an unscrupulous and fraudulent manner and for wrongfully exploiting the artists, composers, and performers who have signed agreements with them."[72] As in the original 1984 lawsuit, Blades also maintained that Masucci used the various entities at his disposal interchangeably. Masucci, he claimed, orchestrated a process through which various entities became parties to the contracts signed by Blades in the form of assignees, licensees, or the like.[73] I cite a portion of the 2002 complaint at length to convey the breadth of Blades's allegations and the implication that a financial conspiracy vexed other artists' and composers' attempts to recover royalties from Fania assignees and successors:

> Masucci and his successors organized these various defendant entities [Fania Records, Vaya Records, Vaya Publishing, Fania Publishing, Musica Latina, and Vev Publishing-Sonido] as part of a complex and illegitimate set of transactions and assignments that were intended to make it exceedingly difficult for the artists and composers who were providing recording and composing services to those entities to obtain royalties and other payment to which they are contractually entitled. . . . Masucci and his successors and assignees further implemented this scheme to defraud these artists and composers by entering into a series of purported sales, transfers, and assignments with certain foreign entities, including Valsyn, an Argentinian/Uruguayan entity, all in the furtherance of their efforts to defeat and defraud the rights of the artists and composers who were under contract with the defendant entities.[74]

Blades suggests that the defendants named in the 2002 lawsuit, all of which were owned by and/or affiliated with Masucci in some way, colluded to create a web of transactions that made it virtually impossible to determine which entity was responsible for artist and composer royalties at any given moment over the course of almost forty years, especially once Masucci created and acquired additional labels, publishing companies, and the manufacturing plant.

| | |
|---|---|
| 1979 | Masucci sells the Fania catalog and all its assets to the Uruguayan company Valsyn; retains distribution rights in United States and Puerto Rico for remaining inventory. |
| | Fania Records and most of its subsidiary labels cease formal operations. |
| 1981 | Masucci registers the Fania trademark and assigns it to Musica Latina, which becomes the company doing business as (d/b/a) Fania. |
| 1984 | *Musica Latina v. Blades* |
| 1986 | Sonido Inc. established; acquires the Fania trademark and all licensing agreements from Musica Latina and begins d/b/a Fania. |
| 1988 | *Blades v. Vaya Records* |
| 1997 | Sonido amends Valsyn license; FEG formed one month later; Sonido transfers all assets to FEG. |
| | FEG files paperwork with the SEC in advance of an IPO for stock in the company. |
| | Masucci dies two days after SEC paperwork filed; NASDAQ registration for FEG withdrawn. |
| | Masucci's estate goes into probate; Melissa Gosnell becomes executor of the estate and trustee for the trust established in Masucci's will for their daughter, Corinne Masucci. |
| 1999 | Sonido extends Valsyn license to 2004. |
| | *Sonido v. David Lugo* (title would change to *Lugo v. Sonido*) |
| 2000 | *LAMCO v. Cárdenas Fernández* |
| 2002 | *Blades v. Fania Records* |

| | |
|---|---|
| **2003** | Valsyn brokers a $45 million deal with Universal Music Group for the Fania catalog; Masucci's estate rejects the offer. |
| | *Roena v. Fania* |
| | LAMCO *v. Cárdenas Fernández* (Appeal) |
| | *Feliciano v. Valsyn* (D.P.R.) |
| **2005** | Morgan Stanley finances Emusica Entertainment Group purchase of the Fania catalog for $11 million; Masucci's estate, now out of probate, acts as the agent for Valsyn. |
| | Emusica begins promoting the catalog using the Fania name and logo. |
| | Emusica discovers a storage unit in upstate New York with audio recordings, masters, photographs, contracts, and other materials. |
| | *Gallo v. Sonido* |
| **2006** | Emusica beings to remaster and reissue Fania classics. |
| | *New York Times* article announces the return of the label "that made salsa hot." |
| | *Feliciano v. Valsyn* (D.P.R., Appeal) |
| | WIPO Arbitration and Mediation Center, "Administrative Panel Decision: *Sonido, Inc. v. MU21C.COM Inc.* Case No. D2006-0685 |
| | Biopic *El Cantante* released; sales of LaVoe material reach upward of 90,000 pieces. |
| | *Masucci v. Gosnell* |
| **2007** | Emusica files trademark Fania with the United States Patent and Trademark Office (USPTO). |
| | Soundtrack for *El Cantante* biopic reaches #1 on *Billboard* charts for Latin Albums and Latin Tropical Albums; peaks at #4 on *Billboard* Top Soundtracks chart. |
| **2008** | Market decline in CD sales prompts Emusica shift toward digital market and access to a global market previously untapped. |
| | *Feliciano v. Valsyn* (S.D.N.Y.) |

| | |
|---|---|
| 2009 | Signal Equity Partners acquires the Fania catalog under the name Codigo Records; begins using the Fania name and logo to promote the catalog. |
| | *Maldonado v. Valsyn* |
| 2011 | Release of remastered limited-edition two-CD/DVD set of *Live at the Cheetah*, vols. 1 and 2, and *Our Latin Thing*. |
| | *Masucci v. Sonido* |
| 2013 | Codigo reports first profitable year for Fania catalog since its purchase in 2005. |
| | *LAMCO v. Spanish Broadcasting* |
| 2014 | Fiftieth anniversary of Fania Records. |
| | Codigo signs with Creative Arts Agency to promote the Fania catalog. |
| | Approximately 60 percent of revenue from Fania catalog derives from music sales; remainder largely from licensing deals and merchandise sales, including remixes of Fania classics. |
| 2018 | Concord Music purchases Fania assets from Codigo; begins d/b/a Fania and using logo. |
| 2022 | Vinyl reissue by Craft Recordings of *Live at the Cheetah*, vol. 1. |
| 2023 | Vinyl reissues by Craft Recordings include |
| | *Asalto Navideño*, vol. 2 |
| | *Indestructible* |
| | *Live at the Cheetah*, vol. 2. |
| 2024 | Sixtieth anniversary of the founding of Fania Records. |

*Note:* Lawsuits are listed by filing date.

The complex web of companies and transactions has largely stymied efforts to seek financial compensation. Lawsuits have been filed in New York and Puerto Rico by various artists, including Cheo Feliciano, Bobby Valentín, Richie Ray, Bobby Maldonado, and Roberto Roena.[75] While several settlements have been reached, the use of secondhand information about Masucci's financial transactions, on which artists have been forced to rely, has hindered efforts to establish an undisputable legal relationship between Masucci and Valsyn, which would have allowed artists to file suit against Masucci's estate.[76] Even Masucci's brother Alex and former vice president of Fania Victor Gallo have relied on secondhand information in their respective lawsuits against Valsyn for unpaid labor, after the 2005 sale of the Fania catalog to Emusica.[77] Blades's success in regaining control over the songs he wrote is an extraordinary exception, not only in relation to Fania but in the music industry generally.

### Conclusion

The legal strategy available to Blades and his lawyers reflects the limits of the legal system and the importance of challenging the assumption that it is legally preferable to disenfranchise any potential collaborators for the sake of protecting the rights of an individual. The proliferation of multiple and overlapping forms of ownership that emerged during the social life of "El Cantante" reveals how the song's creation continued beyond a finite moment during which Blades wrote the initial stanzas. He wrote those verses, after all, as an up-and-coming artist signed to Fania and thus rightly expected to be recognized for his creative labor. Yet Blades's effort to retain complete ownership denied the ways in which LaVoe's own creative labor contributed to the song, which reinforces the limits of existing copyright law. The law obfuscates the economic value of the song, in the form of licensing fees and royalties, that developed through LaVoe's abjection and conflation with the song's narrative subject. It remains important, however, that Blades never challenges LaVoe's right to perform the song, whether in interviews or in documents related to the lawsuit against Sonido. Blades, whose law degree from the Universidad Nacional de Panamá and master's from Harvard Law School likely facilitated his understanding of copyright law, indicted only Fania and its successors in his suits.

As immigrants from Panama and Puerto Rico, Blades and LaVoe, respectively, were inscribed into the gendered and racial/ethnic hierarchies of the United States that originated in colonial structures of power.[78] Blades's rendering of events also shows that LaVoe's abjection within legal narratives cannot be understood outside the ways in which the coloniality of power also structures the relationship *between* the two performers. Puerto Ricans are, as Ramón Grosfoguel elaborates, "doubly colonial"—as colonial and diasporic subjects whose presence in the metropolis remains racialized and criminalized in ways specific to the historical processes that structured the migration of Puerto Ricans to the United States.[79] Blades's subject position as the "writer" of "El Cantante" relies on redeploying hegemonic narratives of LaVoe as a failed citizen subject indebted to the canta-autor's generosity. In fact, Blades included a narrative of the song's trajectory, including the sonero's drug abuse, during his deposition for the 2002 lawsuit against Fania Records and its successors.[80]

Blades's successful reclamation of the rights to his songs after having transferred them to the publishing arm of Fania Records remains an outlier among lawsuits where former artists allege copyright infringement, failure to pay royalties, and breach of contract on the part of Fania, its subsidiaries, and its successors; and his success in each of three lawsuits remains unequaled. The lawsuits between Blades and Fania's successors also stand out because they occurred more than a decade before he would have been able to terminate Fania's rights to his songs. Under the termination rights clause in the Copyright Act of 1976, the creator of a copyrighted work (or their heirs) may reclaim rights transferred to another party after thirty-five years. After termination, any rights transferred return to the creator or their heirs.[81] Moreover, without evidentiary power to the contrary or the willingness of US courts to consider alternative interpretations of what constitutes an author of a joint work, Blades's legal strategy relegates LaVoe to the status of legal nonsubject. LaVoe's racialized performance of masculinity and subjecthood remained illegible within the legal sphere. Blades benefited from the express desire within copyright law to protect the rights of an individual author despite communal collaborative processes and technological developments that produce multiple moments of creativity.

Questions of cultural patrimony potentially expand intellectual property law, encroaching on the public domain, which should be protected. Yet the meaning making within "El Cantante" carries implications for contemporary debates about cultural authority, intellectual property, and intangible cultural heritage. Insofar as music and other forms of artistic expression remain a privileged site for imagining and reenvisioning Latinidad, scholars must engage debates about the ways in which creative subjects, whether as individuals or communities, are constituted in part in relationship to both the legal sphere and the market.[82] Concerns about the intellectual property rights of cultural producers are particularly significant for communities whose histories, like that of Puerto Rico and its diaspora, remain marginal to legal discourses.

I propose, like legal scholar Rosemary Coombe, that the law must be understood as a constellation of images, narratives, and legal conventions that form part of hegemonic power. To that end, my approach to the question of whether "El Cantante" should be considered a joint work under copyright law, or at minimum require a collaborative agreement, recognizes how power is negotiated across musical, social, and legal contexts. To this end, I have examined the narratives, images, and legal conventions third parties have used to establish their authority over LaVoe's creative labor. Rather than attempting to establish the "truth" of these claims, I am interested in how these legal positionalities were established and protected over time and the ways they reify the coloniality of power through which LaVoe's status in the courtroom was (re)presented. Blades, like Lugo and the LaVoe estate, resorted to hegemonic narratives of Puerto Rican abjection. The unwillingness of the court to navigate ambiguity further exacerbated the liminal position of LaVoe within the courtroom in terms of determining whether "El Cantante" constitutes a joint work as defined under the US Copyright Act of 1976. The courtroom, as demonstrated in each of the legal cases, becomes the site for reproducing authority.

For LaVoe's fans, "El Cantante" constituted a personal confession from the singer, one that translated into his being considered the author of the experience narrated within the song. All the same, this authority does not negate Blades's proprietary rights or the public knowledge that he wrote the song's initial verses, thus demonstrating the multiple and sometimes simultaneous modes in which ownership operates. Outside the legal system, the hierarchy between a visionary creator and the mechanical performer is unsustainable. LaVoe is not merely the mechanical device that "speaks in the name of the author" but rather the one endowed with the title of "El Cantante de los Cantantes."[83]

Blades rejected LaVoe's status as creator using the Romantic discourse of author as individual genius encoded within US copyright law, which allowed him to repudiate the status of "El Cantante" as a collaborative endeavor. Blades also benefited financially from LaVoe's recording, performances, and identification with "El Cantante." Finally, Sonido's self-interest aside, Fania's successor failed to protect LaVoe's creative work. As sole creator before the court, Blades now receives all publishing royalties even though the entirety of the song—both the first three verses and the series of two-line verses—forms part of the recording. Of course, Sonido owned the mechanical rights to the song's reproduction, so the label receives royalties when the song is reissued in any form, as in the case of the play *¿Quién mató a Héctor LaVoe?*, the soundtrack to the film biopic *El Cantante*, and the album *Tributo urbano a Héctor LaVoe* (2007).

That Blades never challenged LaVoe's right to perform the song, a possibility under copyright law, recognizes the sonero's cultural authority over "El Cantante" and its meanings.[84] The ability of audiences to accommodate multiple and overlapping definitions of ownership that recognize Blades's role in creating the song while bestowing on LaVoe the moniker of "El Cantante de los Cantantes," however, creates a space of Rican/Struction: a space within which Blades recognizes the song and the experience it narrates not only as his song but as LaVoe's. That both Blades and LaVoe lay claim to the experience it narrates resonates with the listening public, precisely because of the ways salsa's Nuyorican imaginary accommodates the song's dynamic meanings.

# Notes

## Introduction. Rican/Struction: The Social Life of Salsa

Epigraph: From *Brujalicious*, De La Luz Records, 2006.

1    The song was also released on Anthony's album *3.0* three months later.

2    City Lore, "La Marqueta."

3    Aparicio, "Marc Anthony *3.0*," 50–51. The most frequent translation of *gozar* would be "to enjoy" or "to revel in." Anthony's usage conveys a

taking hold of pleasure and of life. It also suggests the substantive *gozo*, which can denote both pleasure and bliss.

4    Vázquez, "Can You Feel the Beat?," 112; Neal, *Songs in the Key*, 110. George came of age in New York City's East Harlem neighborhood in the 1970s and 1980s, listening to Afro-Caribbean and African American music playing on the radio and wafting out of 8-track decks in people's cars.

5    Aparicio, "Marc Anthony *3.0*," 48.

6    Nicknamed La Voz (The Voice) by a dazzled local promoter, Héctor Juan Pérez Martínez assumed the stage name Héctor LaVoe. The spelling reflects the aspirated final-syllable /s/ common to Puerto Rican Spanish. I use LaVoe rather than the alternative Lavoe to emphasize the aesthetic and sociolinguistic context. It also reflects the spelling found on various albums. Any use of the lowercase *v* reflects the spelling in interview transcriptions or essay titles.

7    Valentín-Escobar, "El hombre que respira," 176.

8    On LaVoe's status as a Puerto Rican effigy, see Valentín-Escobar, "El hombre que respira."

9    Benson Arias, "Sailing on the USS *Titanic*," 32; Ayala, "Decline of the Plantation Economy," 77–78; Sánchez Korrol, *From Colonia to Community*, 27.

10   Espiritu, "Home Bound," 47. Diasporic Puerto Ricans continue to have the highest poverty rates and the highest asthma and asthma-related mortality rates among Latinas/os, and they continue to account for disproportionately high numbers of new HIV cases in the United States. Deren et al., "Addressing the HIV/AIDS Epidemic"; Asencio, *Sex and Sexuality*, 9–10; Arcoleo et al., "Longitudinal Patterns."

11   Muñoz, *Cruising Utopia*.

12   Glasser, *My Music Is My Flag*, 3.

13   Historian Frank Guridy characterizes the "US-Caribbean world" as the supranational region of trade networks consolidated during the first four decades after the War of 1898 that extended along the Eastern Seaboard of the United States, the Caribbean Basin, the Gulf of Mexico, and the northern boundaries of South America. As the region became increasingly entangled in the US economic sphere of influence, the translocal linkages within the US-Caribbean world connected cities in the northeastern United States such as New York to other major cities. These trade networks facilitated the flows of Afro-diasporic music to coastal cities such as Caracas, Venezuela, and Cali, Colombia, both of which became nodal points in salsa's increasingly transnational flows by the mid to late 1970s and the mid-1980s, respectively. Guridy, *Forging Diaspora*, 7–8; Waxer, *City of Musical Memory*.

14    Waxer, "Situating Salsa," 5; see also Aparicio, *Listening to Salsa*; Berríos-Miranda, "Is Salsa a Musical Genre?"; Valentín-Escobar, "El hombre que respira"; Rondón, *Book of Salsa*.

15    Sanabria (@mrsalsamovie), "The idea #IzzySanabria had for this #RayBarretto cover."

16    Herrera, *Nuyorican Feminist Performance*, 29–30.

17    Herrera, *Nuyorican Feminist Performance*, 30–31.

18    Normative Puerto Ricanness does not signify a singular ideological position but rather the ways that liberal citizenship informed claims to social, economic, and political rights by Puerto Ricans in both the diaspora and in Puerto Rico, albeit at different historical junctures. As demonstrated in the proceeding chapters, I do not suggest that salsa destabilized all hegemonic mobilizations of Puerto Ricanness, particularly with regard to the gendered and sexual boundaries of Puerto Rican belonging.

19    Tyler, *Revolting Subjects*, 3–5.

20    Jaime, *Queer Nuyorican*, 30.

21    Herrera, *Nuyorican Feminist Performance*, 45.

22    Herrera, *Nuyorican Feminist Performance*, 46; Jaime, *Queer Nuyorican*, 8, 46.

23    Herrera, *Nuyorican Feminist Performance*, 36.

24    Herrera, *Nuyorican Feminist Performance*, 69–70.

25    Herrera, *Nuyorican Feminist Performance*, 32.

26    La Bruja, "Nuyorico Interlude," on *Brujalicious*. El Morro was designed by the Spanish to protect Puerto Rico from pirates and constructed between 1539 and 1790.

27    Glasser, *My Music Is My Flag*, 50–51.

28    Significantly, whereas the emergence and consolidation of the plena occurs between 1900 and 1926 across Puerto Rico, during the next quarter century it also becomes a fixture among New York Puerto Rican communities. See J. Flores, "'Bumbún' and the Beginnings of *Plena* Music," in *Divided Borders*, 85–108.

29    Glasser, *My Music Is My Flag*, 74–78.

30    Pacini Hernández, *Bachata*, 24–25.

31    J. Flores, *Salsa Rising*, 121.

32    Pacini Hernández, "Tale of Two Cities."

33    Y. Flores, interview with the author; Pacini Hernández, "Tale of Two Cities," 82; Glasser, *My Music Is My Flag*, 3.

34    Pacini Hernández, "Tale of Two Cities," 81.

35    J. Flores, *From Bomba to Hip-Hop*, 82, 107–10.

36  Lorrin Thomas, *Puerto Rican Citizen*, 88.

37  Cited in Lorrin Thomas, *Puerto Rican Citizen*, 134–35.

38  *New York Times*, "City Called Haven." These concerns have continued over time. In 2010, all Puerto Rican birth certificates issued before July 1 of that year were invalidated.

39  Grutzner, "City's Puerto Ricans Found Ill-Housed."

40  Lorrin Thomas, *Puerto Rican Citizen*, 160.

41  Lorrin Thomas, *Puerto Rican Citizen*, 159–60.

42  Lorrin Thomas, *Puerto Rican Citizen*, 88.

43  Lorrin Thomas, *Puerto Rican Citizen*, 158–60.

44  Andrés Torres, *Between Melting Pot and Mosaic*, 66; Grosfoguel, *Colonial Subjects*, 149–64; Grosfoguel and Georas, "Latino Caribbean Diasporas," 106–7.

45  Buder, "City School Rolls."

46  Buder, "Racial Patterns Shift in Schools."

47  Briggs, *Reproducing Empire*, 163.

48  See Andrés Torres, *Between Melting Pot and Mosaic*.

49  Lorrin Thomas, *Puerto Rican Citizen*, 150–51.

50  United States Congress, *Communist Activities among Puerto Ricans*, 1515, 1604.

51  Zipp, *Manhattan Projects*, 165–66.

52  Dávila, *Barrio Dreams*, 28; Mele, *Selling the Lower East Side*, 138.

53  Lorrin Thomas, *Puerto Rican Citizen*, 158–60.

54  Mele, *Selling the Lower East Side*, 142–43; V. Rosa, "Colonial Projects," 189–91.

55  Mele, *Selling the Lower East Side*, 129–31; Dávila, *Barrio Dreams*, 31; Zipp, *Manhattan Projects*, 205.

56  Dávila, *Barrio Dreams*, 31.

57  During a two-year period from 1959 to 1961, Puerto Ricans accounted for 76 percent of residents displaced by urban renewal, reflecting policies that characterized them as a "transient" and "vulnerable" population for whom public assistance was not the city's priority. Mele, *Selling the Lower East Side*, 129–31; Dávila, *Barrio Dreams*, 29–31.

58  Zipp, *Manhattan Projects*, 183.

59  Findlay, "Slipping and Sliding," 27. Suárez interviewed Puerto Ricans born in New York during the 1940s, 1950s, and 1960s who moved to San Juan, Puerto Rico.

60  Black Latinas Know Collective, "Statement"; Dinzey-Flores, "Stop Sacrificing Black Latinxs"; Lloréns and Dinzey-Flores, "Replay."

61    Lloréns, *Making Livable Worlds*, 34–35. See also Figueroa-Vásquez, "Survival of a People"; T. Hernández, *Racial Innocence*.

62    Stoever, "Splicing the Sonic Color-Line," 65–68.

63    Stoever, "Reproducing U.S. Citizenship," 783.

64    Sandoval Sánchez, *José, Can You See?*, 23.

65    Tyler, *Revolting Subjects*, 19–46; Hancock, *Politics of Disgust*, 66–67; Mele, *Selling the Lower East Side*, 129–30.

66    Lazzarato, *Making of the Indebted Man*, 11.

67    Tyler, *Revolting Subjects*, 4, 170–71.

68    Quoted in Lorrin Thomas, *Puerto Rican Citizen*, 158.

69    Mele, *Selling the Lower East Side*, 272–73.

70    Dávila, "Culture in the Battlefront," 163–64.

71    Valentín-Escobar, "Bodega Surrealism," 37, 129–30.

72    Quoted in Echeverría Ortiz, "'Where We Were Safe.'"

73    Valentín-Escobar, "El hombre que respira," 165. The section heading means "Let them play salsa," the title of a song by El Gran Combo.

74    Pacheco, interview with the author.

75    Pacheco, "Interview."

76    Lee, "Re-examining the Concept," 13.

77    In cases where a corporation name would normally include a diacritic but none was used by the relevant entity, I have defaulted to the convention used by that party.

78    Gurza, "Fania Tries a Non-salsa Label," 90; Gallo, interview with the author, 2002; Miller, "Crossover Schemes," 192.

79    Fania Entertainment Group, "Securities and Exchange Commission Form SB-2"; Waring, "Fania Records"; Peisner, "Digital Salsa."

80    Gurza, "La Tierra for Latins," 39; Miller, "Crossover Schemes," 192.

81    Lee, "Re-examining the Concept," 14.

82    Pacini Hernández, *Oye Como Va!*, 15.

83    Pacini Hernández, *Oye Como Va!*, 15.

84    Pacini Hernández, *Oye Como Va!*, 20–21.

85    Lowe and Lloyd, "Introduction," 26.

86    Vázquez, *Listening in Detail*, 4–30.

87    Vázquez, *Listening in Detail*, 8.

88    Bongocero José Mangual Jr. assumed the responsibilities of bandleader at LaVoe's request. Mangual, interview with the author.

89    Appadurai, *Social Life of Things*, 5.

90   Ochoa Gautier, *Aurality*, 5.

91   C. García, *Salsa Crossings*.

92   Delgado and Muñoz, "Rebellions of Everynight Life," 9–10.

93   Jaime, *Queer Nuyorican*, 142, 164.

94   Muñoz, *Disidentifications*, 182.

95   I generally refer to public figures by their last name and fans who were not public figures by their first names. Where the use of the last name might cause confusion, I defer to the first name. For example, I refer to Pete "El Conde" Rodríguez as "Pete 'El Conde'" to differentiate him from his contemporary Pete Rodríguez. I refer to Luis "Máquina" as such to distinguish him from the various other persons I interviewed as well as cultural critics who share the last name Flores.

96   Taylor, *Archive and Repertoire*, 129–30.

97   Carby, "Souls of Black Men," 13–16.

98   Vargas, "Ruminations," 718.

99   Vargas, "Ruminations," 715–18; Vargas, "Un Desmadre Positivo," 286.

100  R. Rosa, "Governing Tourism."

101  Sheller, *Consuming the Caribbean*, 177–78.

102  Coombe, "Is There a Cultural Studies of Law?," 37–38.

103  Paul Gewirtz, quoted in Coombe, "Is There a Cultural Studies of Law?," 37.

### Chapter 1. *Our Latin Thing*: Salsa's Nuyorican Histories

1   I say "generally considered" the band's debut because the All-Stars performed at the Red Garter in Greenwich Village in 1968 and released a live recording of the concert, but neither got significant attention, and the band did not appear together again until the Cheetah Lounge concert.

2   Fundora, "Desde nuestro rincón internacional," 36.

3   Rondón, *Book of Salsa*, 59–60.

4   The song is listed as "Introduction theme" on the album. Barretto also released the song on his 1972 album *Que viva la música*.

5   Greenspun, "Doing '*Our Latin Thing*,'" 13.

6   Miller, "Crossover Schemes," 187–88.

7   In her study of New York's Puerto Rican community, Ana Celia Zentella defines "dense" communities as those where "most of the people not only [know] each other's name and apartment number, they also [know] personal histories and considered each other's friends their friends." *Growing Up Bilingual*, 8.

8    Quiroga, "Salsa, Bad Boys, and Brass," 236. Pacheco's flute solo is listed as "Closing Theme" on the album.

9    Glasser, *My Music Is My Flag*, 108.

10   The relationships of business owners like Hernández with local musicians were not without conflict; musicians charged that Victoria took a bigger cut than she should. Glasser, *My Music Is My Flag*, 107–9, 147–49.

11   Quoted in Echeverría Ortiz, "'Where We Were Safe.'" Victoria Hernández's first record store, Almacenes Hernández (aka the Hernández Music Store), closed in 1939 when her family moved to Mexico for two years. Settling in the Bronx in 1941, Hernández opened Casa Hernández at 786 Prospect Avenue and supplemented music sales by providing piano lessons and selling clothing. It was the first location in the New York State Register associated with Puerto Ricans in New York. See Martínez, "La Madrina's Music Store."

12   Pacheco, interview with the author; Cobo, "Wild and Improbable Journey."

13   Pacheco, interview with the author.

14   Gurza, "Hot Latin Dance Music," 90.

15   Pacheco, interview with the author.

16   Lee, "Re-examining the Concept," 13.

17   Pacheco, interview with the author; Gallo, interview with the author, 2002.

18   Melanson, "Fania Concert Is Success," 18.

19   Larry Harlow, quoted in Kent, *Salsa Talks*, 396; Sanabria, "Jerry Masucci on Willie," 5. In its previous incarnation as the Palm Gardens, it was the epicenter of the boogaloo and Latin soul scene.

20   *Record World*, "Gast Brings Fania to Screen," 17.

21   Kent, *Salsa Talks*, 396.

22   Kent, *Salsa Talks*, 396.

23   Pacheco, interview with the author; Harlow, quoted in Kent, *Salsa Talks*, 396; J. Flores, *Salsa Rising*, 182–83.

24   Mercado, interview with the author.

25   Dávila, *Latinos, Inc.*, 46.

26   Mercado, interview with the author.

27   Quoted in Kent, *Salsa Talks*, 399.

28   Mercado, interview with the author.

29   Detailed accounts of the concert may be found in Kent, *Salsa Talks*, 396–400; Rondón, *Book of Salsa*, 41–55; J. Flores, *Salsa Rising*, 175–85.

30    Rodríguez, quoted in Kent, *Salsa Talks*, 397.

31    Mercado, interview with the author.

32    Ocasio, interview with the author.

33    Rondón, *Book of Salsa*, 44.

34    Katz, "Salsa Criticism," 47.

35    "WT/F–True/False Film Fest."

36    Music and Art merged with the High School for the Performing Arts—on which the film *Fame* (1980) was based—in 1984.

37    Harlow, interview with the author.

38    Gast won the 1997 Academy Award for Best Documentary Film for *When We Were Kings*. He filmed the footage for the documentary while in Zaire to film the Fania All-Stars.

39    Slater, "It Was Our Thing."

40    Slater, "It Was Our Thing."

41    The relationship with Good Vibrations also guaranteed sound engineers with experience recording salsa's polyrhythmic arrangements. Sutherland, "Studio Track," 14; Sutherland, "Sessions Get More Sophisticated," L–12; Miller, "Crossover Schemes," 187.

42    Greenspun, "Doing 'Our Latin Thing,'" 13.

43    Melanson and Contreras, "'Latin Thing' Premieres," 10.

44    *New York Magazine*, "Movies around Town," 9; R. Goldstein, "Latin Nabes," 41.

45    Greenspun, "Doing 'Our Latin Thing,'" 13.

46    Rondón, *Book of Salsa*, 59–60.

47    Fundora, "Desde nuestro rincón internacional," 36.

48    Aletti, *"Our Latin Thing,"* 42.

49    Aletti, *"Our Latin Thing,"* 42.

50    Guzmán, "'*Our Latin Thing*?,'" 9.

51    Guzmán, "'*Our Latin Thing*?,'" 9.

52    Berríos-Miranda, "Salsa Music as Expressive Liberation," 165.

53    Slater, "It Was Our Thing."

54    Glasser, *My Music Is My Flag*, 53–54.

55    The spectacularization of abject poverty within *Our Latin Thing* may be contrasted to the 1978 *Viva Loisaida*, which, as Karen Jaime states, "visually and sonically captured" the culture of the Lower East Side. While underscoring the "governmental neglect impacting the area, in *Viva Loisaida* [director Marlis] Member juxtaposes these images of dilapi-

dated buildings and abandoned lots with full-scale murals and artistic productions, including music and poetry." Jaime, *Queer Nuyorican*, 32.

56    Miranda, "Ismael Miranda."

57    Delgado, interview with the author.

58    Singer and Martínez, "South Bronx Latin Music Tale," 182.

59    For additional information on the role of the South Bronx in the development of "Latin" music in New York, see Singer and Martínez, "South Bronx Latin Music Tale." The "Mambo to Hip Hop" tour offered until 2010 by the Point, a cultural arts organization in the Hunts Point section of the Bronx, also provided a historical perspective on the development of Latin music in the South Bronx.

60    Oteri, "Salsa Is an Open Concept."

61    Additional places included the Seventy-Seventh Street entrance to Central Park. Y. Flores, interview with the author. Central Park hosted a variety of music festivals during this period, including the annual Schaefer Festival (1967–76) and the 1973 *Latin N.Y.* concert. Orchard Beach continues to host salsa bands during the summer.

62    Cuchifrito is a popular Puerto Rican stewed dish that, like chitterlings (chitlins), is made with pig intestines.

63    There were also various clubs that catered to different forms of Latin music, such as the Caborrojeño on Upper Broadway, which my mother frequented.

64    R. García, "Salsa Is Exploding," s-2.

65    Kent, *Salsa Talks*, 143.

66    L. Flores, interview with the author.

67    A. Flores, interview with the author.

68    Chris Washburne provides an overview of informal practices within the salsa scene and the drug economy in *Sounding Salsa*.

69    Mangual, interview with the author.

70    Interview with the author.

71    Montalvo, interview with the author.

72    Mangual, interview with the author.

73    A. Flores, "Latin Scene," 56.

74    Harlow, interview with the author.

75    Dávila, *Culture Works*, 189.

76    Mangual, interview with the author; Mercado, interview with the author.

77    This competition among artists was nothing new to the Latin music industry, as the often-reported feuds between Tito Puente and his

contemporaries attest. Harlow, interview with the author; Gallo, interview with the author, 2002. Regarding the competition between Ray Barretto and Eddie Palmieri, see the obituary by Pablo Guzmán, "Ray Barretto."

78  Mercado, interview with the author.

79  Harlow, interview with the author. In a 2002 interview I conducted, Fania executive Victor Gallo claimed that the accountant discovered that Harlow owed the label money.

80  Gallo, interview with the author, 2002.

81  Mercado, interview with the author.

82  Gast has suggested it occurred spontaneously, one of the many scenes captured as the film crew walked through the Lower East Side. Slater, "It Was Our Thing."

83  Interview with the author.

84  Singer and Martínez, "South Bronx Latin Music Tale," 186–87.

85  The Palladium played Latin music and drew its patrons in part from New York's Puerto Rican communities. While this club remains the most documented of the 1950s and 1960s to feature Latin music, a host of smaller clubs, dance halls, afterhours clubs, and theaters provided entertainment in New York's Puerto Rican communities. The Park Palace on 110th Street and Fifth Avenue, nicknamed El Palladium Chiquito (The Little Palladium), was one such example. While the building still stands, a church now occupies the space. For additional information on the Latin music scene prior to salsa, see Glasser, *My Music Is My Flag*. See also the chapter on community settlement patterns in Singer and Martínez, "South Bronx Latin Music Tale."

86  Segarra, interview with the author.

87  Segarra, interview with the author; Echeverría Ortiz, "'Where We Were Safe.'"

88  Harlow, interview with the author.

89  Interview with the author.

90  Segarra, interview with the author.

91  L. Flores, interview with the author, August 6, 2002.

92  Interview with the author.

93  A. Flores, interview with the author.

94  Luciano, interview with the author.

95  Interview with the author. Where I quote or use specific information provided by someone I interviewed, I use their first name. I do not share the names of persons who shared information that they did not

want attributed to them or that might cause indirect harm should they be identified as the source. I do not include individual names when I bring together the recollections and information shared by various people.

96    Interview with the author.

97    Luciano, interview with the author.

98    The term *Marintaiga* (a Spanish phonetic pronunciation) was also common.

99    Hutchinson, "Mambo on 2."

100    A. Flores, interview with the author. For an exploration of the patriarchal discourses of salsa, the listening practices of women, and their exclusion from the histories of salsa, see the groundbreaking analysis by Frances Aparicio, *Listening to Salsa*.

101    Terrace, "Masucci May Try," 27.

102    Luciano, interview with the author.

103    Interview with the author.

104    C. García, "'Don't Leave Me, Celia!,'" 205.

105    Interview with the author.

106    Interviews with the author.

107    Interview with the author.

108    Spain, *Gendered Spaces*, 15–16; Aparicio, *Listening to Salsa*.

109    Y. Flores, interview with the author.

110    A. Flores, interview with the author. Aurora founded the band Zon del Barrio.

111    Aparicio, *Listening to Salsa*, 123.

112    Slater, "It Was Our Thing."

113    Included in the soundtrack as "Cockfight and Interview."

114    Humphrey, *Santería, Vodou and Resistance*, 3.

115    The scene is listed as "Bembé" on the soundtrack.

116    Humphrey, *Santería, Vodou and Resistance*, 3, 11–42.

117    Vega, "Yoruba Orisha Tradition"; Vega, "Ancestral Sacred Creative Impulse," 55; Fernández-Olmos, *Sacred Possessions*, 56.

118    Moten, *In the Break*, 6.

119    Armstrong, "'Effects of Blackness,'" 214.

120    Included in the soundtrack as "Botánica."

121    Within Caribbean discourse, see Benítez Rojo, *La isla que se repite*. See also González, *El país de cuatro pisos y otros ensayos*.

122 Vega, "Ancestral Sacred Creative Impulse," 45. The representation of Black female bodies as excess reifies tropicalizations of the Caribbean elaborated by historians such as Antonio Benítez Rojo, who constructs a Caribbean essence expressed through polyrhythms, improvisation, and lack of reason that surpasses the parameters of Western modernity. While attempting to challenge an investment in whiteness, blackness becomes an essence contained within the prelinguistic: it is ritual, music and rhythm, pleasure, and seduction. This Caribbeanness, in turn, is embodied by Black women, specifically mulattas, who walk in a "certain kind of way," a product of the fragmentation, chaos, and violence that produced the Caribbean as a sign. Benítez Rojo uses "in a certain kind of way" to describe the development of the Caribbean across cultural and linguistic differences. The meta-rhythm he describes is defined by its improvisation and lack of reason and inspired by "two old black women" he saw walk beneath a balcony "in a certain kind of way" that, as Benítez Rojo informs the reader, the author could not describe. "I will say only," he writes, "that there was a kind of ancient and golden power between their gnarled legs, a scent of basil and mint in their dress, a symbolic, ritual wisdom in their gesture and their gay chatter." *La isla que se repite*, 10.

123 Luciano, interview with the author; Vega, "Yoruba Orisha Tradition," 204.

124 Berríos-Miranda, "Salsa Music as Expressive Liberation," 162.

125 *Record World*, "Eve Charlack," 23; *Record World*, "Carol Polizzi," 28; *Record World*, "Gertrude Fredd," 30.

126 Muñoz, *Cruising Utopia*, 151.

127 Miller, "Crossover Schemes," 186.

128 Other advertisers included El Zarape Records, which featured the "Chicano Explosion" of artists in its roster; Columbia Records' ad celebrating Trini López's first Spanish-language album; and the publicity firm for Cheo Feliciano. *Billboard*, "El Cheetah Is All Latino."

129 Its first issue, published in 1973, announced the "Latin explosion" on its cover, similarly to both *Billboard* and *New York Magazine*. The magazine, however, defined that explosion more broadly and inaugurated its publication by reporting on a Latin Arts Festival at the Cheetah that included music, art, poetry, and photography. *Latin N.Y.* featured the work of Puerto Rican writers, photographers, dancers, and fashion designers in addition to following the highs and lows of the Latin music scene. In-depth articles, interviews, and profiles about local and national Latina/o figures filled the magazine's pages alongside articles exploring a variety of topics related to Latinas/os locally, nationally, and, eventually, in Puerto Rico.

130 Miller, "Crossover Schemes," 180–81.

131 *Billboard*, "Latin Album Covers," 30, 35.

132 In 1975, due in no small part to Harlow's efforts, the National Academy of Recording Arts and Sciences (now the Recording Academy of Arts and Sciences) awarded its first Grammy category in Latin music to Eddie Palmieri for *The Sun of Latin Music*.

133 Feeney, "Los Angeles Swings," s-6.

134 Blassor, "Puerto Rico Is Big Contributor"; Contreras, "Puerto Rican Music Scene."

135 Gurza, "Hot Latin Dance Music," 90.

136 Pacini Hernández, *Bachata*, 106–10.

137 Pacini Hernández, *Bachata*, 107–8, 112.

138 Waxer, "Llegó La Salsa," 219 (emphasis in original).

139 Gallo, interview with the author, 2002.

140 Waxer, *City of Musical Memory*; *Billboard*, "Fania Deals at MIDEM," 23; De León, "Fania All Stars Conquer Europe," 34–35, 50.

141 Gurza, "Hot Latin Dance Music," 82; R. García, "Salsa Is Exploding," s-2.

142 Quoted in Miller, "Crossover Schemes," 188.

143 Hansberry, "Nation Needs Your Gifts."

144 Fania, "Harvey Averne"; Rudland, liner notes for *I Can See*.

145 Melanson, "Fania to Romance Black Radio," 1, 11.

146 From a report titled "A Study of the Soul Music Environment Prepared for Columbia Records Group," commissioned by Columbia Records, quoted in Miller, "Crossover Schemes," 183–84.

147 Between 1961 and 1991, Columbia Records released recordings outside North America under the name CBS Records; the latter has no relation to the CBS Records established in 2006.

148 Rondón, *Book of Salsa*, 94–95.

149 Jaji, *Africa in Stereo*, 7.

150 Sheller, *Consuming the Caribbean*, 14.

151 Rondón, *Book of Salsa*, 101.

152 Quoted in Rondón, *Book of Salsa*, 110.

153 Gurza, "Hot Latin Dance Music," 82.

154 Rondón, *Book of Salsa*, 101.

155 Interview with the author. Luciano would eventually be fired for violating a clause in his contract that prohibited "editorializing or politicizing in any way." Sanabria, "Felipe Luciano Loses Radio Show," 40.

156  Young Lords Party, "Music Belongs to the People," 7.

157  Meléndez, *We Took the Streets*, 209.

158  Miller, "Crossover Schemes," 178.

159  Salserísimo Perú, "Expediente salsa."

160  A. Flores, "Who Burned the South Bronx?"

## Chapter 2. "Los Malotes de la Salsa": Salsa Dons and the Performance of Subjecthood

1    Hernández, "Ultimate Willie Colón Interview."

2    González, *Bronx*, 110; Kaiser, "Blacks and Puerto Ricans," A1.

3    Oteri, "Salsa Is an Open Concept."

4    Valentín-Escobar, "Nothing Connects Us All," 211.

5    Colón was certainly not exceptional with regard to his listening practices. Percussionist, arranger, and songwriter Bobby Sanabria, who also grew up in the Bronx, listened to jazz, soul, funk, and rock in addition to Latin music on local radio stations. Felipe Luciano's weekly radio show *Latin Roots* felt "like going to school every Sunday" because he featured interviews with musicians, collectors, and Latin music historians. Sanabria watched drummers like Bobby Rosengarden and Grady Tate play "explosive" solos on programs like *The Dick Cavett Show*, on which he saw other "cutting edge artists" like La Lupe, Frank Zappa, and James Brown. Then, as Sanabria tells it, he "heard Cal Tjader's great group on the radio. . . . Willie Bobo was the timbale player and jazz drummer in that band. Mongo Santamaría, who I also got to record and play for, was in that band. So that was the epiphany, and I said, 'This is what I'm going to do for the rest of my life.'" Crane, "Bobby Sanabria."

6    W. Colón, liner notes for *Asalto Navideño*, deluxe edition.

7    Hernández, "Ultimate Willie Colón Interview."

8    Valentín-Escobar, "El hombre que respira," 165; Berríos-Miranda, "Is Salsa a Musical Genre?," 28.

9    Oteri, "Salsa Is an Open Concept."

10   Valentín-Escobar, "Nothing Connects Us All," 211; Rondón, *Libro de la salsa*, 50.

11   Valentín-Escobar, "El hombre que respira," 165–66.

12   Oteri, "Salsa Is an Open Concept."

13   Valentín-Escobar, "El hombre que respira," 165; Valentín-Escobar, "Nothing Connects Us All," 210–11; Berríos-Miranda, "Salsa Music as Expressive Liberation," 162; Charlie Palmieri, quoted in Berríos-Miranda, "Is Salsa a Musical Genre?," 28; Rondón, *Book of Salsa*, 15–16.

14     I want to thank Gui Duvignau for listening with me and his assistance in providing the language to describe what I heard in Colón's innovative approach to musical arrangements.

15     Valentín-Escobar, "El hombre que respira," 165.

16     A. Flores, liner notes for *El Juicio.*

17     Valentín-Escobar, "Nothing Connects Us All," 211–12.

18     Njoroge, *Chocolate Surrealism*, 129.

19     A. Flores, liner notes for *El Juicio.*

20     A montuno may refer to a semi-improvised instrumental section of a song or repetition of a syncopated piano vamp. It may be accompanied by a repeating chorus or vocal riffs.

21     Oteri, "Salsa Is an Open Concept"; Dove, "On the Trail."

22     The song refers to the BMT, the Brooklyn-Manhattan Transit Corporation, in operation in 1967 when the album was released.

23     *New York Times*, "Puerto Ricans Halt," 32.

24     Zentella, *Growing Up Bilingual*, 41.

25     Quoted in Navas, "Ray Barretto."

26     Aparicio, "On Sub-Versive Signifiers."

27     For a detailed analysis of code-switching, see Valdés, "Social Interaction and Code-Switching Patterns"; Sánchez, *Chicano Discourse*. On Puerto Rican code-switching among youth in New York, see Zentella, *Growing Up Bilingual*.

28     It remains unclear, however, whether LaVoe originated this term or heard it elsewhere.

29     Zentella, *Growing Up Bilingual*, 13.

30     On claims to individual and group rights framed in terms of liberal citizenship, see Lorrin Thomas, *Puerto Rican Citizen.*

31     Sandoval Sánchez, "*West Side Story*," 64.

32     Hernández, "Ultimate Willie Colón Interview."

33     Grosfoguel, Negrón-Muntaner, and Georas, "Beyond Nationalist and Colonialist Discourses," 29.

34     Sanabria, liner notes for *The Hustler.*

35     Stoever, "Reproducing U.S. Citizenship."

36     Valentín-Escobar, "El hombre que respira," 167.

37     The Fulton Fish Market moved to the Hunts Point area of the Bronx in 2005.

38     Valentín-Escobar, "El hombre que respira," 169.

39     hooks, *Art on My Mind*, 64.

40    The relationship between riots and music had already been deployed by Latin soul artist Joe Bataan on his album *Riot* (1968).

41    Latin Music USA, "Chapter 5"; Sanabria, interview with the author, September 17, 2002.

42    Sanabria and Masucci, liner notes for *Fania 1964–1994*; Sanabria, "Latin Album Covers."

43    Aparicio, "La Lupe, La India," 138.

44    Federal Bureau of Investigation, "COINTELPRO Puerto Rican Groups Part 02 of 11."

45    Valentín-Escobar, "El hombre que respira," 138.

46    Rubin, *Jewish Gangsters*, 148.

47    Lima and Picano, *Ambientes*, 33.

48    On the relationship between whiteness and Puerto Rican national identity, see Jiménez Román, "Un hombre (negro) del pueblo"; Lloréns, *Imaging the Great*; Godreau, *Scripts of Blackness*; and Alamo-Pastrana, *Seams of Empire*. On the mid-twentieth-century populist campaign in Puerto Rico that did the same, see Suárez Findlay, *We Are Left*, 25–89.

49    Oteri, "Salsa Is an Open Concept."

50    Salazar, *Mambo Kingdom*, 273.

51    Latin Music USA, "Salsa Revolution"; Oteri, "Salsa Is an Open Concept."

52    On the reciprocal relationship among violence, hypermasculinity, and homosexuality in Puerto Rican cultural production in the United States, see Cruz-Malavé, "What a Tangled Web!"

53    *Latin N.Y.*, "Willie Speaks about His Image."

54    Luciano, "Is the Gangster Image Good?," 2–3.

55    Sanabria, "Rebuttal," 3.

56    *Latin N.Y.*, "A Talk with Willie."

57    *Latin N.Y.*, "Hector LaVoe."

58    The title also belonged to salsa vocalist Ismael Rivera, one of the most prolific and talented soneros of his generation. The song thus laid LaVoe's claim to Afro–Puerto Rican musical traditions while lauding his abilities. See Valentín-Escobar, "El hombre que respira."

59    I build on and extend the arguments of Juan Otero Garabís and Juan Flores about the diasporic meanings of this album. Otero Garabís argues that *Asalto Navideño* interrupts dominant discourses of nationhood in Puerto Rico by introducing itself as part of the archipelago's cultural traditions. He concludes, however, that the cuatro is used opportunistically in this endeavor and that in the course of the album, traditional elements of Puerto Rican identity become displaced. He also maintains

that the album contributes, in one song in particular, to a nostalgic and idyllic recuperation of Puerto Rico. Flores, on the other hand, focuses on the broader diasporic implications of the project, examining both the "loving" and "mildly challenging" way the album addresses the archipelago. He emphasizes the hybridization, or creolization, of traditional Puerto Rican musical forms and the way they interact in the album. I expand on his argument by focusing on how *Asalto Navideño* deploys and undermines official nationalist discourses of Puerto Rico as they construct New York as an authentic Puerto Rican space where the jíbaro is far removed from the Puerto Rican countryside, found in the streets of Latin New York. Otero Garabís, *Nación y ritmo*, 286; J. Flores, *Diaspora Strikes Back*, 154–56.

60    Oteri, "Salsa Is an Open Concept."

61    Afro–Puerto Rican folkloric music such as bomba and plena do not form part of what is referred to as música jíbara, an example of how musical boundaries are perceived through narratives of geographic blackness, which "refers to common spatial, speech, and behavioral practices that segregate and marginalize blackness (and black people) from the national and territorial conceptions of the Puerto Rican nation." Lloréns, *Imaging the Great Puerto Rican*, 16–17.

62    W. Colón, liner notes for *Asalto Navideño*, deluxe edition.

63    J. Flores, liner notes for *Asalto Navideño*.

64    Fiol-Matta, *Great Woman Singer*, 129.

65    J. Flores, *Diaspora Strikes Back*, 154.

66    W. Colón, liner notes for *Asalto Navideño*, deluxe edition.

67    Y. Flores, interview with the author.

68    Salserísimo Perú, "Héctor Lavoe."

69    Luciano, interview with the author.

70    Herrera, *Nuyorican Feminist Performance*, 47.

71    My analysis of the jíbaro in salsa as a Nuyorican figure is in conversation with that of Efraín Barradas in his essay "De lejos en sueños verla."

72    Jiménez Román, "Allá y acá," 11.

73    Net migration to the United States from Puerto Rico was 446,693 and 221,763 during the 1950s and 1960s, respectively. Net migration dropped to 26,683 during the 1970s. The first net in-migration to Puerto Rico happened in the 1950s, reported at 14,000. That number jumped to almost 70,000 during the 1960s and remained relatively steady the following decade, when net in-migration reached almost 60,000. Duany, "Nation, Migration, Identity," 432.

74    Jiménez Román, "Allá y acá," 11.

75  Jiménez Román, "Allá y acá," 11–12. On Puerto Ricans born in the United States and Nuyorican cultural remittances, see J. Flores, *Diaspora Strikes Back*.

76  Jiménez Román, "Allá y acá," 11; Zenón Cruz, *Narciso descubre su trasero*.

77  Sandoval Sánchez, "Puerto Rican Identity," 189.

78  Richardson, *Afro-Latin@ Experience*, 75.

79  J. Flores, *Divided Borders*, 85–88; Quintero Rivera, *Salsa, sabor y control*, 69–72.

80  J. Flores, *Divided Borders*, 85–86.

81  Aparicio, *Listening to Salsa*, 27; Rivero, *Tuning Out Blackness*, 63.

82  Aletti, "Music."

83  Terrace, "Salsa Rhythms Explode."

84  A. Flores, "Radio Lags behind Concerts," 88.

85  Suárez Findlay, *We Are Left*, 183.

86  LaVoe takes these lines from "Lamento Borincano" (Puerto Rican lament), written by songwriter Rafael Hernández while living in New York. Released for the first time in 1930, the song describes "a Puerto Rican campesino (peasant) trying to sell his wares in town and meeting with failure and economic hardship." Díaz Ayala, liner notes for *Lamento Borincano*.

87  Valentín-Escobar, "El hombre que respira," 175–76.

88  Otero Garabís, *Nación y ritmo*, 114–16, 148.

89  Barradas, "De lejos en sueños verla."

90  Williams, *Country and the City*, 43.

91  Puerto Rican author René Marqués set his canonical but infamous novel *La carreta* (*The Oxcart*, 1956) in La Perla, and anthropologist Oscar Lewis included the enclave in his 1966 study of the "culture of poverty," *La Vida*. La Perla remained desperately poor in the ensuing decades amid geographic, social, economic, and racial marginalization. These images of the countryside contrast with the perceived moral denigration of the city, whether in the United States or Puerto Rico, which achieved its full development in *La carreta*. Representations of Puerto Rican criminality and moral deviance also permeated the New York media and social sciences publications of the time. The novel *Down These Mean Streets* (1967), by Piri Thomas, and the play *Short Eyes* (1975), by Miguel Piñero, while portraying the material context in which they were produced, were circulated as images of moral degeneration within US urban Puerto Rican communities.

92  Curet, *Economía política de Puerto Rico*, 205.

93    Bhabha, "Of Mimicry and Man."

94    Miller, "Crossover Schemes," 192–93.

95    I draw here on the conceptualization of sovereignty by Yarimar Bonilla in *Non-sovereign Futures*, as well as the collection of essays *Sovereignty Unhinged*, edited by Deborah Thomas and Joseph Masco.

## Chapter 3. Salsa's Dirty Secret: Liberated Women, Hairy Hippies, and the End of the World

1    La Lupe's full name was Guadalupe Victoria Yolí Raymond.

2    A. Flores, "Orchid in Manhattan," 41.

3    Muñoz, *Cruising Utopia*, 151.

4    Reddy, "Afro-Asian Intimacies."

5    Lowe and Lloyd, "Introduction," 26.

6    Vargas, "Ruminations."

7    Marín, "Artist Essentials." The section heading translates to "You're so pretty."

8    Irigaray, "Women on the Market," 176.

9    Quoted in Rose, "Never Trust a Big Butt," 235.

10   Huyssen, *After the Great Divide*, 47.

11   With regard to how women become objects of exchange in processes in which they do not participate, while men are exempt from being used and circulated like commodities, see Felman, *What Does a Woman Want?*, 52; Irigaray, "Women on the Market."

12   Harrison, "Gendered Politics," 457.

13   Irigaray, "Women on the Market," 176–79; Stockton, *God between Their Lips*, 66; Aparicio, *Listening to Salsa*, 142.

14   Quoted in Padura Fuentes, *Los rostros de la salsa*, 49–50.

15   I am not, however, eliding the historical and structural differences within these communities. Instead, I want to point out the sentimental and even familial relationships among them. The relationship to other countries established prior to the boom by artists such as Rafael Cortijo and Ismael Rivera, who traveled throughout the Caribbean, cannot be ignored either. Rivera's ties to Panama, for example, combine elements of religion, race, and the familial and must be taken into consideration when addressing the transnational nature of the music. Rivera's devotion to El Cristo Negro de Portobelo (the Black Christ of Portobelo), for example, is inscribed within the song "El Nazareno" (The Nazarene, 1974).

16   Pacini Hernández, *Bachata*, 107–8.

17   La Fountain-Stokes, *Queer Ricans*, 1.

18   Sedgwick, *Epistemology of the Closet*, 50.

19   Stockton, *God between Their Lips*, 66.

20   Sedgwick, *Epistemology of the Closet*, 50.

21   Aparicio, *Listening to Salsa*, 125.

22   Aparicio, *Listening to Salsa*, 125–27.

23   Cho, "Popular Abjection," 45.

24   Aparicio, *Listening to Salsa*, 163.

25   Fregoso, "Re-imagining Chicana Urban Identities," 75.

26   Sangria, "Interview," 36–37.

27   Sangria, "Interview," 36–37.

28   Hill Collins, *From Black Power*, 127–30; Ramos-Zayas, *National Performances*, 61; Lloréns, *Making Livable Worlds*.

29   Quoted in Bronx Museum of the Arts, "Women of the Young Lords."

30   Young Lords Organization, "13 Point Program and Platform," 19.

31   Quoted in Bronx Museum of the Arts, "Women of the Young Lords."

32   Young Lords Women's Caucus, "Position Paper on Women," 12–14.

33   Bronx Museum of the Arts, "Women of the Young Lords"; Morales, *Through the Eyes*, 223.

34   Morales, *Through the Eyes*, 43.

35   The group grew out of the Black Lesbian Caucus of the Gay Activist Alliance, which had, in turn, splintered off from the Gay Liberation Front in 1971.

36   CENTRO, "Daisy De Jesus Interview."

37   Delgado and Muñoz, "Rebellions of Everynight Life," 20.

38   Fregoso, "Re-imagining Chicana Urban Identities," 78; Ramos-Zayas, *National Performances*, 51.

39   *Santos* translates to "saints." Here it refers specifically to the deities, or orishas, of Santería.

40   Ramos-Zayas, *National Performances*, 50–51.

41   Rose, "Black Texts / Black Contexts," 226–27; Rose, "Never Trust a Big Butt," 239.

42   Aparicio, *Listening to Salsa*, 163.

43   Aparicio, *Listening to Salsa*, 163.

44   Aparicio, *Listening to Salsa*, 112.

45   Aparicio, *Listening to Salsa*, 122, 130, 155.

46    Aparicio, *Listening to Salsa*, 161.

47    Aparicio, *Listening to Salsa*, 161–63.

48    Harrison, "Gendered Politics," 457.

49    *Guajira* is a Cuban regionalism for a person (female) from the country-side. It also refers to a popular Cuban musical form with themes of life in the countryside. Although the use of *guajira*, a term not used in Puerto Rico, suggests a Cuban origin for the song, its place within the LaVoe corpus functions alongside other songs about the countryside.

50    See especially René Marqués's novel *La carreta* (*The Oxcart*, 1956).

51    I build on Felman's work on the function of women as screens in *What Does a Woman Want?*

52    Aparicio and Valentín-Escobar, "Memorializing La Lupe and Lavoe," 81, 87–88.

53    Muñoz, *Disidentifications*, 193.

54    Abreu, "Más que una reina," 338.

55    Muñoz, *Disidentifications*, 192.

56    The emphasis on bodily excess, alongside commentary on her religious practice within Santería, once again illuminates the racist colonial imaginaries of blackness as sublime: La Lupe inspired terror in men even as they subjected her to their aesthetic judgment and described her as a mere conduit for the careers of men. Rondón, for example, maintains that La Lupe's significance has "less to do with her own talents, composition, and performances" than with the value she imparted to the compositions of Puerto Rican lyricist Tite Curet Alonso. Quoted in Aparicio and Valentín-Escobar, "Memorializing La Lupe and Lavoe," 88–91.

57    Puerto Rican vocalist Myrta Silva, one of the most talented performers of her generation, similarly exceeded normative moral and gendered expectations with a "gritty, hypersexual, and harsh delivery" that characterized "all body" excess. Despite her immense talent and pioneering role in Latina/o television during the 1960s, she "appears as a footnote to a history narrated around male figures, a history written in lockstep with national-popular teleologies of cultural identity and progress." Like La Lupe, Silva's aural, racialized, and gendered transgressions challenged the performance of collective normative masculinity performed through salsa and its policing of gender roles and sexualities. Fiol-Matta, *Great Woman Singer*, 17–22.

58    Aparicio and Valentín-Escobar, "Memorializing La Lupe and Lavoe," 92.

59    Aparicio and Valentín-Escobar contrast La Lupe with Celia Cruz, "whose professional demeanor on stage and mainstream politics have produced a high degree of acceptability by mainstream audiences." However, the "contrasting strategies" mobilized by Cruz and La Lupe should not be

reduced to an opposition between Cruz's "baroque elegance" and La Lupe's radical chusmería. As Aparicio and Valentín-Escobar are careful to point out, each artist challenged eroticizing narratives about Black women. "Memorializing La Lupe and Lavoe," 85. See also Abreu, "Más que una reina," 344–45.

60   Aparicio and Valentín-Escobar, "Memorializing La Lupe and Lavoe," 84.

61   Herrera, *Nuyorican Feminist Performance*, 5; Jaime, *Queer Nuyorican*, 7.

62   Aparicio, *Listening to Salsa*, 135.

63   Rose, "Never Trust a Big Butt," 239; Rose, "Black Texts / Black Contexts," 226–27.

64   Ostberg, "Quest for Masculine?," 225.

## Chapter 4. Puerto Rico's (Un)Freedom: The Soundscape of Nation Branding

Epigraph: Voice-over added to the documentary *Puerto Rico*, directed by Marcos Zurinaga for the 1992 Universal Expo in Seville, when the AHFRHC made the film available on its website.

1    Hernández Colón, "Mensaje del Gobernador," October 12, 1992.

2    Beard, "After $31 Million."

3    Hernández Colón, "Mensaje en la Ceremonia."

4    Rosa, "Governing Tourism," 87–97.

5    Díaz Quiñones, *La memoria rota*, 138–39.

6    Olenski, "Why Music Plays a Big Role."

7    Alamo-Pastrana, *Seams of Empire*, 7.

8    This high-wire act is most clearly encapsulated in the 1991 decision to make Spanish the official language of Puerto Rico during the ceremony celebrating the participation of Puerto Rican soldiers in the Persian Gulf War. Díaz Quiñones, *La memoria rota*, 137–38.

9    Benson Arias, "Sailing on the USS *Titanic*," 32.

10   Sánchez Korrol, *Colonia to Community*, 27.

11   Suárez Findlay, *We Are Left*, 65.

12   Lloréns, *Imaging the Great Puerto Rican*, 111; Rosa, "Governing Tourism," 90.

13   Álvarez-Curbelo, "La conflictividad," 16.

14   Merrill, *Negotiating Paradise*, 239.

15   Quoted in Suárez Findlay, *We Are Left*, 184.

16   The persecution of the Partido Nacionalista de Puerto Rico (Puerto Rico Nationalist Party) and its members took place alongside and in

collusion with US federal repression of nationalists in Puerto Rico during this period. The gag rule was rescinded in 1957. Rosa, "Governing Tourism," 92.

17    Rosa, "Governing Tourism," 88.

18    Rosa, "Business as Pleasure," 89; Díaz Quiñones, *La memoria rota*, 33; Rosa, "Governing Tourism," 92.

19    Rosa, "Governing Tourism," 92–93.

20    Merrill, *Negotiating Paradise*, 212–15.

21    Díaz Quiñones, *La memoria rota*, 27; Briggs, *Reproducing Empire*, 108; Dinzey-Flores, *Locked In, Locked Out*, 32–33; Alamo-Pastrana, *Seams of Empire*, 102.

22    Álvarez-Curbelo, "De la rueda del progreso," 199–200.

23    In the municipalities of Jayuya and Guánica, for example, unemployment reached 34 percent and 38 percent, respectively. In the mid-1980s, economic recovery was limited to those with college degrees. Approximately 12 percent of the Puerto Rican population left for the United States during the 1980s, almost double the amount of the previous decade. Despite widely publicized concerns of a "brain drain," census data suggest that out-migration generally represented an age-and-educational cross section of the general population even when accounting for the overrepresentation of certain specialized fields like nursing and engineering from 1985 to 1990. Rivera-Batiz and Santiago, *Island Paradox*, 47–54, 85; Economic Commission for Latin America and the Caribbean, "Industrialisation Strategy in the Caribbean," 1–3.

24    Economic Commission for Latin America and the Caribbean, "Industrialisation Strategy in the Caribbean," 1.

25    Puerto Rico's exports to the United States, approximately one-third of the gross domestic product in 1970, rose to 67 percent by 1990. Pantojas-García, "'Federal Funds' and the Puerto Rican Economy," 208; Rivera-Batiz and Santiago, *Island Paradox*, 12; Cordero-Guzmán, "Puerto Rico," 79–80; Ruiz, "Impact of the Economic Recession," 125.

26    Economic growth dropped to just 2 percent during the 1973–75 recession that impacted most of the Western Hemisphere. Ruiz, "Impact of the Economic Recession," 125. The United States also decreased investment in labor-intensive initiatives due to its participation in multinational trade agreements such as the Caribbean Basin Initiative (CBI), the various GATT agreements, and discussions already underway that would culminate with the passage of NAFTA and further threaten Puerto Rico's economy. According to Héctor Cordero-Guzmán, by the mid-1980s, 85 percent of Puerto Rico's production was for export, while 45 percent of food consumption was imported from the United States. Jaime Benson

Arias states that multinational agreements with newly industrialized economies and developing nations, however, opened US markets to additional foreign imports and increased competition for US investment. Rivera-Batiz and Santiago, *Island Paradox*, 63; Ruiz, "Impact of the Economic Recession," 125; Cordero-Guzmán, "Puerto Rico," 79–80; Benson Arias, "Sailing on the USS *Titanic*," 31.

27    The CBI is a trade agreement between Caribbean and Central American countries that President Ronald Reagan signed in 1983 in order to support US Cold War–era interests. The passage of NAFTA in 1994 decreased the advantage of Caribbean countries that formed part of the CBI.

28    Under this arrangement, manufacturing plants in other parts of the Caribbean, such as the Dominican Republic, would complete the initial assembly of manufactured goods that required low-skilled workers paid lower wages than they would be in Puerto Rico or the United States. The complementary plant in Puerto Rico was reserved for more highly skilled labor necessary to complete the process. Safa, *De mantenidas a proveedoras*, 27.

29    Hernández Colón also attempted to privatize public utilities and dismantle social welfare. At the time he accepted the invitation to be an individual exhibitor at Expo '92, the governor was trying to privatize the Puerto Rico Telephone Company and its long-distance carrier Telefónica Larga Distancia (TLD) in order to establish interest-bearing funds with monies from the sale. He promised the interest from these "perpetual" funds would be used, first, to modernize Puerto Rico's aging infrastructure, provide adequate sewage systems and drinking water throughout the country, and repair its public schools, some of which did not have enough desks or lacked functioning bathrooms, and second for education reform. Álvarez-Curbelo, "De la rueda del progreso," 199–200; E. Colón, "Lo inacabado, las fronteras, los tránsitos," 249; Hernández Colón, "Mensaje del Gobernador," February 21, 1990.

30    Hernández Colón, "Mensaje del Gobernador," October 11, 1990.

31    Hernández Colón, "Mensaje del Gobernador," October 11, 1990.

32    Estrada Resto, "Atraídos los visitantes."

33    Duany, *Puerto Rican Nation*, 55.

34    Department of Economic Development and Commerce, "Puerto Rico Industrial Development Corporation."

35    Hernández Colón, "P.R. Orden Ejecutiva 5012B."

36    In addition to the governor, the oversight committee consisted of eight members from the private sector and various government representatives, including the secretaries of state and governance. While the private-sector appointees received no remuneration for their service,

the government covered travel expenses to Cartuja to oversee the progress of the pavilion. Hernández Colón, "P.R. Orden Ejecutiva 1990–40"; Hernández Colón, "P.R. Orden Ejecutiva 5012B."

37   Berríos, "Hincan los pilotes"; Rivera-Batiz and Santiago, *Island Paradox*, 109.

38   Berríos, "Hincan los pilotes"; Rivera-Batiz and Santiago, *Island Paradox*, 109; *Caribbean Business*, "Sale of the Century."

39   Estrada Resto, "Exalta Rafael Hernández Colón."

40   Agrait, "El pabellón 'nacional.'"

41   US Census Bureau, "Table 1321."

42   Estrada Resto, "Exalta Rafael Hernández Colón."

43   Hernández Colón, "Mensaje del Gobernador," October 11, 1990.

44   Esparza, "'Qué bonita mi tierra,'" 119.

45   Esparza, "'Qué bonita mi tierra,'" 117–20. The Catholic Church benefited from the intersection of colonial tax policies and financial investments in pharmaceutical companies that supported its heteropatriarchal priorities. On the conflicting perceptions of diasporic Puerto Rican participation, see Negrón-Muntaner, "Twenty Years," 46.

46   Álvarez-Curbelo, "De la rueda del progreso," 199–200.

47   Dávila, *El Mall*, 177.

48   By the late 1960s, many of the malls in large Latin American cities modeled on North American counterparts were anchored by Sears. Dávila, *El Mall*, 46.

49   On the role of the mall in Puerto Rico and Latin America, see Dávila, *El Mall*, 82; Dávila, *Culture Works*, 33–36.

50   Dávila, *El Mall*, 2, 10; Ortiz-Negrón, "Space out of Place," 46.

51   Dávila, *Culture Works*, 33–36.

52   Dávila, *El Mall*, 161.

53   Berríos, "Encerrada la discordia."

54   Berríos, "Encerrada la discordia."

55   The PNP would adopt the neoliberal discourse of free trade and economic progress with which Hernández Colón propelled the pavilion project forward. Puerto Rico's role as an individual exhibitor among other "nations," however, remained incompatible with its pro-statehood political agenda. Pedro Rosselló, Hernández Colón's successor in the governor's mansion, would emphasize Puerto Rico's distinct *American* culture in order to act as a bridge to the rest of the Caribbean and Latin America at the moment when NAFTA was being instituted. Rosselló reoriented Puerto Rico's economic growth toward the United States as

the site of the archipelago's economic potential. The desires to exploit global economic capital and to increase tourism were thus very similar while closely aligned to each party's respective position on Puerto Rico's political status: whether Puerto Rican culture is more American (PNP) or Hispanic (PPD), and, therefore, what it can offer to whom in the new global economy.

56   Hernández Colón, "Mensaje del Gobernador," October 12, 1992.

57   Berríos, "Hincan los pilotes."

58   Oficina de Gerencia y Presupuesto del Estado Libre Asociado de Puerto Rico, "Ley Reguladora del Centro Bancario Internacional."

59   Banco Santander, "Quiénes somos."

60   Hernández Colón, "Mensaje del Gobernador," October 11, 1990.

61   Banco Santander, "Quiénes somos."

62   Hernández Colón, "Mensaje del Gobernador," October 11, 1990. The section heading means "The noble gallantry of mother Spain," a quote from the song "Preciosa" (Lovely, beautiful) by Rafael Hernández.

63   Hernández Colón, "La Españolidad de Puerto Rico."

64   Quoted in J. Flores, *Divided Borders*, 95.

65   J. Flores, *Divided Borders*, 92–98.

66   Estrada Resto, "Predomina la salsa en Sevilla."

67   Duany, "Popular Music in Puerto Rico," 200; Aparicio, *Listening to Salsa*, 69.

68   Rivero, *Tuning Out Blackness*, 3.

69   Dávila, *Sponsored Identities*, 195.

70   A. García, *Cocolos y rockeros*; Aparicio, *Listening to Salsa*, 73; Duany, "Popular Music in Puerto Rico," 200–201.

71   Dávila, *Sponsored Identities*, 189–95.

72   "Reportaje cocolos vs rockeros 1987."

73   Dávila, *Sponsored Identities*, 189–95; Álvarez-Curbelo, "De la rueda del progreso," 198.

74   Dávila, *Sponsored Identities*, 194–95.

75   Hernández Colón, "Mensaje del Gobernador," February 19, 1988.

76   Hernández Colón, "Mensaje del Gobernador," October 28, 1988.

77   Sheller, *Consuming the Caribbean*, 175–76, 191; Clarke, "Mapping Transnationality," 74.

78   Dávila, *Sponsored Identities*, 194–95.

79  These attitudes were also projected onto merengue, a Dominican Afro-Caribbean genre increasingly popular in Puerto Rico during the 1980s.

80  See J. Flores, "Rappin', Writin', and Breakin'"; J. Flores, "'Puerto Rican and Proud'"; J. Flores, "Puerto Rocks"; R. Rivera, "Cultura y poder"; R. Rivera, *New York Ricans*.

81  See R. Rivera, "Policing Morality"; LeBrón, *Policing Life and Death*, 83–113.

82  See LeBrón, *Policing Life and Death*; Paik, *Bans, Walls, Raids, Sanctuary*, 12–13.

83  On urban planning and policing, see Dinzey-Flores, "Criminalizing Communities"; Dinzey-Flores, *Locked In, Locked Out*; LeBrón, *Policing Life and Death*, 26–42.

84  Moreau, "'Puerto Rico es salsa' señores."

85  Elecciones en Puerto Rico, "Referéndum del 8 de diciembre de 1991."

86  Moreau, "'Puerto Rico es salsa' señores."

87  Rivera, "Will the 'Real' Puerto Rican?," 217–22.

88  Luciano, "Lamenta la exclusividad salsera"; Estrada Resto, "Predomina la salsa en Sevilla"; Estrada Resto, "La salsa, nexo con el mundo."

89  Luciano, "Lamenta la exclusividad salsera."

90  *El Nuevo Día*, "Puerto Rico es salsa."

91  D'Astro, "Pabellón de la discordia"; D'Castro, "La salsa en 'guiso español.'"

92  Estrada Resto, "Sin auspiciador la Orquesta Sinfónica."

93  Mattei, "Objeción al lema Boricua"; Estrada Resto, "Odón Alonso, Bellas Artes."

94  Ultimately, the Symphonic Orchestra combined enough private and corporate funding to allow approximately half of its musicians to travel to the Expo and inaugurate Puerto Rico's national day in Seville.

95  Millán Ferrer, "Siguiéndole los pasos."

96  He did, however, perform for the Expo's opening concert, sponsored by the host country alongside the Tito Puente Orchestra, Rubén Blades, and Celia Cruz. Torres Torres, "Problemas con el Pabellón"; Torres Torres, "Bastante activo el sonero."

97  Torres Torres, "Problemas con el pabellón."

98  Estrada Resto, "Predomina la salsa en Sevilla."

99  An increasing amount of scholarship examines the histories of Afro–Puerto Ricans, including Zenón Cruz, *Narciso descubre su trasero*; Lloréns, *Imaging the Great*; Dinzey-Flores, *Locked In, Locked Out*; Ramos-Zayas,

National Performances; Godreau, Scripts of Blackness; Duany, Puerto Rican Nation; La Fountain-Stokes, Queer Ricans; Jaime, Queer Nuyorican; Herrera, Nuyorican Feminist Performance; LeBrón, Policing Life and Death; Jiménez Román, "Un hombre (negro) del pueblo."

100 Lloréns, Imaging the Great, 60.

101 Pedreira, Insularismo, 151.

102 Alamo-Pastrana, Seams of Empire, 107. Carlos Alamo-Pastrana provides an excellent overview of this theme.

103 Suárez Findlay, We Are Left, 48–49.

104 Suárez Findlay, We Are Left, 49.

105 Álvarez-Curbelo, "La conflictividad," 46–47.

106 Ledee, quoted in L. Torres, "Desafinada la selección musical."

107 Cruz-Malavé, "Toward an Art of Transvestism," 142.

108 Fiol-Matta, Great Woman Singer, 129.

109 H. Rodríguez, "¿Debe la salsa representarnos internacionalmente?"

110 H. Rodríguez, "¿Debe la salsa representarnos internacionalmente?"

111 Millán Ferrer, "Siguiéndole los pasos."

112 Estrada Resto, "Predomina la salsa en Sevilla."

113 D'Castro, "La salsa siempre."

114 Estrada Resto, "Atraídos los visitantes."

115 Huron, "Music in Advertising."

116 Kusno, "Rethinking the Nation," 215; Casakin and Bernardo, Role of Place Identity, 186.

117 F. Rodríguez, Catálogo de Arquitectura Contemporánea, 24.

118 F. Rodríguez, Catálogo de Arquitectura Contemporánea, 24–25.

119 The buildings designed by Heinrich (Henry) Klumb and the architectural firm Toro y Ferrer, founded by Osvaldo Toro and Miguel Ferrer, married the appearance of the built environment with the government's investment in education, a process Cardona invoked in the design of the middle structure in the pavilion. Klumb was an architect for the University of Puerto Rico for twenty years, and his work was featured in Architectural Forum in 1964. A year later, Toro-Ferrer was awarded the design of the General Studies Faculty building for the University of Puerto Rico. F. Rodríguez, Catálogo de Arquitectura Contemporánea, 15–16, 24.

120 F. Rodríguez, Catálogo de Arquitectura Contemporánea, 24–25; Casanova, Nuestro Pabellón.

121 Dávila, Sponsored Identities, 169.

122 Álvarez-Curbelo, "De la rueda del progreso," 203–4.

123    Alamo-Pastrana, *Seams of Empire*, 7–9.

124    Suárez Findlay, *We Are Left*, 77, 186.

125    By the 1960s, the government adopted Afro–Puerto Rican vocalist Ruth Fernández as a cultural ambassador. She became, as Fiol-Matta shows, "a symbol of Puerto Rico's modernity and [was] adopted by the government as its official cultural ambassador," whose television programs assumed a pedagogical purpose. Fernández became a "heroic figure within a middle-class ethos, espoused by a heavily white and light-skinned, elite group and funneled to the rest of the population via the state's cultural arm." Fiol-Matta, *Great Woman Singer*, 69–71.

126    Suárez Findlay, *We Are Left*, 69.

127    These practices reflected post–World War II economic development policies in the Western world that combined racist paternal attitudes toward "backward" populations with, as Suárez Findlay notes, "contempt for local cultures and socioeconomic practices." Rodríguez Castro, "Foro de 1940," 77; Suárez Findlay, *We Are Left*, 64–65, 76–77.

128    Díaz Quiñones, *La memoria rota*. "Dead time" refers to the period preceding 1940, the year that the PPD comes into power and Muñoz Marín takes office as the first popularly elected governor of Puerto Rico. The intellectual elite imagined themselves as fulfilling the desires of their predecessors, who, under Spanish colonial rule, advocated for autonomy and an end to slavery. The year 1940 marks Puerto Rico's entrance into modernity (vis-à-vis US economic development policies). Accordingly, the "nation" is no longer defined politically. Instead, nationalism is projected onto the realm of culture.

129    Hernández Colón, "Mensaje del Gobernador," March 8, 1991.

130    Seminario Interdisciplinario de Información y Documentación José Emilio González, "Mensaje de Emilio Cassinello."

131    The Bureau International des Expositions (BIE, International Bureau of Expositions) initially awarded the 1992 Universal Expo to both Chicago and Seville. The organizers for each site had independently submitted applications to the BIE in 1981 and 1982, respectively, to host the Expo in celebration of the quincentennial anniversary of Columbus's arrival in the Americas. While both cities accepted the BIE proposal for dual sites, Chicago eventually pulled out, citing financial and organizational challenges. Spain successfully petitioned for removal of all mentions of Chicago and dual sites from the records of the BIE. As a result of Chicago pulling out, the *Reglamento General de la Exposición Universal 1992* was revised to delete all references to Chicago, any references to conditions created by a dual-site Expo, and a change of date. Expo92.es, "La candidatura de España"; Pablo-Romero Gil-Delgado, *La Exposición Universal de Sevilla 1992*, 73.

132  Pablo-Romero Gil-Delgado, *La Exposición Universal de Sevilla 1992*, 27, 73–74.

133  Castells and Hall, *Technopoles of the World*, 197.

134  Pablo-Romero Gil-Delgado, *La Exposición Universal de Sevilla 1992*, 74, 252; Castells and Hall, *Technopoles of the World*, 197. Countries at Plaza de América: Argentina, Bolivia, Brazil, Colombia, Costa Rica, the Dominican Republic, Ecuador, El Salvador, Guatemala, Haiti, Honduras, Nicaragua, Panama, Paraguay, Peru, and Uruguay.

135  Baklanoff, "Spain's Economic Strategy," 111–18.

136  Pablo-Romero Gil-Delgado, *La Exposición Universal de Sevilla 1992*, 27, 73–74; Castells and Hall, *Technopoles of the World*, 197.

137  Smith, *Moderns*, 127.

138  Pablo-Romero Gil-Delgado, *La Exposición Universal de Sevilla 1992*, 73.

139  The Discovery Pavilion itself, however, was destroyed due to an accidental fire just two months before the Expo opened.

140  Sony, "Sony Annual Report."

141  Junta de Andalucía, "Eventos."

142  This latter structure, currently administered by the Andalucía treasury department and available for conferences and similar events, housed four autonomous pavilions: El Pabellón del Universo, El Pabellón de las Telecomunicaciones, El Pabellón del Medio Ambiente, and El Pabellón de la Energía (Universal Pavilion, Telecommunications Pavilion, Environmental Pavilion, and Energy Pavilion).

143  Díaz Quiñones, *La memoria rota*, 30.

144  *ABC Sevilla*, "Puerto Rico está que arde."

145  Seminario Interdisciplinario de Información y Documentación José Emilio González, "Pabellón de Puerto Rico."

146  Rodríguez Castro, "Divergencias."

147  Aronczyk, *Branding the Nation*, 11.

148  Jennifer Stoever uses the analytic of the "listening ear" to "describe how listening functions as an embodied cultural process that echoes and shapes one's orientation to power and one's posture toward the world." "Splicing the Sonic Color-Line," 65.

149  Sheller, *Consuming the Caribbean*, 177–78.

150  Beard, "After $31 Million."

151  Whether any inquiries were initiated by foreign investors and what may have transpired during those inquires is, however, unclear.

152  The strength of Japan's economy and its rising rate of foreign investment contributed to what Hernández Colón described as "transcendental

events" that positioned Puerto Rico "in the future." However, the US State Department intervened when Puerto Rico agreed with Japan to offer tax subsidies to Japanese corporations to increase foreign investment in the archipelago. Puerto Rico, the State Department stated, "does not have the authority on its own to negotiate or enter into international agreements." Citing the exclusive right of the federal government to negotiate international agreements, the State Department also noted that "the U.S. opposes the principle of tax sparing and does not enter into tax sparing agreements with any country." The same day this statement was sent to the US ambassador to Japan, the US president entered into a tax-sparing agreement with the Marshall Islands and Micronesia. Tolchin, "Deaver's Lobbying for Puerto Rico."

153 Beard, "After $31 Million."

154 Suárez Findlay, *We Are Left*, 47–49, 59–60, 72–76.

155 Otero Garabís, "'Puerto Rico Is Salsa,'" 25; Rivera Nieves, "Poder y obedecer," 264.

156 Sheller, *Consuming the Caribbean*, 23–26.

157 Rodríguez Castro, "Divergencias," 367.

158 Hernandez Colón, "Gobernador R.H.C. firma proyectos Plaza de Salseros."

159 Clarke and Thomas, "Globalization and the Transformations," 4–5.

160 Arroyo, "'Roots' or the Virtualities," 214.

161 Sheller, *Consuming the Caribbean*, 23–26; Franco, *Decline and Fall*, 160.

162 I am referring, in part, to the analysis of attitudes to return migrants and their cultural remittances, and extending it to encompass Black material culture and Black communities in Puerto Rico more broadly. See J. Flores, *Diaspora Strikes Back*, 5.

## Chapter 5. Entre la Letra y la Nota: Becoming "El Cantante de los Cantantes"

1 Gurza, "FBI Raids Alleged Latin Pirate," 10; Gurza, "FBI Looking Into Reports," 81.

2 W. Colón, "Salsa Pioneers," 35.

3 Leoncavallo, *Leoncavallo's I Pagliacci*, prologue.

4 *Latin N.Y.*, "What Happened to Hector LaVoe?," 11; *Latin N.Y.*, "Mail," 8.

5 Salazar, *Mambo Kingdom*, 273.

6 Mirabal, "Héctor LaVoe," 19.

7 Saxon et al., "Ruben Blades," 35.

8   The October 1978 issue of *Latin N.Y.* includes a review of *Comedia* and a note about Blades's upcoming release of "Plástico," a track on the *Siembra* album.

9   Blades, "Interview," pt. 1; Blades, "Interview," pt. 2.

10   Cobo, "Serving Up the Salsa," 18.

11   Gurza, "Dangerous Grooves."

12   Blades, SDRB #8.

13   Blades, SDRB #8.

14   Blades, "Interview," pt, 1.

15   Blades, "Interview," pt. 1.

16   Gallo, interview with the author, 2002.

17   Forrest, "Surmounting the Catch-22 of Promotion," LA-70.

18   Valentín-Escobar, "El hombre que respira," 176.

19   Salserísimo Perú, "Héctor Lavoe."

20   Leogrande, "Salsa Time at Garden."

21   Muñoz, *Cruising Utopia*, 22–32; Taylor, *Archive and Repertoire*, 129.

22   Díaz Ayala, *Si te quieres*, 13–15, 74–75; García Molina, "Nostalgia, Internal Migration," 232.

23   Díaz Ayala, *Si te quieres*, 13–15, 74–75, 115, 213–14.

24   La Fountain-Stokes, *Queer Ricans*, 1.

25   Valentín-Escobar, "Nothing Connects Us All," 218.

26   Appadurai, "Introduction," 19.

27   Oteri, "Salsa Is an Open Concept."

28   The recorded performance at La Clave Club in Hialeah, Florida, on February 19, 1988, was released in 1997 as *Hector LaVoe Live*. See also recorded live performances on YouTube, "Hector Lavoe 'El Cantante' En Vivo/Live" posted by Fania, and "Hector Lavoe Live at the Village Gate 1988. Sings 'El Cantante,'" posted by Primo Discos Digital Services.

29   Appadurai, *Modernity at Large*, 31.

30   Emerson, "Gifts," 26.

31   Whitman, "Chaplin's Little Tramp."

32   Chaluisan, "*Comedia*, Hector LaVoe," 14.

33   Rondón, *El libro de la salsa*, 126.

34   CFDM was a partnership between David Maldonado Productions and Cárdenas Fernández and Associates

35   *LAMCO and ACEMLA v. Cárdenas Fernández and Assocs., Inc.*, 843, 847.

36   *LAMCO and ACEMLA v. Cárdenas Fernández and Assocs., Inc.*, 843.

37 Box 5, Jorge Manuel Carmona Rodríguez to Jerry Masucci, July 12, 1993, *Lugo v. Sonido, Inc.*

38 *LAMCO and ACEMLA v. Cárdenas Fernández*, 843, 847. Similar claims were made in *LAMCO v. Spanish Broadcasting.*

39 Partial Summary Judgement, Sequence 005, *Lugo v. Sonido, Inc.*

40 I came across the handwritten note in 2002, which simply stated that LaVoe transferred his royalties to Lugo for $10. I returned to the archive in 2006 to review additional documents in the case, but the handwritten note was missing. Only the typed document in which LaVoe assigns his royalties to Lugo, which the latter submitted to the court, remained. Agreement between Hector LaVoe and David Lugo, *Lugo v. Sonido, Inc.*; Torres, "'¡Qué lindo es!'"

41 Jorge Manuel Carmona Rodríguez to Jerry Masucci, *Lugo v. Sonido, Inc.*

42 Affidavit of Jorge Manuel Carmona Rodríguez at par. 12–13, *Lugo v. Sonido, Inc.*

43 Reply Affidavit of David Lugo at par. 20–22, *Lugo v. Sonido, Inc.*

44 Reply Affidavit of David Lugo at par. 9–14, *Lugo v. Sonido, Inc.*

45 Lugo Affidavit in Support of Motion for Partial Summary Judgement at par. 4–5, *Lugo v. Sonido, Inc.*

46 Reply Affidavit of David Lugo, Exhibit 3: Request for Psychiatric Services, Lake Sumter Health Center and Hospital Admissions Agreement, *Lugo v. Sonido, Inc.* In a 2021 interview, Lugo stated that he learned LaVoe had AIDS after a physician at Lake Sumter Health Center conducted a physical. Salserísimo Perú, "¿David Lugo se llevó?"

47 Mires, "De la gloria al ocaso."

48 The album cover and references to the album never include the diacritic.

49 Reply Affidavit of David Lugo at par. 11, *Lugo v. Sonido, Inc.*

50 Reply Affirmation at par. 4–5, 29, *Lugo v. Sonido, Inc.*; Affidavit of Jorge Manuel Carmona Rodríguez at par. 12, *Lugo v. Sonido, Inc.*

51 The portion of royalties due to José Pérez, LaVoe's son, was to remain in escrow in order to compensate Sonido for any losses the label might incur due to *LAMCO and ACEMLA v. Cárdenas Fernández et al.*

52 Valentín-Escobar, "El hombre que respira," 163.

53 Esparza, "Qué bonita mi tierra," 109.

54 Roque Ramírez, "Gay Latino Histories."

55 Gallo, interview with the author, 2002.

56 Muñoz, *Cruising Utopia*, 65.

57 Muñoz, *Cruising Utopia*, 65.

58    Reply Affidavit of David Lugo at par. 10, *Lugo v. Sonido, Inc.*

59    Trouillot, *Silencing the Past*, Kindle loc. 535.

60    Vargas, *Dissonant Divas in Chicana Music*, 56.

61    Roque Ramírez, "'Mira, yo soy boricua,'" 277.

62    Sandoval Sánchez, "Politicizing Abjection," 313.

63    Jaime, *Queer Nuyorican*, 37.

64    Like LaVoe's *Revento*, La Bruja's title does not include the diacritic.

## Chapter 6. (Copy)Rights and Wrongs: "El Cantante" and the Legislation of Creative Labor

1    See, for example, Mochkofsky, "It's Time Rubén Blades."

2    Gurza, "*Siembra*," 45.

3    Fania Records, 1976 Standard Songwriters Agreement, *Blades v. Fania Records.*

4    Deposition of Ruben Blades at pp. 56–58, *Blades v. Fania Records.*

5    In musical works, "the sound recording is the sound produced by the performer's rendition of the musical work." Fleet, "What's in a Song?," 1242.

6    Deposition of Victor Gallo at p. 238, *Blades v. Fania Records.*

7    Jaszi, "Is There Such a Thing?," 420.

8    Woodmansee, "On the Author Effect," 28.

9    Cepeda, *Musical ImagiNation*, 43.

10   Agudelo, "Slight U.S. Sales Recovery," 59.

11   Williamson, *Last Fight*. The film starred Blades as a singer-turned-boxer and Colón. It included minor roles for various familiar faces, including Izzy Sanabria (Slim), Professor Joe Torres (as himself), and Don King (as himself). Masucci was also an executive producer on *Vigilante*, which was directed by William Lustig (1982). The film centers Black and white male factory workers who form a vigilante group to deal with crime in their New York neighborhood. Nick Marino, a white worker who declines to join them, seeks his own justice after the Puerto Rican gang leader Federico "Rico" Meléndez (played by Colón), arrested for murdering Marino's son and stabbing his wife, is set free on a suspended sentence by a corrupt judge. Colón and LaVoe recorded the film's soundtrack, which was remastered and released on 180-gram vinyl by Craft Recordings in 2023. Buyers could bundle their purchase with a Fania T-shirt featuring the album cover.

12   Gallo, interview with the author, 2003; Magistrate Judge's Report and Recommendation, at p. 2, *Feliciano v. Valsyn* (2006).

13    Gallo, interview with the author, 2003.

14    WIPO Arbitration and Mediation Center, "Administrative Panel Decision."

15    Fania Entertainment Group, "Securities and Exchange Commission Form SB-2."

16    Fania Entertainment Group, "Securities and Exchange Commission Form SB-2," 16.

17    Fania Entertainment Group, "Securities and Exchange Commission Form SB-2," 24.

18    After Masucci's death, Melissa Gosnell became the trustee of the trust he established under his will and the executor of his estate. The trust beneficiary was Masucci's daughter, Corinne Masucci. *Masucci v. Gosnell.*

19    Gallo, interview with the author, 2003; Fania Entertainment Group, "Securities and Exchange Commission Form SB-2," 22.

20    *LAMCO v. Cárdenas Fernández.*

21    Cobo, "Emusica Buys Fania Holdings," 15.

22    Peisner, "Digital Salsa."

23    Rosen, "Return of Fania," 60; Andre Torres, "Industry Rule #4083."

24    Cobo, "Hot Salsa."

25    Cobo, "Fania Records Targets New Audience."

26    Cobo, "Fania Records Links with !K7."

27    Peisner, "Digital Salsa."

28    Reuters, "Fania Records to Launch."

29    A Fania All-Stars concert scheduled for August 2014 was canceled.

30    Rohter, "It Happened One Night."

31    Concord began as Concord Records in 1973. It became CMG in 2004 when the label merged with Fantasy Inc, which owned multiple catalogs, including the post-Atlantic Stax catalog. Concord, in addition to its live labels, owns an astonishing number of music catalogs from historic labels, which are managed by Concord's Craft Recordings. In addition to the Fania catalog, Concord owns the distribution rights for such iconic artists as Clearwater Revival, John Coltrane, Miles Davis, R.E.M., Joan Baez, Little Richard, Otis Redding, Jewel, Isaac Hayes, John Lee Hooker, Nine Inch Nails, and Paul McCartney (post-Beatles). Concord, "About: Concord Label Group."

32    The all-analog reissues were remastered using the original tapes and, reflecting the ongoing resurgence of vinyl records, pressed on 180-gram audiophile quality vinyl. Each album was released individually and as a bundle, the latter accompanied by limited-edition T-shirts. Craft Record-

ings has since continued to release reissues of Fania recordings, with a select number pressed on 180-gram vinyl, including multiple albums by Colón and LaVoe as well as Joe Bataan's *Gypsy Woman*, Ray Barretto's *Indestructible*, and Ismael Rivera's *Lo último en la avenida* and *Esto fue lo que trajo el barco*, among others.

33  Amended Answers and Counterclaim at p. 28, par. 5, *Musica Latina International, Inc. v. Blades*.

34  The court determined that Blades was owed $10,000 in royalties for two albums, which was paid upon the execution of the settlement agreement. The court also determined that Blades had a $20,000 debit in his royalties account, which Musica Latina would charge against future royalties. Order, Stipulation and Settlement Agreement, *Musica Latina International, Inc. v. Blades*, 1984.

35  First Amended Complaint and Jury Demand, par. 77–77, *Blades v. Fania Records*.

36  Plaintiff's Reply to Amended Counterclaims, Doc. 19, p. 11, *Blades v. Fania Records*; Notice of Motion for Partial Summary Judgement, Doc. 24, p. 2, *Blades v. Fania Records*.

37  Lugo is listed as the copyright claimant in the registration. However, a copyright registration form is not by itself a legally binding document.

38  First Amended Complaint and Jury Demand at p. 15, par. 68–69, *Blades v. Fania Records*.

39  Woodmansee, "On the Author Effect," 27–37.

40  The Statute of Anne (1710) had previously established that copyright would be regulated by the government and the courts.

41  Kretschmer and Kawohl, "History and Philosophy of Copyright," 35.

42  Toynbee, "Musicians," 127.

43  Jaszi, "Is There Such a Thing?," 51–52.

44  Jaszi, "On the Author Effect," 51–52.

45  Barancik, "Childress v. Taylor," 58.

46  Quoted in Barancik, "Childress v. Taylor," 59.

47  Barancik, "Childress v. Taylor," 59.

48  Quoted in VerSteeg, "Defining Author," 1331; quoted in Barancik, "Childress v. Taylor," 58–59.

49  Minority opinions that would not require that the contributions of each party be independently copyrightable remain on the fringe of copyright law. See Fleet, "What's In a Song?," 1249.

50  The ruling in favor of Childress reinforced the majority view in case law, what Russ VerSteeg refers to as the "Marshall-Goldstein standard," for

determining the central tenets of copyright. As VerSteeg explains, the first tenet of the majority view may be found in a statement made by Justice Thurgood Marshall in *Community for Creative Non-Violence v. Reid*: "As a general rule, the author is the party who actually creates the work, that is, the person who translates an idea into a fixed, tangible expression entitled to copyright protection." Paul Goldstein's treatise on copyright law has been generally accepted as the standard for determining a joint work for the purpose of copyright: in order to be an "author," a creator must contribute something that is independently copyrightable. VerSteeg, "Defining Author," 1326–33; Goldstein, *Copyright*, § 4.2.1.2, p. 379.

51    Théberge, "Technology, Creative Practice, and Copyright," 141–44.

52    Woodmansee, "On the Author Effect," 28.

53    Courts have defined *musical composition* in various ways. In terms of "El Cantante," Blades's claim and the legal discussion pertained specifically and exclusively to the lyrics. Sterling, *Intellectual Property Rights*, 324–25; Fleet, "What's in a Song?," 1238–39.

54    The title of the case is *Hart v. Graham* (N.D. Ill. 1917).

55    Leo, "Early Blues and Jazz Authorship," 311–13. Leo did not originate the idea of "distributed authorship," which visual artist Roy Ascott began to use in 1986 in relation to his own work.

56    Blades, "Interview," pt. 1."

57    Franco, "What's Left?," 198.

58    Rohter, "Salsa Star Is Reborn."

59    Boyle, "Ruben Blades."

60    Rohter, "Salsa Star Is Reborn."

61    Rondón, *El libro de la salsa*, 126.

62    See Hegel, *Elements of the Philosophy*.

63    Kant, *Critique of Judgement*, 150 §46.

64    Kant, *Metaphysics of Morals*, 71 §31.

65    "Ruben Blades—El Cantante—Damrosch NYC 8-7-13."

66    C. Rodríguez, "New Old Salsero."

67    IMDb, "Flaco Navaja."

68    C. Rodríguez, "New Old Salsero."

69    Complaint and Jury Demand at p. 4, par. 9, *Blades v. Fania Records*.

70    The corporations could conduct commercial activities and invest in properties in Uruguay. The Sociedad Anónima Finaciera de Inversión (SAFI, Anonymous Financial Society for Investments) designation for these companies was phased out in 2010.

71 Complaint and Jury Demand at p. 6, par. 18, *Blades v. Fania Records.*

72 Complaint and Jury Demand, Introduction, at p. 1, *Blades v. Fania Records.*

73 Memorandum of Law in Support of Defendant's Motion to Add Parties as Defendants in Support of Defendant's Counterclaims at pp. 3–4, *Musica Latina International, Inc. v. Blades.*

74 Complaint and Jury Demand at p. 4, par. 9, *Blades v. Fania Records.*

75 See *Feliciano v. Valsyn* (2008); *Maldonado v. Valsyn, S.A.*; *Roena v. Fania*; *Valentín v. Fania Records.*

76 See *Feliciano v. Valsyn* (2006).

77 *Masucci v. Sonido, Inc.*; *Gallo v. Sonido, Inc.*

78 On race, knowledge, and the coloniality of power, see Quijano, "Coloniality of Power"; Lugones, "Coloniality of Gender."

79 Grosfoguel, *Colonial Subjects*, 131.

80 "Deposition of Ruben Blades" at 56–58, *Blades v. Fania Records.*

81 For a detailed explanation of the parameters for enforcing termination rights, see Leaffer, *Understanding Copyright Law*, 223–64. For a general overview, see Rohter, "Copyright Victory, 35 Years Later."

82 Coombe, "Cultural Agencies," 80–81.

83 Kant, *Metaphysics of Morals*, 72 §31.

84 As the copyright owner for "El Cantante," Blades controls the right to perform the song publicly.

# Sources

## Archives

Amherst College Archives and Special Collections, Marshall Bloom (AC1966) Alternative Press Collection

Archivo Histórico Fundación Rafael Hernández Colón (AHFRHC)

*Descarga Journal*

Discogs, https://discogs.com

Harbor Conservatory for the Performing Arts, Colección Raíces

Harvard University, Rubén Blades Archives

Jacobs, Glenn. *Latin N.Y.* Collection. Personal archive

New York Public Library for the Performing Arts, *Latin N.Y.* Collection

Salserísimo Perú, https://www.salserisimoperu.com/

World Radio History Digital Archive, https://worldradiohistory.com/

## Discography

Anthony, Marc. *El Cantante*. Sony US Latin, 2007.

Anthony, Marc. *3.0*. Sony US Latin, 2013.
   "Vivir mi vida"

Barretto, Ray. *Barretto para bailar*. Riverside Records, 1961.

Barretto, Ray. *Acid*. Fania Records, 1968.

Barretto, Ray. *Barretto Power*. Fania Records, 1971.
   "Right On"

Barretto, Ray. *Que viva la música*. Fania Records, 1972.
 "Cocinando"

Barretto, Ray. *Indestructible*. Fania Records, 1973.

Barretto, Ray. *Tomorrow: Barretto Live*. Atlantic Records, 1976.

Barretto, Ray. *Rican/Struction*. Fania Records, 1979.
 "Adelante siempre voy"

Bataan, Joe. *Gypsy Woman*. Fania Records, 1967.
 "Gypsy Woman"

Bataan, Joe. *Riot*. Fania Records, 1968.

Bataan, Joe. *Subway Joe*. Fania Records, 1968.

Bataan, Joe. *Poor Boy*. Fania Records, 1969.

Bataan, Joe. *Singin' Some Soul*. Fania Records, 1969.
 "Under the Street Lamps"
 "Young, Gifted and Brown"

Bataan, Joe. *Mr. New York and the East Side Kids*. Fania Records, 1971.

Blades, Rubén. *Bohemio y poeta*. Fania Records, 1979.
 "Juan Pachanga"

Blades, Rubén. *El que la hace la paga*. Musica Latina International, 1983.

Blades, Rubén. *Doble filo*. Sonido, 1986.
 "El Cantante"

Blades, Rubén. *Agua de luna*. Elektra Entertainment, 1987.

Blades, Rubén. *The Best*. Sony Discos Inc., 1992.

Brecht, Bertolt, lyricist. *The Threepenny Opera*. Theater am Schiffbauerdamm,
 Berlin, 1928.
 "Mack the Knife"

La Bruja. *Brujalicious*. De La Luz Records, 2006.
 "Nuyorico Interlude"
 "Revento"

Caymmi, Dorival. *Eu Vou pra Maracangalha*. Indústrias Elétricas E Musicais
 Fábrica Odeon S.A., 1957.
 "Maracangalha"

Colón, Willie. *El Malo*. Fania Records, 1967.
 "Chonqui"
 "El Malo"
 "Skinny Papa"
 "Willie Baby"
 "Willie Whopper"

Colón, Willie. *The Hustler*. Fania Records, 1968.
 "The Hustler"

"Qué lío"

"Se acaba este mundo"

"Soñando despierto"

Colón, Willie. *Cosa nuestra*. Fania Records, 1969.

"Ausencia"

"Che che colé"

"Juana Peña"

"Sonero mayor"

"Te conozco"

Colón, Willie. *Guisando / Doing a Job*. Fania Records, 1969.

"Guisando"

"I Wish I Had a Watermelon"

"No me den candela"

"Oíga señor"

"El Titán"

Colón, Willie. *Asalto Navideño*. Vol. 1. Fania Records, 1970.

"Canto a Borinquen"

"La murga"

"Popurri Navideño"

"Traigo la salsa"

Colón, Willie. *The Big Break—La gran fuga*. Fania Records, 1970.

"Abuelita"

"Pa' Colombia"

"Panameña"

"Sigue feliz"

Colón, Willie. *Crime Pays*. Fania Records, 1972.

Colón, Willie. *El Juicio*. Fania Records, 1972.

"Piraña"

"Si la ves"

"Soñando despierto"

"Timbalero"

Colón, Willie. *Asalto Navideño*. Vol. 2. Fania Records, 1973.

"Pescao (Potpourri sambao)"

"Recomendación"

Colón, Willie. *Lo mato (si no compra este LP)*. Fania Records, 1973.

"Calle Luna, Calle Sol"

"Guajira ven"

"Vo so"

Colón, Willie. *The Good, the Bad, the Ugly*. Fania Records, 1975.

"Cazanguero"

"Toma"

Colón, Willie, and Rubén Blades. *Metiendo mano.* Fania Records, 1977.
  "Pablo Pueblo"

Colón, Willie, and Rubén Blades. *Siembra.* Fania Records, 1978.
  "Pedro Navaja"
  "Plástico"
  "Siembra"

Colón, Willie, and Rubén Blades. *Canciones del solar de los aburridos.* Musica Latina International, 1981.

Colón, Willie, and Héctor LaVoe. *Vigilante.* Musica Latina International, 1983.

Cruz, Celia, and Willie Colón. *Only They Could Have Made This Album.* Vaya Records, 1977.

Fania All-Stars. *Live at the Red Garter.* Vol. 1. Fania Records, 1968.

Fania All-Stars. *Live at the Cheetah.* Vols. 1 and 2. Fania Records, 1972.
  "Anacaona"
  "Bembé"
  "Closing Theme"
  "Cockfight and Interview"
  "Introduction Theme" ("Cocinando")
  "Ponte duro"
  "Quítate tú"

Fania All-Stars. *Live at Yankee Stadium.* Vols. 1 and 2. Fania Records, 1975.
  "Bemba colorá"
  "Mi gente"

Fania All-Stars. *Rhythm Machine.* Columbia Records, 1977.
  "Juana Pachanga"

Fania All-Stars. *Live at the Cheetah.* Vol. 1. Craft Recordings, 2022.

Fania All-Stars. *Live at the Cheetah.* Vol. 2. Craft Recordings, 2023.

Gillespie, Dizzy, Chano Pozo, and Gil Fuller. "Manteca." *Manteca.* RCA Victor, 1947.

Hernández, Rafael. "Preciosa." Victor, 1935.

Hernández, Rafael. *Lamento Borincano.* Vols. 1 and 2. Arhoolie Records, 2001.
  "Lamento Borincano," 1930.

Joe Cotto y Su Orquesta. *Dolores.* Magda, 1963.
  "Dolores"

Joe Cuba Sextet. *Wanted Dead or Alive.* Tico Records, 1966.
  "Bang! Bang!"

Khaled. "C'est la vie." Universal Music, 2012.

La Lupe. *Reina de la cancion Latina / Queen of Latin Soul.* Tico Records, 1968.
  "La Tirana"

LaVoe, Héctor. *La Voz*. Fania Records, 1975.
"Un amor de la calle"
"Mi gente"
"Paraíso de dulzura"
"Rompe saragüey"
"El Todopoderoso"

LaVoe, Héctor. *De ti depende*. Fania Records, 1976.
"Mentira"
"Periódico de ayer"

LaVoe, Héctor. *Comedia*. Fania Records, 1978.
"Bandolera"
"El Cantante"
"Comedia"

LaVoe, Héctor. *Héctor, Yomo y Daniel: Feliz Navidad*. Fania Records, 1979.
"Mr. Brownie"

LaVoe, Héctor. *Lo que pide la gente*. Musica Latina, 1984.

LaVoe, Héctor. *Revento*. Musica Latina International, 1985.
"La fama"

LaVoe, Héctor. *Héctor LaVoe Live*. JMM Records, 1997.

LaVoe, Héctor. *Cantante: The Originals*. Fania, 2007.

LaVoe, Héctor. *A Man and His Music*. Fania, 2010.

Orchestra Harlow. *Abran paso!* Fania Records, 1971.
"Abran paso"

Orchestra Harlow. *Hommy: A Latin Opera*. Fania Records, 1973.

Original Dixieland "Jass" Band. *Dixieland Jass Band One-Step*. Victor, 1917.
"Livery Stable Blues"

Pacheco, Johnny. *Cañonazo*. Fania Records, 1964.

Palmieri, Eddie. *Justicia*. Tico Records, 1970.
"Everything Is Everything"
"Justicia"

Palmieri, Eddie. *Sentido*. Mango Records, 1973.
"Puerto Rico"

Palmieri, Eddie. *The Sun of Latin Music*. Coco Records, 1973.

Palmieri, Eddie, with Harlem River Drive. *Live at Sing Sing*. Vol. 1. Tico Records, 1972.

Palmieri, Eddie, with Harlem River Drive. *Live at Sing Sing*. Vol. 2. Tico Records, 1974.

Quiñones, Domingo. *¿Quién mató a Héctor LaVoe?* RMM Records, 1999.

Rivera, Ismael. *Esto fue lo que trajo el barco*. Tico Records, 1972.

Rivera, Ismael. *Lo último en la avenida.* Tico Records, 1972.

Rivera, Ismael. *Traigo de todo.* Tico Records, 1974.
"El Nazareno"

Rodríguez, Pete "El Conde." *De Panamá a New York / From Panama to New York.* Alegre Records, 1970.

Rodríguez, Pete. *I Like It Like That.* Alegre Records, 1967.

Roberto Roena y su Apollo Sound. *La 8va maravilla.* International Records, 1977.
"Para ser rumbero"

Roberto Roena y su Apollo Sound. *9.* International Records, 1977.
"Nadie sabe"

Santana, Carlos. *Carlos Abraxas.* CBS Records, 1970.
"Oye como va"

Sonora Ponceña. *Fuego en el 23.* Inca Records, 1969.
"Fuego en el 23"

Various. *Tributo urbano a Héctor LaVoe.* Emusica, 2007.

**Interviews with Public Figures**

*Unless otherwise noted, all interviews were conducted by the author in New York.*

Amadeo, Willie. July 14, 2002.

Barreiro, Vicente. July 12, 2002.

Bonilla, Richie. August 4, 2003.

Calderón, Henry. July 23, 2002.

Candelario, Charlie. July 14, 2002.

Delgado, Jimmy. September 9, 2002.

DJ Berto. July 12, 2002.

Flores, Aurora. September 16, 2002.

Flores, Elliot "Yeyito." September 11, 2002.

Flores, Luis "Máquina." July 14 and August 22, 2003.

Gallo, Victor. August 8, 2002, and September 10, 2003.

Harlow, Larry. September 9, 2002.

Luciano, Felipe. July 25, 2002.

Mangual, José, Jr. August 26, 2003.

Marín, Orlando. September 9, 2003.

Marrero, Nicky. September 8, 2003.

Mercado, Ralph. August 29, 2002.

Montalvo, Eddie. September 9, 2003.

Morales, Frankie. August 27, 2003.

Ocasio, Nydia. December 20, 2007.

Pacheco, Johnny. September 15, 2002.

Pagán, Dylcia. Phone interview. August 19, 2003
René, Angel. July 25, 2002.
Rodríguez, Ángel. August 5, 2002.
Sanabria, Izzy. Union City, NJ, September 17, 2002.
Segarra, Arnie. September 9, 2002.
Solá, Vicky. July 14, 2002.
Suárez, Efraín. July 13 and July 16, 2002.
Valdez Jr., Alfredo. August 24, 2003.
Valentín, Dave. Phone interview, August 22, 2003.

## Cited Lawsuits

*Bach v. Longman* (1777) 2 Cowp. 623.
*Blades v. Fania Records*, No. 1:2002-cv-07042 (S.D.N.Y. filed September 5, 2002).
*Blades v. Vaya Records*, No. 10693/88 (N.Y. Sup. filed May 27, 1988).
*Childress v. Taylor*, 945 F.2d 500 (2d Cir. 1991).
*Community for Creative Non-Violence v. Reed* (490 U.S. 730 1989).
*Donaldson v. Becket* (1774) Hansard, 1st ser., 17 (1774): 953–1003.
*Feliciano v. Valsyn, S.A.*, No. civ 04–1809 PG, 2006 WL 3718177.
*Feliciano v. Valsyn, S.A.*, No. 1:2008-cv-09583 (S.D.N.Y. filed November 7, 2008).
*Feliciano v. Valsyn, S.A.* 2006 U.S. Dist. App. LEXIS 108185 (D.P.R. filed October 4, 2006).
*Gallo v. Sonido, Inc.*, No. 603940/2004 (N.Y. Sup. filed 2005).
*Hart v. Graham* (N.D. Ill. 1917).
*Latin American Music Co. and ACEMLA v. Cárdenas Fernández and Assoc., Inc.*, 2 F. App'x 40 (1st Cir. 2001).
*Latin American Music Co. v. Cárdenas Fernández and Assocs., Inc.*, 60 F. App'x 843, 847 (1st Cir. 2003).
*Latin American Music Co. v. Spanish Broadcasting*, 232 F. Supp. 3d 384 (S.D.N.Y. 2017).
*Lugo v. Sonido, Inc.*, No. 99/115246 (N.Y. Sup. filed July 7, 1999).
*Maldonado v. Valsyn, S.A.*, 2009 U.S. Dist. App. LEXIS 90920, 2009 WL 3094888 (S.D.N.Y. filed September 23, 2009).
*Masucci v. Gosnell.* No 0602438/2006, N.Y. Slip Op. 32446 (N.Y. Sup. 2007).
*Masucci v. Sonido, Inc.*, No. 603594/2005, N.Y. Slip Op 33892 (N.Y. Sup. 2011).
*Musica Latina International, Inc. v. Blades*, No. 84 civ. 0719, 1984 App. WL 336 (S.D.N.Y. filed May 21, 1984).
*Roena v. Fania*, No. 3:03-cv-01484 (D.P.R. filed May 1, 2003).
*Valentín v. Fania Records*, No. 3:02-cv-02298 (D.P.R. filed August 27, 2002).
WIPO Arbitration and Mediation Center, "Administrative Panel Decision: *Sonido, Inc. v. MU21C.COM Inc.* Case No. D2006–0685.

## Liner Notes

Colón, Willie. Liner notes for *Asalto Navideño*, deluxe edition.

Díaz Ayala, Cristóbal. Liner notes for *Lamento Borincano*, vols. 1 and 2.

Fania. Liner notes for *The Last Fight*.

Flores, Aurora. Liner notes for *El Juicio*. Fania.

Flores, Juan. Liner notes for *Asalto Navideño*, vol. 1.

Luciano, Felipe. Liner notes for *Tomorrow: Barretto Live*. Atlantic Records, 1976.

Rodríguez, Pete. Liner notes for *El Malo*. Fania Records, 1967.

Rudland, Daniel. Liner notes for *I Can See*.

Sanabria, Izzy. Liner notes for *The Hustler*. Fania Records, 1968.

Sanabria, Izzy, and Gerald Masucci. Liner notes for *Fania 1964–1994*

## Videography/Filmography

Brooks, Richard, dir. *Blackboard Jungle*. Metro-Goldwyn-Mayer, 1955.

Chaplin, Charlie. *The Circus*. United Artists, 1928.

Ferland, Guy, dir. *Dirty Dancing: Havana Nights*. Lionsgate, 2004.

Frankenheimer, John, dir. *The Young Savages*. United Artists, 1961.

García, Ana María, dir. *Cocolos y rockeros*. Du Art Film and Video, 1992.

Gast, Leon, dir. *Our Latin Thing*. Fania Records, 1972.

Gast, Leon, dir. *When We Were Kings*. PolyGram Filmed Entertainment, 1996.

Gast, Leon, and Jerry Masucci, dirs. *Salsa*. 1976. Movies and Pictures International, 1993.

Haines, Randa, dir. *Dance with Me*. Columbia TriStar, 1998.

"Hector Lavoe 'El Cantante' En Vivo/Live." YouTube, October 22, 2015. https://www.youtube.com/watch?v=6DNPN9BukTY.

"Hector Lavoe Live at the Village Gate 1988. Sings 'El Cantante.'" YouTube, September 21, 2016. https://www.youtube.com/watch?v=y40OXQAQ8SE.

Hussein, Waris, dir. *The Possession of Joe Delaney*. Haworth Productions and ITC Entertainment, 1972.

Ichaso, Leon. *El Cantante*. Picturehouse, 2006.

Latin Music USA. "Chapter 5: *Our Latin Thing* and the Fania All-Stars." *Latin Music USA*. PBS, October 12, 2009. Accessed December 15, 2014. http://www.pbs.org/wgbh/latinmusicusa/02/05.html.

Latin Music USA. "The Salsa Revolution." *Latin Music USA*. PBS, October 12, 2009. Accessed December 15, 2014. http://www.pbs.org/wgbh/latinmusicusa/index.html#/en/wat/02/03.

Levy-Hinte, Jeff, dir. *Soul Power*. Antidote Films, 2008.

Lustig, William, dir. *Vigilante*. Magnum Motion Pictures, 1982.

Maysles, David, Albert Maysles, and Charlotte Zwerin, dirs. *Gimme Shelter*. Direct Cinema, 1970.

Mires, Fran, exec. prod. "De la gloria al ocaso." *Ocurrió así*. Telemundo WNJU-TV, 1993.

Molina Casanova, Luis, dir. *Nuestro Pabellón*. 1992.

Momber, Marlis. *Viva Loisaida*. Gruppe Dokumentation and Tylis, 1978.

Parker, Alan, dir. *Fame*. United Artists, 1980.

Rossen, Robert, dir. *The Hustler*. 20th Century Fox, 1961.

"Ruben Blades—El Cantante—Damrosch NYC. 8-7-13." YouTube, August 7, 2013. https://www.youtube.com/watch?v=g95306RmDg4.

*SDRB #8*. Webcast, August 13, 2007. Accessed September 29, 2014, https://myspace.com/rubenbladescom/video/show-de-ruben-blades-8/28735753.

Wadleigh, Michael, dir. *Woodstock*. Warner Bros., 1970.

Williamson, Fred, dir. *The Last Fight*. Best Film and Video, 1983.

Wise, Robert, and Jerome Robbins, dirs. *West Side Story*. Mirisch Pictures and Seven Arts Productions, 1962.

Zurinaga, Marcos, dir. *Puerto Rico*. Puerto Rico Industrial Development Company, 1992.

## Bibliography

*ABC Sevilla*. "Puerto Rico está que arde." June 23, 1992. Accessed April 23, 2015. http://hemeroteca.abcdesevilla.es/nav/Navigate.exe/hemeroteca/sevilla/abc.sevilla/1992/06/23/024.html.

Abreu, Christina D. "Más que una reina: Race, Gender, and the Musical Careers of Graciela, Celia, and La Lupe, 1950s–1970s." *Journal of Social History* 52, no. 2 (2018): 332–52.

Agrait, Rechani. "El pabellón 'nacional': Las parejas que bailan salsa en Sevilla no curarán ni un solo niño en el hospital pediátrico." *El Nuevo Día*, April 28, 1992.

Agudelo, Carlos. "Slight U.S. Sales Recovery Seen." *Billboard*, October 30, 1982.

Alamo-Pastrana, Carlos. *Seams of Empire: Race and Radicalism in Puerto Rico and the United States*. Gainesville: University Press of Florida, 2016.

Aletti, Vince. "Music: Some Like It Hot." *New York Magazine*, August 7, 1972.

Aletti, Vince. "Our Latin Thing." *Rolling Stone*, August 31, 1972.

Alexander, Michelle. *The New Jim Crow: Mass Incarceration in the Age of Colorblindness*. The New Press, 2013.

Álvarez-Curbelo, Silvia. "De la rueda del progreso al pabellón de Sevilla: Las propuestas estatales de identidad nacional." In *Polifonía salvaje: Ensayos de cultura y política en la postmodernidad*, edited by Silvia Álvarez-Curbelo, Irma N. Rivera Nieves, and Carlos Gil, 195–205. San Juan, Puerto Rico: Editorial Postdata, 1995.

Álvarez-Curbelo, Silvia. "La conflictividad en el discurso político de Luis Muñoz Marín: 1926–1936." In *Del nacionalismo al populismo: Cultura y política en Puerto Rico*, edited by Silvia Álvarez-Curbelo and María Elena Rodríguez Castro, 13–36. Río Piedras, Puerto Rico: Ediciones Huracán, 1993.

Aparicio, Frances. "The Blackness of Sugar: Celia Cruz and the Performance of (Trans)Nationalism." *Cultural Studies* 13, no. 2 (April 1999): 223–36.

Aparicio, Frances. "La Lupe, La India, and Celia: Toward a Feminist Genealogy of Salsa Music." In *Situating Salsa: Global Markets and Local Meanings in Latin Popular Music*, edited by Lise Waxer, 135–60. New York: Routledge, 2002.

Aparicio, Frances. *Listening to Salsa: Gender, Latin Popular Music, and Puerto Rican Cultures.* Hanover, NH: Wesleyan University Press, 1998.

Aparicio, Frances. "Marc Anthony 3.0: Toward a Critical Salsa Romántica." In *Rhythm and Power: Performing Salsa in Puerto Rican and Latino Communities*, 47–58. New York: Center Press, Center for Puerto Rican Studies, 2017.

Aparicio, Frances. "On Sub-Versive Signifiers: Tropicalizing Language in the United States." In *Tropicalizations: Transcultural Representations of Latinidad*, edited by Susana Chávez-Silverman and Frances R. Aparicio, 194–212. Hanover, NH: University Press of New England, 1997.

Aparicio, Frances, and Wilson Valentín-Escobar. "Memorializing La Lupe and Lavoe: Singing Vulgarity, Transnationalism and Gender." CENTRO *Journal* 16 (2004): 79–101.

Appadurai, Arjun. "Introduction: Commodities and the Politics of Value." In *The Social Life of Things: Commodities in Cultural Perspective*, edited by Arjun Appadurai, 3–63. Cambridge: Cambridge University Press, 1986.

Appadurai, Arjun. *Modernity at Large: Cultural Dimensions of Globalization.* Minneapolis: University of Minnesota Press, 1996.

Appadurai, Arjun, ed. *The Social Life of Things: Commodities in Cultural Perspective.* Cambridge: Cambridge University Press, 1986.

Arcoleo, Kimberly J., Colleen McGovern, Karenjot Kaur, Jill S. Halterman, Jennifer Mammen, Hugh Crean, Deepa Rastogi, and Jonathan M. Feldman. "Longitudinal Patterns of Mexican and Puerto Rican Children's Asthma Controller Medication Adherence and Acute Healthcare Use." *Annals of the American Thoracic Society* 16, no. 6 (June 2019): 715–23.

Armstrong, Meg. "'The Effects of Blackness': Gender, Race, and the Sublime in Aesthetic Theories of Burke and Kant." *Journal of Aesthetics and Art Criticism* 54, no. 3 (1996): 213–36.

Aronczyk, Melissa. *Branding the Nation: The Global Business of National Identity.* New York: Oxford University Press, 2013.

Arroyo, Jossianna. "'Roots' or the Virtualities of Racial Imaginaries in Puerto Rico and the Diaspora." *Latino Studies* 8, no. 2 (June 2010): 195–219.

Asencio, Marysol. *Sex and Sexuality among New York's Puerto Rican Youth.* Boulder, CO: Lynne Rienner, 2002.

Ayala, César J. "The Decline of the Plantation Economy and the Puerto Rican Migration of the 1950s." *Latino Studies Journal* 7, no. 1 (Winter 1996): 61–90.

Baklanoff, Eric N. "Spain's Economic Strategy toward the 'Nations of Its Historical Community': The 'Reconquest' of Latin America?" *Journal of Interamerican Studies and World Affairs* 38, no. 1 (1996): 105–27.

Banco Santander. "Quiénes somos." Santander, 2014. Accessed February 19, 2015. http://www.santander.pr/QuienesSomos/Historia.aspx.

Banet-Weiser, Sarah. *Authentic^{TM}: The Politics of Ambivalence in a Brand Culture*. New York: New York University Press, 2012.

Barancik, Karen. "Childress v. Taylor, 945 F.2d 500 (2nd Cir. 1991)." *DePaul Journal of Art, Technology and Intellectual Property Law* 2, no. 2 (Spring 1992): 58–59.

Barradas, Efraín. "De lejos en sueños verla: Visión mítica de Puerto Rico en la poesía neorrican." *Revista Chicano-Riqueña* 7, no. 3 (1979): 46–56.

Beard, David. "After $31 Million, Puerto Rico Unloads Fair Pavilion For $4 Million." AP News, July 15, 1993.

Benítez Rojo, Antonio. *La isla que se repite: El Caribe y la perspectiva posmoderna*. Hanover, NH: Ediciones del Norte, 1989.

Benson Arias, Jaime. "Sailing on the USS *Titanic*: Puerto Rico's Unique Insertion to Global Economic Trends." In *None of the Above: Puerto Ricans in the Global Era*, edited by Frances Negrón-Muntaner, 29–38. New York: Palgrave Macmillan, 2007.

Bernstein, Leonard, Jerome Robbins, Arthur Laurents, and Stephen Sondheim. *West Side Story*. New York: Amberson, 1957.

Berríos, Nelson Gabriel. "Encerrada la discordia en el pabellón." *El Nuevo Día*, October 13, 1990.

Berríos, Nelson Gabriel. "Hincan los pilotes del pabellón de Sevilla." *El Nuevo Día*, December 10, 1990.

Berríos-Miranda, Marisol. "Is Salsa a Musical Genre?" In *Situating Salsa*, edited by Lise Waxer, 23–50. New York: Routledge, 2002.

Berríos-Miranda, Marisol. "Salsa Music as Expressive Liberation." *CENTRO Journal* 16, no. 2 (2004): 159–73.

Bhabha, Homi. "Of Mimicry and Man: The Ambivalence of Colonial Discourse." *October* 28 (Spring 1984): 125–33.

*Billboard*. "El Cheetah Is All Latino." November 25, 1972.

*Billboard*. "Fania Deals at MIDEM." February 16, 1974.

*Billboard*. "Latin Album Covers Reflect Music's Sophistication." July 27, 1974.

*Billboard*. "Latin Chart Action Recap for 2nd Half of 1977." January 14, 1978.

*Billboard*. "Rubén Blades: Buscando América." January 26, 1985.

Black Latinas Know Collective. "The Statement." Black Latinas Know Collective, April 30, 2019. https://www.blacklatinasknow.org.

Blades, Rubén. "Interview: A Visit with Ruben Blades, Part 1." Interview by Bruce Polin. *Descarga Journal*, December 1, 1996.

Blades, Rubén. "Interview: A Visit with Ruben Blades, Part 2." Interview by Bruce Polin. *Descarga Journal*, December 1, 1996.

Blassor, Lorraine. "Puerto Rico Is Big Contributor." *Billboard*, June 12, 1976.

Bonilla, Yarimar. *Non-Sovereign Futures: French Caribbean Politics in the Wake of Disenchantment*. Chicago: University of Chicago Press, 2015.

Boyle, Chris. "Ruben Blades." *Elite Traveler* (blog), August 11, 2009. https://www.elitetraveler.com/leaders-in-luxury/ruben-blades.

Brecht, Bertolt, and Kurt Weill. "Mack the Knife." *The Threepenny Opera*. Theater am Schiffbauerdamm, Berlin, 1928.

Briggs, Laura. *Reproducing Empire: Race, Sex, Science, and U.S. Imperialism in Puerto Rico*. Berkeley: University of California Press, 2003.

Bronx Museum of the Arts. "Women of the Young Lords: The Revolution within the Revolution." YouTube, July 23, 2015. https://www.youtube.com/watch?v=xLs4dsG4DQc.

Buder, Leonard. "City School Rolls Expected to Soar." *New York Times*, January 26, 1958.

Buder, Leonard. "Racial Patterns Shift in Schools; Non-Negro and Non-Puerto Rican Exodus Rises." *New York Times*, June 7, 1966.

Cabrera, Pablo. *¿Quién mató a Héctor LaVoe? / Who Killed Héctor LaVoe?* 47th Street Theatre, 1999.

Carby, Hazel. "The Souls of Black Men." In *Race Men*, 9–44. Cambridge, MA: Harvard University Press, 2000.

*Caribbean Business*. "Sale of the Century." March 18, 1993.

Carter, Dan T. *The Politics of Rage: George Wallace, the Origins of the New Conservatism, and the Transformation of American Politics*. New York: Simon and Schuster, 1995.

Casakin, Hernan, and Fátima Campos Bernardo. *The Role of Place Identity in the Perception, Understanding, and Design of Built Environments*. Oak Park, IL: Bentham Science Publishers, 2012.

Castells, Manuel, and Peter Hall. *Technopoles of the World: The Making of 21st Century Industrial Complexes*. New York: Routledge, 1994.

CENTRO: Centro Oral History Project (COHP) / Latino Educational Media Center (LEMC). "Daisy De Jesus Interview." Center for Puerto Rican Studies Library and Archives, Hunter College, CUNY, January 16, 2008. https://centroca.hunter.cuny.edu/Detail/collections/154.

Centro de Bellas Artes Luis A. Ferré. "Historia." 2014. Accessed May 7, 2015. https://www.cba.pr.gov/historia/.

Cepeda, María Elena. *Musical ImagiNation: U.S.-Colombian Identity and the Latin Music Boom*. New York: New York University Press, 2010.

Chaluisan, Luis. "Comedia, Hector LaVoe." *Latin N.Y.*, October 1978.

Childress, Alice. *Moms*. 1986. Alexandria, VA: Alexander Street Press. https://search.alexanderstreet.com/view/work/bibliographic_entity%7Cbibliographic_details%7C3606536.

Cho, Michelle. "Popular Abjection and Gendered Embodiment in South Korean Film Comedy." In *Abjection Incorporated: Mediating the Politics of Pleasure and Violence*, edited by Maggie Hennefeld and Nicholas Sammond, 43–63. Durham, NC: Duke University Press, 2020.

City Lore. "La Marqueta (Formerly Park Avenue Market)." Place Matters. Accessed February 8, 2024. https://citylore.org/neighborhood/east-harlem/.

Clarke, Kamari Maxine. "Mapping Transnationality: Roots Tourism and the Institutionalization of Ethnic Heritage." In *Globalization and Race: Transformations in the Cultural Production of Blackness*, edited by Kamari Maxine Clarke and Deborah A. Thomas, 74–96. Durham, NC: Duke University Press, 2006.

Clarke, Kamari Maxine, and Deborah A. Thomas. "Globalization and the Transformations of Race." In *Globalization and Race: Transformations in the Cultural Production of Blackness*, edited by Kamari Maxine Clarke and Deborah A. Thomas, 1–34. Durham, NC: Duke University Press, 2006.

Cobo, Leila. "Emusica Buys Fania Holdings." *Billboard*, August 27, 2005.

Cobo, Leila. "Fania Records Links with !K7 for Overseas Deals." *Billboard*, October 1, 2010.

Cobo, Leila. "Fania Records Targets New Audience with Classics." *Billboard*, July 7, 2010.

Cobo, Leila. "Hot Salsa." *Billboard*, November 21, 2009.

Cobo, Leila. "Serving Up the Salsa: Fania's Lavoe Bonanza Making an Impact at Retail." *Billboard*, September 1, 2007.

Cobo, Leila. "The Wild and Improbable Journey of Fania Records." *Billboard*, August 22, 2014.

Colón, Eliseo R. "Lo inacabado, las fronteras, los tránsitos: Práctica teórica y crítica cultural." CIC *Cuadernos de Información y Comunicación* 4 (1989): 249–57.

Colón, Willie. "Salsa Pioneers, Scribes of Society." *New York Newsday*, July 3, 1993.

Coombe, Rosemary. "Cultural Agencies: The Legal Construction of Community Subjects and Their Rights." In *Making and Unmaking Intellectual Property*, edited by Mario Biagioli, Peter Jaszi, and Martha Woodmansee, 79–98. Chicago: University of Chicago Press, 2011.

Coombe, Rosemary. "Is There a Cultural Studies of Law?" In *A Companion to Cultural Studies*, edited by Toby Miller, 36–62. Malden, MA: Blackwell, 2001.

Concord. "About: Concord Label Group." June 11, 2020. https://concord.com/about/.

Contreras, Antonio. "Puerto Rican Music Scene Growth Rivals Mainland Pace." *Billboard*, July 27, 1974.

Cordero-Guzmán, Héctor. "Puerto Rico: Lessons from Operation Bootstrap." In *Free Trade and Economic Restructuring in Latin America: A NACLA Reader*, edited by Fred Rosen and Deidre McFayden, 78–83. New York: Monthly Review Press, 1995.

Crane, Jason. "Bobby Sanabria: Afro-Cuban Storyteller." All about Jazz, March 24, 2008. https://www.allaboutjazz.com/bobby-sanabria-afro-cuban-storyteller-bobby-sanabria-by-jason-crane.

Cruz-Malavé, Arnaldo. "Toward an Art of Transvestism: Colonialism and Homosexuality in Puerto Rican Literature." In ¿Entiendes? Queer Reading, Hispanic Writings, edited by Emilie L. Bergmann and Paul Julian Smith, 137–67. Durham, NC: Duke University Press, 1995.

Cruz-Malavé, Arnaldo. "What a Tangled Web! Masculinity, Abjection, and the Foundations of Puerto Rican Literature in the United States." In Sex and Sexuality in Latin America, edited by Daniel Balderston and Donna J. Guy, 234–49. New York: New York University Press, 1997.

Curet, Eliezer. Economía política de Puerto Rico: 1950 a 2000. San Juan, Puerto Rico: Ediciones M.A.C., 2003.

D'Astro, Tony. "Pabellón de la discordia." El Nuevo Día, April 23, 1992.

D'Astro, Tony. "La salsa en 'guiso español.'" Claridad, May 1, 1992.

D'Castro, Alex. "La salsa siempre nos ha representado." Claridad, June 12, 1992.

Dávila, Arlene M. Barrio Dreams: Puerto Ricans, Latinos, and the Neoliberal City. Berkeley: University of California Press, 2004.

Dávila, Arlene M. "Culture in the Battlefront: From Nationalist to Pan-Latino Projects." In Mambo Montage: The Latinization of New York City, edited by Agustín Laó-Montes and Arlene M. Dávila, 159–82. New York: Columbia University Press, 2001.

Dávila, Arlene M. Culture Works: Space, Value, and Mobility across the Neoliberal Americas. New York: New York University Press, 2012.

Dávila, Arlene M. El Mall: The Spatial and Class Politics of Malls in Latin America. Berkeley: University of California Press, 2016.

Dávila, Arlene M. Latinos, Inc.: The Marketing and Making of a People. Berkeley: University of California Press, 2012.

Dávila, Arlene M. Sponsored Identities: Cultural Politics in Puerto Rico. Philadelphia: Temple University Press, 1997.

De Jesús, Anthony, and Madeline Pérez. "From Community Control to Consent Decree: Puerto Ricans Organizing for Education and Language Rights in 1960s and '70s New York City." CENTRO Journal 21, no. 2 (2009): 7–31.

De León, Carlos. "The Fania All Stars Conquer Europe." Latin N.Y., March 1976.

Delgado, Celeste Fraser, and José Esteban Muñoz. "Rebellions of Everynight Life." In Everynight Life: Culture and Dance in Latin/o America, edited by Celeste Fraser Delgado and José Esteban Muñoz, 9–32. Durham, NC: Duke University Press, 1997.

Department of Economic Development and Commerce. "Puerto Rico Industrial Development Company." Puerto Rico Industrial Development Company. Accessed May 30, 2017. http://www.pridco.pr.gov.

Deren, Sherry, Camila Gelpí-Acosta, Carmen E. Albizu-García, Ángel González, Don C. Des Jarlais, and Salvador Santiago-Negrón. "Addressing the HIV/ AIDS Epidemic among Puerto Rican People Who Inject Drugs: The Need for a Multiregion Approach." American Journal of Public Health 104, no. 11 (November 2014): 2030–36. https://doi.org/10.2105/AJPH.2014.302114.

Díaz Ayala, Cristóbal. *Si te quieres por el pico divertir: Historia del pregón lati- noamericano*. San Juan, Puerto Rico: Ediciones Cubanacán, 1988.

Díaz Quiñones, Arcadio. *La memoria rota*. Río Piedras, Puerto Rico: Hura- cán, 1993.

Dinzey-Flores, Zaire. "Criminalizing Communities of Poor, Dark Women in the Caribbean: The Fight against Crime through Puerto Rico's Public Housing." *Crime Prevention and Community Safety* 13, no. 1 (February 2011): 53–73.

Dinzey-Flores, Zaire Zenit. *Locked In, Locked Out: Gated Communities in a Puerto Rican City*. Philadelphia: University of Pennsylvania Press, 2013.

Dinzey-Flores, Zaire Z. "Stop Sacrificing Black Latinxs: The Census and the Racial Mis-Count of Latinxs." *Black Latinas Know Collective Blog*, March 31, 2023. https://www.blacklatinasknow.org/post/stop-sacrificing-black-latinxs -the-census-the-racial-mis-count-of-latinxs.

Dove, Ian. "On the Trail of a New York Sound." *Billboard*, December 14, 1974.

Duany, Jorge. "Nation, Migration, Identity: The Case of Puerto Ricans." *Latino Studies* 1, no. 3 (2003): 424–44.

Duany, Jorge. "Popular Music in Puerto Rico: Toward an Anthropology of 'Salsa.'" *Latin American Music Review / Revista de Música Latinoamericana* 5, no. 2 (October 1, 1984): 186–216.

Duany, Jorge. *The Puerto Rican Nation on the Move: Identities on the Island and in the United States*. Chapel Hill: University of North Carolina Press, 2002.

Duncan, Nancy. "Renegotiating Gender and Sexuality in Public and Private Spaces." In *Body Space: Destabilizing Geographies of Gender and Sexuality*, edited by Nancy Duncan, 126–44. New York: Routledge, 1996.

Echeverría Ortiz, Marcos. "'Where We Were Safe': Mapping Resilience in the 1970s Salsa Scene." The Latinx Project at NYU, July 13, 2023. https:// www.latinxproject.nyu.edu/intervenxions/where-we-were-safe-mapping -resilience-in-the-1970s-salsa-scene.

Economic Commission for Latin America and the Caribbean. "Industri- alisation Strategy in the Caribbean: Lessons from the Puerto Rican Ex- perience." United Nations, September 2004. https://www.cepal.org/en /publications/38416-industrialisation-strategy-caribbean-lessons-puerto -rican-experience.

Elecciones en Puerto Rico. "Referéndum del 8 de diciembre de 1991." Accessed September 14, 2023. https://electionspuertorico.org/referencia/referendum91 .html.

Emerson, Ralph Waldo. "Gifts." In *The Logic of the Gift: Toward an Ethic of Gen- erosity*, edited by Alan D. Schrift, 25–27. New York: Routledge, 1997.

Esparza, René. "'Qué bonita mi tierra': Latinx AIDS Activism and Decolonial Queer Praxis in 1980s New York and Puerto Rico." *Radical History Review*, no. 140 (May 2021): 107–41.

Espiritu, Yen Le. *Home Bound: Filipino American Lives across Cultures, Com- munities, and Countries*. Berkeley: University of California Press, 2003.

Estrada Resto, Nilka. "Atraídos los visitantes por la realidad Boricua." *El Nuevo Día*, April 26, 1992.

Estrada Resto, Nilka. "Exalta Rafael Hernández Colón los valores del Pabellón." *El Nuevo Día*, April 22, 1992.

Estrada Resto, Nilka. "La salsa, nexo con el mundo." *El Nuevo Día*, April 22, 1992.

Estrada Resto, Nilka. "Odón Alonso, Bellas Artes y Roselín Pabón." *El Nuevo Día*, March 7, 1992.

Estrada Resto, Nilka. "Predomina la salsa en Sevilla." *El Nuevo Día*, February 18, 1992.

Estrada Resto, Nilka. "Sin auspiciador la Orquesta Sinfónica." *El Nuevo Día*, February 19, 1992.

Expo92.es. "La candidatura de España." February 1, 2006. http://www.expo92 .es/laexpo/index.php?seccion=historia.

Fania. "Harvey Averne." Accessed July 6, 2023. https://fania.com/artist/harvey -averne/.

Fania. "Hector Lavoe 'El Cantante' en Vivo/Live." YouTube, uploaded March 18, 2016. https://www.youtube.com/watch?v=MRZJwsgZ5VE.

Fania Entertainment Group. "Securities and Exchange Commission Form SB-2." December 19, 1997. http://www.secinfo.com/dsvrb.828q.5.htm.

Federal Bureau of Investigation. "COINTELPRO Puerto Rican Groups Part 02 of 11." FBI Records: The Vault. Accessed April 21, 2016. https://vault.fbi.gov/cointel -pro/puerto-rican-groups/cointel-pro-puerto-rican-groups-part-02-of-11.

Feeney, Geraldo. "Los Angeles Swings to Salsa Beat." *Billboard*, June 12, 1976.

Felman, Shoshana. *What Does a Woman Want? Reading and Sexual Difference.* Baltimore: Johns Hopkins University Press, 1993.

Fernández-Olmos, Margarita. *Sacred Possessions: Vodou, Santería, Obeah, and the Caribbean.* New Brunswick, NJ: Rutgers University Press, 2000.

Figueroa-Vázquez, Yomaira C. "The Survival of a People: Afro-Puerto Ricans and the Reparation of the Imagination." Public lecture at the University of Wisconsin–Madison, December 5, 2023.

Findlay, Eileen J. "Slipping and Sliding: The Many Meanings of Race in Life Histories of New York Puerto Rican Return Migrants in San Juan." *CENTRO Journal* 24, no. 1 (2012): 20–43.

Fiol-Matta, Licia. *The Great Woman Singer: Gender and Voice in Puerto Rican Music.* Durham, NC: Duke University Press, 2017.

Fleet, Gabriel Jacob. "What's in a Song? Copyright's Unfair Treatment of Record Producers and Side Musicians." *Vanderbilt Law Review* 61, no. 4 (May 2008): 1235–79.

Flores, Aurora. "Latin Scene." *Billboard*, August 20, 1977.

Flores, Aurora. "Once-Hot Biz of Salsa Sound Is a Cold Note." *New York Daily News*, July 14, 1987.

Flores, Aurora. "An Orchid in Manhattan: N.Y. Femme Winning Her Battle for Sex Equality." *Billboard*, February 5, 1977.

Flores, Aurora. "Radio Lags behind Concerts in Salsa Exposure." *Billboard*, November 12, 1977.

Flores, Aurora. "Who Burned the South Bronx?" *Hispanic Affairs*, August 1984.

Flores, Juan. *The Diaspora Strikes Back: Caribeño Tales of Learning and Turning*. New York: Routledge, 2008.

Flores, Juan. *Divided Borders: Essays on Puerto Rican Identity*. Houston: Arte Público, 1993.

Flores, Juan. *From Bomba to Hip-Hop: Puerto Rican Culture and Latino Identity*. New York: Columbia University Press, 2000.

Flores, Juan. "'Puerto Rican and Proud, Boyee!': Rap, Roots and Amnesia." *Iberoamericana (1977–2000)* 21, no. 3/4 (67/68) (1997): 168–78.

Flores, Juan. "Puerto Rocks: Rap, Roots, and Amnesia." In *That's the Joint! The Hip-Hop Studies Reader*, edited by Murray Foreman and Mark Anthony Neal, 69–86. New York: Routledge, 2004.

Flores, Juan. "Rappin', Writin', and Breakin'." *CENTRO Journal* 2, no. 3 (Spring 1988): 22–31.

Flores, Juan. *Salsa Rising: New York Latin Music of the Sixties Generation*. New York: Oxford University Press, 2016.

Forrest, Ricardo. "Surmounting the Catch-22 of Promotion and Distribution." *Billboard*, November 3, 1979.

Franco, Jean. *The Decline and Fall of the Lettered City: Latin America in the Cold War*. Cambridge, MA: Harvard University Press, 2002.

Franco, Jean. "What's Left of the Intelligentsia? The Uncertain Future of the Printed Word." In *Critical Passions: Selected Essays*, edited by Mary L. Pratt and Kathleen Newman, 196–207. Durham, NC: Duke University Press, 1999.

Fregoso, Rosa Linda. "Re-imagining Chicana Urban Identities in the Public Sphere, Cool Chuca Style." In *Between Women and Nation: Nationalisms, Transnational Feminisms, and the State*, edited by Norma Alarcón, Coren Kaplan, and Minoo Moallem, 70–91. Durham, NC: Duke University Press, 1999.

Fundora, Tomás. "Desde nuestro rincón internacional." *Record World*, July 29, 1972.

García, Cindy. "'Don't Leave Me, Celia!': Salsera Homosociality and Pan-Latina Incorporation." *Women and Performance: A Journal of Feminist Theory* 18, no. 3 (2009): 199–213.

García, Cindy. *Salsa Crossings: Dancing Latinidad in Los Angeles*. Durham, NC: Duke University Press, 2013.

García, Rudy. "Salsa Is Exploding." *Billboard*, June 12, 1976.

García Molina, Andrés. "Nostalgia, Internal Migration and the Return of Cuban Street-Vendor Songs." *Culture, Theory and Critique* 61, no. 2–3 (July 2020): 229–45.

Gautier Benítez, José. "A Puerto Rico (Regreso)." 1878. In *Colección de poemas clásicos de Puerto Rico*, 74–76. Puerto Rico Ebooks, 2007. Kindle.

Glasser, Ruth. *My Music Is My Flag: Puerto Rican Musicians and Their New York Communities, 1917–1940.* Berkeley: University of California Press, 1997.

Glazer, Nathan, and Daniel Patrick Moynihan. *Beyond the Melting Pot: The Negroes, Puerto Ricans, Jews, Italians, and Irish of New York City.* Cambridge, MA: MIT Press, 1974.

Godreau, Isar P. *Scripts of Blackness: Race, Cultural Nationalism, and U.S. Colonialism in Puerto Rico.* Urbana: University of Illinois Press, 2015.

Goldstein, Paul. *Copyright: Principles, Laws, and Practices.* New York: Little, Brown, 1989.

Goldstein, Richard. "The Latin Nabes." *Billboard*, August 7, 1972.

González, Evelyn. *The Bronx.* New York: Columbia University Press, 2004.

González, José Luis. *El país de cuatro pisos y otros ensayos.* Río Piedras, Puerto Rico: Ediciones Huracán, 1989.

Greenspun, Roger. "Screen: Doing *Our Latin Thing* as Documentary: Leon Gast Production Opens at Cine 2 Film Is Based on Fania Concert at Cheetah." *New York Times*, July 21, 1972.

Grosfoguel, Ramón. *Colonial Subjects: Puerto Ricans in a Global Perspective.* Berkeley: University of California Press, 2003.

Grosfoguel, Ramón, and Chloé S. Georas. "Latino Caribbean Diasporas in New York." In *Mambo Montage: The Latinization of New York City*, edited by Agustín Lao-Montes and Arlene M. Dávila, 97–118. New York: Columbia University Press, 2001.

Grosfoguel, Ramón, Frances Negrón-Muntaner, and Chloé S. Georas. "Beyond Nationalist and Colonialist Discourses: The Jaiba Politics of the Puerto Rican Ethno-Nation." In *Puerto Rican Jam: Rethinking Colonialism and Nationalism*, edited by Frances Negrón-Muntaner and Ramón Grosfoguel, 1–36. Minneapolis: University of Minnesota Press, 1997.

Grutzner, Charles. "City Puerto Ricans: Complex Problem." *New York Times*, October 3, 1949.

Grutzner, Charles. "City's Puerto Ricans Found Ill-Housed." *New York Times*, October 4, 1949.

Guridy, Frank Andre. *Forging Diaspora: Afro-Cubans and African Americans in a World of Empire and Jim Crow.* Chapel Hill: University of North Carolina Press, 2010.

Gurza, Agustín. "Cayre and Fania End '77 Strong: Other Latins Line Up." *Billboard*, January 14, 1978.

Gurza, Agustín. "Dangerous Grooves." *Los Angeles Times*, July 29, 2007.

Gurza, Agustín. "Fania Tries a Non-salsa Label." *Billboard*, October 2, 1976.

Gurza, Agustín. "FBI Looking into Reports That Latin Tape Piracy Accelerating." *Billboard*, February 4, 1978.

Gurza, Agustín. "FBI Raids Alleged Latin Pirate." *Billboard*, June 4, 1977.

Gurza, Agustín. "The Hot Latin Dance Music." *Billboard*, November 12, 1977.

Gurza, Agustín. "*Siembra*: A New Era for Salsa." *Latin N.Y.*, April 1979.

Gurza, Agustín. "La Tierra for Latins: Fania Finds the 'Perfect' Studio." *Billboard*, November 13, 1976.

Guzmán, Pablo. "Ray Barretto, 1929–2006: Mi Amigo, Latin Music's Most Intellectual Cat, Made Sure We Listened." *Village Voice*, February 27, 2007.

Guzmán, Pablo "Yoruba." "*Our Latin Thing*?" *Palante*, August 4–17, 1972.

Hackworth, Jason. *The Neoliberal City: Governance, Ideology, and Development in American Urbanism*. Ithaca, NY: Cornell University Press, 2006.

Hancock, Ange-Marie. *The Politics of Disgust: The Public Identity of the Welfare Queen*. New York: New York University Press, 2004.

Hansberry, Lorraine. "The Nation Needs Your Gifts." Address to Reader's Digest / United Negro College Fund creative writing contest winners, New York, May 1, 1964.

Harrison, Faye V. "The Gendered Politics and Violence of Structural Adjustment: A View from Jamaica." In *Situated Lives: Gender and Culture in Everyday Life*, edited by Louise Lamphere, Helena Ragoné, and Patricia Zavella, 451–68. New York: Routledge, 1997.

Hegel, Georg Wilhelm Friedrich. *Elements of the Philosophy of Right*. London: George Bell and Sons, 1821.

Hernández, Al Carlos. "The Ultimate Willie Colón Interview." *Herald de Paris*, February 14, 2010. http://www.heralddeparis.com.

Hernández, Tanya K. *Racial Innocence: Unmasking Latino Anti-Black Bias and the Struggle for Equality*. Boston: Beacon, 2022.

Hernández Colón, Rafael. "Gobernador R.H.C. firma proyectos Plaza de Salseros." February 19, 1988. Cassette #185. AHFRHC.

Hernández Colón, Rafael. "La Españolidad de Puerto Rico." *ABC Sevilla*, May 20, 1988.

Hernández Colón, Rafael. "Mensaje del Gobernador del Estado Libre Asociado de Puerto Rico Honorable Rafael Hernández Colón con motivo de la presentación del 'Proyecto Ventana al Mundo' del pabellón nacional de Puerto Rico en la Exposición Universal Sevilla 1992." March 8, 1991. AHFRHC.

Hernández Colón, Rafael. "Mensaje del Gobernador del Estado Libre Asociado de Puerto Rico Honorable Rafael Hernández Colón con motivo de las primeras jornadas universitarias puertorriqueñas sobre la comunidad europea e iberoamericana." October 11, 1990. AHFRHC.

Hernández Colón, Rafael. "Mensaje del Gobernador del Estado Libre Asociado de Puerto Rico Honorable Rafael Hernández Colón con motivo del cierre de la Exposición Universal Sevilla '92." October 12, 1992. AHFRHC.

Hernández Colón, Rafael. "Mensaje del Gobernador del Estado Libre Asociado de Puerto Rico Honorable Rafael Hernández Colón en la firma de la Resolución Conjunta 3043 de la Cámara para la construcción de la Plaza de la Salsa." February 19, 1988. AHFRHC.

Hernández Colón, Rafael. "Mensaje del Gobernador del Estado Libre Asociado de Puerto Rico Honorable Rafael Hernández Colón en la inauguración de Plaza de los Salseros." October 28, 1988. AHFRHC.

Hernández Colón, Rafael. "Mensaje del Gobernador del Estado Libre Asociado de Puerto Rico Honorable Rafael Hernández Colón sobre 'El Fondo Especial para la Educación.'" February 21, 1990. AHFRHC.

Hernández Colón, Rafael. "Mensaje en la ceremonia de los proyectos de ley para fortalecer la cultura Puertorriqueña." July 20, 1988. AHFRHC.

Hernández Colón, Rafael. "Mensaje en los Actos de Inauguración del Pabellón de P.R. en la Exposición Universal Sevilla '92." April 20, 1992. AHFRHC.

Hernández Colón, Rafael. "P.R. boletín administrativo 1991–68." Office of the Governor, October 11, 1990. AHFRHC.

Hernández Colón, Rafael. "P.R. orden ejecutiva 5012B." May 12, 1988. AHFRHC.

Hernández Colón, Rafael. "P.R. orden ejecutiva 1990–40." 1990. AHFRHC.

Herrera, Patricia. *Nuyorican Feminist Performance: From the Café to Hip Hop Theater*. Ann Arbor: University of Michigan Press, 2020.

Hill Collins, Patricia. *From Black Power to Hip Hop: Racism, Nationalism, and Feminism*. Philadelphia: Temple University Press, 2006.

hooks, bell. *Art on My Mind: Visual Politics*. New York: New Press, 1995.

Humphrey, Paul. *Santería, Vodou and Resistance in Caribbean Literature: Daughters of the Spirits*. Studies in Hispanic and Lusophone Cultures 12. Cambridge, UK: Modern Humanities Research Association, 2019.

Huron, David. "Music in Advertising: An Analytic Paradigm." *Musical Quarterly* 73, no. 4 (January 1989): 557–74.

Hutchinson, Sydney. "Mambo on 2: The Birth of a New Form of Dance in New York City." *CENTRO Journal* 16, no. 2 (October 2004): 108–37.

Huyssen, Andreas. *After the Great Divide: Modernism, Mass Culture, Postmodernism*. Bloomington: Indiana University Press, 1986.

IMDb. "Flaco Navaja." Accessed July 28, 2021. http://www.imdb.com/name/nm1500029/bio.

Irigaray, Luce. "Women on the Market." In *The Logic of the Gift: Toward an Ethic of Generosity*, edited by Alan D. Schrift, 174–89. New York: Routledge, 1997.

Jaime, Karen. *The Queer Nuyorican: Racialized Sexualities and Aesthetics in Loisaida*. New York: New York University Press, 2021.

Jaji, Tsitsi Ella. *Africa in Stereo: Modernism, Music, and Pan-African Solidarity*. Oxford: Oxford University Press, 2014.

Jaszi, Peter. "Is There Such a Thing as Postmodern Copyright?" In *Making and Unmaking Intellectual Property: Creative Production in Legal and Cultural Perspective*, edited by Mario Biagioli, Peter Jaszi, and Martha Woodmansee, 413–28. Chicago: University of Chicago Press, 2011.

Jaszi, Peter. "On the Author Effect: Contemporary Copyright and Collective Creativity." In *The Construction of Authorship: Textual Appropriations in Law and Literature*, 29–56. Durham, NC: Duke University Press, 1994.

Jennings, James, and Francisco Chapman. "Puerto Ricans in the Community Control Movement: An Interview with Luis Fuentes." In *The Puerto Rican Movement: Voices from the Diaspora*, edited by Andrés Torres and José Emiliano Velázquez, 280–95. Philadelphia: Temple University Press, 1998.

Jiménez Román, Miriam. "Allá y Acá: Locating Puerto Ricans in the Diaspora(s)." *Diálogo* 5, no. 1 (March 2001): 11–13.

Jiménez Román, Miriam. "Looking at That Middle Ground: Racial Mixing as Panacea?" In *A Companion to Latina/o Studies*, edited by Juan Flores and Renato Rosaldo, 325–36. Malden, MA: Blackwell, 2007.

Jiménez Román, Miriam. "Un hombre (negro) del pueblo: José Celso Barbosa and the Puerto Rican 'Race' towards Whiteness." CENTRO *Journal* 8, no. 1–2 (1996): 8–29.

Junta de Andalucía. "Eventos." Pabellón del Futuro. Accessed July 15, 2015. http://www.pabellondelfuturo.es/.

Kaiser, Charles. "Blacks and Puerto Ricans a Bronx Majority." *New York Times*, April 19, 1976.

Kant, Immanuel. *Critique of Judgement*. Translated by J. H. Bernard. New York: Hafner, 1951.

Kant, Immanuel. *Metaphysics of Morals*. Cambridge: Cambridge University Press, 1996.

Kapper, Arturo. "Latin Scene." *Billboard*, May 26, 1973.

Katz, Marco. "Salsa Criticism at the Turn of the Century: Identity Politics and Authenticity." *Popular Music and Society* 28, no. 1 (2005): 35–54.

Kent, Mary. *Salsa Talks: A Musical Heritage Uncovered*. Altamonte Springs, FL: Digital Domain, 2005.

Kretschmer, Martin, and Friedmann Kawohl. "The History and Philosophy of Copyright." In *Music and Copyright*, edited by Simon Frith and Lee Marshall, 21–53. New York: Routledge, 2004.

Kusno, Abidin. "Rethinking the Nation." In *The Sage Handbook of Architectural Theory*, edited by C. Greig Crysler, Stephen Cairns, and Hilde Heynen, 213–30. Thousand Oaks, CA: SAGE, 2012.

La Fountain-Stokes, Lawrence. *Queer Ricans: Cultures and Sexualities in the Diaspora*. Minneapolis: University of Minnesota Press, 2009.

Latin Jazz Network. "Interview with Bobby Sanabria." Accessed July 2, 2003. http://www.latinjazznet.com/special_feature/questions/bobby_sanabria.htm.

*Latin N.Y.* "Hector LaVoe." August 1973.

*Latin N.Y.* "Mail." August 1977.

*Latin N.Y.* "A Talk with Willie." August 1973.

*Latin N.Y.* "What Happened to Hector LaVoe?" July 1977.

*Latin N.Y.* "Willie Speaks about His Image." August 1973.

Lazzarato, Maurizio. *The Making of the Indebted Man: An Essay on the Neoliberal Condition*. Los Angeles: Semiotext(e), 2012.

Leaffer, Marshall A. *Understanding Copyright Law*. 7th ed. Durham, NC: Carolina Academic Press, 2019.

LeBrón, Marisol. *Policing Life and Death: Race, Violence, and Resistance in Puerto Rico*. Oakland: University of California Press, 2019.

Lee, Stephen. "Re-examining the Concept of the 'Independent' Record Company: The Case of Wax Trax! Records." *Popular Music* 14 (January 1995): 13–31.

Leo, Katherine M. "Early Blues and Jazz Authorship in the Case of the 'Livery Stable Blues.'" *Jazz Perspectives* 12, no. 3 (September 2020): 311–38.

Leogrande, Ernest. "Salsa Time at Garden." *New York Daily News*, September 5, 1977.

Leoncavallo, Ruggero. *Leoncavallo's I Pagliacci (Opera Journeys Libretto Series)*. 1892. Edited by Burton D. Fisher. Coral Gables, FL: Opera Journeys, 2006.

Lewis, Oscar. *La Vida: A Puerto Rican Family in the Culture of Poverty: San Juan and New York*. New York: Vintage Books, 1966.

Lima, Lázaro, and Felice Picano. *Ambientes: New Queer Latino Writing*. Madison: University of Wisconsin Press, 2011.

Lloréns, Hilda. *Imaging the Great Puerto Rican Family: Framing Nation, Race, and Gender during the American Century*. Lanham, MD: Lexington Books, 2014.

Lloréns, Hilda. *Making Livable Worlds: Afro-Puerto Rican Women Building Environmental Justice*. Seattle: University of Washington Press, 2021.

Lloréns, Hilda, and Zaire Z. Dinzey-Flores. "The Replay: White Passes and Black Exclusions in Latinidad." *Black Latinas Know Collective Blog*, January 9, 2021. https://www.blacklatinasknow.org/post/the-replay-white-passes-and-black-exclusions-in-latinidad.

López, Edrik. "Nuyorican Spaces: Mapping Identity in a Poetic Geography." *CENTRO Journal* 17, no. 1 (Spring 2005): 203–19.

Lowe, Lisa, and David Lloyd. "Introduction." In *The Politics of Culture in the Shadow of Capital*, edited by Lisa Lowe and David Lloyd, 1–32. Durham, NC: Duke University Press, 1997.

Luciano, Felipe. "Is the Gangster Image Good for Willie Colón?" *Latin N.Y.*, August 1973.

Luciano, María Judith. "Lamenta la exclusividad salsera en el pabellón." *El Nuevo Día*, February 19, 1992.

Lugones, María. "The Coloniality of Gender." *Worlds and Knowledges Otherwise* (*WKO*), 2 (Spring 2008), 1–17. https://globalstudies.trinity.duke.edu/projects/wko-gender.

Marín, Bobby. "Artist Essentials: Willie Colón." Fania. Accessed February 25, 2024. https://fania.com/artist-essentials/willie-colon/.

Marqués, René. *La carreta: Drama en tres actos*. San Sebastian Auditorium, New York, 1953.

Marqués, René. *La mirada*. Río Piedras, Puerto Rico: Editorial Antillana, 1975.

Martínez, Elena. "La Madrina's Music Store: Victoria Hernández and the Beginnings of Puerto Rican Music in New York, Centro de Estudios Puertorriqueños." *Centro Voices*, February 25, 2015.

Mattei, Julia. "Objeción al lema Boricua en la Expo." *El Nuevo Día*, July 28, 1992.

Melanson, Jim. "Fania Concert Is Success as an All-Star Delight." *Billboard*, September 8, 1973.

Melanson, Jim. "Fania to Romance Black Radio." *Billboard*, January 6, 1973.

Melanson, Jim. "'Latin Thing' Premieres." *Billboard*, August 12, 1972.

Melanson, Jim, and A. Contreras. "Latin Scene." *Billboard*, December 16, 1972.

Mele, Christopher. *Selling the Lower East Side: Culture, Real Estate, and Resistance in New York City*. Minneapolis: University of Minnesota Press, 2000.

Meléndez, Miguel. *We Took the Streets: Fighting for Latino Rights with the Young Lords*. New York: St. Martin's, 2003.

Merrill, Dennis. *Negotiating Paradise: U.S. Tourism and Empire in Twentieth-Century Latin America*. Chapel Hill: University of North Carolina Press, 2009.

Millán Ferrer, Alida. "Siguiéndole los pasos a Gilberto Santa Rosa." *Claridad*, June 12, 1992.

Miller, Karl Hagstrom. "Crossover Schemes: New York Salsa as Politics, Culture, and Commerce." In *R&B, Rhythm and Business: The Political Economy of Black Music*, edited by Norman Kelley, 192–217. New York: Akashic Books, 2005.

Mirabal, Carmen. "Héctor Lavoe: No soy drogadicto." *Salsa Magazine* 1, no. 2 (ca. 1976): 18–19. Harbor Conservatory for the Performing Arts, Colección Raíces.

Miranda, Ismael. "Ismael Miranda: 'Eterno Niño Bonito' de La Salsa." *Primera Hora*. Accessed September 17, 2004. http://www.primerahora.com.

Mochkofsky, Graciela. "It's Time Rubén Blades Was Accepted into the American Canon." *New Yorker*, October 6, 2023. https://www.newyorker.com/news/daily-comment/its-time-ruben-blades-was-accepted-into-the-american-canon.

Mora, Richard. "'Dicks Are for Chicks': Latino Boys, Masculinity, and the Abjection of Homosexuality." *Gender and Education* 25, no. 3 (2003): 340–56.

Morales, Iris. *Through the Eyes of Rebel Women: The Young Lords 1969–1976*. New York: Red Sugarcane Press, 2016.

Moreau, Inés. "'Puerto Rico es salsa' señores." *El Nuevo Día*, February 3, 1992.

Moten, Fred. *In the Break: The Aesthetics of the Black Radical Tradition*. Minneapolis: University of Minnesota Press, 2003.

Muñoz, José Esteban. *Cruising Utopia: The Then and There of Queer Futurity*. New York: New York University Press, 2009.

Muñoz, José Esteban. *Disidentifications: Queers of Color and the Performance of Politics*. Minneapolis: University of Minnesota Press, 1999.

Murray, Derek Conrad. "Post-Black Art and the Resurrection of African American Satire." In *Post-Soul Satire: Black Identity after Civil Rights*, edited by

Derek C. Maus and James J. Donahue, 3–21. Jackson: University Press of Mississippi, 2014.

Navas, Danilo. "Ray Barretto: Barretto Power." Latin Jazz Network, December 18, 2020. https://latinjazznet.com/featured/ray-barretto-barretto-power/.

Neal, Mark Anthony. *Songs in the Key of Black Life: A Rhythm and Blues Nation.* New York: Routledge, 2003.

Negrón-Muntaner, Frances. "Twenty Years of Puerto Rican Gay Activism: An Interview with Luis 'Popo' Santiago." *Radical America* 25, no. 1 (March 1991): 39–51.

Negus, Keith. *Music Genres and Corporate Cultures.* New York: Routledge, 1999.

New York Civil Liberties Union. "Stop-and-Frisk Data." New York Civil Liberties Union, 2024. https://www.nyclu.org/en/stop-and-frisk-data.

*New York Magazine.* "Movies around Town." August 7, 1972.

*New York Times.* "City Called Haven for Illegal Aliens." December 21, 1949.

*New York Times.* "Puerto Ricans Halt a School Meeting." January 14, 1969.

Njoroge, Njoroge M. *Chocolate Surrealism.* Caribbean Studies Series. Jackson: University Press of Mississippi, 2016.

*El Nuevo Día.* "Puerto Rico es salsa: El disparate del siglo." July 14, 1992.

Ochoa Gautier, Ana María. *Aurality: Listening and Knowledge in Nineteenth-Century Colombia.* Durham, NC: Duke University Press, 2014.

Oficina de Gerencia y Presupuesto del Estado Libre Asociado de Puerto Rico. "Ley Reguladora del Centro Bancario Internacional." February 16, 2017, 22.

Olenski, Steve. "Why Music Plays a Big Role When It Comes to Branding." *Forbes*, February 6, 2014.

Ortiz-Negrón, Laura L. "Space out of Place: Consumer Culture in Puerto Rico." In *None of the Above: Puerto Ricans in the Global Era*, edited by Frances Negrón-Muntaner, 39–50. New York: Palgrave Macmillan, 2008.

Ostberg, Jacob. "The Quest for Masculine To-Be-Looked-at-Ness? Exploring Consumption-Based Self-Objectification among Heterosexual Men." In *The Routledge Companion to Marketing and Feminism*, edited by Pauline Maclaran, Lorna Stevens, and Olga Kravets, 222–38. New York: Routledge, 2022.

Oteri, Frank J. "Willie Colón: Salsa Is an Open Concept." New Music Box, March 1, 2009. https://nmbx.newmusicusa.org/willie-colon-salsa-is-an-open-concept/.

Otero Garabís, Juan. *Nación y ritmo: "Descargas" desde el Caribe.* San Juan, Puerto Rico: Ediciones Callejón, 2000.

Otero Garabís, Juan. "'Puerto Rico Is Salsa': Propositions, Appropriations, and Interpretations of a Popular Genre." *Journal of Latin American Cultural Studies* 5, no. 1 (1996): 25–31.

Pablo-Romero Gil-Delgado, María del Pópulo. *La Exposición Universal de Sevilla 1992: Efectos sobre el crecimiento económico Andaluz.* Seville: Universidad de Sevilla, 2002.

Pacheco, Johnny. "Interview: A Visit with Maestro Johnny Pacheco." *Descarga Journal.* November 27, 2001.

Pacini Hernández, Deborah. *Bachata: A Social History of Dominican Popular Music*. Philadelphia: Temple University Press, 1995.

Pacini Hernández, Deborah. *Oye Como Va! Hybridity and Identity in Latino Popular Music*. Philadelphia: Temple University Press, 2010.

Pacini Hernández, Deborah. "A Tale of Two Cities: A Comparative Analysis of Los Angeles Chicano and Nuyorican Engagement with Rock and Roll." CENTRO *Journal* 11, no. 2 (Spring 2000): 70–93.

Padura Fuentes, Leonardo. *Los rostros de la salsa: Entrevistas con las principales figuras musicales del Caribe*. Mexico City: Editorial Planeta Mexicana, 1999.

Paik, A. Naomi. *Bans, Walls, Raids, Sanctuary: Understanding U.S. Immigration for the Twenty-First Century*. Oakland: University of California Press, 2020.

Pantojas-García, Emilio. "'Federal Funds' and the Puerto Rican Economy: Myths and Realities." CENTRO *Journal* 19, no. 2 (Fall 2007): 206–23.

Pedreira, Antonio. *Insularismo*. Río Piedras, Puerto Rico: Editorial Edil, 1992.

Peisner, David. "Digital Salsa: The Surprising Rebirth of Legendary Latin-Music Label Fania Records." *Fast Company*, June 5, 2014. https://www.fastcompany.com/3031260/digital-salsa-the-surprising-rebirth-of-legendary-latin-music-label-fania-records.

Piñero, Miguel. *Short Eyes: A Play*. New York: Hill and Wang, 1975.

Primo Discos Digital Services. "Hector Lavoe Live at the Village Gate 1988. Sings 'El Cantante.'" YouTube, uploaded September 21, 2016. https://www.youtube.com/watch?v=y4oOXQAQ8SE.

Quijano, Aníbal. "Coloniality of Power and Eurocentrism in Latin America." *International Sociology* 15, no. 2 (2000): 215–32.

Quiñones, Maritza. "Queridas Hermanas." *Black Latinas Know Collective Blog*, November 29, 2020. https://www.blacklatinasknow.org/post/queridas-hermanas.

Quintero Rivera, Ángel G. *Cuerpo y cultura: Las músicas "mulatas" y la subversión del baile*. Madrid: Iberoamericana Editorial Vervuert, 2009.

Quintero Rivera, Ángel. G. *Salsa, sabor y control! Sociología de la música "tropical."* Havana: Casa de las Américas, 1998.

Quiroga, José. "Salsa, Bad Boys, and Brass." In *None of the Above: Puerto Ricans in the Global Era*, edited by Frances Negrón-Muntaner, 233–40. New York: Palgrave Macmillan, 2007.

Rama, Angel. *La ciudad letrada*. Hanover, NH: Ediciones del Norte, 1984.

Ramos-Zayas, Ana Y. *National Performances: The Politics of Class, Race, and Space in Puerto Rican Chicago*. Chicago: University of Chicago Press, 2003.

*Record World*. "Carol Polizzi: Pride and Purpose." November 1, 1975.

*Record World*. "Eve Charlack: The Production Story." November 1, 1975.

*Record World*. "Gast Brings Fania to Screen." November 1, 1975.

*Record World*. "Gertrude Fredd: Keeping Records Straight." November 1, 1975.

Reddy, Vanita. "Afro-Asian Intimacies and the Politics and Aesthetics of Cross-Racial Struggle in Mira Nair's Mississippi Masala." *Journal of Asian American Studies* 18, no. 3 (2015): 233–63.

"Reportaje cocolos vs rockeros 1987." YouTube, uploaded June 10, 2008. https://www.youtube.com/watch?v=Ugr-adcn5RM.

Reuters. "Fania Records to Launch First-Ever Latin Music App for Spotify as Part of 50th Anniversary Celebrations." April 24, 2014.

Richardson, Jill Toliver. *The Afro-Latin@ Experience in Contemporary American Literature and Culture: Engaging Blackness*. New York: Palgrave Macmillan, 2016.

Rivera, Raquel Z. "Cultura y poder en el rap puertorriqueño." *Revista de Ciencias Sociales* 4 (January 1998): 124–46.

Rivera, Raquel Z. *New York Ricans from the Hip Hop Zone*. New York: Palgrave Macmillan, 2003.

Rivera, Raquel Z. "Policing Morality, Mano Dura Style: The Case of Underground Rap and Reggae in Puerto Rico in the Mid-1990s." In *Reggaeton*, edited by Raquel Z. Rivera, Wayne Marshall, and Deborah Pacini Hernández, 111–34. Durham, NC: Duke University Press, 2009.

Rivera, Raquel Z. "Will the 'Real' Puerto Rican Culture Please Stand Up? Thoughts on Cultural Nationalism." In *None of the Above: Puerto Ricans in the Global Era*, edited by Frances Negrón-Muntaner, 217–31. New York: Palgrave Macmillan, 2007.

Rivera-Batiz, Francisco, and Carlos E. Santiago. *Island Paradox: Puerto Rico in the 1990s*. New York: Russell Sage Foundation, 1996.

Rivera Nieves, Irma N. "Poder y obedecer: Cambios en el ejercicio del poder gubernamental en Puerto Rico." In *Polifonía salvaje: Ensayos de cultura y política en la postmodernidad*, edited by Silvia Álvarez-Curbelo, Irma N. Rivera Nieves, and Carlos Gil, 261–75. San Juan, Puerto Rico: Editorial Postdata, 1995.

Rivero, Yeidy M. *Tuning Out Blackness*. Durham: Duke University Press, 2005.

Rodríguez, Carolina. "New Old Salsero." *New York Daily News*, July 18, 2007.

Rodríguez, Francisco Javier. *Catálogo de arquitectura contemporánea de Puerto Rico / Contemporary Architecture in Puerto Rico, 1993–2010*. Guaynabo, Puerto Rico: American Institute of Architects, 2014.

Rodríguez, Héctor. "¿Debe la salsa representarnos internacionalmente?" *Claridad*, June 12, 1992.

Rodríguez Castro, María Elena. "Divergencias: De ciudadanos a espectadores culturales." *Revista de Crítica Literaria Latinoamericana* 23, no. 45 (1997): 365–80.

Rodríguez Castro, María Elena. "Foro de 1940: Las pasiones y los intereses se dan la mano." In *Del nacionalismo al populismo: Cultura y política en Puerto Rico*, edited by Silvia Álvarez-Curbelo and María Elena Rodríguez Castro, 61–106. Río Piedras, Puerto Rico: Ediciones Huracán, 1993.

Rohter, Larry. "A Copyright Victory, 35 Years Later." *New York Times*, September 10, 2013.

Rohter, Larry. "It Happened One Night at the Cheetah." *New York Times*, August 21, 2011.

Rohter, Larry. "A Salsa Star Is Reborn after a Break for Politics." *New York Times*, November 27, 2009.

Rondón, César Miguel. *The Book of Salsa: A Chronicle of Urban Music from the Caribbean to New York City*. Chapel Hill: University of North Carolina Press, 2008.

Rondón, César Miguel. *El libro de la salsa: Crónica de la música del Caribe urbano*. Caracas, Venezuela: Merca Libros Editorial Arte, 1980.

Roque Ramírez, Horacio N. "Gay Latino Histories / Dying to Be Remembered: AIDS Obituaries, Public Memory, and the Queer Latino Archive." In *Beyond El Barrio: Everyday Life in Latina/o America*, edited by Gina M. Pérez, Frank A. Guridy, and Adrian Burgos, 103–28. New York: New York University Press, 2010.

Roque Ramírez, Horacio N. "'Mira, yo soy boricua y estoy aquí': Rafa Negrón's Pan Dulce and the Queer Sonic Latinaje of San Francisco." *CENTRO Journal* 19, no. 1 (Spring 2007): 275–313.

Rosa, Richard. "Business as Pleasure: Culture, Tourism, and Nation in Puerto Rico in the 1930s." *Nepantla: Views from South* 2, no. 3 (2001): 449–88.

Rosa, Richard. "Governing Tourism: Representation, Domination and Freedom in Puerto Rico: 1949." *Global South* 6, no. 1 (2012): 87–97.

Rosa, Vanessa. "Colonial Projects: Public Housing and the Management of Puerto Ricans in New York City, 1945–1970." In *Critical Dialogues in Latinx Studies: A Reader*, edited by Ana Y. Ramos-Zayas and Mérida M. Rúa, 186–96. New York: New York University Press, 2021.

Rose, Tricia. "Black Texts / Black Contexts." In *Black Popular Culture*, edited by Michelle Wallace and Gina Dent, 223–26. Seattle: Bay, 1992.

Rose, Tricia. "Never Trust a Big Butt and a Smile." In *Black Feminist Cultural Criticism*, edited by Jacqueline Bobo, 233–54. Malden, MA: Blackwell, 2001.

Rosen, Jody. "The Return of Fania, the Record Company That Made Salsa Hot." *New York Times*, June 4, 2006.

Rubin, Rachel. *Jewish Gangsters of Modern Literature*. Urbana: University of Illinois Press, 2000.

Ruiz, Angel L. "The Impact of the Economic Recession on the Puerto Rican Economy: An Input-Output Approach." *Caribbean Studies* 16, nos. 3–4 (October 1976): 125–48.

Safa, Helen Icken. *De mantenidas a proveedoras: Mujeres e industrialización en el Caribe*. San Juan: Editorial de la Universidad de Puerto Rico, 1998.

Salazar, Max. *Mambo Kingdom: Latin Music in New York*. New York: Schirmer Trade Books, 2002.

Salserísimo Perú. "¿David Lugo se llevó a la fuerza a Héctor Lavoe de Florida?" YouTube, uploaded September 30, 2020. https://www.youtube.com/watch?v =oDEPyM49kYI&ab_channel=Salser%C3%ADsimoPer%C3%BA.

Salserísimo Perú. "Exclusivo: Los secretos de Fania contados por Carmen Mirabal, exrelacionista pública del sello." YouTube, uploaded December 12, 2023. https://www.youtube.com/watch?v=UmiL5hdOTPU&ab_channel =Salser%C3%ADsimoPer%C3%BA.

Salserísimo Perú. "Expediente salsa: 'Fuego en el 23' y la historia real del clásico de La Sonora Ponceña." YouTube, uploaded June 12, 2021. https://www.youtube.com /watch?v=A6eLKCWS2iE&ab_channel=Salser%C3%ADsimoPer%C3%BA.

Salserísimo Perú. "Héctor Lavoe: La historia jamás contada de 'Che che colé.'" YouTube, uploaded June 7, 2020. https://www.youtube.com/watch?v =_qyoP3DrjzE.

Sanabria, Izzy. "Felipe Luciano Loses Radio Show." *Latin N.Y.*, May 1975.

Sanabria, Izzy. "Jerry Masucci on Willie." *Latin N.Y.*, August 1973.

Sanabria, Izzy. "Latin Album Covers Reflect Music's Sophistication." *Billboard*, July 27, 1974.

Sanabria, Izzy. "Rebuttal." *Latin N.Y.*, August 1973.

Sanabria, Izzy (@mrsalsamovie). "The idea #IzzySanabria had for this #RayBarretto cover came from the literary classic, Gulliver's Travels." X (formerly known as Twitter), March 2, 2017. https://twitter.com/mrsalsamovie/status /837308224491700224.

Sánchez, Rosaura. *Chicano Discourse*. Rowley, MA: Newbury House, 1983.

Sánchez Korrol, Virginia. *From Colonia to Community: The History of Puerto Ricans in New York City*. Berkeley: University of California Press, 1983.

Sandoval Sánchez, Alberto. *José, Can You See? Latinos On and Off Broadway*. Madison: University of Wisconsin Press, 1999.

Sandoval Sánchez, Alberto. "Politicizing Abjection: In the Manner of a Prologue for the Articulation of AIDS Latino Queer Identities." In *Passing Lines: Sexuality and Immigration*, edited by Bradley S. Epps, Keja Valens, and Bill Johnson González, 311–19. Cambridge, MA: Harvard University, David Rockefeller Center for Latin American Studies, 2005.

Sandoval Sánchez, Alberto. "Puerto Rican Identity Up in the Air: Air Migration, Its Cultural Representations, and Me 'Cruzando El Charco.'" In *Puerto Rican Jam: Rethinking Colonialism and Nationalism*, 189–208. Minneapolis: University of Minnesota Press, 1997.

Sandoval Sánchez, Alberto. "*West Side Story*: A Puerto Rican Reading of 'America.'" In *Latin Looks*, edited by Clara E. Rodríguez, 164–79. New York: Routledge, 1997.

Sangria, Marc. "Interview with a Liberated Latin Woman." *Latin N.Y.*, February 1975.

Saxon, Anne, Adela López, Mary B. Hoffman, and Mercedes Acosta. "Ruben Blades: Superman of Salsa." *Latin N.Y.*, February 1979.

Sedgwick, Eve Kosofsky. *Epistemology of the Closet*. Berkeley: University of California Press, 1990.

Seminario Interdisciplinario de Información y Documentación José Emilio González. "Mensaje de Emilio Cassinello, comisario general de la EXPO 92." YouTube, June 23, 1992. https://www.youtube.com/watch?v=Hx12rcqc68E.

Seminario Interdisciplinario de Información y Documentación José Emilio González. "Pabellón de Puerto Rico—Espectáculos—Día Nacional de Puerto Rico." YouTube, June 23, 1992. https://www.youtube.com/watch?v=fQFxHrtqwW8.

Shapiro, Peter. *Turn the Beat Around: The Secret History of Disco.* New York: Faber and Faber, 2005.

Sheller, Mimi. *Consuming the Caribbean: From Arawaks to Zombies.* New York: Routledge, 2003.

Singer, Roberta L., and Elena Martínez. "A South Bronx Latin Music Tale." *CENTRO Journal* 16, no. 1 (Spring 2004): 176–204.

Slater, Russ. "It Was Our Thing, *Our Latin Thing*: An Interview with Leon Gast." *Sounds and Colors*, November 29, 2011. https://soundsandcolors.com.

Smith, Paul Julian. *The Moderns: Time, Space, and Subjectivity in Contemporary Spanish Culture.* Oxford: Oxford University Press, 2000.

Sony. "Annual Report 1992." December 30, 2015. https://www.sony.com/en/SonyInfo/IR/library/ar/1992-E.pdf .

Spain, Daphne. *Gendered Spaces.* Chapel Hill: University of North Carolina Press, 1992.

Sterling, J. A .L. *Intellectual Property Rights in Sound Recordings, Film and Video.* London: Sweet and Maxwell, 1992.

Stockton, Kathryn Bond. *God between Their Lips: Desire between Women in Irigaray, Brontë, and Eliot.* Stanford, CA: Stanford University Press, 1994.

Stoever, Jennifer. "Reproducing U.S. Citizenship in Blackboard Jungle: Race, Cold War Liberalism, and the Tape Recorder." *American Quarterly* 63, no. 3 (September 2011): 781–806.

Stoever, Jennifer. "Splicing the Sonic Color-Line: Tony Schwartz Remixes Postwar Nueva York." *Social Text* 28, no. 1 (Spring 2010): 59–85.

Suárez Findlay, Eileen J. *We Are Left without a Father Here: Masculinity, Domesticity, and Migration in Postwar Puerto Rico.* Durham, NC: Duke University Press, 2014.

Sutherland, Sam. "Sessions Get More Sophisticated, Experimental." *Billboard*, November 25, 1972.

Sutherland, Sam. "Studio Track." *Billboard*, September 30, 1972.

Swift, Jonathan. *Gulliver's Travels.* New York: Harper, 1950.

Taylor, Diana. *The Archive and the Repertoire: Performing Cultural Memory in the Americas.* Durham, NC: Duke University Press, 2003.

Terrace, Ray. "Masucci May Try to Top Garden Hit." *Billboard*, August 17, 1974.

Terrace, Ray. "Salsa Rhythms Explode on the Southern California Market." *Billboard*, July 27, 1974.

Théberge, Paul. "Technology, Creative Practice, and Copyright." In *Music and Copyright*, edited by Simon Frith and Lee Marshall, 139–56. New York: Routledge, 2004.

Thomas, Deborah A., and Joseph Masco, eds. *Sovereignty Unhinged: An Illustrated Primer for the Study of Present Intensities, Disavowals, and Temporal Derangements*. Durham, NC: Duke University Press, 2023.

Thomas, Lorrin. *Puerto Rican Citizen: History and Political Identity in Twentieth-Century New York City*. Chicago: University of Chicago Press, 2010.

Thomas, Lynnell L. "'People Want to See What Happened': *Treme*, Televisual Tourism, and the Racial Remapping of Post-Katrina New Orleans." *Television and New Media* 13, no. 3 (2012): 213–24.

Thomas, Piri. *Down These Mean Streets*. New York: Knopf, 1967.

*Time*. "Puerto Rico: The Bard of Bootstrap." June 23, 1958.

Tolchin, Martin. "Deaver's Lobbying for Puerto Rico Brought Reprimand from Shultz." *New York Times*, June 3, 1986.

Torres, Andre. "Industry Rule #4083: Andre Torres." Red Bull Music Academy, September 5, 2013. Accessed September 17, 2014. http://www.redbullmusicacademy.com/magazine/industry-rule-andre-torres.

Torres, Andrés. *Between Melting Pot and Mosaic: African Americans and Puerto Ricans in the New York Political Economy*. Philadelphia: Temple University Press, 1995.

Torres, Arlene. "La gran familia puertorriqueña 'ej prieta de beldá' (The Great Puerto Rican Family Is Really Black)." In *Blackness in Latin America and the Caribbean: Eastern South America and the Caribbean*, edited by Arlene Torres and Norman E. Whitten, 285–306. Bloomington: Indiana University Press, 1998.

Torres, Edgar. "'¡Qué lindo es!' . . . un legado musical." Fundación Nacional para la Cultura Popular, September 19, 2014. https://prpop.org/2014/09/que-lindo-es-un-legado-musical/.

Torres, Luis Angeli. "Desafinada la selección musical del pabellón Boricua en Sevilla." *El Nuevo Día*, February 22, 1992.

Torres Torres, Jaime. "Bastante activo el sonero y bolerista Cheo Feliciano." *El Nuevo Día*, April 19, 1992.

Torres Torres, Jaime. "Problemas con el Pabellón." *El Nuevo Día*, March 2, 1992.

Toynbee, Jason. "Musicians." In *Music and Copyright*, edited by Simon Frith and Lee Marshall, 123–38. 2nd ed. New York: Routledge, 2004.

Trouillot, Michel-Rolph. *Silencing the Past: Power and the Production of History*. Boston: Beacon, 1995. Kindle.

Tyler, Imogen. *Revolting Subjects: Social Abjection and Resistance in Neoliberal Britain*. London: Bloomsbury, 2013.

United States Congress. *Communist Activities among Puerto Ricans in New York City and Puerto Rico. Hearings*. Washington, DC: US Government Printing Office, 1960.

US Census Bureau. "Table 1321. Puerto Rico—Summary: 1990 to 2010." September 5, 2013. Accessed May 12, 2015. http://www.census.gov/compendia /statab/2012/tables/12s1321.pdf.

Valdés, Guadalupe. "Social Interaction and Code-Switching Patterns: A Case Study of Spanish/English Alternation." In *Spanish in the United States: Sociolinguistic Aspects*, edited by Jon Amastae and Lucía Elías-Olivares, 209–29. Cambridge: Cambridge University Press, 1982.

Valentín-Escobar, Wilson. "Bodega Surrealism: The Emergence of Latina/o Artivists in New York City, 1976–Present." PhD diss., University of Michigan, 2011.

Valentín-Escobar, Wilson A. "El hombre que respira debajo del agua: Trans-Boricua Memories, Identities, and Nationalisms Performed through the Death of Héctor Lavoe." In *Situating Salsa: Global Markets and Local Meanings in Latin Popular Music*, edited by Lise Waxer, 161–86. New York: Routledge, 2002.

Valentín-Escobar, Wilson A. "Nothing Connects Us All but Imagined Sounds: Performing Trans-Boricua Memories, Identities, and Nationalisms through the Death of Héctor Lavoe." In *Mambo Montage: The Latinization of New York City*, edited by Agustín Lao-Montes and Arlene M. Dávila, 207–34. New York: Columbia University Press, 2001.

Vargas, Deborah R. *Dissonant Divas in Chicana Music: The Limits of La Onda.* Minneapolis: University of Minnesota Press, 2012.

Vargas, Deborah R. "Ruminations on Lo Sucio as a Latino Queer Analytic." *American Quarterly* 66, no. 3 (2014): 715–26.

Vargas, Deborah R. "Un Desmadre Positivo: Notes on How Jenni Rivera *Played* Music." In *Contemporary Latina/o Media: Production, Circulation, Politics*, edited by Arlene Dávila and Yeidy M. Rivero, 285–302. New York: New York University Press, 2014.

Vázquez, Alexandra T. "Can You Feel the Beat? Freestyle's Systems of Living, Loving, and Recording." *Social Text* 28, no. 1 (102) (2010): 107–24.

Vázquez, Alexandra T. *Listening in Detail: Performances of Cuban Music.* Refiguring American Music. Durham, NC: Duke University Press, 2013.

Vega, Marta Moreno. "The Ancestral Sacred Creative Impulse of Africa and the African Diaspora: Ase, the Nexus of the Black Global Aesthetic." *Lenox Avenue: A Journal of Interarts Inquiry* 5 (1999): 45–57.

Vega, Marta Moreno. "The Yoruba Orisha Tradition Comes to New York City." *African American Review* 29, no. 2 (1995): 201–6.

VerSteeg, Russ. "Defining Author for Purposes of Copyright." *American University Law Review* 45 (1995): 1323–66.

Waring, Charles. "Fania Records: How a New York Label Took Salsa to The World." *uDiscover Music* (blog), January 13, 2023. https://www.udiscovermusic.com /stories/fania-records-story/.

Washburne, Christopher. *Sounding Salsa: Performing Latin Music in New York City*. Philadelphia: Temple University Press, 2008.

Waxer, Lise. *The City of Musical Memory: Salsa, Record Grooves and Popular Culture in Cali, Colombia*. Middletown, CT: Wesleyan University Press, 2002.

Waxer, Lise. "Llegó La Salsa: The Rise of Salsa in Venezuela and Colombia." In *Situating Salsa: Global Markets and Local Meanings in Latin Popular Music*, edited by Lise Waxer, 219–46. New York: Routledge, 2002.

Waxer, Lise. "Situating Salsa: Latin Music at the Crossroads." In *Situating Salsa: Global Markets and Local Meanings in Latin Popular Music*, edited by Lise Waxer, 3–22. New York: Routledge, 2002.

Whitman, Alden. "Chaplin's Little Tramp, an Everyman Trying to Gild Cage of Life, Enthralled World." *New York Times*, December 26, 1977.

Williams, Raymond. *The Country and the City*. Oxford: Oxford University Press, 1975.

Woodmansee, Martha. "On the Author Effect: Recovering Collectivity." In *The Construction of Authorship: Textual Appropriations in Law and Literature*, edited by Martha Woodmansee and Peter Jaszi, 15–28. Durham, NC: Duke University Press, 1994.

"wT/F—True/False Film Fest." Accessed September 28, 2013. http://truefalse .org/wtf/leon-gast-discusses-pugilism.php.

Young Lords Organization. "13 Point Program and Platform." *Palante*, May 8, 1970.

Young Lords Party. "Music Belongs to the People." *Palante*, January 29, 1971.

Young Lords Women's Caucus. "Position Paper on Women." September 25, 1970.

Zenón Cruz, Isabelo. *Narciso descubre su trasero: El negro en la cultura puertorriqueña*. Humacao, Puerto Rico: Editorial Furidi, 1975.

Zentella, Ana Celia. *Growing Up Bilingual: Puerto Rican Children in New York*. Malden, MA: Blackwell, 1997.

Zipp, Samuel. *Manhattan Projects: The Rise and Fall of Urban Renewal in Cold War New York*. Oxford: Oxford University Press, 2012.

# Index

audiences, 10, 34–38, 50, 133, 234;
Black, 62; Blades's, 214, 243;
Colón's, 84, 94, 98; diverse, 10;
Fania All-Stars and, 61; Latin
American and Caribbean, 40,
115–16, 216, 228; LaVoe's, 190, 196,
211, 216; mainstream, 63, 265n59;
Nuyorican, 53, 80, 231; *Our Latin
Thing* and, 59, 220; Puerto Rican,
22, 80, 179, 215, 231; rap's, 157;
salsa's, 64, 71; Santería and, 58
authenticity, 39, 100, 186–87; coquí as
symbol of Puerto Rican, 162; cultural, 32, 99; elite culture and, 164;
of LaVoe's signature, 201; nationalism and, 125
authority, 5, 26, 68–69, 122, 134, 200,
216, 228–29, 231, 242; colonial,
170; cultural, 26, 206, 232–34, 241,
243; male spheres of, 119; narrative, 214; paternal, 174; patriarchal,
55, 119, 124; of Puerto Rico, 173,
274n152
authorship, 215–16, 224–27, 232; dis-
tributed/distributive, 227, 281n55.
*See also* "El Cantante"
autonomy, 140–41, 143, 149–50, 160,
170, 273n128; of salseras, 54

Barney Google's, 43, 44*f*
Barradas, Efraín, 108, 261n71
Barretto, Ray, 6–7, 29–33, 37, 44, 47, 51,
62, 66; *Barretto Power*, 80; Blades
and, 183, 213; "Cocinando," 30–31;
*Indestructible*, 279n32; *Our Latin
Thing* and, 58, 112; Palmieri and,
253n77; *PS 52* and, 42; *Que viva la
música*, 250n4; *Rican/Struction*,
7, 10*f*, 78; *Sesame Street* and, 61;
Young Lords and, 65
Bataan, Joe, 62; *Gypsy Woman*,
279n32; *Mr. New York and the East
Side Kids*, 79; *Poor Boy*, 76–77, 78*f*;
*Riot*, 38, 259n40; *Subway Joe*, 83
Benelux Union, 40, 61
*Billboard*, 40, 44, 47, 59–60, 62, 110,
113, 214, 256n129; Hot Latin LPS
chart, 65, 198, 238; Latin 50 chart,

199; Latin music chart, 184; special
issue on salsa, 59–60, 106
Blackness, as excess, 58, 255n12; and
La Lupe, 133–34; narratives of, 168,
172, 174; tropicalization of, 58; in
relation to geographic regions,
98–99, 261n61; as sublime, 57, 134
Black Puerto Ricans, 13, 15–16, 153,
160, 164, 170
Blades, Rubén, 5, 25–26, 46, 64–65,
178–80, 183–88, 206, 213–16, 221–23,
226, 228–36, 280n53, 282n84;
"Cazanguero," 222–23; *Doble
filo*, 222, 229, 234; Expo '92 and,
271n96; "Juan Pachanga," 64, 228;
*Last Fight*, 278n11; LaVoe and, 26,
186–88, 214, 222, 228–34, 240–43;
lawsuits, 237–38; "Ligia Elena,"
222–23, 228; *Metiendo mano*, 183,
188, 213; "Pablo Pueblo," 213–14,
222–23, 228; "Pedro Navaja," 214,
222, 234; "Plástico," 222–23, 275n8;
pregones of, 230, 234; royalties,
214, 221–22, 241–42, 279n34;
*Siembra*, 183, 188, 214, 222, 275n8.
*See also* "El Cantante"; SDRB (*El
show de Rubén Blades*)
Bobo, Willie, 11, 258n5
bolero, 121, 130, 172, 198
bomba, 72–75, 106, 110, 163, 172, 260n61
boogaloo, 6, 11, 18, 50, 73, 79–80,
251n19
brass (instruments), 64, 99, 128
Bronx, 6, 13, 43, 49, 52, 54, 71–72,
87, 97, 212, 250n11, 258n5; Hunt's
Point, 252n59, 259n37; Longwood,
34; South Bronx, 42, 67, 94, 118,
252n59
Brooklyn, 14, 38, 52, 54; Fulton Fish
Market, 87; Hotel St. George, 43;
Red Hook, 36

Caborrojeño, 50, 253n63
Campbell, Paula, 186, 188
campo. *See* countryside
capital, 19, 35, 118, 142, 144, 148, 173,
269n55; cultural, 102, 226; culture
and, 141, 154; European, 149, 152;

human, 168–69; internationalized, 140–41, 147, 152, 176; mobility, 117; racial, 16; social, 228

capitalism, 142–43, 167

Cardona, Segundo, 165–66, 272n119

Cartuja, 139, 152, 164, 268n36; See also Expo '92

Catholicism, 57, 168, 170

cbs Records, 62–64, 178, 257n147

cfdm Theatrical Productions, 199–200, 223, 276n34

charanga, 6, 11, 50, 74

Cheetah Lounge, 33, 35, 43, 49, 58–59, 112–13; Fania All-Stars concert at, 23–24, 29, 32, 36–38, 40, 47–48, 56, 69–71, 220, 250n1; Latin Arts Festival at, 256n129; Latin Music Awards at, 60. See also *Our Latin Thing*

Chez José, 49–52

Chez Sensual, 43, 113

Chico East, 43, 45*f*

*Childress v. Taylor*, 225–26, 280n50

chisme, 209; archive of, 210

Christopher's, 43, 113

chusmería, 24, 133–34, 265n59

citizenship, 25, 151; consumer, 150; failed, 179; liberal, 81, 259n30; productive, 22; racialized, 114; US, 143

*Claridad*, 148, 158–59, 163–64

cocolos, 154–55, 162

Codigo, 20, 184, 218–20, 239

Cold War, 14–15, 144; anxieties, 143; policies of, 3; US interests in, 267n27

collective memory of salsa, 53, 215

Colombia, 61, 116, 118, 246n13, 273n134

Colón, Willie, 2, 29, 46, 50–51, 66, 70–76, 79–80, 94–102, 118, 163, 258n14; *Asalto Navideño*, 91, 98, 100–102, 111, 116, 121, 239, 260n59; "Ausencia," 121–22, 127; *The Big Break—La gran fuga*, 78, 87–89, 90*f*–92*f*, 115; Blades and, 178, 183, 186, 188, 213–14, 216, 221, 228; "Calle Luna, Calle Sol," 96, 108–10; *Cosa nuestra*, 46, 75, 79, 86–87, 88*f*, 127; *Crime Pays*, 85, 91, 96; *The Good, the Bad, the Ugly*,

87, 89*f*, 91, 213; *Guisando/Doing a Job*, 76, 85, 86*f*, 98; *The Hustler*, 78, 83–87, 123; "The Hustler," 84, 98, 119; "Juana Peña," 87, 127; *El Juicio*, 75, 91, 93, 94–95*f*; *Last Fight*, 278n11; LaVoe and, 23–25, 70, 74–76, 80–82, 85–90, 93–101, 108, 110, 113–17, 119–21, 126–27, 130–32, 134, 179–80, 195, 229, 233, 278n11, 279n32; listening practices of, 258n5; *Lo mato (si no compra este LP)*, 91, 93, 96, 109, 131; *El Malo*, 73–76, 78–79, 81–84; "El Malo," 75, 82, 84, 98, 110; *Metiendo mano*, 183, 188, 213; "No me den candela," 126; *Only They Could Have Made This Album*, 198; professional trajectory of, 43; "Oíga señor," 87, 119; "Pa' Colombia," 116–17; "Panameña," 115–17; "Recomendación," 121, 126; "Señora Lola," 119; ; *Siembra*, 183, 188, 214, 222, 275n8; "Sonero mayor," 75, 97–98; "Timbalero," 102, 119

colonialism, 2, 99, 102, 106, 124, 153, 174; homosexuality and, 161; and Antonio Pedreira, 160, 174; and Luis Muñoz Marín, 160–61, 174; US, 6, 160. See also imperialism

coloniality of power, 5, 26, 241–42

Columbia Records, 62–63, 256n128, 257n147

Columbus, Christopher, 140, 151–52, 169, 273n131

commerce, 117, 144

commercialization, 22; of plena, 106; of Puerto Rico, 158; of rap, 117; of salsa, 32–33, 63, 69, 211

commodification, 22, 69, 117; of creative labor, 223; of the nation, 175; of salsa, 24

competition, 47, 115, 118, 253n77; "El Cantante" and, 194; Fania All-Stars and, 36; masculinity and, 70, 119; in *Our Latin Thing*, 36, 53, 70, 96; salsa and, 194; for US investment, 144–45, 267n26. *See also* merengue

imperialism: Spanish, 169–70; US, 61, 63, 102, 125
improvisation, 36, 53, 58, 68, 107, 231, 255n122; Anthony and, 3; copyright law and, 226–27; LaVoe and, 75, 193, 210, 226–27, 232–33; Navaja and, 234; Piñeiro and, 8; plena and, 106. *See also* descargas
infrastructure, 168; Fania Records and, 18, 117; in Puerto Rico, 142, 144, 146, 268n29; technological, 169
Instituto de Cultura Puertorriqueña (ICP), 148, 154–56
intellectual property, 215; law, 241; rights, 242; scholars, 227
intertextuality, 81, 87, 229

Jaime, Karen, 8, 211, 252n55
Jaszi, Peter, 216, 225
jazz, 6–7, 30, 32, 43, 63, 71, 80, 227; Colón and, 72–73, 258n5; Latin, 6, 10; salsa and, 99, 163. *See also* Gillespie, Dizzy; Grillo, Frank "Machito"
jíbaros, 53, 98–102, 108, 132, 162–63, 172, 179, 194, 260n59; tragic, 232. *See also* música jíbara
Jiménez, Manuel "El Canario," 9, 192
Jiménez Román, Miriam, 103–4
juvenile delinquency, 14, 157

Khaled, 1–2

labor, 4, 268n28; creative, 187–88, 215–16, 224, 226, 232–33, 240, 242; force, 109, 140, 144; low-wage, 142; market, 13; surplus, 9, 191
La Bruja, 9, 212, 277n64
La Fountain-Stokes, Lawrence, 119, 193
la gran familia puertorriqueña (the grand Puerto Rican family), 159–60, 174
La Lupe, 113, 133–34, 258n5, 262n1, 265nn56–57, 265n59
Latin America, 2, 21, 192, 198, 214–16, 228; bolero in, 130; Fania's reach into, 19; investment in, 170; malls

in, 269n49; Puerto Rico as democracy's laboratory in, 3, 144; record sales in, 221; salsa in, 118; sound and listening practices in, 23; women's bodies and geography of, 115
Latin American Music Company (LAMCO), 199–200
Latinidad, 2, 4, 117, 133, 241; queer, 212
Latin music, 11, 18–21, 32–34, 38–40, 43, 49–51, 62–63, 85, 106, 182, 212, 227, 253n63, 258n5; app, 219; *Billboard* charts, 184; Fania's dominance of, 216; gatekeepers of, 84; Grammy category in, 256n132; industry, 18, 20–21, 47, 253n77; labels, 23, 59, 75; markets, 19, 59, 178; musical practices in, 11, 18–19, 57, 73; producers, 35; promoters, 199; Santería and, 57; scene, 23, 32, 36, 38–39, 42, 55, 70–71, 76, 98, 113, 179, 181, 186, 188, 254n85, 256n129; social hierarchies of, 82; South Bronx and, 252n59
Latin New York, 5, 11, 18, 23–24, 26, 60, 70, 77, 132, 260n59; Colón and, 51, 81, 97; Fania Records and, 24, 69; *Our Latin Thing* and, 29–30, 32–33, 39–41, 58, 69; women in, 8
*Latin N.Y.*, 7, 47, 59–60, 95–97, 123, 214, 256n129; ads in, 44–45f; Blades and, 183, 275n8; concert (1973), 253n61; LaVoe and, 181–82
Latin soul, 2, 6, 10, 18, 62, 76, 251n19. *See also* Bataan, Joe; La Lupe
*La Vida*, 13, 262n91
LaVoe, Héctor, 2–3, 29, 33, 42, 46, 66, 106–7, 110, 178–84, 189–95, 198, 203–12, 215, 222–23, 226–27, 238, 245n6, 246n8, 259n28, 262n86; AIDS and, 203, 207–8, 211–12, 277n46; "Bandolera," 128–31; Blades and, 26, 186–88, 214, 222, 228–34, 240–43; as "El Cantante de los Cantantes," 3, 179, 184, 216, 232–33, 242–43; Colón and, 23–25, 70, 74–76, 80–82, 85–90, 93–101, 108, 110, 113–17, 119–21,

Masucci, Gerald "Jerry," 18–20, 34–35, 37–38, 40, 47–48, 60, 178, 217–18; Blades and, 186, 221, 235–36; *El Cantante* and, 183; estate of, 19, 218, 237–38, 240, 278n18; *El Juicio* (Colón) and, 93; *The Last Fight* and, 216; *Our Latin Thing* and, 63; Polizzi and, 59; *Vigilante* and, 278n11. *See also* Musica Latina International; Sonido; Uptite Records; Valsyn; Vaya Publishing; Vaya Records

Meléndez, Miguel "Mickey," 18, 65

Mercado, Ralph, 35–36, 47, 203

merengue, 60–61, 94, 99, 118, 156, 270n79

mestizaje, 98, 156, 176

Mexico, 2, 250n11

migrants: Puerto Rican, 12–13, 71, 100; return, 104, 275n163. *See also* immigrants

migration, 61, 130; of Latin(a/o) American communities, 118; Puerto Rican, 3–4, 9–14, 82, 103–5, 142, 144, 241, 261n73, 267n23; as betrayal, 161; to Puerto Rico, 106; *See also* (de)afuera

Miller, Karl Hagstrom, 66, 110

Miranda, Ismael, 29, 38, 42, 53, 56, 58, 71, 141

modernity, 63, 142–43, 165, 172, 228; architecture as instrument of, 166; capitalist, 128; performance of, 4; Puerto Rican, 110, 143, 170, 174–75, 272n125; Puerto Ricans as impediments to, 8; Puerto Rico's entrance into, 3, 99, 108, 143, 150, 167–68, 273n128; Spain's jump toward, 170; Western, 255n122

Montalvo, Eddie, 42–43, 46–47, 183

Morales, Iris, 125

mujer perdida, 130, 133

muñocismo, 142, 167–68

Muñoz, José Esteban, 24, 126, 133, 191, 209

Muñoz Marín, Luis, 3, 99, 142–43, 160, 167, 174, 273n128. *See also* muñocismo

music, 9–11, 17–18, 22–26, 29, 30–31, 37, 41–43, 49–50, 53, 68–69, 106, 111, 117–18, 154–55, 162–64, 176–77, 194, 204, 219, 226, 228, 241, 245n4, 252n55; Afrodiasporic, 246n13; awards, 60; Blackness and, 255n122; Blades's, 222, 229; Colón's, 71–73, 75, 97–98; critics, 232; Cuban, 6, 11; executives, 61, 65, 211; festivals, 33, 48, 61, 71, 140, 154–55, 253n61, 256n129; folkloric (*see* música jíbara); LaVoe's, 70, 98, 114, 192, 212; Palmieri's, 80; pregones and, 192; Puerto Rican, 5–6, 72–74, 158, 164, 167, 171–72, 175; rights, 220; riots and, 259n40; Rivera's, 263n15; sales, 239, 250n11; Spanish-language, 20, 32–33, 118; supermarket, 64; tropical, 61, 216. *See also* boogaloo; copyright; copyright law; funk; Latin soul; merengue; plena; popular music; R&B; rap; rock music; soul

música jíbara (folkloric music), 98–101, 260n61

Musica Latina International, 19–20, 214, 217–18, 221–22, 229, 236–37, 279n34

musicality, 11, 24, 31, 51, 115; Colón's, 71, 73, 98; LaVoe's, 212; *Our Latin Thing* and, 47; Roena's, 37; urban, 18

música típica (folkloric music), 71, 98–101, 116, 154–55, 162; Afro-Puerto Rican, 260n61

music industry, 5, 20–21, 26, 35, 40, 47, 113, 134, 179, 213, 240; Latin, 18, 20–21, 47, 253n77

national imaginary, 16, 86, 153, 161

nationalism, 108, 125, 143, 150; cultural, 99, 110, 124–25, 141, 149, 158, 161, 172, 273n128; global, 167, 172, 176; patriarchal, 135; political, 143; Puerto Rican, 66, 90; white, 176

nation branding, 149, 172, 177; campaign, 25, 140–41, 148, 165, 175

New Rican Village, 17–18

standard songwriter's agreement
(SSA), 200–201, 214, 222–25, 229,
236
Stoever, Jennifer, 16, 274n148
Suárez Findlay, Eileen, 142, 160,
248n59, 272n127
subjecthood, 94, 121–22, 134–35; heteronormative, 117, 134; masculinist, 131, 174; performance of, 25,
70, 87, 93, 111, 113–14, 135, 206, 241;
racialized, 131, 134–35; threats to,
127, 131, 198
subjectivity, 24; colonial, 9; Diaspo-
Rican, 105; jíbaro, 179; Latina/o, 208;
male, 90; Nuyorican, 26, 66, 69,
179, 215; Puerto Rican, 9; racialized, 161; surplus, 25; violent, 135
sublime, 57, 134. See also La Lupe
sucias, 114, 131

tax incentives, 142, 144–45, 173
Thomas, Lorrin, 12, 14, 259n30
Tico Records, 19, 59
Típica 73, 7, 47, 178
Tito Puente Orchestra, 133, 271n96
Tjader, Cal, 7, 50, 258n5
Torin, Symphony Sid, 32, 36
Toro, Yomo, 87, 100
tourism, 158; Cuba and, 63; Panama
and, 229; Puerto Rico and, 143,
146–47, 149, 173–74, 269n55
transatlantic slave trade, 63, 170
tropicalization, 58, 158, 175, 255n122

Universal Expo (1992). See Expo '92
Universidad Nacional de Panamá,
213, 240
Uptite Records, 19, 62
urban renewal, 14–15, 26, 248n57;
housing and, 15, 157, 168
Uruguay, 217, 235, 273n134, 281n70
US Copyright Office, 199, 223

Valentín, Bobby, 19, 35–36, 39, 44, 48,
240
Valentín-Escobar, Wilson, 3, 73–75,
86, 90, 108, 133, 265n59; on plena,
193–94; on salsa, 6, 71

Valsyn, 20, 200, 217–18, 222, 235–40
Vargas, Deborah, 25, 210–11
Vaya Publishing, 20, 214, 221–22,
236
Vaya Records, 19, 62, 213–14, 221–22,
235–36
Venezuela, 61, 118, 235; Caracas, 40,
246n13
Vev Publishing, 20, 214, 236
violence, 13–14, 82, 96, 128–30, 133,
260n52; "Bandolera" and, 128–30;
"Calle Luna, Calle Sol" and, 96,
110; the Caribbean and, 255n122;
colonial, 144, 255; Hernández
Colón's policies and, 170, 176;
"El Malo" and, 92; public housing developments and, 155; sonoridad and, 82, 129. See also
los malotes de la salsa; women:
name-calling

Waxer, Lise, 6, 61
Westside Latino, 218–19
West Side Story, 15–16, 41, 81, 83, 84f,
147, 165
white flight, 13, 16, 71
whiteness, 8, 15, 24, 98, 106, 140–41,
167, 255n122; heteropatriarchal,
94; Hispanophile, 175; jíbaro
and, 101
women, 8, 13, 34, 57–59, 112–17, 123–28,
130–32, 134–35, 172, 179, 181; as
activists, 65, 126, 149; Black, 57,
102, 255n122, 265n59; bolero and,
121–22, 130; of color, 124–26; as
commodities, 263n11; disobedient, 25; Hernández Colón's policies and, 170; liberated, 121, 123;
listening practices of, 254n100;
masculine, 120; name-calling and,
127–31; in Our Latin Thing, 48, 56,
112–13; Puerto Rican, 12, 124–26,
172; rights of, 212; roles of in salsa
scene, 55–57, 113; salsa and, 53–55;
as screens, 264n51; violence and,
128–30. See also La Bruja; Cruz,
Celia; La Lupe; sucias; Young
Lords: Women's Caucus

World War II, 10–13, 18, 46, 53, 142, 272n127

Yépez, Tomás, 161–62

Young Lords, 17, 30, 43, 65–66; *Palante*, 40, 65; Women's Caucus, 124–25. *See also* Guzmán, Pablo

"Yoruba"; Luciano, Felipe; Meléndez, Miguel "Mickey; Morales, Iris; Oliver, Denise

Zenón Cruz, Isabelo, 104, 271n99

Zentella, Ana Celia, 78, 81, 250n7, 259n27